GOLDEN MOUTH

GOLDEN MOUTH

The Story of John Chrysostom—
Ascetic, Preacher, Bishop

J. N. D. Kelly

Cornell University Press
Ithaca, New York

First published 1995 by Cornell Unversity Press

Library of Congress Cataloging-in-Publication Data

Kelly, J. N. D. (John Norman Davidson)
  Golden mouth : the story of John Chrysostom, ascetic, preacher,
bishop / J. N. D. Kelly.
      p.   cm.
  Includes bibliographical references and index.
  ISBN 0-8014-3189-1 (alk. paper)
  1. John Chrysostom, Saint, d. 407. 2. Christian saints–Turkey–
Biography. I. Title.
BR1720-C5K45 1995
270.2'092–dc20
  [B]   95-1444

Printed in Great Britain

Contents

Preface

It may surprise readers to learn that this is the first comprehensive study of John Chrysostom to be published in this country since 1880, when W.R.W. Stephens's classic *Saint John Chrysostom, His Life and Times* appeared. One reason for this apparent neglect may be that the field, both here and abroad, has for more than sixty years been dominated by C. Baur's erudite two-volume biography, published in German at Munich in 1929/30 and in an (execrable) English translation in 1959. Meanwhile, so far from standing still, Chrysostom studies have been exceptionally active in every department during the past five decades. To give but two examples out of many, our knowledge of the Syrian asceticism by which John was attracted as a young man has been greatly enriched by scholars like G.M. Colombás, P. Canivet, and S. Brock, while É. Demougeot, J.H.W.G. Liebeschuetz, G. Albert, and others have provided us with a fuller understanding of the political setting of his episcopate. Slow but steady progress has been made (mainly by *Sources chrétiennes*) in the production of critical editions of his treatises, and F. van Ommeslaeghe's rehabilitation of 'Martyrios' as a primary source for his life counts as a major event.

Three considerations have been in my mind in preparing this book. In the first place, I wanted to repay an old debt. The Hensley Henson lectures which I gave in Oxford in 1979/80 were devoted to aspects of John, but since I was not wholly satisfied with my treatment of them, I did not publish the lectures, as is expected, at the time. A primary object, therefore, has been to fulfil this obligation at last. Secondly, however, it occurred to me that the most sensible way of doing this would be to incorporate the substance of the lectures, with modifications, in a more general survey of John and his career. This I have done in Chapters 2, 3, and 16, although I doubt whether even I could now disentangle the old from the new. Thirdly, as I was already convinced of the need for a fresh study of John which would take account of recent scholarly developments, I welcomed the opportunity to do what I could to provide one, not least because it would enable me to present a more realistic appraisal of his complex personality than the conventional one, as well as to put forward one or two interpretations of my own. I should like to have included some tentative discussions of the intellectual presuppositions underlying John's thinking, perhaps also of certain of his specifically theological ideas which still need clarification; but advancing years were insistent that I should leave these to younger scholars.

Many friends have encouraged and helped me in my work, but two to whom I am particularly indebted are David Taylor, who not only let me consult him on Syriac matters, but critically read three chapters, and Nigel Wilson, who generously lent me books unavailable in the Bodleian Library, and went to the trouble of studying select passages of John's works in order to discuss with me the supposed Attic qualities of his style. Others to whom I gladly offer thanks are Professor Cyril Mango, who recommended to me the 9th-century mosiac image of John Chrysostom (from the north tympanum of Hagia Sophia) which is reproduced on the jacket; Peter Hayward, of the cartographical department of the Oxford School of Geography, who, on the basis of material I supplied, prepared the two city plans; and Alice Gibbons, who gave me unsparing assistance in photocopying my typescript.

I pay a special tribute to Colin Haycraft, chairman of Duckworth and most congenial of publishers, who often discussed the book with me, prodded me when I was deflected by other projects, and just before his sudden death posted me the proofs along with my original typesecript meticulously copy-edited by himself.

Finally I must ask readers to be indulgent with the inconsistencies in my spelling of Greek proper names. All my life I have been impatient with the patronising way with which we westerners present Greek names in their Latin forms, and in my old age I decided to break free from it, adopting the principles used by my stand-by mini-encyclopedia, *Der Kleine Pauly*. Unfortunately I have sometimes deviated from its high standards – for example, printing Chalkedon but shying away from Nikaia.

13 November 1994
Feast (in the east) of
St John Chrysostom

J.N.D.K.

Abbreviations

AASS	*Acta Sanctorum* (Antwerp 1643 ff.; Venice 1734 ff.; Paris 1863ff.)
AB	*Analecta Bollandiana*
ACO	E. Schwartz, *Acta conciliorum oecumenicorum*
Baur	C. Baur, *John Chrysostom and his Time* (ET London 1959), 2 vols
BSS	*Bibliotheca Sanctorum* (Rome 1961-1970)
BZ	*Byzantinische Zeitschrift*
CCL	*Corpus christianorum, Series Latina*
CIL	*Corpus inscriptionum Latinarum*
CQ	*Classical Quarterly*
CSCO	*Corpus scriptorum christianorum orientalium*
CSEL	*Corpus scriptorum ecclesiasticorum Latinorum*
CT	Theodosian Code
DHGE	*Dictionnaire d'histoire et de géographie ecclésiastique*
ET	English translation
GCS	*Die griechischen christlichen Schriftsteller*
GRBS	*Greek, Roman, and Byzantine Studies* (Durham, N. Carolina)
HE	*Historia ecclesiastica*
HJG	*Historisches Jahrbuch der Görresgesellschaft*
HTR	*Harvard Theological Review*
JRS	*Journal of Roman Studies*
JTS	*Journal of Theological Studies*
JW	P. Jaffé, *Regesta pontificum Romanorum* (2nd ed. by G. Wattenbach)
LXX	Septuagint
Mansi	J.D. Mansi, *Sacrorum conciliorum nova et amplissima collectio*
MGHAA	*Monumenta Germaniae historica, Auctores antiquissimi*
Moulard	A. Moulard, *Saint Jean Chrysostome, sa vie, son oeuvre* (Paris 1949)
MSR	*Mélanges de science religieuse*
OCA	*Orientalia christiana analecta* (Rome)
OCP	*Orientalia christiana periodica* (Rome)

PG	Migne's *Patrologia Graeca*
PL	Migne's *Patrologia Latina*
PLRE	*The Prosopography of the Later Roman Empire* (Cambridge)
PSyr	*Patrologia Syriaca*
PW	Pauly-Wissowa-Kroll, *Realencyclopädie der classischen Wissenschaft*
RAC	*Reallexikon für Antike und Christentum*
REA	*Revue des études anciennes*
REB	*Revue des études byzantines*
REL	*Revue des études latines*
RHE	*Revue d'histoire ecclésiastique*
SC	*Sources chrétiennes* (Paris)
SM	*Studia monastica* (Montserrat)
ST	*Studi e testi* (Rome)
TAPA	*Transactions and Proceedings of the American Philological Association*
Tillemont	Lenain de, *Mémoires pour servir à l'histoire des six premiers siècles* (Venice 1732), vol. xi
TM	*Travaux et mémoires* (Paris)
TU	*Texte und Untersuchungen*
VC	*Vigiliae christianae*
ZKTh	*Zeitschrift für Katholische Theologie*
ZNTW	*Zeitschrift für die neutestamentliche Wissenschaft*

1

The Early Years

I

In the middle of the fourth century AD Antioch, in the province of Syria (now Antakya, in south Turkey, capital of the vilayet of Hatay), was reckoned one of the most prosperous and splendid cities of the Roman empire.[1] Founded in 300 BC by Seleukos I Nikator, one of Alexander the Great's generals, it occupied a spectacular site, mainly on the left bank of the river Orontes as it flowed south-west to the sea some 30 km away, but also on the right bank and on an island (long disappeared through silting) formed by a loop of the river; the walls surrounding it extended some 10 km. Immediately to the south-east rose the thickly wooded slopes of Mount Silpios (508 m), at first gradually but then precipitously, like a towering wall. Laid out on the favoured checker-board plan, its main street was paved with marble, embellished with two-storeyed colonnades, and lit with oil-fed lamps by night; and it was justly proud of its magnificent buildings, abundant water-supply and public baths (eighteen, one for each ward), theatres and hippodrome. Eight kilometres to the south-west the main road led to Daphne (Harbiye), a picturesque garden-suburb with elegant villas, refreshing springs (still in use), and a temple of Apollo famous for its oracle; here Olympic games were regularly held.

Its position on the great commercial highway from Asia to the Mediterranean, its connection with the nearby port of Seleukeia, and the agricultural products of its intensively cultivated hinterland made Antioch wealthy, supplied with goods of every kind. It also possessed a mint and an arms factory. At the same time it maintained a vigorous intellectual and cultural life, being admired for its schools and professors. In addition, it was the administrative and military key-point of the Roman east. Here resided not only the governor (*consularis*) of the province of Syria, but the count (*comes*) of Oriens, the vast civil diocese[2] which, from Valens' reign (364-78), comprised fifteen provinces and extended from Mesopotamia to the borders of Egypt. Here too, because of the importance of the city as a base for warlike operations against Persia, the military commander for

[1] See G. Downey, *A History of Antioch in Syria* (Princeton 1961); J.H.W.G. Liebeschuetz, *Antioch* (Oxford 1972).
[2] For reasons of administrative efficiency Diocletian had grouped the provinces in twelve huge *dioikeseis*.

Oriens (*magister militum per Orientem*) had his headquarters with a powerful supporting garrison. The emperors themselves, with their court and army of functionaries, often made Antioch their temporary capital, sometimes for prolonged periods, staying in the huge palace which Diocletian (284-305) had constructed on the island.

By ancient standards Antioch was a large city, smaller than Rome, but comparable in size with Constantinople and Alexandria, although it was rapidly being overtaken by the former as the fourth century advanced. Its built-up area was densely inhabited, and its population (although such calculations are notoriously difficult to substantiate) has been estimated as falling between 150,000 and 300,000.[3] It was a mixed and also cosmopolitan community, and while Greek was the language in general use, the peasants in the surrounding country were Syriac-speaking. In general it was affluent, and while about a tenth of the population was abjectly poor,[4] this was probably a smaller proportion than for other comparable cities. At this time it was an increasingly Christian stronghold. While professing pagans were numerous, especially in the professional and upper classes, and there was a substantial, well organised and confident Jewish element,[5] with a synagogue at Daphne as well as one in the city, there can be no doubt that the majority of citizens were Christians, and that this majority was reflected on the city council.[6] They recalled with pride that the apostles Peter and Paul had both worked at Antioch, and that it was there, according to Acts 11.26, that believers had been first called Christians. Ecclesiastically the council of Nicaea (325), in its sixth canon, had recognised that the see of Antioch, like those of Rome and Alexandria, enjoyed a special precedence, and throughout the fourth century its bishop, although his jurisdiction over them remained vague and ill-defined, was looked up to by the bishops of the entire civil diocese of Oriens as their leader.

With a Christian population of this size it was inevitable that there should be several Christian churches in fourth-century Antioch,[7] although a self-consciously pagan writer like Libanios would scorn to mention them in the detailed, affectionate description of the city he published in 360.[8] Much the grandest was the octagonal Great Church, or Golden Church, begun by Constantine in 327 and completed under his son Constantius II; it was dedicated on 6 January 341 on the occasion of the meeting of an important council. This remarkable building, of exceptional size and beauty, was crowned by a shallow, gilded dome of impressive height. It almost certainly stood on the island in the Orontes, adjacent to the imperial

[3] So Liebeschuetz, op. cit., 92-6.
[4] We owe this figure to John himself (*In Matt. hom.* 66.3: *PG* 58.630), who also suggests that the very rich too amounted to a tenth.
[5] See esp. R.L. Wilken, *John Chrysostom and the Jews* (Berkeley 1983), 34-65.
[6] P. Petit, *Libanius et la vie municipale à Antioche au ivme siècle* (Paris 1955), 200-3.
[7] W. Eltester, 'Die Kirchen Antiochias im iv. Jahrhundert', *ZNTW* 36 (1937), 251-86.
[8] *Or.* 11.196-272 (Förster 1.504-35).

palace; its site included a substantial guest-house and canteens for feeding the poor. In addition, in the main town between the river and Mount Silpios, there were three or four parish churches of which the most frequently mentioned was the Palaea, or Old Church, a basilica constructed between 313 and 324 but replacing one going back to the third century which had been destroyed in Diocletian's persecution (303-12). Some claimed it had been founded by the apostles, but in fact it owed its name to having been the leading church of the city before the building of the Great Church. There was, thirdly, a small church in the old town which, as we shall see,[9] the separatist but orthodox group known as the Eustathians were permitted to use. In addition, there were a number of martyrs' shrines, testifying to the rapid growth of the cult of martyrs in the first half of the fourth century. Since they were erected over the bodies of martyrs or housed their remains, they were required by law to be outside the city walls. The most noteworthy were the cemetery church outside the gate leading to Daphne, the great *martyrion* which formed the centre-piece of the cemetery outside the Romanesian gate to the north, the *martyrion* of St Babylas on the right bank of the Orontes (to be erected in 379),[10] and the shrine of the Maccabees, the seven Jewish brothers and their mother who, under Antiochos Epiphanes, had suffered death *c.* 168 BC for refusing to eat pork (2 Macc. 7), and had come to be treated as prototypes of Christian martyrs.

The citizens of Antioch had a reputation for pleasure-seeking, worldliness, fickleness and cynicism; among other diversions they had a passion for horse-racing and the theatre, and in spring and summer they streamed out to Daphne for relaxation or amusement. By contrast the desert regions near the city, the higher slopes and peaks of Mount Silpios and the other mountains on its outskirts, were becoming peopled by hermits and monks who, in obedience to what they conceived to be the call of Christ, had turned their backs on civilisation and the vanities of the world. The monastic ideal, with its summons to throw off the entanglements of ordinary life, not least the attractions of sex, had been sweeping through the Christian east since the beginning of the fourth century; nowhere had it caught on more effectively than in Syria, and nowhere did it assume more bizarre forms. The sophisticated citizens of Antioch, Christian and non-Christian alike, might view the often uncouth monks of the neighbourhood with contempt and revulsion, but the masses venerated them, and when they appeared in the city at times of crisis, even the highest government officials found it prudent to treat them with respect. The more noteworthy drew constant streams of visitors to their cells and retreats, seeking counsel or help or merely eager to gaze on the holy man.

[9] See below, p. 12.
[10] See below, p. 41.

II

It was at Antioch that John, later to be designated Chrysostom, or Golden Mouth,[11] because of his dazzling effectiveness as a pulpit orator, was born and was to spend almost fifty years of his life. Various dates between 344 and 354 have been proposed for his birth, but while certainty is impossible the one which seems to fit most of the known facts is 349.[12] If this is correct, he was considerably junior to Basil of Caesarea, Gregory of Nazianzos, and Basil's younger brother, Gregory of Nyssa, the three outstanding Greek-language Christian thinkers and preachers of the fourth century, the first two of whom were born around 330 and the third about 335. He was very slightly junior too, to his great Latin contemporary, Jerome,[13] who was to stay in or near Antioch in the 370s without, apparently, meeting him but was to assail him mercilessly in later life, and probably much the same age as Theophilos (b. *c.* 345), the imperious patriarch of Alexandria who was to be the main instrument of his downfall. From the historian Sokrates[14] (*c.* 380 – *c.* 450) we learn that his father was called Sekoundos and his mother Anthousa, both people reckoned to be of good family in the city. While the latter is a thoroughly Greek name, Sekoundos despite its deceptively Greek spelling is a Latin one, and invites the guess that his father may have been of Roman stock. This is borne out by the fact that he also had an aunt, probably his father's sister, called Sabiniana,[15] a Latin name too. Years later his disciple and biographer Palladios was to come across her in Antioch, a venerable lady 'who conversed intimately with God'. In addition, he had an elder sister whose name has not survived and who, so far as we know, was to play no part in his subsequent story.[16]

There can be no doubt that John's family, if not of the foremost rank, was well placed socially, and also very comfortably off. Where exactly they lived we have no means of knowing, but the dozens of villas which excavations have uncovered, in the city itself and in its suburbs, with their richly coloured mosaic floors and elegant lay-out, give a vivid impression of the life style of the more well-to-do citizens. It has been widely assumed, on the basis of a report by Palladios,[17] that his father held the important position of military commander for Oriens, being therefore a very prominent personage indeed. But this reading of the passage is now regarded as mistaken. What Palladios in fact meant, it would appear, is that Sekoundos and his forbears had served with distinction in the *officium*, or secretariat, of the

---

[11] The nickname was applied to several admired orators, and to John, in the east and west generally, from the fifth century.
[12] See Appendix B.
[13] Most scholars place his birth *c.* 347, but there is a case for its being much earlier.
[14] 6.3: John nowhere names them himself.
[15] Palladios, *Hist. Lausiaca*, 41 (Butler 129).
[16] Palladios, *Dial.* 5 (SC 341.104).
[17] *Dial.* 5 (SC 341.104).

commander-in-chief. In other words, he did not, as the military commander for Oriens did, rank as a senator of the highest grade, to be dignified after about 365 with the honorific title of 'illustrious', nor indeed was he a general at all. Rather, he was a responsible, top-class civil servant.[18] This is in harmony with John's own statement,[19] to be made many years later, that he and a boyhood friend of his named Basil had been equally matched in possessing moderate affluence and a similar family background. It also agrees with the claim which he put into his mother's mouth, in the sequel to the same passage, that she had not frittered away his father's estate (evidently it was not enormous) in order to give him a liberal education, but had paid for it out of her own (apparently ample) dowry.

His family, his mother at any rate if not his father, was Christian. This is clearly suggested in the section of his later apologetic essay *Priesthood* referred to above; in addition, we possess a graphic reminiscence of his from his teens (to be related shortly) which implies that Anthousa was known to be a Christian. In spite of this he was not baptized in infancy; following the practice widely accepted in those days, his family deferred his baptism, and (as we shall see) it was only as a young man approaching twenty that he took the momentous step of offering himself for it. By that time his father Sekoundos was long dead; he had died, as John himself records,[20] shortly after his son's birth, when Anthousa was about twenty. Like many devout Christians (pagans too) of that epoch, she set her face resolutely against a second marriage, and as a result the responsibility both of managing her household and of bringing up her children devolved wholly on her. Years later, in a passage which, for all its emotional overtones, was almost certainly based on authentic reminiscences, he was to represent her recalling her struggles, as an inexperienced young woman, with indolent or mischievous servants, rapacious relatives and extortionate tax-collectors, and also the consolation she had derived, when he was still a baby unable to speak, first of all from God's ever-present help, and then from the striking resemblance she wistfully imagined she could trace between his and his dead father's features.[21]

III

In the same passage John portrays Anthousa as complaining that, while it was bad enough for a young widow to be left with a baby daughter, it was infinitely worse to be left with an infant son. In the one case she was at least spared expense and anxiety, but the cost of educating a boy (to mention nothing more) could be crippling. Beyond the fact that she faced

---

[18] See A.H.M. Jones, *HTR* 46 (1953), 71: an article now generally accepted.
[19] *De sacerdotio* 1 (*SC* 272.62).
[20] *De sacerdotio* 1 (*SC* 272.66); *Ad viduam iun.* 2 (*PG* 48.624).
[21] *De sacerdotio* 4 (*SC* 272.68).

the challenge, we have no direct information about the earlier stages of John's schooling and must have recourse to conjecture. Thus he must have spent his infant years at home, picking up what he could from nurses, servants, above all his mother. After that, like other Christian boys of his social standing, he must have followed, with his young friend and comrade Basil (as he himself records among the youthful reminiscence from which we have been drawing), the educational programme universally accepted in the Graeco-Roman world of his day[22] – which in fact had scarcely undergone any serious modification since the fourth century before Christ. This involved attending, at the age of seven or thereabouts, the elementary school, where children learned reading, writing and simple arithmetic, and then, from about ten to fourteen or fifteen, the grammar school. Here a boy was given a thorough grounding in Greek classical literature, especially the poets, but also prose-writers and orators; Homer, Euripides, Menander and Demosthenes were the four pillars. In striking contrast to much modern English practice, he was drilled in grammar and syntax, and was expected to learn long passages by heart and to be able to comment on them. Nor was the subject-matter – the mythology, history, etc. – neglected, still less the moral and practical lessons that could be drawn from it. The content of the works studied was inevitably pagan, and thoughtful Christians were becoming increasingly conscious of the incompatibility of such a curriculum with an upbringing based on the scriptures. As yet no arrangements existed for this outside the child's home and church, and ordinary Christian parents like Anthousa had no practicable alternative to sending their sons to the traditional schools.

The third stage was the school of rhetoric, which boys normally entered when they were fourteen or fifteen (in some cases later),[23] and in which they were trained in all aspects of the arts of composition and public speaking, including the actual preparation and delivery of speeches of different kinds. At this point there is a momentary break in the general cloud enveloping John's youth, for Sokrates records that at Antioch he had Libanios as his professor of rhetoric and attended the lectures of Andragathios on philosophy.[24] Sokrates adds that among his fellow-pupils were Theodore, who was later to become bishop of Mopsuestia (an important see in Cilicia) and a remarkable commentator on scripture, and Maximos, future bishop of Seleukeia, the nearby seaport. Nothing is known of Andragathios, but Libanios (314-393) was the distinguished professor, fine stylist and man of letters who occupied the official chair of rhetoric at Antioch from 354 until his death, and whose letters and speeches provide a detailed, fascinating picture of political, social, and economic life in the city. A convinced pagan

[22] For this paragraph see H.I. Marrou, *Histoire de l'éducation dans l'antiquité* (6th ed., Paris 1965), esp. 243-64.
[23] The normal age of Libanios' pupils was 14 to 18: see A.J. Festugière, *Antioche païenne et chrétienne* (Paris 1959), 187 n. 4.
[24] 6.3.

devoted to traditional values, openly contemptuous of the new official religion, although enjoying good relations with many who professed it, he was the friend and admirer of the apostate emperor Julian, and viewed the progress of Christianity with acute dismay. The veracity of Sokrates' testimony has sometimes been questioned, but needlessly. While a large majority of Libanios' students were pagans, they undoubtedly included a number of Christians,[25] and that John was one of these, likely enough in itself quite apart from Sokrates' report, is confirmed by striking imitations of the master which have been detected in his earlier writings.[26]

In his early thirties John was to tell a story which coheres perfectly with everything we know of Libanios' character and personality, and thus provides further confirmation of Sokrates' witness. 'When I was still a young man', he was to write, 'I recall the admiration which my professor – incidentally, the most superstitious of men – publicly expressed for my mother. In his usual way he questioned the bystanders about my origins, and when he learned that I was the son of a widow, he inquired of me both my mother's age and the length of her widowhood. When I replied that she was forty years old, and that it was twenty years since she had lost my father, he was astounded and, looking round at the company, exclaimed, "Great heavens, what remarkable women are to be found among the Christians!" '[27]

Any reconstruction of John's schooling is inevitably conjectural, devoid for the most part of hard facts; but we are able in some degree to gauge its impact from his writings and sermons. Latin formed no part of his curriculum, but he is likely to have picked up at least a smattering of it if (as will be argued in the next chapter) he was already setting his sights on the higher civil service. Latin was still the official language of the empire in the east, and he himself was to remark on its usefulness for someone training for the bureaucracy.[28] But his chief debt to his teachers was for the classic purity of his Greek diction and the astonishing elegance of expression he acquired from them. If a junior contemporary like Isidore of Pelusion (d. *c.* 435), himself a highly polished writer, could wax lyrical on the music of his prose,[29] modern connoisseurs of Greek literature have united in acclaiming him 'an almost pure Atticist', the only prose author of his epoch who can stand comparison with Demosthenes.[30] If this judgment

---

[25] See P. Petit, *Les étudiants de Libanius* (Paris 1957), 196.

[26] See C. Fabricius, *Zu den Jugendschriften des J. Chrysostomos* (Lund 1962), 119-211; also *Symbolae Osloenses* 33 (1957), 135f.

[27] *Ad viduam iun.* 2 (*PG* 48.601). The description of Libanios as 'superstitious' is realistic: he was always consulting the gods about his health, etc. See A.J. Festugière, op. cit., 409; PW XII (2).1540.

[28] *Adv. oppug. vitae mon.* 3.5 (*PG* 47.357).

[29] *Ep.* 4.224 (*PG* 78.1317-18).

[30] See, e.g., O. Bardenhewer, *Geschichte der altkirchlichen Literatur* (Freiburg i. Br. 1912) 3, 353, who cites an enthusiastic encomium by U. von Wilamowitz-Moellendorff.

is accepted, it must be with the reservation that John used a language which, in syntax but even more in vocabulary, had moved beyond that of the fourth century BC. This said, it remains true that his earlier writings reveal that he had gained at school a first-rate working knowledge of the most admired authors of the classical period and regularly looked to them as models. The three who had greatest influence on him, as indeed on his master Libanios, were Demosthenes, Plato and Homer, in that order.[31] This legacy of his boyhood education is all the more striking in view of the deeply critical attitude which, as we shall discover, he was to develop towards Hellenistic culture. Similarly, his treatises and sermons alike give proof, abundant although sometimes underrated in the past, that he was thoroughly familiar with, and prepared to exploit as the occasion demanded, all the oratorical and stylistic devices which often appear artificial to modern taste but which were strenuously inculcated in the fourth-century schools of rhetoric. His skill in these techniques of the so-called Second Sophistic gives credence to the anecdote reported by Sozomen that, when Libanios was dying and his friends inquired who should succeed him in his chair of rhetoric, he answered, 'It ought to have been John had not the Christians stolen him from us.'[32]

IV

These years of John's childhood and adolescence were full of incident and excitement for both Antioch and its Christian inhabitants. The emperors – Constantius II (337-61); Gallus (351-4), whom Constantius as Augustus appointed as Caesar, or junior emperor, with responsibility for the east while he himself was occupied with the west; Gallus' half-brother Julian (361-3); Jovian (363-4); Valens (364-78) – were frequent, sometimes regular, residents in the palace on the island on the Orontes. The amenities of Antioch, not least its excellent climate, made it a favourite resort, but it was also their military base for the war with Persia; and for much of the time the city was crowded with troops.[33] The strain put on its resources could be crippling, and we hear of a famine during Gallus' stay, a severe economic crisis during Julian's.[34] It was from Antioch that Julian, brought up as a Christian but now a militant pagan, led the Roman army to the eastern front on 5 March 363, only to be struck down by the banks of the Tigris on 26 June. It was to Antioch that his hastily acclaimed successor, Jovian, after concluding a humiliating peace with Persia, felt obliged to

---

[31] For these statements see C. Fabricius, op. cit., esp. 143-9.
[32] 8.2. See also T.E. Ameringer, *The Stylistic Influence of the Second Sophistic on the Panegyrical Sermons of St John Chrysostom* (Washington 1921).
[33] Libanios, *Or.* 11.177-8 gives a vivid picture of these throngs of soldiers in 360.
[34] See G. Downey, 'The Economic Crisis at Antioch under Julian the Apostate' (in P.R. Coleman (ed.), *Studies in Roman Social and Economic History* (Princeton 1921)).

retreat for a brief, uncomfortable stay. These events must have left their imprint on John's consciousness, especially Julian's unexpected death. A pagan, and personal friend of the emperor's like Libanios was, of course, shattered by the news, but in Christian circles it was greeted with uninhibited rejoicings in churches and theatres alike. As a lad of fourteen John must have listened with tingling ears to the exultant shouts of 'God and his Christ have triumphed.'[35]

Such jubilation was understandable in view of the tense atmosphere which had been building up among Christians in Antioch ever since the brilliant, serious-minded young emperor's arrival there on 18 July 362. Exactly a month before reaching it, on 17 June, he had published an edict which, though apparently innocuous, effectively banned professing Christians from teaching in schools.[36] Its unconcealed object was to undermine the growing influence of Christians among the educated class. In the course of his uneasy stay in the city he had completed his skilfully argued, if repetitive, intellectual critique of Christianity, *Against the Galilaeans*, and had developed increasingly anti-Christian policies. Two of his measures in particular (as we shall later discover) left an indelible impression on John's imagination. The first was his removal, in autumn 362, of the remains of Babylas, a celebrated local martyr and bishop (d. *c*. 250), from the new shrine close to the temple of Apollo at Daphne to which his bigoted brother Gallus, in an attempt to check the licence of that pleasure-resort, had translated them from the cemetery outside the south walls, and his return of them to their original resting place. He was instigated to do this by reports he had received that Apollo's oracle had been reduced to silence and its precinct polluted by the proximity of dead bodies, but his action outraged Christian feeling. When the temple and its hallowed image of the god were mysteriously destroyed by fire shortly afterwards (22 October), the blame was inevitably placed on Christians, and Julian's attitude hardened. He set up an exceptionally harsh investigation to discover the perpetrators,[37] had the Golden Church shut down and allowed its liturgical vessels to be confiscated. But far more shocking to Christian sentiment were the overtures he made to the Jews, especially his programme, energetically undertaken early in 363, for having the Temple at Jerusalem, which had been razed to the ground by the Romans in AD 70, restored with government help and the Jewish sacrificial system restarted in it.[38] To Christians this seemed a blasphemous attempt not only to revive the faith which Christianity had (as they saw it) fulfilled and so superseded, but also to demonstrate the falsity of sayings of Christ recorded in the gospels which were

---

[35] Theodoret, *HE* 3.28.1-2 (*GCS* 44.206).
[36] CT 13.3.5. For his own amplification of the edict see the fragmentary *Letter* 42 (Bidez 162), 73-5.
[37] Ammianus Marcellinus (22.13.2) speaks of 'quaestiones ... solito acriores'.
[38] See, e.g., R.L. Wilken, *John Chrysostom and the Jews* (University of California 1983), 138-48.

interpreted as prophesying that the Temple would never be rebuilt. Their suspicions were well grounded, for one of Julian's chief motives was 'to refute the Christians and prove that Jesus was not divine'.[39]

Julian's brief reign dealt a blow to the confidence of Christians, not least in Antioch where much of it was spent, which was to linger in their consciousness for decades. Accustomed for half a century to Christian emperors who had actively supported their cause, they now found themselves ruled by a militant pagan who not only decreed general toleration for all religions (pagans, Jews, Christians – heretics as well as orthodox), but withdrew the privileges and immunities previous emperors had granted them, reopened the temples and ordered the return of any that had been seized by Christians, and reintroduced the worship of the ancient gods and public sacrifices in their honour. No less ominous were the violent reprisals which both pagans and Jews, whose temples and holy places Christians had violated at will, felt free to exact just so soon as they sensed the way the wind was blowing.[40] Thoughtful Christians (and we must include the youthful John among them) must have felt a cold shudder of apprehension as it dawned on them how much vitality there still was in paganism, and how precarious the position of the church was.

V

Meanwhile the Christian community in Antioch had interior worries of its own at which we must briefly glance if we are to understand John's subsequent activities. Basically, they sprang from the ways in which the hotly argued debate about the nature of the Trinity – more precisely, about the relation of the Son to the Father, and then somewhat later about the status of the Holy Spirit – was evolving in the eastern church, but they were exacerbated from time to time by the shifts of government policy.

A generation earlier the landmark council of Nicaea (325) which Constantine the Great had summoned had decreed that, while the Godhead was one and indivisible, the Son was 'of the same essence' or being as the Father. Its object had been to eliminate the contention of the famous heretic Arius (*Areios*) that the Son was a creature, superior to other creatures, but inferior in essence or being to the Father. Since then the situation had become more complicated. While a determined minority remained passionately loyal to the strict Nicene definition, the great majority suspected this of having 'Sabellian'[41] implications, i.e. of confusing the Father and the Son and regarding the Godhead as an undifferentiated unity. In order, therefore, to emphasise their distinction as 'persons' (*hupostaseis*), they pre-

---

[39] Ibid., 143.
[40] For a few, well chosen examples see J. Lieu, J. North and T. Rajak (eds.), *The Jews among Pagans and Christians* (London and New York 1992), 104.
[41] From Sabellius, an otherwise unknown early third-century Roman theologian who taught such a doctrine.

ferred to describe their relationship in terms of 'likeness in all respects', or even simply of 'likeness'. These formulae, especially the latter, had the immense advantage, from the government's point of view, of being acceptable not only to moderate churchmen generally but also to moderate Arian churchmen. For this reason emperor Constantius II, who shared his father Constantine's understandable eagerness to achieve as wide a measure of Christian unity as possible, had the Homoean (from *homoios*, i.e. like) compromise canonised as the official teaching of the church at separate councils of eastern and western bishops held in 359, and then confirmed at a great united council held at Constantinople in 360. Two further developments which were taking place about this time and a little later deserve note. First, after its earlier setback at Nicaea, Arianism had not only made itself respectable by sheltering under the Homoean formula, but in the fifties and sixties, as a protest against this compromise, was being brilliantly expounded in a revised, radical form by Aetios and Eunomios, who argued that the Son was in fact 'unlike' the Father (hence the soubriquet 'Anomoean', from *anomoios*, i.e. unlike), being altogether different from him in essence. Secondly, in reaction to this, an increasing number of eastern Christians who wished to maintain the Nicene principle of the Son's full divinity were beginning to rally round the affirmation that, while there were three distinct persons (*hupostaseis*) in the Godhead, the three were one in essence or being (*ousia*).

These theological tensions were reflected, with painful distortions, among the Christians of Antioch. Half a dozen years after Nicaea, probably in 331,[42] the opponents of the council's teaching had succeeded in getting its stubbornly Nicene-minded bishop, Eustathios, ejected, and for many years a succession of prelates more or less openly sympathetic to Arianism, usually in its more moderate forms, officially controlled the see. A small group, uncompromisingly devoted to the Nicene 'of one essence' and known after their banished leader as Eustathians, kept themselves apart under the hard-line priest Paulinos. The great majority, however, despite their distaste for Arianism in its various forms, for some years maintained uneasy communion with the bishops, but in the 350s and early 360s, given a lead by two highly educated, ascetic laymen Diodore and Flavian (we shall hear more of both later), who openly proclaimed the equality of the Son and the Spirit with the Father, began adopting a more independent stance.

Thus the Christian community which John knew as a schoolboy and student was deeply divided. There seems little doubt that he and his family adhered to the party of Diodore and Flavian; he was soon, as we shall see in the next chapter, to put himself under Diodore's spiritual wing. In 360 the see of Antioch fell vacant owing to the translation of the Arianizing Eudoxios to Constantinople. With the agreement of the court and the ruling

[42] For the date, about which there is much debate, see M. Spanneut, *DHGE* 16.17; he bases himself on Theodoret, *HE* 2.31.11-12 (*GCS* 44.173).

Homoean group the choice fell on Meletios, formerly bishop of Sebaste (Sivas) in Armenia, a man of intellectual distinction and a born leader, but he almost at once made it apparent by his preaching that, while prepared to employ Homoean language, he was much more sympathetic to Nicaea than his sponsors had bargained for. In spite of his immense popularity he was therefore exiled to Armenia only a few weeks after his installation;[43] understandably emperor Constantius would only have bishops who subscribed to the Homoean creed which had only recently been promulgated in the most solemn fashion as the church's official teaching. The new bishop appointed in his place was Euzoios, an avowed Arian and one of Arius' earliest collaborators (he was, however, steadily moderating his tone). A large section of the community, however, continued to regard Meletios as their true chief pastor, and preferred to hold their services outside the city.

Constantius died on 3 November 361. His successor, Julian, had no interest in favouring any one Christian faction; rather he found amusement in the divisions of Christians. One of his first acts, as we noted above, was to publish an edict of general toleration, which included an amnesty for orthodox Christians who had been driven into exile by his Arian predecessor.[44] In the resulting free-for-all Meletios was able to come back to Antioch in 362, but before he did so the priest Paulinos had been consecrated bishop by Lucifer of Cagliari, a zealous partisan of the extreme Nicene position, who had also been enabled by the emperor's cynical clemency to return from banishment. Thus the schism was made worse, for, in addition to the Arianizing government nominee occupying the official throne, there were now two 'orthodox' bishops of Antioch, Paulinos representing the die-hard Nicene stance, and Meletios (though exiled again in 365, he managed to reside in the city from 367 to 371) championing the full divinity of the Son, but expressing it in terms of the new, increasingly popular 'three hypostases' theology. Euzoios, we should note, made no attempt to have Paulinos exiled, and even allowed him the use of a small church in the old town. The motive is said to have been respect for him personally,[45] but it was also a skilful move to make things difficult for the much more dangerous Meletios.

The division between the Meletians and the Eustathians was particularly unfortunate, for both groups were united in their opposition to every kind of Arianism and in their adhesion to the essentials of the Nicene creed. What made matters worse was that the most important see in the eastern part of the empire, Alexandria, recognised only Paulinos as lawful bishop, and on its advice the Roman popes adopted the same line and cold-shouldered Meletios and his successor. This tragic legacy of schism, which

---

[43] Scarcely thirty days, John reports in *Hom. in Melet.* 1 (*PG* 50.516), where he also records the extraordinary devotion he inspired in such a short time.

[44] See J. Bidez and F. Cumont, *Iuliani imperatoris epistulae et leges* (Paris 1922), nos 43-5.

[45] Sokrates 4.2.

grew more intense in the reign of the Arian-minded Valens (364-78), was to embitter church life in the Syrian metropolis throughout the whole of John's life there; indeed, its dying embers were not to be extinguished until long after his death.[46]

[46] See below, p. 290.

2

The Young Ascetic

I

As a boy and teenager John's figure remains largely in the shadows, and we catch few if any reliable glimpses of his personality or activities. The picture changes strikingly when he reaches the end of his schooldays, and from this date we can follow his development in at any rate broad outline. In his apologia *Priesthood*,[1] written some twenty or so years later, he was to set down some illuminating reminiscences of critical moments in his life as a young man, and we shall draw on these. Their trustworthiness has sometimes been questioned, but it is difficult to believe that he could have written anything but the truth about himself in a work designed to be read by, and to convince, people among whom he had lived, and many of whom had known him personally, most of his life.

First, then, it seems clear that he completed his rhetorical studies under Libanios in 367,[2] when Flavius Valens, a bigoted, deeply superstitious Christian who actively supported Arianism in its Homoean form,[3] was now Augustus in charge of the eastern parts of the empire (364-78). The normal time for leaving school was towards the end of July, August and September being vacation months. According to Palladios, he was now eighteen; his own story about his mother, reproduced on p. 7 above, might suggest that he was twenty, but he was an inveterate rounder off of numbers. Palladios adds that he was a young man of more than ordinary intellectual ability, and his conduct seems to have been exemplary since in later life his detractors were unable, in spite of energetically raking over his past, to discover any youthful misdemeanours.[4] He still lived at home with his mother Anthousa, and while he had numerous friends, much the closest was the youthful Basil who has already been mentioned.[5] Coming from the same social background, they had been brought up together and had attended the same schools; they were always in each other's company, and shared a common outlook on most things, being both keen Christians. So

---

[1] *De sacerdotio* 1.1-3 (*SC* 271.60-76). The other main sources for this and the next section are Palladios, *Dial.* 5 (*SC* 341.105-10); Sokrates, 6.3; Sozomen, 8.3.

[2] For the chronology see Appendix B.

[3] See above, p. 11.

[4] See below, p. 204.

[5] See above, p. 5.

John was later to record in vivid passages which recapture the intimate friendship of the two young men, the one (himself) quick-tempered and self-assertive, the other more sensible and equable. In important respects, he admits, they differed. He himself was assiduous in his attendance at the law-courts, following the cases conducted there with excited interest; in addition, like the majority of the citizens of Antioch, he was passionately fond of the theatre. Basil had not the least concern for such things; he was so devoted to his books that he scarcely ever ventured out into the city square.

This reference to his habit as a student of hanging around the law-courts early gave rise to the inference that his ambition at this time must have been to practise at the bar. Sokrates, followed by Sozomen, drew this conclusion, the former adding for good measure that his adolescent enthusiasm had been checked when he realised how hard-worked a barrister was, and also how frequently he could be led into conniving at injustice. In fact, it was natural enough for a young man studying rhetoric to pay regular visits to the law-courts; and the value of an acquaintance with the law was not confined then, any more than today, to the legal profession. We have perhaps a more accurate clue to the career for which he was preparing himself in Palladios' remark that 'he was given a thorough training in rhetoric with a view to the service of the divine oracles (*ton theion logion*)'. The last three words seem at first sight to mean, and were in the past generally interpreted as meaning, the holy scriptures (the sense they most frequently bear in Palladios); but this makes nonsense of the passage, since a rhetorical education was neither necessary nor, in the view of strict Christians, desirable for the ministry of God's word. It also ignores the contrast which Palladios draws in the very next sentence between John's earlier, presumably secular, interests, and the sacred studies to which he was to turn in reaction on leaving Libanios' school.

There has therefore been widespread acceptance for the proposal that the correct rendering of 'divine oracles' is 'imperial pronouncements', i.e. rescripts, letters and constitutions emanating from the imperial chancellery, ultimately from the emperor.[6] Such documents were regularly described in Latin as 'sacred oracles (*sacra oracula*)' in the late empire, and the Greek adjective for 'divine' (*theios*), like its Latin equivalent, very commonly carried the alternative meaning 'imperial'. On the assumption that this was what Palladios had in mind, the career for which John was being trained as a youth, no doubt by his own choice and with his mother's approval, was service as one of the clerks of the *sacra scrinia*, i.e. the influential and much sought after secretariats which assisted the appropriate ministers in drafting official rescripts and constitutions, sometimes also legislation. This was a branch of the civil service for which a first-class literary education was indispensable, since government pronouncements

[6] A.H.M. Jones, *HTR* 46 (1953), 171-3.

needed to be clothed in clear and dignified prose, and for which practical experience of the law-courts was useful. Socially it ranked well above the secretariat of the commander-in-chief, in which John's father had served, for the successful clerks who came to the top in each of the *scrinia* ended their days with the rank of senators.

II

While this may have been the glittering career originally planned for him, it was not the one to which John was eventually to devote himself. In the passage already cited Palladios makes it plain that John's graduation from school coincided with a radical change in his whole mental attitude. He rebelled, Palladios states, against his liberal arts teacher,[7] an expert in 'meretricious verbiage', who had claimed his attention hitherto and, 'becoming intellectually a full-grown man, he fell in love with sacred studies', i.e. became absorbed with the scriptures. This dramatic switch is reflected in John's own reminiscences, for he was to record that, when he and his comrade Basil had completed their formal education, they decided 'to embrace the blessed life of solitaries and the true philosophy' (i.e., in the language of educated Christians of that time, the life of withdrawal, contemplation, scripture reading). Basil's enthusiasm for this, he confessed, was at first much the more intense; his own fluctuated wildly, as he was alternately distracted by worldly excitements, and then drawn back to higher pursuits. Although their friendship remained firm, there was a temporary break in their intimacy. We cannot gauge how long this lasted, but the time came when John was at last able, through his friend's influence, to drag himself out of his involvement with frivolous concerns. Basil received him with open arms, devoted himself wholly to him and laid bare a plan he had been pondering for some time, that they should abandon their parental homes and set up house together. His persuasions won John over, and the two made all the arrangements to carry out their project. It was only Anthousa who, with her tearful entreaties that John should not, in effect, leave her a widow for a second time but should stay at home with her as long as she lived, finally frustrated it.

Although often nowadays neglected, this passage throws light on what seems to have been a turning-point in John's acceptance of committed Christianity; it also illustrates one of the forms this might take for educated young men in fourth-century Antioch. It was about the same time, as we learn from Palladios in the text already cited, that John fell under the influence of 'blessed Meletios the confessor, who then ruled the church of Antioch'. This description was not strictly accurate, for the government nominee who was official bishop was the Arianizing Euzoios (361-76);

---

[7] The genitive singular, given by the G group of MSS, is preferable on grammatical grounds to the accusative plural printed by most editors. See *SC* 341.107 n. 3.

nevertheless, from 360 until his formal restoration in 378, Meletios was looked to as their leader by the main body of 'orthodox' Christians in Antioch,[8] who held their services in the open air, first on the slopes of the mountain, then on the banks of the Orontes, finally in the military exercise ground (*polemikon gumnasion*) outside the north gate.[9] In spite of Valens' decree (5 May 365) ordering back into exile the bishops whom Julian the Apostate had permitted to return,[10] Meletios seems to have contrived to remain in the city, probably because the emperor had been prevented from taking up residence there because of his preoccupation with the revolt (28 September 365) of the would-be usurper Prokopios, and then with a punitive war against the Goths who had supported him.[11] According to Palladios, 'he took notice of the gifted young man, was greatly attracted by the beauty of his character, and encouraged him to be continually in his company'. This close association of John with Meletios in fact marked another important stage in his spiritual development as a Christian. Palladios records that he now took the momentous step of offering himself for baptism, and after that was in regular attendance on the bishop for around three years. With the touching faith of a hero-worshipper Palladios later claimed that he could not believe that 'from the hour of his baptism John ever swore or made others take oaths, ever spoke evil of anyone, or told lies, or cursed, or tolerated frivolous talk'.[12]

In the fourth-century church the customary time for administering baptism was the night preceding the dawn of Easter. On the assumption that John left Libanios' school in mid-summer 367, the most probably date for his baptism would be Easter 368. Some of those who accept 349 as the date of his birth prefer to opt for Easter 367, implying that he left Libanios before the end of the school year and proceeded to the sacrament immediately; but on the face of it this seems precipitate, and in any case is not supported by any evidence. Others insist that he must have had a catechumenate, or period of organised preparation, of at least two years; but this is to overlook the fact that, while a two-year catechumenate was normally required of converts from paganism, the children of Christian parents were treated as catechumens from birth.[13] For these intensive instruction in Christian faith and morals during the preceding Lent was usually considered sufficient. The date 368 would also allow for John's three years' attendance on Meletios as an assistant mentioned by Palladios, for the harassed bishop was obliged to return into exile, at his family estate in Armenia, when Valens at last arrived and set up his headquarters in Antioch in late autumn 371. It was almost certainly Meletios who super-

---

[8] See above, p. 12.
[9] Theodoret, *Hist. rel.* 2 (*SC* 234.228).
[10] See above, pp. 10 and 12.
[11] So E. Schwartz, *ZNTW* 34 (1935), 168; 170 n. 82.
[12] *Dial.* 19 (*SC* 341.380).
[13] See Baur, 1.85 (with n. 8).

vised John's Lenten instruction and officiated at his baptism, for these
tasks counted among a bishop's chief responsibilities.

III

Palladios gives no hint of the form John's attendance on Meletios took, but
we may reasonably infer that he acted as the bishop's aide, or one of his
aides, in carrying out his liturgical, pastoral and administrative functions.
From a different quarter, however, we have some valuable information
which, as well as confirming the intensification of his religious commitment, goes a little way towards filling in our picture of his activities and
state of mind during this critical period (368-72) of his life.

Our informant is the historian Sokrates, who, without mentioning
Meletios' interest in him, reports that, when John had turned his back on
a secular career, he abandoned ordinary social life in favour of 'the life of
tranquillity – *ton hesuchion bion*', i.e. the life of ascetic withdrawal –
adopted the attire (the coarse, sleeveless robe known as the *lebiton*) and
the abstracted, solemn mode of walking affected by Christian 'monks', and
applied himself to bible study and to making frequent visits to church for
prayer.[14] He was inspired, Sokrates remarks, by the example of Evagrios,
a man who cannot now be identified, but who had studied under the same
professors and had a little earlier made a similar break. Already showing
the power to influence people which was always to characterise him, John
persuaded two friends who had also been fellow-students with him under
Libanios, Theodore and Maximos, to join him in renouncing any idea of a
life spent in making money and instead to embrace one of gospel simplicity.
We know nothing of Maximos except that he was to become bishop of
Seleukeia in Isauria (Silifke). Theodore, however, of whom we shall hear
more shortly, was to become bishop of Mopsuestia, in Cilicia (Misis, almost
30 km east of Adana), from 392 to 428, and one of the most brilliant (and
controversial) theologians and scripture expositors of the eastern church.

Sokrates adds that, in their zeal for spiritual excellence, John and his
two friends set themselves to study its principles under Diodore and
Carterios, who were at that time in charge of an ascetic school or schools
(*asketerion* or *asketeria*: it is not clear whether he used the singular or
plural). The Carterios mentioned here is otherwise unknown, but Diodore
was the orthodox leader whom we met (along with his colleague Flavian)
as a layman in the previous chapter,[15] and who had meanwhile (between
361 and 365), with Flavian, been ordained priest by Meletios. He was well
qualified to give instruction in asceticism, for the privations to which he
had subjected himself were so extreme that he had ruined his physical

---

[14] 6.3: see Sozomen 8.2.
[15] See above, p. 11.

health – earning him a mocking rebuke from Julian the Apostate in 363,[16] who attributed his emaciated appearance and bodily discomforts to the merited anger of the gods. That John had studied under Diodore has sometimes been questioned, but he himself was to confirm it many years later when Diodore, now bishop of Tarsos, visited Antioch and he acclaimed him from the pulpit as his spiritual father and teacher.[17] It is more than likely that he owed to him (among others) the marked preference he was to show in mature life for the literal, as opposed to the allegorical, method of interpreting scripture. The latter was widely popular, especially in Alexandrian circles, as a means of evading difficulties in the sacred text, but Diodore was a sharp critic of allegorising and championed straightforward, historical exegesis, while allowing that the historical events could foreshadow spiritual realities later to be revealed.

It is an intriguing question what exactly this *asketerion* was, in which upper-class, deeply religious young Christians of Antioch, like John and Theodore (John supplies us elsewhere with some further names), picked up their grounding in ascetic commitment and the understanding of scripture under Diodore's direction. Scholars have often assumed that it must have been a monastery, i.e. a community of monks living together under a rule, but this suggestion must be ruled out. As Meletios' deputy, in charge of the church during his absences, Diodore had too much on his hands to be the superior of a religious house. John, too, was still living at home with his mother, and was carrying out a range of practical duties for Meletios or his deputy. Nor is there any evidence, literary or archaeological, for the existence of a monastery within the walls of Antioch at this early date.[18] On the other hand, if Diodore's *asketerion* was not a monastery proper, it seems to have had certain unmistakably 'monastic' features. As we shall shortly discover,[19] the young men who frequented it regarded one another as 'brothers', as 'members' of a 'body', and on entering it they were enrolled on an official list (*katalogos*). When they joined it the members made a covenant or pact (*sunthekai*) with Christ by which they bound themselves to renounce marriage and a range of indulgences normally accepted by men of their class.

It seems more realistic, therefore, to envisage Diodore's pupils as a close-knit fellowship of dedicated Christians who, while staying in their separate homes and living in the world, accepted self-imposed rules of rigorous self-denial and met together, probably in some private house, to pray, study the bible and hear expositions of it, and be counselled by the master in ascetic withdrawal. Writing more than half a century later, when conditions had changed somewhat, it is understandable that Sokrates

---

[16] *Letter* 90 (to Photinos of Sirmium: Bidez 174-5).
[17] *Laus Diodori* (*PG* 52.761-6).
[18] Cf. P. Canivet, *Le monachisme syrien selon Théodoret de Cyr* (Paris 1977), 50-1.
[19] See below, p. 23.

should have used to describe the group a term which was not strictly applicable to it. Nevertheless, in the eyes of contemporaries its members were 'monks' (*monachoi*), for the Greek word, like its Syriac equivalent *ihidaya*, had a wider connotation then than it has today. It embraced not only (a) hermits and (b) religious organised in a community, but also fervent Christians who, while still moving around in the world, were striving to live a life as far as possible detached from it, focused wholly on God.[20] Their ideals and practices, it may be suggested, illustrate, in a Greek-speaking milieu, the peculiarly Syrian genre of asceticism practised by the 'sons of the covenant' or 'daughters of the covenant' (*benai qyama* or *benat qyama*) of whom we hear from fourth- and early fifth-century Syrian writers, notably Aphrahat and Rabbula of Edessa.[21] While the institution took a variety of forms, the 'sons of the covenant' often formed small brotherhoods attached to a local church and lived with its clergy; alternatively, they could stay with their relations, as apparently John did, or else completely alone. Without exception they entered into a pact or covenant with Christ, and bound themselves to remain celibate, abstain from wine and meat, wear a distinctive dress, and devote themselves to prayer; secular employment was forbidden for them. For discipline and support they generally depended on the local clergy, as John's group looked to Diodore for counsel and leadership, and they were expected to assist the clergy in liturgical, administrative and pastoral functions. They formed a pool to which local bishops readily turned when they needed new clergy for their churches. The expression 'sons of the covenant' had different nuances at different times, but when John was a young man its meaning admirably described the form of ascetic commitment which he and his fellow-students adopted.

IV

Two literary works by John, the earliest from his pen that have survived, may fairly be traced to this period. In a striking way they both illustrate the religious ideals which were then pervading his mind and, if correctly interpreted, throw light on his relations with one of the close friends mentioned in the previous section.

The first is the short essay known as *A King and a Monk Compared*.[22]

---

[20] G.M. Colombás, 'El concepto de monje y vida monastica hasta fines del siglo v', *SM* 1 (1959), 338-42.

[21] E.G.S. Jargy, *OCP* 17 (1951), 304-420; A. Vööbus, *Church History* 30 (1961), 19-27; S. Brock, *Syriac Perspectives and Late Antiquity* (London 1984), 1-19. A key text is Aphrahat's sixth *Demonstration* (*PSyr* 1.239-312).

[22] *Comparatio regis et monachi* (*PG* 47.387-392). For an English trans. see D.G. Hunter, *A Comparison between a King and a Monk* (Lampeter 1988), who dates it (p. 39) 'not long after 379', partly because he does not think John's enthusiasm for monasticism developed so early as has been argued above.

Although its authenticity has sometimes been doubted,[23] this is an attempt to show that, contrary to appearances and popular belief, it is not the emperor, but the monk living alone and surrendered wholly to God, who is true king. The monk (the term is used with its wide connotation) has got the better of human passions and desires, but the emperor, though ruling the world and robed in purple, is still enslaved to them. Both wage war, but the monk conquers evil demons and rescues people from paganism and heresy, the emperor fights with barbarians only to further his avarice and ambition. The monk spends his day in bible study and the night, after a frugal repast, conversing with God; the emperor is in conference all day with heavy-drinking military men, and spends the night sleeping off the effects of rich banquets. While the monk is welcomed by rich and poor with open arms, the emperor is dreaded by his subjects because of the exactions he has to make and his soldiers' brutal behaviour. He can distribute gold when so disposed, but the monk bestows richer gifts – the grace of the Spirit, release from demonic possession, comfort in affliction. Death itself, the thought of which terrifies the emperor, causes no worry to the monk, who long ago renounced the things for the sake of which most men desire life. And their prospects in the next world are immeasurably different. The monk can expect to be received by the Lord who provided the pattern of this blessed form of life; even if he has been a good ruler, the emperor can only look for a more modest reward, while if he has been an evil one, the torments he must face are beyond description.

Graphically written, but showing awkwardnesses of style which differentiate it from John's later work, the piece, which has all the air of a laboured school composition, is a Christian variation on the ancient paradox beloved by the Stoics that it is only the wise man who is truly free, intelligent, rich, sovereign. As such it leaves the impression that John wrote it quite soon after leaving Libanios' classroom. This is borne out, first, by the fact that it is a clear example, carried out according to all the rules, of what was known technically as a 'comparison (*sunkrisis*)', i.e. one of the dozen or so *progumnasmata*,[24] or preliminary exercises traditionally used in teaching rhetoric in schools; secondly, by the inclusion, in a piece only a few pages long, of no fewer than four striking phrases taken from his recent professor's speeches.[25] As well as supporting an early date, the patently artificial character of the essay is an argument against those who place it *either* in his period (372-8) of monastic retreat to Mt Silpios (hardly a propitious time in any case for literary composition), *or* after his return to

---

[23] See J.A. de Aldama, *Repertorium pseudochrysostomicum* (Paris 1965), 327; also *Clavis patrum Graecorum* 2.4500. The stylistic blemishes giving rise to these doubts seem better explained by the immaturity of the work.
[24] On these see PW Suppl. VII.118f.
[25] See C. Fabricius, *Symbolae Osloenses* 33 (1957), 135f. All four passages (from Orations 13 and 64, and the *Apology of Socrates*) date from 362-3, when Julian was resident in Antioch, and applaud either his or Sokrates' ascetic or simple habits.

Antioch, when his writings were to be both much more mature and more in contact with real life. In fact, it reads like an attempt by a relatively inexperienced enthusiast to persuade his friends to resist the allurements of a career in the imperial bureaucracy, with its opportunities for wielding secular power, and embrace instead the 'true philosophy'[26] of ascetic commitment. It has been proposed,[27] with some plausibility, that it was addressed in particular to his comrade Theodore, who (it would seem) was probably born in 352, entered Libanios' school in 366 and left it to join the ascetic group counselled by Diodore in 368/9, when he was sixteen or seventeen. If our little piece was written in 368, when John was a leading member of the group, it could not fail to have been devoured by his younger friend, and may have contributed to his conversion.

This is, of course, speculation, but there can be little doubt that the second of John's literary productions from this period, the longish letter known as *To Theodore When He Fell Away*,[28] was directed to this Theodore. Both Hesychios of Jerusalem, writing in the 430s, and Sozomen a little later, report[29] that John sent the future bishop of Mopsuestia when still a young man a letter which, from their summary of its contents, seems identical with this one; the only reasons for rejecting their evidence arise from supposed chronological considerations which have been shown to be insubstantial.[30] As it has come down, our letter is attached to a much lengthier work bearing the same title, of which it purports to be the second book.[31] There is nowadays agreement that the two are in fact independent. The longer piece is not a letter but a treatise, and is more mature theologically; and while there is a broad similarity of subject-matter, viz. an appeal to a lapsed ascetic to return to his vocation, it is evident that the persons admonished, and their situations, are markedly different. The letter, it is clear, was not drafted (a widely held assumption which was one of the causes of the alleged chronological difficulties) when John was living as a hermit or semi-hermit in the mountains outside Antioch, but when he and Theodore were associated with a group of other ascetically motivated Christians in the city. On the other hand, internal evidence demands that the treatise (which nowhere mentions Theodore's name) should be placed some sixteen or seventeen years later.

It is the letter which alone concerns us here. It is linked, we should note,

---

[26] For 'philosophy' used in this sense see also *De sacerdotio* 1.2 (*SC* 272.62), with A.M. Malingrey's note.
[27] R.E. Carter, 'Chrysostom's *Ad Theodorum lapsum* and the early chronology of Theodore of Mopsuestia', *VC* 16 (1962), 87-101. By 1967 (*Studia Patristica* 10 = *TU* 107) Carter had come to doubt the authenticity of *Comparatio*.
[28] *Ad Theodorum lapsum* 2: *PG* 47.309-16: also in *SC* 117 (ed. J. Dumortier).
[29] 8.2: for Hesychios see Mansi ix.248.
[30] R.E. Carter, art. cit. 92-5.
[31] *PG* 47.277-308. For its independence see J. Dumortier's discussion in *SC* 117; R.E. Carter, art. cit., 88-92.

with *A King and a Monk Compared* by the similarity of some of its themes, and indeed seems to refer to it in a passage pointedly contrasting power, wealth and reputation with the true freedom enjoyed by the Christian.[32] What prompted John to write it was the fact that Theodore (it slips out that he was not yet twenty years old), after joining his ascetic group and creating an edifying impression by his ardour in mortifications and scripture study, had thrown it all up. Family business had claimed his attention; later we learn that his thoughts were turning to marriage. Hence John wrote to him, in highly charged grief rather than anger, reproaching him with indifference (*rathumia*) and urging him to think again and rejoin the fraternity; his friends Valerios, Florentios, Porphyrios and others are all praying for him. He reminds him that he had forsworn extravagant food and clothes, and dismissed all thought of his family rank and wealth from his mind. The letter throws precious light on a personal crisis in the early career of the future famous exegete and bishop of Mopsuestia, but it also confirms the picture of John's spiritual fellowship we set out in the previous section. John upbraids his young friend with 'erasing his name from the list (*katalogos*) of brothers' and 'trampling on the contract (*sunthekai*) he had entered into with Christ'.[33] Marriage, he concedes, may in general be honourable, but for Theodore it would amount to adultery since he has 'joined himself to the heavenly bridegroom'. There is no question here of vows taken by a monk in a monastery (as some interpreters suppose), but still less is John's language intended to be purely figurative (as others argue). Rather it evokes distinctive features of the characteristically Syrian 'sons of the covenant',[34] and confirms that this was the pattern of ascetic brotherhood to which John and his circle belonged.

John's message to Theodore was that, if he had momentarily yielded to the Devil's seductions, he need only turn his gaze to heaven, and Christ would rescue him. Serious Christians a couple of generations later were filled with admiration for his letter, the pious Sozomen exclaiming that in both diction and sentiments it was more divine than the mind of man could conceive.[35] Theodore evidently thought so too, for Sozomen adds that, when he had pondered it, he once again abandoned his property, said goodbye to thoughts of marriage and, saved by John's wise counsel, returned to the life of true philosophy.

---

[32] See R.E. Carter, art. cit., 93f. The passage referred to is the opening of sect. 3 (*PG* 47.312).
[33] *Ad Theodorum lapsum* 2.1 (*PG* 47.309).
[34] See above, p. 20.
[35] 8.2.

3

Retreat to the Mountains

I

Palladios reports that, after serving as bishop Meletios' personal aide for 'about three years',[1] John was appointed an official reader (*anagnostes*: *lector* in Latin), in the eastern churches the lowest order of the clergy, ranking immediately below that of deacons. Although Palladios does not explicitly say so, his language implies that it was Meletios, not an otherwise unknown bishop Zeno as stated by Sokrates,[2] who ordained him. This is what we should have expected if, as our chronology requires, the ordination or promotion (it was the latter verb, *proagein*, that the biographer preferred) took place in 371, since Meletios was still in Antioch for most of that year. Emperor Valens had made brief stays in the city in 370, possibly also in early 371, during which Meletios may have gone into temporary hiding. When Valens, however, set up his winter quarters there in late autumn 371,[3] and was clearly set for continuous residence except for military expeditions in summer, he could no longer afford to play fast and loose with the decree of 5 May 365 expelling the bishops whom Julian the Apostate had permitted to regain their sees, and was obliged to go into definitive exile. He was to remain in his Armenian homeland until the emperor's death in the disastrous battle against the Goths at Adrianople (Edirne) on 9 August 378.

Meletios must have foreseen well in advance that he was faced with an indefinite absence from his flock. It was therefore desirable to reinforce the ranks of the local clergy, and after his three years of probation John must have seemed marked out for recruitment to it. As a reader he had the specific functions of reading the Old Testament lesson and the epistle at mass, but further responsibilities are likely to have devolved upon him now that he belonged, however modestly, to the official body of the clergy.

II

Years later John was to record two dramatic incidents which, although they cannot be precisely dated, must have happened quite soon after his admis-

---

[1] *Dial.* 5 (*SC* 341.108).
[2] 6.3.
[3] Cf. PW II: 7A.2115 (A. Nagl).

sion as a reader. One of them, of little or no importance in itself, vividly recaptures the atmosphere of stark terror which gripped Antioch during the winter of 371/2 and for many months thereafter; the other was to have a profound and lasting impact on his own career.

He was to recount the first in a sermon delivered at Constantinople some thirty years later. Long ago when he was 'still a mere lad', he recalled,[4] he was walking with a friend through the gardens alongside the Orontes on his way to a martyr's shrine when his companion noticed a white object floating on the water. It looked like a piece of linen, but when they saw that it was in fact a book they vied with each other in sporting rivalry to fish it out. When they had got hold of it and turned a page, they discovered to their horror that it was covered with magical formulae. Its terrified owner had tried to get rid of it, but they knew that even so he had been arrested and executed. Panic reigned in Antioch at the time, for the government, alarmed by the exposure of a conspiracy to ascertain by divination when the emperor would die and what the name of his successor would be, was holding a succession of ferocious investigations, trials and executions of everyone even remotely suspected of being involved.[5] Anyone dabbling in sorcery or magic arts, or possessing books dealing with such potentially treasonable subjects, was liable to summary action. The city was everywhere patrolled by soldiers on the lookout, and as they handled the incriminating codex the young men saw one approaching. Rigid with fear, they managed to conceal it, and when he had passed on his way they flung it back into the river. Their escape from almost certain death, John was to assure his rapt congregation, was but one out of countless instances of God's merciful intervention which should incite human beings to greater love for him.

Our knowledge of the second, intrinsically much more important incident comes exclusively from the autobiographical passages of his dialogue *Priesthood* (written 390/1) on which we drew extensively in the previous chapter. In these he describes,[6] in his liveliest narrative style, how when he was a reader still living at home, almost certainly after Meletios' departure for exile, he and his comrade Basil heard a report that the responsible church authorities were planning to seize them both and have them ordained under duress (such press-ganging of apparently suitable young men for the ministry was not uncommon at the time). Their intention was, in all probability, to ordain them priests; the widely held view that they were to be consecrated bishops, unlikely in itself, is traceable to John's preoccupation with the episcopal office in important later sections of the dialogue. The correct reading in the key passage (1.6) is probably not

---

[4] *Hom. in Act.* 38.5 (*PG* 60.274f.). John was 22 or 23, but his use of *meirakion* ('mere lad') was flexible: see Appendix B.

[5] For a full, up-to-date account of the affair, see J. Matthews, *The Roman Empire of Ammianus* (London 1989), 219-20.

[6] *De sacerdotio* 1.3 (*SC* 272.72-6).

episkopes ('episcopate'), but *hierosunes* ('priesthood'), an inclusive term applying in the appropriate context to both the presbyterate and the episcopate.[7]

Both young men, John relates, were filled with dismay by the news. John, however, while convinced of his own utter unworthiness, had no doubt at all that Basil was eminently suited for the priestly office. So he resorted to what has impressed most modern students as a dishonourable stratagem.[8] Although he and Basil made a solemn agreement to act in unison, either both of them accepting or both declining ordination, he privately decided to go his own way even if it meant letting his friend down. Thus when the bishop arrived, Basil submitted under protest to being ordained, being convinced that in view of his promise John too would accept ordination; indeed, bystanders confirmed that he had already done so. In fact, he had gone into hiding. Basil was shattered when he discovered the deception, and reproached him bitterly, only to be assured by John (who was highly amused by the success of his ploy) that he had acted in the way he had out of regard for the church's best interests. What he had done, he argued, should properly be described as 'prudent management' (*oik-onomia*), doing what is best in difficult circumstances, rather than as a deceitful act. In certain circumstances, he suggested, 'a well-timed deception, undertaken with a morally good intention', could be the proper course for a Christian.[9] He then proceeded to illustrate, at great length and with a casuistical expertise which has often embarrassed his admirers, how invaluable deceits (*apatai*) planned 'with a salutary purpose' can be in war, in medical practice, even in the conduct of family life and relations with one's friends.[10]

Ordinary readers are usually struck by the freshness and naturalness of John's narrative, and by the countless lifelike touches it contains. They find in these traits a guarantee of its general veracity, even allowing for the freedom he clearly allowed himself in setting down his recollections. The impression of authenticity is heightened, as the dialogue proceeds, by his deeply emotional account of the public reaction to his refusal to be ordained. The prominent people who had put him forward were outraged by what they regarded as gross discourtesy. In the community he was accused on every hand of arrogance and vain ambition for spurning this public service; not a soul would come forward to defend him. Even Basil found himself implicated in his disgrace, and complained that he had had to go into hiding, for every time he ventured into the street he risked being upbraided for John's conduct; no one would believe that he had not been fully aware what his close friend and comrade was up to.[11]

[7] Cf. A.M. Malingrey, *SC* 272 (Paris 1980), 72f.
[8] *De sac.* 1.5-7 (*SC* 272.88-98).
[9] *De sac.* 1.7 (*SC* 272.90).
[10] *De sac.* 1.6-7 (*SC* 272.90-8).
[11] See the remarkable passage 1.4 (*SC* 272.76-87).

By contrast the majority of Chrysostom scholars this century (there have been welcome signs of a reaction recently)[12] have been inclined to dismiss this entire section of John's treatise, with almost all the rest of the seemingly autobiographical material it contains, as 'a literary fiction' without historical basis, a dramatic lead-up to the eloquent exposition of the dignity and responsibilities of priesthood which, as they maintain, was his sole concern,[13] and which itself, as everyone would admit, while purporting to be John's rejoinder to Basil some twenty years back, really represents his mature views at the time of writing. In support of their scepticism they point out, first, that none of our usual authorities shows any knowledge of what must have been, if it ever took place at all, an extremely important episode in John's life. Secondly, they argue that if a young man like Basil was so closely involved in John's affairs, it is surprising that no other record of his existence seems to have survived, and that no mention of him can be found elsewhere in John's writings. Thirdly, they make much of the fact that in a Platonic-style dialogue, the genre to which everyone agrees *Priesthood* belongs, it is quite normal for the *mise-en-scène* to be largely invented.[14]

Of these three arguments (there are others of less weight) the first is scarcely persuasive. Sokrates and Sozomen had access to only a few, apparently random facts about John's youthful experiences, while it would be absurd to expect Palladios' compressed summary (half a dozen sentences) to include everything of significance. He makes no mention, for example, of either the key role of Diodore as John's ascetic mentor or of the close friendship between John and Theodore. It was his practice, in any case, to pass discreetly over anything likely to show his hero in an unfavourable light. The second carries scepticism too far. The inability to identify a relatively obscure individual in a world about which hard information is so sparse would not in itself be an argument against his existence. As it happens, however, there is a Basil known to history whom, while proof is out of the question, scholars from Tillemont to the present day have recognised as one who might well have been John's comrade.[15] This was the Basil who attended the council of Constantinople (381) as bishop of Raphaneae (Rafniye), a garrison town on the road from Emesa (Homs) to Antioch. If John's friend was ordained about 371, he could have been bishop of Raphaneae by 381. Some have even read John's comforting promise, in the last paragraph of the dialogue,[16] that he will give him his

[12] See the remarks of A.M. Malingrey in *SC* 272.19-22.

[13] For a summary of current attitudes see J. Quasten, *Patrology* (Maryland 1960) 3, 462. A. Nägele, *HJG* 37 (1916), 1-48 remains an influential statement of the sceptical case.

[14] J. Stiglmayr, 'Die historische Unterlage der Schrift des hl. Chrysostomus über das Priestertum', *ZKTh* 41 (1917), 413-49, is a convincing refutation of this case. It is a neglected study.

[15] E.g. A.M. Malingrey, op. cit., 7-10.

[16] *De sac.* 6.13 (*SC* 272.362).

presence and counsel frequently as a coded message that at the time of its
composition Basil was exercising his ministry not far from Antioch.

As regards the third argument, the dialogue form certainly gave John a
free hand in shifting the scenery of his story, improvising conversational
exchanges and lengthier speeches, and the like. But, written as it was for
a community in which he had grown up and was now a leading presbyter,
it did not license him to impose on his readers the report of an attempted
ordination which was an entire fabrication. More seriously, the argument
rests on a failure to recognise the true character of *Priesthood*. Cast in the
form of a dialogue, it is really an essay in self-vindication, an *apologetikos
logos* as it is often described in early MSS, designed to justify, in face of the
criticism and hostility it had aroused and which had probably persisted for
years, his apparently frivolous rejection of the priestly office long ago.
Modern students have tended to regard it exclusively as a magnificent
description of that office in all its aspects. It is that in full measure, but
when he wrote it John's overriding concern was to assure the Antiochene
public that, contrary to the misrepresentations he had suffered from as a
young man, his only motive for turning the priesthood down had been his
conviction at the time that he was utterly unfit for it. His statement is an
intensely personal one – the passion vibrating through it can be sensed by
readers today – but it would have been laughed out of court at Antioch,
where many were still alive who had known him as a young man, and would
have bemused readers elsewhere, if the spurned ordination which he
claimed had inspired it was in fact nothing more than a 'dramatic fiction'.

III

If scepticism about John's youthful reminiscences seems ill-founded, we
must accept that in 371/2 a determined attempt was made by the church
authorities in Antioch to have him ordained. We must also accept, although
the fact has been generally ignored by historians, that his successful
resistance aroused widespread indignation and resentment. Quite soon,
probably, after this dramatic incident he took the decision, as he was to
recall about a decade later,[17] 'to quit the city and make for the huts of the
monks' (*tas skenas ton monachon*). Palladios, who must have obtained his
information from John, was more specific, reporting that when he was a
reader 'he betook himself to the nearby mountains',[18] i.e. to Mt Silpios. He
suggests that John had two motives. First, he had conscientious scruples
that the tasks he was undertaking in the city were not sufficiently demanding; secondly, he was troubled by the difficulty he had in controlling his
burgeoning sexuality. The former must be set in the context of the severe
disruption caused to the orthodox community by Meletios' enforced return

[17] *De compunctione* 1.6 (*PG* 47.403): written 381/2 after his return to Antioch.
[18] *Dial.* 5 (*SC* 341.108).

to exile in late 371. Several of his clergy seem to have left Antioch about the same time; in 372, for example, we find that Diodore had joined the bishop in Armenia.[19] If anything, the church desperately needed trained manpower, but the leaders who remained may have had qualms about asking the young reader who had recently rejected ordination to assume additional responsibilities. The second is perhaps confirmed by John's own confession, in the closing pages of *Priesthood*,[20] that at this time he was still the prey to 'vicious passions' (*epithumiai atopoi*); it was only his closeted life and deliberate avoidance of, among other things, frequent meetings with women that prevented them from erupting.

By themselves these two reasons provide a sufficient explanation of his decision. He had been drawn, as we have seen,[21] to 'the blessed life of solitaries' ever since leaving Libanios' school; to migrate to the mountains was a logical further step. But it is reasonable to surmise that there was another, perhaps even more compelling reason for his withdrawal, which Palladios as a hero-worshipper did not think it necessary to record. Although he was confining himself, as he claimed in the vivid reminiscence cited above, to a tiny room, making himself unsociable and avoiding company as much as possible, his resolve to make a complete break with the community in which his credit had sunk so low can be readily understood.

Silpios was the obvious region for him to retreat to. Its north-eastern slopes, with their barren cliffs of lime and chalk and the inhospitable hinterland, had for some time been the favourite resort of religiously-minded Antiochenes seeking escape to a more intense life of communion with God. So numerous were they that the historian-theologian Theodoret, a native of Antioch (b. *c.* 393) and later bishop of Kyrrhos, in north Syria, an industrious chronicler of the heroes of Syrian asceticism, was to declare that they had made the whole area as beautiful as a flower-decked meadow.[22] Palladios, who had almost certainly gleaned his information from John, reports that he there fell in with an elderly Syrian, an expert in ascetic self-mastery, placed himself under his tutelage and spent the next four years with him, struggling against the onset of sensual passions.[23] John himself, in the retrospective text already cited, gives a rare self-deprecatory glimpse of the petty things he was tempted to fret about as he embarked on his new life:[24] 'I couldn't stop fussing and trying to discover where I'd get my supply of necessary items, whether I'd be able to eat fresh bread each day and whether I'd be obliged to use the same oil for both my lamp and my food, whether I'd have a wretched diet of lentils forced on me,

[19] Cf. Basil of Caesarea, *Ep.* 99.3 (ed. Y. Courtonne, 1, 217).
[20] *De sac.* 6.12 (*SC* 272.342-6).
[21] See above, p. 16.
[22] *HE* 4.28.3 (*GCS* 44.269).
[23] *Dial.* 5 (*SC* 341.108-10).
[24] *De compunctione* 1.6 (*PG* 47.403).

and be assigned some back-breaking task – being ordered, for example, to dig, or carry logs or water, or perform all sorts of services of that kind. In a word, my great worry was about the time that would be allowed me for spiritual recreation' (*anapausis*).

IV

So far as particular events or experiences are concerned, John's life during these four critical years (372-6) remains a complete blank to us, but we can form a fairly clear, if general, picture of its pattern. It is sometimes assumed that he spent them alone with his Syrian guru; after all, beyond remarking that he modelled himself on the old man's tough self-discipline, that is all Palladios actually tells us. But his summary statement should not be taken as necessarily complete. John's own fragmentary reminiscence of his move quoted above makes it plain that it was not to isolation but to some kind of community. He speaks there of 'the huts of the monks', and implies that there would be people who would assign him tasks and supervise his behaviour. These hints are confirmed, and fleshed out with detail, by several homilies which he was to preach in Antioch after his ordination in 386, and in which, with starry-eyed enthusiasm, he was to hold up the monks settled on Silpios as an inspiring example to his worldly congregation.[25] His descriptions of their manner of life and their conduct are uncritically eulogistic; he was recalling his own time spent among them with affectionate nostalgia, and could not bring himself to admit that human frailties could exist among such paragons. But his accounts of the structures and routines of these settlements can be accepted as authentic recollections of the one to which he himself had belonged during those four years.

The picture he draws is of what was, in essence, a multiple hermitage, with numerous small huts or cells grouped closely together. In a vivid image he likens them to the serried tents of a military camp, with the difference that there were no glittering spears with saffron mantles fastened to them planted by the monks' hovels. Each monk had his own hut assigned to him; he remained in it alone throughout the night and much of the day. It seems likely that John and his Syrian guide occupied adjacent cells. But while each retained his independence in a way characteristic of Syrian monasticism, the monks were far from being hermits or anchorites in the strict sense. There were certain clearly defined communal arrangements to which they were all expected to adhere. Thus before daybreak, so soon as the cock crowed, their superior (*proestos*) went his rounds and, with a light touch of his foot, awakened the inmates of the huts. They all got up – no need to dress, for sleeping naked was banned – and together, with arms

[25] *In Matt. hom.* 55.5-6; 68.3-5; 69.3-4; 70.5; 72.3-4; *In I Tim. hom.* 14.3-6 (*PG* 58.545-50; 643-8; 651-4; 660-2; 670-4; *PG* 62.574-80).

upraised, chanted psalms of praise and gratitude to God. Their day was in fact divided into four parts, and at the end of each they assembled to glorify God in unison with psalm-singing (John uses the Greek terms for terce, sext, nones and vespers).[26]

After these acts of worship the monks returned each to his own cell to study the scriptures, meditate on them and on God himself, or on the contrast between the visible and the invisible world. The rule of silence was strictly observed. But there were also practical tasks they took in hand – digging the ground, watering and planting it, plaiting straw to make baskets, weaving coarse cloth, copying books. The substantial profits they made from this work they devoted to poor relief. There were also visitors to be received and entertained. Their sole meal, taken by most (it would seem) in common, came in the evening. Some took only bread and salt, others added a little oil, the more enfeebled ate green vegetables (*lachana*) and dried lentils (*ospria*). Their clothing was equally simple, consisting for the most part of goat-skins and camel-skins. In their cells they slept on straw spread on the bare ground, but sometimes with no roof except the sky above them.

Scholars have sometimes claimed that it was during his four years in such a community that John wrote several of his ascetic treatises.[27] These include *A King and a Monk Compared* and *To Theodore When He Fell Away*, which we noticed in the last chapter, but also certain others at which we shall glance in the next. As it happens, internal evidence makes it much more plausible that these texts originated when John was in Antioch, in direct contact with the individuals addressed or the problems treated. It is, however, difficult, in the light of his fairly detailed descriptions of the monastic routine, to find a place in it for such extensive literary activity; it is even harder to picture him carrying it out in the tiny cell, lacking all but the most basic facilities, which he must have occupied. Hardest of all, perhaps, is it to envisage him being allowed to devote himself to such a time-consuming, essentially private employment in a community in which the tasks carried out by the members seem to have been largely shared. One wonders whether those who attribute the composition of such lengthy works to John's monastic period have been led astray by the misleading parallel of his contemporary Jerome, a very different, élitist figure, who during part of this time was installed in his cave with his library at not far distant Chalcis, and was able to keep on writing to his friends and studying books to his heart's content.[28]

In fact, if we wish to form a realistic idea of how John and his fellow-monks spent the greater part of their time, we should recall that the ideal at which they aimed was to maintain, as far as possible, uninterrupted

---

[26] *In I Tim. hom.* 14.4 (*PG* 62.576D: *trite, hekte, ennete, hesperinai euchai*).

[27] E.g. A. Moulard, *Saint Jean Chrysostome* (Paris 1949), 34-7.

[28] J.N.D. Kelly, *Jerome* (London 1975), ch. vi.

communion with God. This ideal was well expressed in the counsel which Eusebios, the early fifth-century leader of just such a community at Koruphe, a cone-shaped mountain dominating the plain of Tell 'Ade just east of Antioch, gave to his disciples. 'He exhorted them', Theodoret records, 'to keep up their converse with God uninterruptedly, without allowing a single moment to be exempt from this activity. While they should carry out the exercises prescribed by their rule, they should, during all the breaks between these throughout the entire day, go each by himself, and under the shade of a tree or beside a rock or wherever else he could find some tranquillity, standing erect or lying on the ground, should pray to the Master and implore him for salvation.'[29] How far they succeeded in living up to these high standards, no one can tell, but John shared them to the full, claiming in one passage that the task of monks was that of Adam before the Fall, to converse continually with God, with absolute frankness and a conscience free from guilt.[30]

V

After four years of semi-communal monasticism John switched to a much more rigorous, demanding programme. For this stage our sole informant is Palladios, who relates that, when he had mastered his sensual passions, 'not so much by strenuous self-discipline as by spiritual insight', he went off by himself to a cave in the mountain and lived there alone for 'thrice eight months, seeking complete escape from the world'.[31] He adds that he passed most of that long span without sleeping, learning the Old and New Testaments by heart, and that for the entire two years he never lay down by night or day. He was allowing himself, we may assume, only the most meagre diet, with long spells of fasting. It is little wonder that, as a result of his self-mortification, he severely damaged his health; as Palladios puts it, 'his gastric regions were deadened, and the functions of his kidneys were impaired by the intense cold'. For the rest of his life John was to suffer from rushes of blood to the head, stomach trouble and insomnia, and to be extremely sensitive to winter cold.

Scholars have sometimes speculated on what drove John to seek complete isolation in this way. The fanciful theory has even been propounded that he wanted to hide himself from leading Christians in the Antiochene community who were still over-eager to recruit him for the ordained ministry. There is, however, no need to hunt around for any other explanation than the obvious one, his yearning for a less distracted, richer, ever more continuous converse with God. We should note that among the distinctive features of Syrian asceticism at this time was the conviction

[29] *Hist. phil.* 4.5 (*SC* 234.300-2).
[30] *Hom in Matt.* 68.2 (*PG* 58.643-4).
[31] *Dial.* 5. (*SC* 341.110).

that the supreme perfection was to be found in the entirely secluded life; 'it was the solitary virtuoso', as a contemporary scholar has remarked, 'who dominated the scene'.[32] Even in the community in which John had spent his first four years, we saw that each of the monks had his own cell, and spent prolonged periods all alone in it. In fact, as another scholar has noted, the communal monastery in fifth-century Syria could be regarded simply as 'a school for solitaries, the training ground in which the future champions of asceticism prepared themselves'.[33] Some of these Syriac monasteries had 'the curious custom of choosing out their more advanced members for the life of complete seclusion, wholly consecrated to the things of God. These were the monks of the first class, the authentic ones, the specialists in mortification and continuous prayer, the only ones in whom writers of the time like Theodoret were interested.'

So in withdrawing to his lonely cave, once he felt sure he had won control of his physical nature, John was taking a step which contemporaries accepted as natural for an advanced ascetic. Theodoret, who had studied the behaviour, and indeed idiosyncrasies, of such heroes at first hand, has a passage which provides an instructive commentary.[34] There are several ladders, he remarked, by which aspirants to higher religion can ascend to heaven. There are, of course, those who fight their battle in groups; they win an incorruptible crown. 'There are others, however, who embrace the life of complete isolation and train themselves to hold converse all alone by themselves with God. Cutting themselves off from all human consolation, they in this way find themselves acclaimed as victors. Some of these live in huts, others in wretched hovels, celebrating God's praises. Others too prefer to dwell in caverns or in holes in the rocks.'

The punishing regimen to which John, by Palladios' account, subjected himself while shut up in his cave, though striking modern students as bizarre to the point of absurdity, was also entirely in keeping with everything we know about the practices of Syrian solitaries of that period. Denying oneself sleep, with its 'most sweet tyranny', was a highly prized form of self-mortification among them.[35] Their supreme objective was, as far as possible, to commune with God continually, and any practice or indulgence that stood in the way of this was to be rigorously excluded. Thus any device that reduced sleep, or made the short periods of inevitable rest as uncomfortable as possible, was welcomed; the ideal, rarely of course achieved, was complete sleeplessness. Similarly, the practice of continually standing (technically known as *stasis*) was much in vogue in the second half of the fourth and the first half of the fifth centuries. Several of the holy men whose portraits figure in Theodoret's gallery practised this for years

---

[32] S. Brock, *Syrian Perspectives in Late Antiquity* (London 1984), 13.
[33] G.M. Colombás, *El Monacato Primitivo* I (Madrid 1974), 138.
[34] *Hist. rel.* 27 (*SC* 257.216-18).
[35] E.g. Theodoret, *De caritate* 3 (*SC* 257.262).

on end; in reporting on them he distinguished between those who stood erect without interruption and the weaker spirits who divided the day between standing and sitting.[36] According to some, the rationale of the practice was that it was improper for the slave to lie down in the presence of his master. How deeply entrenched it was is impressed on the traveller today when, visiting the Syrian Orthodox abbey of Qartmin (still in use) in the Tur Abdin region of south-east Turkey, he is shown a cell containing a narrow alcove, as high as a man, which was carefully constructed in the fifth or sixth century to assist a recluse to remain perpetually standing.[37]

John had probably envisaged himself as glorifying God, like other contemporary solitaries, in his lonely cell, perhaps also guiding others to follow his example, for the rest of his life. But it was not so to be. When he realised, Palladios reports, that the breakdown of his health made further progress in self-mortification impracticable, he returned to the city.[38] Palladios does not conceal his satisfaction. It was the Saviour's providence, he claimed, which, exploiting his enfeebled condition for the benefit of the church, obliged him to abandon his cave. We need not doubt that it was his wretched state of health that prompted the move. It is likely, as we shall see,[39] that pressures from outside helped to reinforce his decision, but Palladios' account provides a sufficient general explanation. A suggestion which should be rejected is that, while ill health played its part, the real reason for his return was disillusionment with the monastic life, the conviction that he was cut out for active service to the church rather than a purely contemplative role.[40] Such a view is impossible to reconcile with the admiration he lavishes on monks not only in the homilies drawn on in the previous section, which he preached after his ordination in 386, but in such a work as *Against the Enemies of Monasticism*,[41] which he was to write shortly after settling again in Antioch. It is, perhaps, significant that the advocates of this line tend to date this work, almost certainly mistakenly, to the four years he spent in a monastic settlement.

The chief objection to their interpretation, however, is that it rests on a misunderstanding of John's conception of what being a monk entails. On the one hand, he never seems to have wavered from the belief that monks, whether living in community or as solitaries, are (perhaps he meant, have the best chance of being) perfect Christians; as he repeatedly claimed, they live the life of angels and as such are beacons to ordinary people. Not that he viewed them as totally withdrawn from the world; just occasionally he could express exasperation when a monk, asked to undertake some service

---

[36] Theodoret, *Hist. rel.* 27 (*SC* 257.216-18).
[37] See A. Palmer, *Monk and Mason on the Tigris Frontier* (Cambridge 1990), 98-9, where the Syriac *Life of Barsawmo* is referred to for the rationale of the practice.
[38] *Dial.* 5 (*SC* 341.110).
[39] See below, p. 37.
[40] E.g. A. Moulard, op. cit., 38f.
[41] *Adv. oppugnatores vitae monasticae*, *PG* 47.349-86.

for the church, showed selfish concern that his 'spiritual leisure' might be interrupted.[42] On the other hand, he was insistent that Christians in the world should, as far as their circumstances allowed, accept exactly the same standards of perfection as monks. Scripture, he pointed out, nowhere mentions the expressions 'living in the world' (*biotikos*) and 'monk' (*monachos*); the distinction was a purely human invention. The reason for this is that Christ's 'great and marvellous precepts', the ideals implied in the Beatitudes and held up before men in the gospels, are addressed to all his followers alike. Thus the monastic calling, in the wider sense, is just as imperious an obligation, and just as practicable an option, in the crowded city as in a cavern or on the mountainside. It is as much within the reach of the married man, living with his wife and rearing children, as of the single man, provided he conducts his relations with his wife becomingly.[43]

John's attitude, it is apparent, contained an ambiguity which he never attempted to resolve. It meant, however, that when he left his cave and resumed city life he did not conceive of himself as ceasing to be a monk. As deacon, priest and bishop he not only remained a monk at heart (what, after all, was a monk but a Christian striving to live out the gospel to the full?), but continued, as far as his new situation permitted, to practise his routine of monastic austerities – for example living alone as much as possible. Consistently with this, he never hesitated as bishop, when the needs of the church seemed to warrant it, to call monks from their seclusion and either ordain them and associate them with his ministry or employ them as missionaries. However romantically he could idealise monks in their secluded retreats, he could never, with his wider understanding of the monastic vocation, envisage them as standing apart from the church and its predicaments. As he was to put it eloquently, 'Nothing more truly characterises the man who believes in and loves Christ than that he is concerned for his brothers and exerts himself for their salvation. Let all the monks who have withdrawn to the mountain peaks and have crucified themselves to the world heed these words. Let them back up the church's leaders with all the powers at their command, encouraging them by their prayers, their sympathy, their love. Let them realise that if, placed though they are so far away, they fail to sustain with all their efforts those whom God's grace has exposed to such anxieties and dangers, their life has lost all its point and their religious devotion has been shown up as useless.'[44]

[42] *De compunctione* 1.16 (*PG* 47.403).
[43] *Adv. oppugn. vitae mon.* 3.14; *In Matt. hom.* 7.7; *In Heb. hom.* 7.4 (*PG* 47.373; 58.81f.; 63.67f.).
[44] *De incomp.* 6.2f. (*PG* 48.752).

4

Deacon and Pamphleteer

I

By the time John got back to Antioch, probably in the last quarter of 378, momentous changes affecting the Christian population were under way in the city as in the eastern empire generally. The death of Emperor Valens in battle at Adrianople (9 August 378) signalled the collapse of his policy of actively supporting a Homoean or even Arianizing interpretation of Christianity, which had driven a wedge between the eastern and (pro-Nicene) western parts of the empire. On hearing the news his 19-year-old nephew Gratian, emperor in the west since 367 and an adherent of the orthodox Nicene doctrine, immediately issued a decree from Sirmium (Sremska Mitrovica, west of Belgrade) permitting the return of all exiled bishops and proclaiming freedom of worship for all but a few extremist sects.[1] The brilliant general Theodosius, whom he then summoned from retirement in Spain to lead an expedition against the Goths south of the Danube, and whom after its signal success he promoted Augustus of the east on 19 January 379, was an even more resolute upholder of the full Nicene teaching. Through his influence Gratian's edict of toleration was replaced, on 3 August 379, by one outlawing all forms of heresy;[2] like Constantine the Great, he believed that the emperor's first duty was to maintain the unity of the church. Then on 28 February 380 he decreed[3] that all his subjects should conform to the faith preached by St Peter to the Romans and now taught by pope Damasus and by Peter of Alexandria (he included Peter because it was with Alexandria among the eastern churches that Rome customarily dealt), i.e. the belief in the one Godhead of three co-equal persons subsisting in trinity. Anyone deviating from this was branded as a heretic. He thus made plain his resolve to reorganise the church in his realms on the basis of Nicene orthodoxy, and thereby re-establish religious unity with the west.

Meanwhile Meletios, taking advantage of Gratian's edict, had returned to Antioch from his Armenian exile. The orthodox community, with the exception of Paulinos' tiny hard-line Nicene group, joyfully received him

[1] Sokrates 5.2; Sozomen 7.1: referred to in CT 16.5.5.
[2] CT 16.5.5.
[3] CT 16.1.2.

back as their legitimate bishop, and the military commander Sapores, imperial commissioner for church affairs, recognised him as such. It seems likely that he also handed over the city churches to him, but it has been argued that he must have waited until early 381, when an imperial rescript specifically ordered the surrender of catholic churches everywhere to their bishops.[4] Meletios met no opposition from Dorotheos, the Arian appointed to succeed Euzoios as bishop in 376;[5] he may have left the city when Valens marched north against the Goths in 378. The elderly but intransigent Paulinos presented greater difficulties, since he was the bishop recognised by Rome and Alexandria. Meletios, however, was irenically disposed, and after discussions they reached an agreement under which Paulinos recognised him as bishop of the see while he himself retained the title as pastor of his own church and congregation. It is inconceivable that the agreement, which Paulinos had little option but to accept, included the right to the succession in the event of Meletios predeceasing him,[6] although this compromise seems to have been canvassed in the west.[7] Meletios thus ended – only temporarily, as it soon appeared – the Antiochene schism. For the moment, however, he was establishing his leadership not only in Antioch but throughout most of the east, where he was the outstanding orthodox bishop since the death of Basil of Caesarea on 1 January 379. As such he was increasingly trusted by Theodosius, and increasingly exerted an influence on his theological policies. When the great council which the emperor summoned to Constantinople met in May 381, it was Meletios whom he singled out, by the extraordinary deference with which he greeted him in the presence of the assembled bishops, as his choice for its president.[8]

II

John's return to Antioch cannot have been long after Meletios' arrival there and reassumption of office. Although it was forced on him by the collapse of his health, it would be unrealistic to exclude a connection between the two events. It was clearly a major concern of Meletios to rebuild his congregation, and church life in the Syrian capital generally, under a staff of reliable clergy. There can have been few whom he was more eager to recruit than his former trusted reader, notwithstanding his refusal to accept ordination six years back. Once he had satisfied himself about John's motives for refusing, it is likely that he put pressure on him to exchange active service in the city for a solitary life for which his physique made him manifestly unsuited.

[4] CT 16.5.6.
[5] Sokrates 5.3; Sozomen 6.37.
[6] So Sokrates 5.5; Sozomen 7.3.
[7] Cf. Ambrose, *Epp.* 12.6; 13.2.
[8] Theodoret, *HE* 5.7 (*GCS* 44.286-7).

These must remain tempting surmises. What is certain is that, once back in Antioch, after a period (it need not have been prolonged) which we must allow for the restoration of his health, John resumed his old position as a reader in Meletios' entourage. From that moment until early 386, some eight years later, we can trace with confidence the broad outline of his career, but have practically no detailed facts or events, apart from his literary activities, with which to fill it. The cardinal points we can be sure of are these. First, he continued as a reader for two years after his return. Reporting this, Palladios chooses his words with care: 'He assisted at the altar for three more years, in addition to the three',[9] i.e. the three prior to his retreat to the mountains. Secondly, he was then ordained by Meletios to the diaconate,[10] the rank in the Christian ministry immediately below the priesthood. Assuming the accuracy of the figures, we can date this advancement to the closing months of 380, more probably to the opening weeks of 381. It cannot have been later, for by the end of January or very soon thereafter Meletios was in Constantinople;[11] he wished to be at the emperor's right hand as preparations went ahead for the council, over which he was to preside and at which he was to die without ever setting eyes on either Antioch or John again. Finally, five years later, probably in the opening weeks of 386,[12] he was to be ordained priest by Flavian, who as layman and priest has already appeared in these pages,[13] and whom, on the unexpected death of Meletios, the council, to the distress of its new president Gregory of Nazianzos, now bishop of Constantinople, had appointed bishop of Antioch. Gregory had pleaded that there should be no election but that the succession be allowed to pass to Paulinos; such a gesture would have gratified the west, and abolished the Antiochene schism once and for all. But the bishops, all of them orientals, were determined to make no concessions to Rome, always indifferent to the needs of the east, and its uncompromising protégé Paulinos. The result was that Rome refused to recognise Flavian and excommunicated his consecrators, and the division at Antioch was renewed with enhanced bitterness.[14]

Meletios' death must have been a personal blow to John; in later addresses he was more than once to give vivid expression to his admiration for him. As a deacon he is likely to have taken a modest part in the extraordinary solemnities accompanying the interment of the bishop's remains, brought back by ship from Constantinople, alongside those of Babylas in the new *martyrion* which he had helped to build with his own

[9] *Dial.* 5 (SC 341.110).
[10] Palladios, loc. cit.
[11] See A.M. Ritter, *Das Konzil von Konstantinopel und sein Symbol* (Göttingen 1965), 35.
[12] For the date see Baur, 1.180.
[13] See above, pp. 11 and 18.
[14] Sozomen 7.11.

hands for his venerated predecessor.[15] It was under Flavian, however, with whom his relations were to be exceptionally warm, that he was to serve the remaining years of his diaconate. With the other deacons (there were usually seven assisting a bishop, but we cannot be sure of the number at Antioch) he now had a prominent role at divine service, reciting for example the intercessory prayers, but also seeing that the unbaptised left the church before the central part of the mass. The deacons were also expected to exclude unsuitable persons (e.g. flagrant sinners) from the holy table, and John himself clearly attached importance to this task. 'If a general, a consul, even he who wears the imperial diadem comes forward unworthily,' he later advised deacons, 'you must stop him; your authority is greater than his.'[16]

While deacons were not allowed to preach, they assisted with the instruction of catechumens, and had a role in the baptismal service. But most of their real work lay outside the sanctuary. Closely attached to the bishop's person, they were expected to help him in all aspects of his pastoral work, to be (as an ancient collection of church law expresses it)[17] 'his ear, his mouth, his heart, his soul'. In particular, they acted for him in looking after the poor, the sick and mentally deranged ('demoniacs'), widows and orphans, Christians who might be in prison. In the second half of the fourth century this had become an enormous responsibility. A few years later, when the position had probably not altered greatly, John was to claim that, while the church in Antioch had an income 'not exceeding that of one very rich man and one very moderately wealthy man', it had to maintain upwards of three thousand widows and virgins, not to mention a host of prisoners in gaol, people who were sick or in hospital, others who were impoverished or maimed, others still who crouched by the altar in desperate need of food and clothing.[18] It is sometimes stated that the management of the church's property, including its cemeteries, was a further burden shouldered by the deacons, but in John's time, as his own language makes plain, this was in the main administered at Antioch (in contrast, for example, to Rome) by the priests.[19]

These generalities help us to form some idea of John's day-to-day activities as a deacon during these years; in his contemporary writings we can catch occasional glimpses of him dealing with a particular situation or individual. In one passage, for example, he recalls how he had succeeded in persuading a teenager, the son of a father who wanted him to join up as a soldier and a devout mother who longed to see him a monk, to return from the monastic settlements on Mt Silpios and practise asceticism unostentatiously at home, thereby avoiding a family crisis which might have had

[15] Sozomen 7.10: also *In Bab. hom.* 3 (*PG* 49.533).
[16] *In Matt. hom.* 82.6 (*PG* 58.744).
[17] *Apostolic Constitutions* II.44 (F.X. Funk, I.139).
[18] *In Matt. hom.* 66.3 (*PG* 58.630).
[19] E.g. *In Matt. hom.* 85.3 (*PG* 58.762).

drastic repercussions on the whole ascetic community as well as himself.[20]
(The story, incidentally, shows the lad acting out one of those 'well-
intentioned deceptions' of which, as we have seen,[21] John approved.) In
another, trying to reconcile a young man who has become a victim to
epilepsy to his lot, he begs him to reflect on the much more appalling
sufferings of a couple of people whom he names, and whose condition he
describes in realistic detail.[22] The case of the one, an old man who has been
afflicted for fifteen years, is all the more pitiful because he has a clear
perception of his plight, that of the other because all his friends have ceased
calling on him because of the stench of his room. Alternatively, he should
visit the local hospital and then the prison, with their miserable inmates,
or go to the public baths and observe the half-naked, diseased wretches
clustering around the entrances, with only dung and straw for shelter, their
bodies shivering with cold and their teeth chattering as they try to move
passers-by to pity. It would be even more effective for him to call at the
poor-house outside the walls, and see men and women wasting away with
agonising, incurable diseases like elephantiasis and cancer, who because
of them are prohibited from entering the city and denied access even to
washing facilities and other basic necessities.

John's descriptions are so personal, etched with such precision and
poignant detail, that they are clearly not the colourful flourishes of a
rhetorician, but snapshots of actual human beings in their humiliation and
agony. They reflect his compassionate impressions as he went his rounds.

III

Though not yet licensed to preach, nothing prevented John from wielding
his pen as an author. It is even possible that the desire to enlist his
assistance in that capacity was one of Meletios' reasons for wanting him
back in the capital. In fact, we have a sizeable collection of pamphlets,
letters and essays which, although their individual dates cannot usually
be fixed with precision, almost certainly belong to the period between his
return and his ordination as priest in 386. Though commonly classified as
his ascetic works, they cover quite a variety of topics, including the
problems of marriage and of human suffering, and anti-pagan polemics.
They are all written with consummate rhetorical artifice, reminding us that
he was still, and would always remain, under the influence of the professor
on whom he had scornfully turned his back. A review of them, however
cursory, is demanded not only because they form an important part of his
literary legacy, but because they throw light on his state of mind and his
understanding of Christianity at this critical stage of his development.

---

[20] *Adv. oppugn. vitae mon.* 3.12 (*PG* 47.368-76).
[21] See above p. 26.
[22] *Ad Stagirium ascetam a daemone vexatum* 3.12f. (*PG* 47.489-91).

Let us start with two apologies, the first of which has the clumsy title *St Babylas, in Refutation of Julian and the Pagans.*[23] Its theme, developed with bravura and sometimes tedious repetitiveness, is the assertion that the source of Christianity's victory over paganism is the power of Christ, which is just as visible today as when he was alive on earth. For evidence John points to the remains of Babylas, the defiant bishop of Antioch martyred *c.* 250, which, when translated from the old city cemetery to the garden suburb of Daphne, had first caused licence and frivolity to cease there, then reduced the nearby oracle of Apollo to silence, and finally, when returned by the outraged emperor Julian to their former resting-place, had struck back by making the god's famous temple go up in flames and by destroying his great chryselephantine statue.[24] The discourse contains vivid descriptions of Babylas' heroism and brutal execution, gloats over the weakness of Apollo when faced with the martyr's invincible power, upbraids Julian for sacrilege in daring to move his holy body and derisively tears to pieces the lament which Libanios (a sincere pagan who felt genuinely shattered by the event) had composed for the destruction of the temple. A problem which evidently worried thoughtful Christians, why Julian had not been immediately struck down by the divine wrath, is answered by reminding them that God is always merciful, allows time for a change of heart, but if it fails to come punishes ruthlessly. The message hammered home is that pagans should be persuaded, by the contrast between the laughable ineffectiveness of the old gods and the extraordinary miracles which Christ continues to work through his saints, to transfer their allegiance to him.

Meletios, we know, had a deep veneration for his predecessor Babylas, and was already planning the construction of a magnificent new shrine for his remains on the north side of the Orontes. It is likely that he commissioned John to prepare the discourse as part of a campaign to promote a reinvigorated orthodoxy drawing inspiration from the local hero. Since it contains no hint of the projected shrine, work on which must have begun later in the year, we can safely date it to the early months of 379. John's claim to be writing in the twentieth year after the burning of Apollo's temple can be explained by his inveterate habit of rounding off numbers.[25] Older doubts about its authenticity, based mainly on its supposed stylistic inferiority to John's acknowledged writings, have been convincingly disproved.[26] As it stands the treatise provides indirect evidence of the strength of the pagan minority in Antioch in the late 370s. Only the tension between it and the Christians can explain, for example, John's intemperate on-

---

[23] *De s. Babyla c. Iulianum et Gentiles* (*PG* 50.533.572): critical edition by M. Schatkin, *SC* 362 (Paris 1990).
[24] See above, p.9.
[25] For this habit, with examples, see C. Baur, *ZKTh* 52 (1928), 404 n. 5.
[26] See M. Schatkin's article in *Kyriakon: Festschrift Johannes Quasten* (Münster 1970), 1,474-89.

slaught on his old professor Libanios, who was still alive and in the city. For all his mockery and scornful assumption that paganism had been finally defeated, it is evident that its momentary resurgence under Julian still fills him with anxiety.

The second apology, *Christ's Divinity Proved against Jews and Pagans*,[27] is rather shorter. As it has come down, its argument is directed exclusively against pagans; it is clear, from occasional remarks he makes, that John intended a section specifically aimed at Jewish critics, but he never seems to have completed it. We have no firm clues to its date, for the juxtaposed statements[28] that Julian belongs to 'our generation' and that more than four hundred years have elapsed since the Temple at Jerusalem was destroyed (AD 70) suggest that John was being more than usually reckless with figures. But its resemblance to *Babylas* both in style and in certain themes points to a date not long after it, perhaps early in John's diaconate.[29] Better planned and much less diffuse than its sister work, it contains passages of splendid eloquence, and like *Babylas* witnesses to the continued vitality of the conflict between Christianity and paganism. The argument is also interesting, for John disclaims any intention of appealing to Christ's role in creation or to the miracles he worked in his lifetime; he admits that, if he did, educated pagans would dismiss his claims with incredulity. Instead, as in *Babylas*, he asserts that the source of Christianity's victory over paganism and Hellenic culture generally, as over Judaism, is the active power of Christ. That this power is divine, he argues, is convincingly shown as much in the fulfilment of the Old Testament prophecies as in that of Christ's own predictions that nothing would ever prevail against his church and that the Jewish Temple would be utterly destroyed. The spread of the church and its growing strength are evident for all to see, as is the desolation of the Temple at Jerusalem. The reflective pagan can only conclude that, if Christ were not God, if he were not a mighty God, it is inexplicable that his worshippers, in spite of being harried so cruelly, should have increased to such a multitude, and that the Jews who insulted and crucified him should have been so completely humbled.[30]

IV

Two treatises, *Contrition of Heart*[31] and *To Stageirios*,[32] which are best classified as pastoral, bring us close to the heart of John's understanding of Christian commitment. The former looks back, perhaps with just a hint of disenchantment, to his recent sojourn with the monks, while in the latter,

---

[27] *Adv. Iudaeos et Gentiles demonstratio quod Christus sit deus (PG* 48.813-38).
[28] Cap. 16 *(PG* 48.835).
[29] Cf. A. Lukyn Williams, *Adversus Iudaeos* (Cambridge 1935), 136.
[30] *Dem.* 17 *(PG* 48.838).
[31] *De compunctione (PG* 47.393-432).
[32] *Ad Stag. (PG* 47.423-94).

which Sokrates attributes to his diaconate,[33] he admits to being confined to his home. It therefore seems probably that he wrote both as a young deacon.

The theme of *Contrition*, developed with eloquence and pathos in two complementary books, is the Christian's need of a humble and penitent heart, constantly aware of his sins and of the terrible judgment awaiting him, sustained always by a burning love for Christ. One by one John analyses the gospel commands – commands which, he insists (somewhat unconvincingly), are not really onerous – and remorselessly lays bare the way Christians whittle them down, observe them in a purely external sense, or quite frankly ignore them. The trouble is that they are still victims of pride and complacency, taken up wholly with worldly satisfactions. Businessmen go to endless trouble to make material gains, but Christians, to whom heaven is promised, are reluctant to make any sacrifices to obtain it. This applies just as much to clergy and monks as to lay folk. An informed outsider could be excused if he concluded that Christ has no more determined enemies than his so-called 'crucified' disciples. What Christians need is the true contrition which gives wings to the soul. Like Paul, they should be fired by the passionate yearning for Christ which raised him to the third heaven. Like David, they should humble themselves in tears and throw themselves penitently on God's mercy.[34]

John's pleadings are remarkable for the uncompromising, almost fanatical note which runs through them. He was already, and for the rest of his career was to remain, scornfully impatient of anything less than total commitment to the gospel. The second treatise, a work of extraordinary diffuseness in three books, deals with the problem of personal suffering. It was addressed to Stageirios, a young friend of John's who, after becoming a monk (a noticeably slack one, always boasting of his upper-class background), had suffered an alarming epileptic seizure – possession by a demon, as people in those days assumed.[35] His condition, with all its distressing symptoms of convulsions,[36] foaming at the mouth, and falling to the ground, had proved incurable, in spite of his consulting an exceptionally holy exorcist and praying at renowned martyrs' shrines. The despairing man was driven to question God's providence, even to consider suicide. Nothing like this had happened to him during his earlier playboy existence; friends of his, leading indulgent lives, who had been similarly afflicted had been quickly, and permanently, cured. What made things worse was the fear that, if his rich, truculent father discovered the plight he was in (his mother had so far managed to conceal it), he would vent his indignation on the monastic community. Little wonder that he was utterly dejected, and

---

[33] 6.5.

[34] *De comp.* 2.2-3 (*PG* 47.413-15).

[35] See, e.g., *RAC* 5.830f.

[36] For a remarkable description, see 1.1 (*PG* 47.426 ad fin.).

that John wrote to him (he could not visit him, being obliged by a splitting headache to remain at home) to console him and help him to see his misfortunes in perspective.

His opening remarks must have given the sufferer a jolt. Stageirios' troubles, he said, were certainly calculated to disturb the mind, but only a mind 'that is slack, uninstructed, and indolent'.[37] He then launched out on an immense examination of the divine purpose in adversity, urging Stageirios to recognise the loving hand of providence in his trials. The onslaughts of his demon cannot really harm him if he bears them in a spirit of penitence; God indeed permits them so as to give men an opportunity to do better, also to lighten their burden of punishment in the next world. By all accounts there has already been a significant improvement in Stageirios' whole demeanour and ascetic commitment.[38] A sovereign remedy for his depression is to reflect on the famous figures of the bible, who all had to put up with afflictions far worse than his and from those sufferings won the privilege of free access to God.[39] As for Stageirios himself, his depression results from his assessing his condition by worldly standards and not by sound reasoning. When his epilepsy throws him to the ground in full view of his comrades, he blushes with shame; but the only fall which should make a man ashamed is falling into sin. The true victim of demonic possession is not the epileptic who bears his lot with Christian dignity; it is the man addicted to sensuality, greed, envy and the rest.[40]

Throughout, John's teaching is that suffering such as Stageirios' is not an evil in itself; it is God's providential chastisement, intended to bring out the best in him, or even to help him expiate his sins in this world. 'The time for depression is not when we suffer adversity, but when we commit what is wrong ... It is our sins which separate God from us and make him our enemy, while the punishments he inflicts reconcile him to us, and cause him to be merciful and come close to us.'[41] Some of John's themes, such as his suggestion of the redemptive effects of suffering, are patently Christian. But it can hardly escape notice that others, e.g. his pleas that things which are commonly reckoned evil are not really such, or that a man's only experience of genuine evil is when he chooses to do wrong, are not so much Christian as Stoic in inspiration. This is scarcely surprising, for his thinking (as is now widely recognised),[42] like that of other Christian writers of his time and earlier, was steeped in the popular Stoicism which pervaded the culture in which he, and they, had been brought up.

[37] *Ad Stag.* 1.1 (*PG* 47.426).
[38] 1.10; 2.1 (*PG* 47.447f.; 449f.).
[39] For the expression see *Ad Stag.* 2.5 ad init. (*PG* 47.454).
[40] *Ad Stag.* 2.2-3 (*PG* 47.450-1).
[41] *Ad Stag.* 3.14 (*PG* 47.491-4).
[42] See, e.g., M. Spanneut, art. 'Epiktet', *RAC* 5.599-681.

V

We now come to three pieces concerned with celibacy, marriage, and sexuality generally. The longest and most comprehensive is the treatise *Virginity*.[43] The ideal of virginity it presents and its rather extreme treatment of the subject link it with other ascetic works which John produced shortly after his return from the mountain, and suggest a date around 381/2. It was addressed, apparently, to women who had already embraced the virgin state. Its aim was to demolish the doubts of critics of virginity by highlighting its special dignity (*axioma*), and to impress on dedicated virgins both its demands and its signal rewards. The modern reader[44] should recall that in the fourth century, with the ascetic movement in full swing, countless earnest Christians felt themselves called to a life of complete abstinence from sex, sometimes in community but as often as not without separating themselves from society. They found inspiration in, for example, Jesus' commendation (Matt. 19.12) of those who renounced sexual activity for the sake of the kingdom of heaven, and in St Paul's remark (1 Cor. 7.7) that he wished everyone could remain unmarried like himself. For decades virginity had been a popular theme with preachers and pamphleteers, and it was natural that John, a committed celibate himself, should seek to encourage others to walk the same austere path.

He starts off with an attack on extremists who reject marriage altogether – a pre-emptive strike intended to parry possible accusations of being an extremist himself. They show, he argues, a Manichaean contempt for the natural order created by God, and by downgrading marriage diminish the achievement of those who choose celibacy as the nobler way.[45] He then moves to a sustained eulogy of virginity itself, defining it as more than abstinence from sex: it involves also purity of soul and consecration to Christ. He is aware of its difficulties: 'One must walk on burning coals without being scorched, on a naked sword without being wounded, since lust is as overpowering as fire and steel.'[46] But these can be overcome, and the rewards it bestows are beyond price, here serenity of soul and continual converse with God,[47] hereafter the blessedness of the elect. In a word, it transforms human beings into angels, among whom there is no marriage (Matt. 22.30).[48] By contrast, the best he can say of marriage is that it is, 'for those who choose to use it rightly, a haven of chastity, preventing human nature from relapsing into bestiality'. John's frank advice to those

---

[43] *De virginitate: PG* 48.533-96: crit. ed. by H. Musurillo and B. Grillet, *SC* 125 (Paris 1966), where the date etc. are fully treated.
[44] See above all P. Brown's penetrating and wide-ranging study, *The Body and Society* (London 1989), which only came to the writer's notice after he had drafted these sections.
[45] *De virg.* 8 (114-18).
[46] *De virg.* 27.1 (176-8).
[47] *De virg.* 68.1 (338).
[48] *De virg.* 11.1 (126).

who can curb their sensuality by spiritual discipline is not to marry at all.[49] He reels off a formidable (but, for a fourth-century rhetorician, fairly conventional) catalogue of the discomforts inseparable from marriage, ranging from petty jealousies to the pains of childbirth, all of which distract a man and his wife from heavenly things.[50] They are far worse than any trials a virgin has to face – trials which, in fact, bring her joy since she endures them for Christ. The truth is, marriage was no part of the original divine intention. Sexuality had no place in Paradise, but came into its own after the Fall, when God ordained marriage for the continuation of the race and as a brake on incontinence.[51]

Some two-thirds of *Virginity* is an extended commentary on St Paul's well-known discussion of sexual matters in 1 Cor. 7, but it is noticeable that, wherever possible, John seeks to play down any expression of the Apostle's which presents marriage in an indulgent light. For example, he grudgingly accepts his suggestion (1 Cor. 7.16) that a wife may be able to save her husband,[52] but points out that the very form of his question implies that the possibility is a remote one; in any case it is one not likely to be achieved by their having intercourse. Again, he perversely interprets St Paul's advice to spouses (1 Cor. 7.5) not to abstain from intercourse except as a temporary measure as a covert encouragement to continence.[53] One would not expect a positive evaluation of sexuality from a Christian writer of this period, but the view John takes here (he was to modify it somewhat in later pronouncements) is almost wholly negative. It is noticeable that, while relying so heavily on St Paul, he nowhere in this work appeals to the famous passage in Ephesians (5.21-31) in which the union of man and wife is compared to that between Christ and the church. An equally negative feature of the pamphlet is the disparaging view of women which it takes. It was woman, John argues, who, in the person of Eve, subjected man to death, and women who were the undoing of Old Testament heroes like Samson and Solomon.[54] Woman, he agrees, was created to be man's helper (Gen. 2.18), and she still fulfils that role in bearing children and satisfying his sexual desires. But when it comes to serious things, she is only a hindrance.[55]

To a Young Widow and *Single Marriage* can be treated more briefly.[56] Linked together in the manuscript tradition, the latter used to be regarded as the sequel to the former, but they are distinct in genre and circumstance.

---

[49] *De virg.* 9.1 (120).
[50] *De virg.* 51-72.
[51] *De virg.* 14-15 (136-48).
[52] *De virg.* 47.1-2 (262-4).
[53] *De virg.* 29 (184-8).
[54] *De virg.* 46.2 (258).
[55] 46.5 (262).
[56] *Ad viduam iuniorem* and *De non iterando coniugio: PG* 48.599-610; 609-20: critical edition by B. Grillet and G. Ettlinger, *SC* 138 (Paris 1966).

The former is a letter written to comfort a lady of rank suddenly bereaved of her husband Therasios, a young soldier with brilliant prospects. It can with confidence be dated 380/1 since it mentions the desperate campaign of the recently crowned (379) emperor Theodosius against the invading Goths, but not his crushing defeat of them in 382.[57] The latter is a treatise for young widows in general, didactic in tone and devoid of personal allusions. It seems later than and complementary to *Virginity*, to which it makes a passing reference.[58] and may perhaps be dated *c.* 382. Both alike deal with the specifically Christian problem of the remarriage of widows. In pagan society, while widowhood enjoyed respect, remarriage was accepted as normal, and was strongly encouraged by Roman law. In the gospels there is not a word against it, but St Paul (1 Cor. 7.30), while approving it provided the new partner is a Christian, suggests that the widow would be happier if she stays as she is. Later epistles attributed to him advise younger widows to remarry (1 Tim. 5.14) but forbid clergy and widows on the official list to do so (1 Tim. 3.2; 12; 5.9), presumably because it indicates a sensual propensity. These rigorist hints were eagerly taken up by the early church, and by the fourth century all serious Christian thinkers in the east deplored second marriages as a carnally inspired deviation from the Christian ideal.

The letter falls into the rhetorical category of *consolatio* or *logos para-muthetikos*, much cultivated in antiquity, which combined eulogies of the deceased with stock arguments intended to help the bereaved to bear their loss. John tries his hand at it here with the skill of an expert, but also, since he knew the couple personally, with occasional touches of real feeling. For example, after evoking the horror and anxiety with which the massacres being carried out by the Goths in nearby Thrace had filled the capital, he reminds his correspondent of the numberless other young women whose husbands have been cut down in battle and who have never seen their bodies again.[59] She at least has watched over Therasios in his illness, has listened to his last words, has been able to kiss his eyes when he lay dead, and has shed tears at his grave. The treatise, on the other hand, with its artifices of style, its recourse to fictitious dialogue and its dramatic inter-rogations, belongs to the rhetorical genre known as *enkomion*, and lacks any personal note.

While each has distinct emphases, the theme of both is identical, the praise of the widow who rejects the temptation to marry again. In both the excesses of language and argument noticeable in *Virginity* are absent, and the disparagement of sexuality is toned down; their common teaching is that widowhood is as much superior to a second marriage as virginity is to marriage. In the letter the positive aspects of widowhood are brought out.

---

[57] *Ad vid. iun.* 4 (*SC* 138.138-40).
[58] *De non iter. coniug.* 1 (*SC* 138.166).
[59] *Ad vid. iun.* 4-5 (*SC* 138.132-44).

For example, the true widow is joined in holy union with Christ;[60] if she perseveres, she will be reunited with her husband, not for a short time but for endless ages, not in a union of mortal bodies but of bodies glorified as the faces of Moses (Ex. 34.29) and of Christ himself (Matt. 17.2) were once transfigured with light.[61] The treatise, in its more formal way concedes the legitimacy of a second marriage since St Paul himself expressly allowed it, but argues that it is a sign, not indeed of licentiousness (*aselgeia*), but of a weak, sensual spirit unable to rise above the earthly.[62] It is a sophism to claim that, since marriage is a good thing, it must be good to remarry if one's husband dies. The essence of marriage consists, not in physical union (if it did, fornication would count as marriage), but in a woman being content with one man, a conjugal bond in virtue of which the two become 'one flesh' (Matt. 19.5). This means that, if a widow admits another man to her house, she is not indeed guilty of fornication, but both her original husband and her new one are 'deprived of the esteem and affection due from a wife to her husband'.[63] John was evidently troubled by St Paul's wish (1 Tim. 5.14) that younger widows should marry and bear children, but extricated himself from the difficulty by pleading, somewhat speciously, that the widows the Apostle was addressing were only weak-willed ones with sensual proclivities.[64] Such second marriages, he held, were a concession to human frailty, not to be condemned, but certainly not to be applauded. By contrast, the young widows who win God's approval are those who are resolved to remain such and who, detaching themselves from earthly interests, embrace the angelic existence appropriate to those who have Christ himself as their bridegroom.[65]

VI

We should also, notwithstanding Palladios' dating them to the start of his episcopate,[66] assign to John's diaconate two associated treatises,[67] one addressed to men and the other to women, denouncing the cohabitation of monks and virgins. Constantinople is ruled out by John's disclaimer[68] in the former of episcopal rank (he is not a spiritual judge but just a doctor

---

[60] *Ad vid. iun.* 2 (*SC* 138.122).
[61] *Ad vid. iun.* 3 (*SC* 138.128-30).
[62] *De non iterando* 2 (*SC* 138.168).
[63] *De non iterando* 2 (*SC* 138.168-70).
[64] *De non iterando* 3 (*SC* 138.176-8).
[65] *De non iterando* 6 (*SC* 198-200).
[66] *Dial.* 5 (*SC* 341.118).
[67] *C. eos qui subintroductas habent virgines* and *Quod regulares viris cohabitare non debeant* (*PG* 47.495-514; 514-52): crit. ed. by J. Dumortier, *Jean Chrysostome: les cohabitations suspectes* (Paris 1955). For their date see J. Dumortier, *MSR* 6 (1949), 247-52. See also the valuable analysis by E.A. Clark in *Church History* 46 (1977), 171-85.
[68] *C. eos* 2 (*PG* 47.496).

offering advice), by a reference[69] to monks loaded with chains making for the mountain peaks (a spectacle foreign to the capital but familiar at Antioch), and by the fact that his strictures are not addressed specifically to clergy (as Palladios states) but more generally to monks.[70] The case for Antioch, however, is clinched by Jerome's famous *Letter* 22 ('On Preserving Virginity') to his protégée Eustochium. Not only is its title borrowed from that of John's second treatise, which was originally named 'How to Preserve Virginity',[71] but it contains[72] a scarcely veiled criticism of John's extravagant ranking, in that treatise, of the faithful virgin with the Cherubim and Seraphim.[73] Jerome, we should note, hounded from his desert retreat, was at Antioch from 376/7 to 380,[74] staying probably with his friend and patron Evagrios, and like him an adherent of Paulinos' little sect and an ardent opponent of Meletios. It was probably from Evagrios or other friends that, settled in Rome, he obtained information about John's two pamphlets.[75] As his letter to Eustochium was composed in spring 384, we can safely date these to 382/383.

The living together in 'spiritual marriage' of men and women vowed to abstention from sex had had a long history in the church. We already come across it at Corinth among the Christians whose sexual problems Paul addressed in 1 Cor. 7.25-38 (John, we note, did not interpret the passage in this sense, although his older contemporary Ephraem did).[76] The practice was much in vogue among earnest Christians in the fourth century, and while enthusiasm for virginity was ostensibly the prime motive, it also had practical advantages. A woman who had opted for virginity while still living in the world (there were as yet no convents for women) might, if she had no male relatives to whom to turn, need someone to look after her financial affairs and otherwise act as her protector. Who more suitable than a 'brother' likewise dedicated to celibacy? Similarly a monk who had not withdrawn to a monastery might need a housekeeper, someone to prepare his food, wash his clothes and so on. (A surprisingly high proportion of the zealous Christians we know about in that period belonged to the very affluent class, and were accustomed to lavish domestic service.) An obvious candidate for the role was a woman vowed to virginity. Such ménages, based on a convergence of needs as well as on a common spiritual ideal, were apparently as numerous at Antioch as at other Christian centres. The

---

[69] *C. eos* 5 (*PG* 47.501).

[70] *C. eos* 9 (*PG* 47.508: cf. *andros monazontos*).

[71] See J. Dumortier, art. cit., 250 n.3.

[72] *Ep.* 22.2 (*CSEL* 54.146).

[73] *Quod regul.* 6 (*PG* 47.527).

[74] J.N.D. Kelly, *Jerome* (London 1975), 75-8.

[75] He cannot have received copies of them, for in 393 he was to claim (*De vir. ill.* 129) that, while John was said to have several works to his credit, the only one he had read was *Priesthood*. See below, p. 83.

[76] *S. Ephraemi Syri Commentarii in Epistulas Divi Pauli* (Latin translation from Armenian: Venice 1893), 62.

official church, however, had quickly come to frown on them, and a whole series of synods had legislated against them. The council of Nicaea (325), for example, had, in its third canon, specifically forbidden a cleric of whatever rank to have any woman other than his mother, sister, aunt or someone equally above suspicion, resident with him.

At Antioch it was a question, apparently, of lay folk sharing house, and the church authorities must have decided that it was time to intervene. It was with their encouragement, probably, that, in these two skilfully argued tracts (they are in effect one), John weighed in against the practice, calling on supposedly consecrated men and women to abandon what he assured them was a morally dangerous mode of life, one which moreover was bound to expose them to misunderstanding and even ridicule. He wrote with a mixture of friendly appeal, brutal realism and stinging sarcasm. His main argument is that for two people of different sex to continue living together, under the same roof and in such close personal relations, is humanly impossible without succumbing to sexual passion and so compromising their vocation. Even if physical intercourse is avoided, which John seems prepared to concede, cohabiting without it only leads to a state of permanent sexual arousal. Weaker brethren are thus imperilled, and scandal damaging to the community is inescapable. Characteristically, he is most severe to the female partners. Called to be brides of Christ, they move about among their men folk with alluring walks and seductive glances more appropriate to courtesans. Their virginity is only nominal; their bodies may remain physically intact, but both they and their male companions are guilty of sexual sin in their hearts.[77] He is dismissive of the pretexts advanced to justify these spiritual unions. If a monk really needs help with household tasks, a fellow-monk would be preferable to a virgin, and would raise none of the embarrassing problems she inevitably does. On the other hand, a well-off woman requiring advice and assistance with her business affairs would do better to marry than put herself under the protection of a monk, who so far from playing the part of her banker ought to be counselling her to scorn riches and embrace poverty. If the man pleads that it is a poor woman he is succouring, there are plenty of elderly or maimed women around to whom he should be giving shelter rather than chasing the pretty young ones.[78]

John's scorn, and also his disparagement of the female sex, come out most vividly in some of the derisive cameos he sketches. One is of the monk, supposedly an athlete of Christ and bearing his cross, who spends his time in trivial womanish chatter with his partner, running errands to the jewellery or perfumery shops for her, with her sandals, girdles and hairnets hanging for all to see in his house. He has become her eunuch (John

---

[77] See esp. *Quod regul.* 1 and 3 (*PG* 47.515; 519-20).
[78] *C. eos* 6-7 (*PG* 47.502-5).

is an incorrigible sexist), or (to vary the image) a toothless, maneless lion.[79] In another he expatiates on the embarrassing encounters, during the night or the early morning, when they cross from one room to the other (it is likely that the man sleeps naked), or again when the monk visits the virgin when she is sick and, getting in ahead of female servants, performs services for her which only women can decently carry out. 'These may be small things, but they bring to birth big coals of lust.'[80] Such behaviour gives the church a bad name, brings virginity into disrepute, and gives occasion to mockery and coarse jokes among pagans. His advice to a monk is to reject with contempt any 'criminal liaison' now, so that hereafter, 'when bodily passions have been done away with and the tyranny of lust is quenched', he and his virgin sister may, with a clear conscience, enjoy an entirely pure and holy intercourse with one another as they share the (sexless) life of angels.[81] With almost mystical fervour he exhorts the virgin 'to forget this criminal liaison and the partner who sinfully cohabits with her', bearing in mind that she has a heavenly bridegroom – indeed, lover (he does not shrink from the term *erastes*, with its sexual overtones) – who will be captivated by her immaculate beauty, and for whom it will be worth making any sacrifices here on earth.[82]

VII

There remains one further piece, *Against the Enemies of Monasticism*,[83] which can be safely attributed to this astonishingly productive period. One of John's most elaborate works, in three books, it illustrates not only the extreme irritation which the proselytising activities of monks were causing in leading circles in Antioch, but also the disenchantment he himself was feeling with traditional Hellenic culture and education. The only clue to its date is his complaint that monks should suffer harassment at a time when the reigning emperors are 'devout Christians' (*ton basileon en eusebeia zonton*).[84] This cannot refer, as Montfaucon proposed,[85] to the Arianizing Valens, in spite of his having been responsible for legislation directed against monks who used their vocation as an excuse for avoiding public duties.[86] In John's parlance the expression must denote orthodox, i.e. Nicene-minded, emperors, and would most naturally refer to Gratian and Theodosius I. As the latter was proclaimed on 19 January 379 and the

---

[79] *C. eos* 9-10 (*PG* 47.507-10).

[80] *Quod regul.* 8 (*PG* 47.528-9).

[81] *C. eos* 13 (*PG* 47.513-14).

[82] *Quod regul.* 9 (*PG* 47.531-2).

[83] *Adv. oppugnatores vitae monasticae: PG* 47.319-86. There is no critical edition, but a good English translation by David G. Hunter (Lampeter 1988).

[84] *Adv. oppugn.* 1.2 (*PG* 47.321).

[85] *PG* 47.317-18.

[86] CT 12.1.63 (1 Jan. 370: renewed 373). It seems to have applied only to Egypt.

former murdered at Lyons on 25 August 383, a date somewhere between these points would seem most probable.

John was provoked to write the treatise, he explains, by the hostility and actual violence shown by professing Christians in the city, many of them baptised, to monks from the nearby mountains. In a dramatic paragraph[87] he describes how, in the market-place or in doctors' consulting rooms, in fact wherever people gather to gossip, you could find one man boasting that he was the first to beat up a monk, another that he had been the first to track down his hut, a third that he had spurred the magistrate into action against the holy men, a fourth that he had dragged them through the streets and seen them locked up in gaol. The bystanders were vastly amused by the recital of these gallant exploits. The people involved, it emerges, were upper-class citizens who were getting fed up with the success the monks were having in recruiting their teenage sons to the harsh life of their settlements. So 'they harry those who introduce other people to our philosophy, forbidding them with fearsome threats to open their mouths, much less give anyone instruction in it'. John professed himself doubly shocked that such outrages were being perpetrated at a time when the emperors were orthodox Christians.

In springing to the monks' defence he argues that, so far from being persecuted, they deserve to be imitated, since they exemplify the authentically Christian life. A city like Antioch, though possessing law-courts and laws, is really full of corruption, whereas 'the desert teems with the fruit of philosophy', i.e. genuine Christianity.[88] So a father, Christian or indeed pagan, could not find better teachers for his children than monks. To prove the point, John, in his second book, imagines a highly placed, wealthy pagan whose only son, a young man of first-rate prospects, has been lured away to the austere life of a monastery. Dispensing with scripture and relying wholly on examples from classical literature,[89] he begs the distraught man not to be shattered by what, correctly interpreted, is a matter for congratulation. Through following the monks' instructions, his son can attain true riches, greatness, happiness, health – all the blessings a fond parent could hope for. The boy may even become more gentle and considerate to his father![90] He will certainly be rewarded with a life free from turmoil, a harbour untroubled by storms.[91] To reach this satisfying conclusion John freely exploits (it is interesting to note) the ancient Stoic paradox that it is only the sage – as he saw it, the Christian ascetic – who possesses what is truly good and worthwhile.

If much of this has the air of a sophisticated exercise, John tackles the central issue of the validity of traditional culture in his third book, where

[87] *Adv. oppugn.* 1.2 (*PG* 47.322).
[88] *Adv. oppugn.* 1.7 (*PG* 47.328).
[89] *Adv. oppugn.* 2.3-5 (*PG* 47.334-40).
[90] *Adv. oppugn.* 2.9 (*PG* 47.344).
[91] *Adv. oppugn.* 10 (*PG* 47.347f.).

he deals with a Christian father faced with the same predicament. The most awful responsibility, he claims, which God imposes on parents is to bring their children up properly.[92] Yet most fathers, when they urge them to get down to their books of rhetoric, are really only concerned for their having a successful career. Instead of warning them against love of money and worldly ambition and holding up the gospel ideals before them, they surround them with superfluous luxuries and give fine names to practices like theatre-going and horse-racing, which are really vicious.[93] Worse still, pederasty is so rampant in schools, homosexuality in the city, that a youth can hardly escape unscathed.[94] The result is a society which is rotten through and through, in contrast with which the monks in their ascetic retreats live the life of angels, enjoying true freedom from care, true peace, true happiness.[95] Hence John proposes a radical programme, that parents should entrust their children to monks from the start. He rejects the suggestion that they should first attend the school of rhetoric, and having completed the course there should then take up 'philosophy' with the monks; by that time they would be irretrievably lost.[96] A liberal arts education can do more harm than good; the first Christians never had one, indeed were sometimes illiterate, and yet they overturned the world. 'True wisdom and true education consist only in the fear of God.'[97]

Later John accepts a compromise,[98] although it is a somewhat unrealistic one: that the young men, after living for ten, or even twenty, years in a monastery, should return like well-trained athletes to the city, and there share the blessings they have received with their parents, their home, their fellow-citizens. This sprawling, wide-ranging essay reveals a revulsion from traditional education and culture, indeed from ordinary family life, its values and aspirations which is without parallel in other Christian intellectuals of the period, such as Basil of Caesarea, and which his readers must have found astounding. He was, we should recall, a young man still full of fervour for the stern, uncompromising monastic life in which he had recently been immersed; he was also driven to propose extreme measures which he must have known to be impracticable by his disgust at the meretricious attractions of life in the great city. A decade later, when he came to write *On Vain Glory and How Parents Should Educate Children*,[99] we find him in a more practical frame of mind. A priest of pastoral experience, John had now abandoned (except as a wistful dream) all idea

[92] *Adv. oppugn.* 3-4 (*PG* 47.351-4).
[93] *Adv. oppugn.* 5-7 (*PG* 47.356-60.
[94] *Adv. oppugn.* 3.8 (*PG* 47.360-3).
[95] *Adv. oppugn.* 3.11 (*PG* 47.366).
[96] *Adv. oppugn.* 3.11 (*PG* 47.366).
[97] *Adv. oppugn.* 3.12 (*PG* 47.368).
[98] *Adv. oppugn.* 3.18 (*PG* 47.380).
[99] *De inani gloria et de educandis liberis*: see below, pp.85-7.

of packing children off to monasteries for their schooling.[100] He is as insistent as ever on the need for a thoroughly Christian education based on the scriptures, but he now recognises that it is in the home that children must receive it and that the duty of instructing them falls primarily on their father.

[100] *De inani gloria* 19 (*SC* 188.102-4).

5

Preacher's First Year

I

With this impressive literary output to his credit, John's promotion in the church of Antioch could not be delayed much longer. Although Palladios could be an uncritical admirer, his later comment[1] that his hero was now becoming renowned as a brilliant teacher whose counsel people found helpful in coping with life's bitterness sounds like an accurate assessment of his growing prestige as a pastor. From his own point of view he had finally overcome his scruples about accepting more responsible clerical office. Bishop Flavian, therefore, now in the fifth year of his episcopate, ordained him to the priesthood. The date cannot be fixed with precision, but since Palladios adds that he served the Antiochene church for twelve years before becoming bishop of Constantinople (February 398), his ordination should probably be placed early in 386, at any rate before the opening of Lent on 15 February. This is confirmed by John himself, for in a sermon delivered on 13 or 14 March 387 he claims that this is now the second year that he has been preaching.[2] He was thirty-seven years old, at the height of his intellectual and spiritual development.

The sermon John preached on the day of his ordination,[3] the first in his long career as a preacher, has been preserved intact. Even today the reader can sense the atmosphere of expectation in the congregation when he stepped forward to the ambo of the Golden Church to speak. He began by expressing incredulity ('Is this night? Am I dreaming?') that a mere 'stripling' (*meirakiskos*), 'panic-stricken ... quite inexperienced in public speaking', should be raised to 'such a height of authority'. Soon he was abjectly protesting that, burdened with sin as he was, he could not presume to dedicate these first-fruits of his oratory, as he would have wished, to God. But all was not lost; instead he would glorify God by singing the praises of one of his 'comrades in the Lord's service'. By this neat transition he switched to what he had always intended as his main theme, a fulsome eulogy of Flavian. With extravagant hyperbole he extolled the bishop's disdain for high living and riches, his absolute self-mastery, his austerities,

---

[1] *Dial.* 5 (*SC* 341.110).
[2] *Hom. ad pop. Antioch.* 16.2 (*PG* 49.164).
[3] *PG* 48.693-700: critical edition by A.M. Malingrey, *SC* 272.367-419 (Paris 1980).

his vigilant care for the church, his virtues 'which no human voice but only one inspired by the Spirit could express'. The loss of Meletios had made his flock inconsolable, but Flavian seemed like Meletios restored from the dead. John concluded by begging the people to pray both for Flavian, 'our father, master, shepherd, pilot', and for himself, once a solitary but now dragged into the limelight, with 'this formidable, crushing yoke' placed on his shoulders.[4]

Modern readers tend to find rhetoric like this turgid and artificial, but John was deploying the stock-in-trade of the ancient genre *encomium* as modified by Christian orators.[5] By fourth-century standards his address was a small masterpiece. We may be sure that Flavian did not feel in the least embarrassed by the exaggerated compliments, and that the huge audience savoured with relish the carefully arranged periods and contrived repetitions, the recherché vocabulary and the skilful use of commonplaces (*topoi*) dear to practised orators. But even the modern reader can overhear, rising above the literary conventions, John's authentic voice when, for example, he exclaims that 'nothing, nothing so impedes our advance to heaven as wealth and all the evils which flow from it',[6] or when he depicts the church's sense of deprivation at Meletios' untimely death.

II

As a priest John had a larger range of responsibilities than as a deacon.[7] While the bishop, if present, presided at mass, with the priests (we have no clue to their number at Antioch) concelebrating with him, when he was absent (as the elderly Flavian not infrequently was) one of the priests officiated as 'president' (*proestos*). As such he gave the liturgical greeting 'Peace be with you' to the congregation, and John himself confirms that he often fulfilled this role.[8] At Antioch the priests also, it seems, collaborated with the bishop in administering the property of the see. John apparently found this an irksome and uncongenial duty, for a few years later we find him grumbling that, as a result of the meanness of the laity, the Antiochene church was obliged to own farms, real estate, houses for letting, carriages for hire, packhorses and mules, and the clergy had to employ themselves, to the neglect of the care of souls, on tasks properly belonging to rent collectors, accountants, and petty tradesmen.[9]

John's principal functions as a priest, however, were preaching and giving instruction to the people. There would always be a sermon, on

[4] *SC* 272.418.
[5] Cf. Th. Payr's study in *RAC* 5.332-43.
[6] *SC* 272.406; 414.
[7] For the duties of priests at Antioch see P. Rendinck, *La cura pastorale in Antiochia nel iv secolo* (Rome 1970), esp. 175-80.
[8] *In Matt. hom.* 32.6 (*PG* 57.385).
[9] *In Matt. hom.* 85.3-4 (*PG* 57.761-4).

occasion several, after the gospel at mass on Sundays and major feast-days, but also, it seems, on Fridays and Saturdays. There were also addresses on weekdays in Lent and Easter week immediately before the evening service or vespers, as well as at special celebrations. In addition, a priest was expected to give courses of instruction to candidates preparing for baptism, and to assist in administering, or himself to administer, that sacrament. Other pastoral duties inevitably fell to him, but in John's case it is certain that from the start Flavian, now in his late seventies, had a special role in view for his newly ordained priest. He had apparently singled him out to be not only the city's preacher *par excellence*, but also his own personal assistant. John himself made this clear in a revealing remark in one of his sermons. He reckoned it, he declared, a more signal honour than any crown or diadem that the bishop who had ordained him was reluctant to appear anywhere unaccompanied by his spiritual son; he therefore had the privilege of escorting him wherever he went.[10]

So for almost twelve years, from 386 to late 397, John stood out as the leading pulpit orator of Antioch, building up an unrivalled reputation. The Syrian capital was amazingly addicted to sermons. You could not find another city anywhere, he once observed, which had such a passion (he used the adverb *erotikos*) for them;[11] and he often inveighed bitterly against the crowds which flocked to church exclusively to listen to the preacher, only to rush off before the awesome climax when Christ would reveal himself in the holy mysteries.[12] As Flavian's personal aide John preached in whatever churches the bishop visited in the course of his duties; while this would be most often the Golden Church, we know that he frequently held forth in the Palaia, or Old Church, once at any rate in 'the new church'[13] (probably a recent building in the suburbs), on occasion at martyrs' shrines. There are indications, however, that he had a regular congregation which he regarded as peculiarly his own, and from which he felt it a wrench to be parted.[14] This is likely to have been the Golden Church, which was Flavian's cathedral.

A large number of sermons delivered in the first year or so of his ministry have come down to us. Their freshness and frequent informality suggest that they have survived broadly in the form in which they were preached, no doubt taken down (as Sokrates reports and other evidence confirms)[15] by stenographers as he spoke and afterwards, in most cases, revised before publication by himself. It is generally agreed that he preached extempore; a late biographer has preserved a reminiscence that, when he went to the ambo, people were amazed that he had no scrap of paper or book in his

---

[10] *In illud, In faciem hom.* 1 (*PG* 51.371-2).
[11] *In prod. Iud. hom.* 1.1 (*PG* 49.373).
[12] E.g. *De incomp. dei nat. hom.* 3.6 (*PG* 48.725).
[13] *In illud, In faciem hom.* 1 (*PG* 51.371).
[14] Ibid.
[15] 6.4: see also the short note inserted at the beginning of the Homilies on Hebrews (*PG* 63.9).

hand but held forth impromptu, something they had never seen before.[16] This is borne out by the numerous improvisations they contain, such as rebukes for chattering or inattention, comments on the weather, references to outbursts of applause, even warnings against pickpockets.[17] As they provide graphic evidence not only of John's style of oratory but also of the varied issues which engaged him at the time, it seems appropriate to pass some representative examples in quick review. His later output as a preacher was so enormous that in subsequent chapters we shall only single out particular addresses for attention when they throw significant light on his opinions or career.

III

Within weeks, possibly days, of his ordination Lent began (Monday 16 February).[18] John had been chosen to give a course of homilies on Genesis, the book from which it was already the custom for the lessons before vespers on weekdays to be taken. Eight of these have been preserved,[19] most of them delivered on successive days; he must have preached many more, but the rest have all been lost, although the eight contain references to one or two of them. That he was still a novice when he gave them is charmingly confirmed by his apology for his apparent presumption in tackling such great issues; in doing so, he explains, he was placing his trust, not in his own abilities, but exclusively in the prayers of his superiors and of the congregation before him.[20]

The core of each is the discussion of some knotty or controversial point of doctrine or interpretation which has been thrown up by the text just read. In the first, for example, John defends the biblical teaching that the material order has been created out of nothing.[21] The adversaries he has in view are, first, pagans in general, whose rejection of it leads them inevitably to idolatry, and then the Manichees (a dualist group which in the fourth century proved intellectually attractive to many Christians – including, for many years, Augustine), who claimed that matter is uncreated and eternal, a principle antagonistic to Spirit. If creation from nothing is hard to understand, he suggests, it is at least as difficult to grasp how our bodies were formed out of earth, or for that matter how the food we eat is transformed into flesh and blood. What we need is a recognition of the limits

---

[16] George of Alexandria: see F. Halkin, *Douze récits byzantins sur s. Jean Chrysostome* (Brussels 1977), 115.

[17] *De incomp.* 4.6 (*PG* 48.735).

[18] E. Schwartz, 'Christliche und jüdische Ostertafeln', *Abhandl. K. Gesellschaft der Wiss. zu Göttingen*, phil.-hist. Kl. NF 8 (1905), 171.

[19] *PG* 54.581-620 (to be distinguished from the 67 homilies on Genesis printed in the same volume).

[20] *In Gen. sermo* 2.1 (*PG* 54.586).

[21] *PG* 54.581-4.

of human knowledge, and a firm trust in scripture. The doctrine of creation also helps us to understand the wretchedness of the human condition, and so to escape the pessimism to which, he claims, Manichaeism condemns its adherents. The abuse he heaps on Manichees ('dogs which say nothing but are mad with rabies ... Don't look at their show of moderation, but at the monster behind the mask')[22] leaves the impression that he was worried about their possible influence on his flock. He had good reason for fear, for Manichaeism was widely diffused in Syria at this time;[23] as a missionary religion it was making converts everywhere. It was to remain a constant target for him.

In the next two homilies,[24] analysing 'Let us make man in our image and likeness' (Gen. 1.26), he first argues against Jewish critics that the plural verb proves that God had with him an only-begotten Son who co-operated in his creative works. He then explains that the creation of man in God's 'image' (*eikona*) does not imply an anthropomorphic view of the Godhead. The image is not of essence or being, but of authority (*arche*), for God has given man domination over the rest of creation. On the other hand, his 'likeness' (*homoiosis*) indicates that he should be kind and gentle (*hemeros kai praos*) as he is. In the fourth[25] he sets out what, in his view, Genesis teaches about the relative positions of the sexes. When he created woman, God made her 'of equal honour' with man, appointing her his helper (Gen. 2.18). Not just an ordinary helper, he points out, like the horses and cattle which in different ways help men, but 'a helper fit for him', words which stress her equality with him. When tempted, however, woman abused her position and showed herself unfit for rule, and God therefore condemned her to a subordinate role. Even so, God mercifully tempered his sentence, for while decreeing (Gen. 3.16) that her husband would rule over her, he made her lot easier by adding, 'Your desire shall be for your husband', meaning that in her troubles he would be her refuge and consolation. He then goes on to interpret the Apostle's refusal to allow women to teach or to wield authority over men (1 Tim. 2.12) in the light of the Genesis story: on the great occasion when she exercised authority over him and tried to teach him, the results were disastrous.

In the sixth and seventh he grapples with the problem why the tree in the Garden was called 'of the knowledge of good and evil' since Adam was clearly aware of moral distinctions before eating its fruit. His solution is that 'We know evil before committing it, but understand it more clearly after committing it, and more clearly still when we are punished.'[26] So it was that by eating the forbidden fruit Adam attained full knowledge of the wickedness of disobedience.

---

[22] *In Gen. sermo* 7.4 (*PG* 54.613).
[23] Cf. e.g. P. Brown, *JRS* 59 (1969).
[24] *In Gen. sermo* 2 and 3 (*PG* 54.587-90; 590-2).
[25] *In Gen. sermo* 4.1 (*PG* 54 .594-5).
[26] *In Gen. sermo* 7.2-3 (*PG* 54.611).

In these sermons John is examining a host of scripture texts; as we should expect of an Antiochene who had been a student under Diodore and a friend of Theodore, he shows himself in general a stickler for literal exegesis as he understands it[27] (the resulting interpretations are sometimes bizarre). Yet so far from being a dry-as-dust academic lecturer, he is always striving to make the bible come alive to ordinary people. Exposition apart, he intersperses his addresses with vivid passages of human interest. The opening of the first, for example, is a prose poem lyrically celebrating, first, the joy felt by seafarers and farmers at the arrival of spring, and then the even more thrilling excitement of earnest Christians when the season of fasting begins. Whenever the bishop is present, John is sure to salute him with obsequious compliments. One evening, when it is getting dark and the congregation is distracted by the sacristan bringing in lights, he is quick to rebuke it for neglecting the much more splendid and salutary light he is kindling from God's word.[28] Elsewhere we find him impressing on children the duty of gratitude to their parents, extolling the joys of fasting, urging his audience to be diligent in bible-study and alms-giving, and especially to be generous to the wretched poor crowding on either side as they go out, and not rush past them as if they were 'pillars, not human bodies ... lifeless statues, not breathing human beings'.[29] Again and again he exhorts his hearers (this could evoke thunderous applause)[30] to repeat his message to their households over the supper with which they would break their fast, thereby transforming their homes into churches, indeed into heaven itself.

IV

In September of the same year John embarked on a more specifically doctrinal series of sermons, aimed at countering the propaganda of the Anomoeans. As was noted earlier,[31] these were radical Arians who taught that, so far from being 'one in essence with', or even 'like', the Father, the Word was wholly 'unlike' (*anomoios*: hence their nickname) him. Along with other Arians, they exploited to the full every text in the New Testament which seemed to imply (as great numbers did) the Son's inferiority to or dependence on the Father. In the early 360s, however, their doctrine had been developed by the brilliant logician Eunomios (d. 395) into a rationalistic system of which the centre-piece was the complete knowability of God. The Father, he argued,[32] alone possesses Godhead; ingenerate himself, he created the Word and imparted to him, not his divinity, but his activity,

[27] See below, p. 95.
[28] *In Gen. sermo* 4.3 (*PG* 54.597).
[29] *In Gen. sermo* 5.3 (*PG* 54.602-3).
[30] *In Gen. sermo* 7.1 (*PG* 54.508).
[31] See above, p. 11.
[32] For a summary of his position see M. Spanneut, *DHGE* 15.1399-405.

thus making him his instrument for bringing other creatures into existence. Since 'ingenerateness' exhaustively defines God's being, and since according to his theory of language words fully express the essence of the things they denote,[33] man can have as complete a knowledge of God as he has of himself.[34] It follows equally that there can be no resemblance whatever between the Father, whose essence is ingenerateness, and the Son, who by definition is generate.

As presented by Eunomios, Anomoeism had been exhaustively criticised by John's older contemporaries, Basil of Caesarea and Gregory of Nyssa. Even so, while other forms of Arianism were in retreat after the re-establishment of orthodoxy in 378, it was still a force to be reckoned with in Antioch in the early 380s. Numbers of intelligent Christians were attracted by its simplicity and logical clarity as well as by its genuine soteriological concern. It posed a sufficient threat for John to single it out as a prime target. It is interesting that he lets it out that he had been meditating an onslaught on the Anomoeans for some time, but had postponed it because he had noticed the enjoyment they took in his sermons and did not wish 'to frighten away the quarry'.[35] Eventually they actually pressed him to debate the difference between their beliefs and his, and he eagerly took up the challenge. But he did so, he avowed, in a deliberately irenical, constructive spirit, hoping to heal these people 'infected with error' rather than let them succumb to their sickness.[36] 'Nothing', he remarked with an uncharacteristic rejection of aggressiveness, 'is more effective than moderation and gentleness.'

As a result five addresses have come down to us,[37] originally delivered (as their numerous allusions to the liturgy make clear) at mass on Sundays between September 386 and early 387. The pervasive theme of all five, but treated in special detail in the first and third, is one which Basil of Caesarea and Gregory of Nyssa had developed with skill and eloquence, viz. the limits of human understanding and its inability to apprehend the essence of God. How could it, John pleads forcefully in the third,[38] since God's being is inaccessible even to angels and archangels, since he dwells (as Paul expressed it in 1 Tim. 6.16) 'in unapproachable light'? He thus confronted head-on Eunomios' central tenet, on which the whole system of advanced Anomoeism rested. He backed his argument with a host of texts from the bible, but also by reminding his audience that man is ignorant of the real nature not only, for example, of the sky above his head, but of his own soul.[39]

[33] See J. Daniélou, 'Eunome l'Arien et l'exégèse neo-platonicienne du Cratyle', *REG* 69 (1956), 412-32.
[34] Cf. his remarkable statement quoted by Sokrates, 4.7.
[35] *De incomprehensibili dei natura* 1.6 (*PG* 48.707). Critical edition by A.M. Malingrey, with introduction by J. Daniélou, in *SC* 28bis (Paris 1970).
[36] *De incomp.* 6-7 (*PG* 48.707-8).
[37] *De incomp. PG* 48.701-48.
[38] *De incomp.* 3.3-5 (*PG* 48.721-5).
[39] *De incomp.* 2.7 (the sky); 5.4 (the soul) (*PG* 48.717-18; 740-1).

John is aware, of course, that he was laying himself open to the charge of agnosticism, and even represents Anomoean critics as objecting, 'Are you then ignorant of what you worship?' But he has his rejoinder ready, based on Paul's statement (1 Cor. 13.9 and 12) that we now 'know in part'. There is a knowledge which men can have of God, but it is not knowledge of his essence (that only the Son possesses), but knowledge that he exists and knowledge of his action in the world.[40] In all this he was sketching a doctrine which was to become fundamental in eastern Christianity, and which was to be conveyed to the west by the writings of the mystical theologian known as Pseudo-Dionysius (c. 500).[41]

What gives these three addresses much of their power and strange fascination is their evocation of the transcendence and impenetrable mystery of the divine being. In the fourth and fifth John turns to the specifically theological questions of the relationship, first, of the Son, and then of the Spirit, to the Father. Appealing again to a few key-texts (notably the claims in John 1.18 that the only-begotten Son, who is in the bosom of the Father, has made him known, and in 1 Cor. 2.11 that no one comprehends the thoughts of God except the Spirit of God), he seeks to demonstrate, in refutation of the Anomoeans, not only that the Son and the Spirit are alone in having complete knowledge of the Father, but that they both share his divinity, being only distinguished from him as persons (*hupostaseis*).[42] We may be sure that his eager audience found his case convincing, for even if it missed the nuances of his close critique of Eunomios,[43] it is likely that it found his confident, if uncritical, handling of the texts irresistible. Much of his argument followed lines of thought already laid down by Basil and Gregory of Nyssa, but while they addressed élite groups John had a unique populist flair for making abstruse concepts and complex exegesis accessible to the ordinary folk crowding his church.

V

Several times John pleads with his congregation to hold out a brotherly hand to the Anomoeans, to pray fervently that 'they may desist from their madness'.[44] No such conciliatory note can be overheard in the eight addresses[45] incorrectly (but not inappropriately) entitled *Against the Jews* at which we must now glance.

On the Wednesday (2 September 386)[46] following the Sunday on which he had inaugurated his anti-Anomoean course John felt constrained to interrupt it in order to declaim against Christians who found themselves

[40] E.g. *De incomp.* 1.5 (*PG* 48.706).
[41] On him see I.P. Sheldon-Williams, *Cambridge History of Later Greek and Early Medieval Philosophy*, 1967, 457-72.
[42] *De incomp.* 5.2-3 (*PG* 48.737-9).
[43] J. Daniélou brings some of this out in his commentary in *SC* 28bis.
[44] *De incomp.* 5.5 (*PG* 48.743).
[45] *Adversus Iudaeos: PG* 48.843-942. ET by P.W. Harkins (Washington 1977). For an illuminating discussion see R.L. Wilken, *John Chrysostom and the Jews* (London 1983).
[46] For the dates of this and other sermons see E. Schwartz, art. cit. 169-83.

irresistibly attracted to the faith and ceremonial practices of their Jewish fellow-citizens. There was, as we noted earlier,[47] a sizeable and, it appears, socially influential Jewish minority in Antioch, with synagogues both in the city and out at Daphne, and what spurred the anxious pastor into action was the imminent approach of the great sequence of Jewish autumn feasts and fasts – the Feast of Trumpets (New Year), then the Day of Atonement ten days later, finally the week-long Feast of Tabernacles. The Antiochene Jews were not standoffish, still less confined to a ghetto, but celebrated these solemn occasions publicly, apparently welcoming outsiders. From experience John knew how fascinatedly many Christians flocked to watch them, even to participate in them. Many, as he ruefully admitted, 'hold Jews in deep respect and regard their way of life (*politeia*) as deserving reverence'.[48] Some, for example, to his unconcealed horror,[49] considered an oath taken in a synagogue especially binding, while others consulted rabbis when sick and found their cures effective (as John confesses they sometimes were, though protesting that they were obtained by amulets, magical incantations, and the like). He therefore exerted himself, in this first homily and in a second preached several days later (aimed particularly at people who practised circumcision), to give a stern warning to such backsliders. How could they have the face, after cavorting with those who had shed Christ's blood, to return to church and partake of that very blood at the altar?[50] The numbers implicated must have been large, for he was to insist next year that careless talk about them could be damaging for morale.[51]

These tirades reveal John as a master of unscrupulous, often coarse invective.[52] His object, of course, is to convince his hearers of the folly, the sheer apostasy, of taking any part whatever in Jewish rituals. But to achieve this pastoral aim he paints the Jews themselves, their religion and their social habits in repulsive colours.[53] Through rejecting the Saviour foretold in their own scriptures they have forfeited the status of children and been reduced to that of dogs, to which, ironically, Jesus had once assigned the Gentiles (Matt. 15.26). The hardness of heart which, according to Acts 7.51, caused them to resist the Spirit itself resulted from their bestial gluttony and drunkenness, as Moses had made plain when he exclaimed (Deut. 32.15), 'Israel ate, and was gorged and made sleek.' On their feast-days they descend to shameless sensuality, dancing in the city squares with naked feet and leading processions of perverts and tarts. There is nothing holy in their synagogues; they are no better than theatres

---

[47] See above, p. 2.
[48] *Adv. Iud.* 1.3 (*PG* 48.847).
[49] *Adv. Iud.* 1.3 (*PG* 48.848).
[50] *Adv. Iud.* 2.3 (*PG* 48.861).
[51] *Adv. Iud.* 8.4 (*PG* 48.983).
[52] See esp. M. Simon, *Verus Israel* (Paris 1948), 256-63.
[53] All citations in this paragraph are taken from *Adv. Iud.* 1.

(in John's eyes cesspools of immorality), brothels or dens of thieves. The fact that they house the books of Moses and the prophets does not sanctify them, any more than the heathen temple of Serapis at Alexandria, where those same books are kept, is thereby made holy. The Jews' souls have become the dwelling-places of demons: not surprisingly, since they are the 'Christ-killers' (*Christoktonoi*) who did not shrink from slaying the Lord. God himself, speaking through his prophets, has branded their worship as abominable; they themselves should be shunned as a filthy plague threatening the entire world.

In proof of these ferocious claims John marshals a battery of mainly Old Testament texts in which God rebuked Israel and criticised its sacrificial system. He makes his point by isolating them from the particular situations to which they originally applied and gratuitously giving them a general reference. To give two examples, when members of his congregation plead that there is surely 'something solemn and grand' about the Jewish festivals, he flings back at them Amos' (5.21) dismissive, 'I hate, I despise your feasts',[54] without explaining the context of the prophet's rebuke. Again, his warning to the backsliders that the people with whom they wish to consort are 'those who shout "Crucify him, crucify him"', and who say "His blood be upon us and our children" ' (he cites the verbs in the present tense), rests on the unspoken assumption that their Jewish neighbours, indeed the Jews everywhere at any time, are to be identified with the handful to whom the evangelists attributed these cries.[55] He is so distressed by the Judaizers' disloyalty that he begs his auditors to be diligent in tracking them down – women searching out women, men men, slaves slaves, freemen freemen, even children children – so that, when next they come together for the liturgy, they may receive commendation from himself and, far more important, a reward from God exceeding all description and amply compensating them for any trouble they have taken.[56] On 31 January 387 John delivered a third homily *Against the Jews* which is traditionally included in the series inaugurated by the two mentioned above.[57] Actually, while inveighing incidentally against the Jews, it has a somewhat different objective, viz. to induce a small group of Christians in Antioch who continued the age-old Syrian custom of celebrating Easter 'with the Jews', i.e. on the Sunday following the Passover on 14 Nisan, to give up the practice, which had been forbidden by the council of Nicaea (325), and fall into line with the rest of the church. Did they really consider the Jews wiser than the fathers who met at the council with Christ himself guiding their decisions?[58] In any case the Jews had no right to be celebrating the Passover now in Antioch, since Moses had forbidden its celebration anywhere except in Jerusalem (Deut.

---

[54] *Adv. Iud.* 1.7 (*PG* 48.853).
[55] *Adv. Iud.* 1.5 (*PG* 48.850).
[56] *Adv. Iud.* 1.8 (*PG* 48.856).
[57] *Adv. Iud.* 3 (*PG* 48.861-72).
[58] *Adv. Iud.* 3.3 (*PG* 48.865).

16.5-6). In autumn of the same year, however, when his Jewish fellow-citizens were preparing once again to observe their traditional fasts and feasts, John felt a fresh urge to break away from the scriptural exposition on which he was then engaged: 'Again the wretched Jews, most pitiful of mankind, are about to fast; again it is incumbent to protect the church's flock.'[59] The five addresses he then delivered are conventionally included in the cycle.

In general, these are more theological in content, somewhat more moderate in tone. In the first, or fourth (they are best cited by their traditional numbers), he challenges Christians tempted to participate in Jewish rituals to reflect on what they are doing.[60] 'Surely the difference between us and Jews is not trifling? ... Why do you try to mix what cannot be mixed? They crucified the Christ whom you worship.' Later he enlarges on the consideration which he had urged in the third, and which recurs several times in the series, viz. that in keeping these fasts and festivals the Jews of Antioch are violating their own law, since it is insistent (again he appeals to Deut. 16, among other texts) that their observance is tied to Jerusalem and the Temple, now destroyed.[61] It is a plea, we should observe, which would have cut little ice with contemporary Judaism, which had its own solutions to problems created by the loss of the Temple.[62] In the fifth he widens the perspective, returning to a central theme of his earlier apologetic writings, that the supreme proof that Christ is truly God is his prediction that Jerusalem would be captured and the Temple destroyed.[63] His argument is that the fulfilment of this prophecy, ratified by the failure of all attempts (including most signally the Emperor Julian's) to rebuild the Temple, taken in conjunction with Malachi's prophecy (1.11-12) that a pure worship would be offered, not in any one place and still less at Jerusalem, but 'from the rising of the sun to its setting', decisively proves that the Jewish religion has been superseded by the Christian one.[64]

The sixth and seventh homilies continue the theme that the old dispensation has been supplanted by the new, while the eighth is largely an exhortation to his audience to extend a helping hand to weaker brethren who may have slipped. In the sixth, however, John abandons reasoned debate and resumes his earlier vituperative style. Explaining the present wretched plight of the Jews, he declares, with Ezekiel 23.5-9 among his witnesses, that they had always been sinners and blasphemers. They adored the golden calf, attempted more than once to murder Moses, sacrificed their children to demons, persecuted their prophets, and finally

---

[59] *Adv. Iud.* 4.1 (*PG* 48.871).
[60] *Adv. Iud.* 4.3 (*PG* 48.875).
[61] *Adv. Iud.* 4.4-6 (*PG* 48.876-81).
[62] See R.L. Wilken's discussion, op. cit., 148-53.
[63] See above, p. 42.
[64] *Adv. Iud.* 5.11-12 (*PG* 48.900-4).

shed the precious blood of the Messiah, so committing the supremely infamous crime which leaves them no hope of pardon.[65]

These homilies, with their scurrilous attacks on the Jews (he kept them up, whenever opportunity offered, throughout his career), have distressed modern readers, who have speculated how much, given the wide diffusion and popularity of his writings, they must have fuelled the cruelly repressive attitudes to Judaism adopted by later Christianity. In his own day, however, there was nothing exceptional about them – except, of course, their oratorical bravura. So far from being original, the arguments they deploy reflect a tradition of Christian polemic which can be traced back, in east and west alike, to the late first century, when the church separated itself from the synagogue. Since Christians, following Paul's lead, now claimed to have displaced the Jews as God's chosen people, as the true Israel, it was logical that they should represent them as traitors to their own scriptures and as having thus forfeited the promises originally made to them. Equally it was in the church's interest, since it had appropriated the Jewish bible and regarded the blessings it contained as applying exclusively to itself, to do everything in its power to discourage its members from too cosy relations with their Jewish neighbours, who might all too easily open their eyes to a quite different interpretation of it, and thus tempt them from their allegiance. There is, in fact, plenty of evidence, in (for example) the legislation of the councils of Elvira (306)[66] and Laodikeia (431),[67] and in the so-called Apostolic Constitutions (fourth cent.: of Syrian provenance),[68] both of the fascination Jewish practices continued to have for susceptible Christians, and of the efforts the church authorities made to keep the two communities apart. John's homilies vividly illustrate how real this danger was in a pluralistic city like Antioch, where Jews and Christians jostled against each other in their daily lives and the Jews, apparently, welcomed the presence of Christians at their celebrations.

After all the abuse he had heaped upon them, it is ironical that many years later, when his own career lay in ruins, John was to acknowledge that the Jews of Constantinople counted among his sympathisers.[69]

VI

Among John's most carefully crafted sermons were those he preached either at celebrations in honour of holy persons or martyrs, or on great feast-days. Several such from his first twelve months as a priest have survived. As well as illustrating his oratorical skills, they throw intriguing light on the forms of Christian devotion he was concerned to promote.

[65] *Adv. Iud.* 6.2 (*PG* 48.905-7).
[66] Canons 26 and 49 (Hefele, *Histoire des conciles* 1, 235; 249).
[67] Canons 37 and 38 (Hefele, op. cit., 1, 1019).
[68] 2.61.1; 5.17; 8.47.70 (Funk 175; 287-8; 584).
[69] *Ep.1 ad Innocentium: SC* 342.86.

In the former category we should place five panegyrics of local saints:[70] the 15-year-old Pelagia who *c.* 283, to frustrate a threat to her virginity, had flung herself to death from the roof of her home (8 October 386); Ignatios, second bishop of Antioch and author of seven remarkable letters, torn to pieces *c.* 107 by lions in the Colosseum at Rome (17 October 386); Philogonios, an advocate promoted *c.* 316 as twenty-second bishop of the see (20 December 386); the martyr Lucian, exegete and theologian (7 January 387); and Meletios, Flavian's predecessor and John's own patron (12 February 387). All these were spoken at the shrines where the saints' relics were preserved. In the case of Meletios, for example, this was the one he had had built for Babylas on the north side of the Orontes, and where his own body had been interred at his request.[71] Pelagia's shrine was some distance from the city, making it necessary for the faithful to troop out to it in procession – and for John to admonish them to behave with decorum, without dancing, laughter, or tipsy loutishness, which would provoke criticism from heretics who might be in the crowd.[72] The core, often the larger part, of these panegyrics consists of a graphic recital of the valiant life, achievements, and (where appropriate) sufferings of their hero or heroine. But John always made a point of appealing to his auditors to imitate their heroism, sometimes also of impressing on them the wonderful relief from life's afflictions, of whatever kind, they would be able to obtain by coming close to, or actually touching, with faith, the caskets housing their remains.[73] In all of them he is stressing, sometimes by implication, but on occasion directly, the enriching fellowship which their devotees on earth can have with the blessed saints.

Striking examples of the second category are the three sermons which John preached on Whitsunday (Pentecost) and Christmas 386, and on Epiphany (6 January) 387.[74] In each of these dazzling orations he holds together several loosely related themes. In the first, for example, he not only explains how the outpouring of the Holy Spirit on the apostles (which Pentecost celebrates: see Acts 2) transformed them into angelic beings armed with supernatural powers, but argues on the basis of this that the gift of the Spirit to sinful men can effect their reconciliation with God.[75] He then turns on the heretics who deny that the Spirit is fully divine (an active group, apparently, in Antioch). Their denial makes a mockery of the privileges Christians believe they enjoy (forgiveness of sins, access to God in prayer, etc.), and indeed (this was a characteristic touch) of the authority of the bishop presiding at this service, since all these depend on his being

---

[70] *De s. Pelagia* (*PG* 50.579-84); *In s. mart. Ignatium* (*PG* 50.587-96); *De beato Philogonio* (*PG* 48.747-56); *In s. Meletium* (*PG* 50.519-26); *In s. Lucianum. mart.* (*PG* 50.515-20). For their dates (in brackets), see E. Schwartz, art. cit., 173-9.

[71] See above, p. 38.

[72] *De s. Pelagia* 4 (*PG* 50.585-6).

[73] See esp. *In s. mart. Ignat.* 5 (*PG* 50.595-6).

[74] *De s. Pentecoste hom.*; *In diem natalem dom. nostri Iesu Christi*; *De baptismate Christi et de Epiphania* (*PG* 50.453-64; 49.352-62; 363-72).

[75] *De s. Pentecoste* 1.2-3 (*PG* 50.456-7).

the Spirit of God.[76] In his prologue he had pointedly reminded his hearers that, while Christians observe three principal feasts (Epiphany, Easter, Pentecost), they are not tied to three fixed days as the Jews were when Moses commanded them to appear thrice yearly before God (Ex. 23.17): the spiritual realities these feasts express remain valid, and should be kept in mind, every day of the year.[77] Later he tackles a problem on which, he says, people were often seeking enlightenment: why the wonders so evident at the first Pentecost are no longer available. His solution is that in those days, when men were emerging from Judaism and paganism, they needed physical signs to bolster their faith; mature Christians are aware that the miracles of grace are spiritually discerned.[78] Finally, seizing on the comparison of the Spirit to 'tongues as of fire' (Acts 2.3), he winds up his homily with a vivid picture of the Spirit burning up a man's sins as fire destroys thorns, and of the day of judgment which, however menacing, a man can face with confidence if he has purged his sins by the grace of the Spirit whom God has sent.[79]

The topics treated in the Epiphany address are even more variegated. One which stands out is the question why the baptism of Jesus, and not his birth, is called his 'epiphany', i.e. manifestation. John's answer is that his true nature was not revealed to mankind when he was born, but when the Holy Spirit descended on him at his baptism (cf. John 1.26 and 1.33-4).[80] But it is the Christmas sermon which, for reasons which will become clear, is historically the most important of the three. Exceptionally long, although Flavian was booked to follow with another address, it contains a blistering attack on pagans who ridicule the Christian claim that 'God was born in flesh', although their own objects of worship, artefacts of stone or wood, are by comparison utterly contemptible.[81] It concludes with a passionate appeal to the congregation to come with fear and trembling, with a clean conscience, without pushing or shoving or brawling, to the dread table at which men, dust and ashes as they are, receive Christ's body and blood.[82] These digressions apart, it is exclusively concerned with promoting, and giving reasons for, the celebration of Christ's nativity on 25 December. The key-note is struck in the opening paragraph, where John expresses his joy that the practice of observing it on this day, prevalent in the west (so he claims) from earliest times, has at last been accepted in Antioch (witness the vast congregation present in the church), in spite of the fact that 'it is not yet ten years since the significance of the day became known to us'.[83]

---

[76] *De s. Pentecoste* 1.4 (*PG* 50.458-9).
[77] *De s. Pentecoste* 1.1 (*PG* 50.453-4).
[78] *De s. Pentecoste* 1.4 (*PG* 50.459).
[79] *De s. Pentecoste* 1.5 (*PG* 50.460-1).
[80] *De baptismo Christi* 2 (*PG* 49.365-6).
[81] *In diem natalem* 6 (*PG* 49.358-60).
[82] *In diem natalem* 7 (*PG* 49.360-2).
[83] *In diem natalem* 1 (*PG* 49.351-2).

Many in his audience, John freely admits, are puzzled and sceptical about the legitimacy of this novel and exciting feast. To convince them that 25 December was the actual date of Christ's birth he appeals first to the rapid and widespread acceptance of that date. This surely suggests that it cannot be of mere human contrivance; it must be 'from God' (he cites Gamaliel's remark in Acts 5.39-9) for otherwise it could never have won recognition so quickly. Secondly, he argues that, since 'we have received this date from the Romans', we can safely assume it to be correct since they have access to the official records kept at Rome of the census which the governor Quirinius conducted at the time of the birth (Luke 2.1-7).[84] Thirdly, he devotes the bulk of his sermon to an elaborate, somewhat bizarre computation based on the stories in Luke's gospel (1.5-56) of the promise made by the angel of the Lord to the priest Zechariah that his wife Elizabeth, now past the age of child-bearing, would give birth to a son (John the Baptist), and the announcement six months later to the Blessed Virgin that she will conceive and bear a son.[85] On the assumption that Zechariah was high priest, and as such could only enter the holy of holies of the Temple once a year, in September, he deduces that Mary must have conceived Jesus six months later, i.e. in March, and given birth to him nine months after that, i.e. around 25 December. John presents his argument with panache and, considering the complexity of his scriptural evidence, surprising clarity. Unfortunately his whole case hinges on the premiss that Zechariah was high priest, and this is completely fallacious.

In spite of what John says about its antiquity, Christmas was a comparatively recent feast, originating indeed in the west at Rome, but only around 330.[86] Almost certainly it was intended to be a Christian counter to the widely popular pagan festival of the birthday of the Unconquered Sun (*Sol Invictus*), observed in the west at the winter solstice on 25 December. John confirms this connection in his opening paragraph, where he exclaims that, while it is exciting to watch the sun bestriding the earth and scattering its rays on all mankind, it is much more so to see the Sun of Righteousness (Malachi 4.2: a title regularly applied to Christ) pouring out his radiance from our human flesh and enlightening our souls.[87] Its emergence soon after the council of Nicaea (325) is also significant: there can be little doubt that the orthodox Nicene party saw it as a liturgical rebuff to Arianism. This is borne out by evidence supplied by sermons of Gregory of Nazianzos and Gregory of Nyssa,[88] both champions of the Nicene renaissance, that, in spite of the nativity having been hitherto commemorated at Epiphany in the east, Christmas had been introduced both at Constanti-

---

[84] *In diem natalem* 2 (*PG* 49.352-3).
[85] *In diem natalem* 3-5 (*PG* 49.354-8).
[86] See, e.g., B. Botte, *Les origines de la Noël et de l'Épiphanie* (Louvain 1932).
[87] *In diem natalem* 1 (*PG* 49.351).
[88] B. Botte, op. cit., 26-31.

nople and in Asia Minor by 380, i.e. at the time of the restoration of orthodoxy by Theodosius the Great. John's sermon is fully in line with this, with its vigorous and repeated assertion that it was God himself who was made flesh.

A further point deserving note is the sermon's clear implication that Christmas was being observed for the first time at Antioch in 386. Against this it has been objected that John's remark that 'it is scarcely ten years since this day became fully known to us' indicates that the feast had been established there for several years. This, however, is to read far too much into his words. Correctly interpreted, they refer simply to the appreciation at Antioch of the full significance of 25 December, not to its adoption as a feast. Indeed, the celebration of Christmas there before 386 cannot be reconciled either with his enthusiasm that 'today at last' the great day he has been longing to see has arrived, or with his assurance in his Pentecost address earlier in the year that the church has three great feasts – Epiphany, Easter and Pentecost (no mention of Christmas) – the theme of the first being Christ's appearance on earth 'as a child'.[89] What surely clinches the matter is the notice he gave,[90] only a few days before in his panegyric of Philogonios, of the imminent approach of 'the most solemn and awesome of all festivals, which one would not be wrong to designate "the metropolis" of all festivals, the birth of Christ in flesh', from which all other great feasts take their origin and derive their meaning. For this great, seemingly unprecedented occasion he begged everyone to abandon his home and pack the church.

It is tempting to speculate whether the continuing schism between the official church in Antioch and the minute hard-line group presided over by Paulinos played any part, one way or the other, in the introduction of the new feast. Although we cannot be certain, it is more than likely that the Paulinians, or Eustathians, who were alone recognised by the holy see and maintained close ties with it, already celebrated the nativity on 25 December. If so, this would probably have seemed to many in Flavian's congregation an excellent reason for resisting its adoption. Others, however, aware that rapprochement with Rome was in the church's long-term interest, and recalling that Meletios and his party had been careful to build doctrinal bridges with the west,[91] may have seen some advantage in not lagging behind Rome's protégé in a matter of such symbolical importance. These conflicting positions may well have stimulated the sharp debates to which John refers,[92] and may even have delayed recognition of the feast for some time. Unfortunately we have no means of answering these questions. It remains interesting, however, that John, who was chosen by the authorities

---

[89] *De s. Pentecoste* 1.1 (*PG* 50.454).
[90] *De beato Philogonio* 3 (*PG* 48.752-3).
[91] See above, p. 37.
[92] *In diem natalem* 1 (*PG* 49.352).

to explain the new feast to the general public and win support for it, went out of his way to highlight the authority of Rome (a line of argument not used by other eastern leaders). The feast, he claimed, had been observed at Rome from earliest times, the Romans were uniquely qualified to know the precise date of the nativity, and it was they 'who have now transmitted reliable knowledge of it to us'.

6

An Anxious Lent

I

Less than two months after his Christmas sermon, on Sunday 21 February 387, John harangued the congregation in the Old Church on Paul's advice to Timothy, 'Drink a little wine for your stomach's sake' (1 Tim. 5.22), taking occasion to criticise 'our simpler brothers' who, when they see people getting drunk and behaving disgracefully, call for a ban on wine. Wine, he pointed out,[1] is God's creation; it is not the mere use of it that causes drunkenness, but immoderate indulgence in it. In his peroration he called on Christians, if they should come across someone blaspheming God, to rebuke him sharply, if necessary striking him in the face: 'Make your fist holy by that blow.' He was booked to preach again on the Saturday and Sunday following, and on Monday 1 March, the first day of Lent, to embark on a course of Lenten homilies. But on the intervening Thursday, or perhaps Friday, there was a sudden explosion of popular violence in Antioch which was to fill the city with horror, and then with fear only gradually yielding to hope, through all the weeks of Lent until the arrival of Easter.[2]

Our information about the riot and its sequel, it is worth noting, comes almost exclusively from John's Lenten sermons and five 'speeches' (nos 19, 20, 21, 22, 23) of his former tutor Libanios, who was also in Antioch during the crisis. Of these latter all but *Oration* 23 were composed after the affair had been settled; they were probably intended, in Libanios' manner,[3] not for public delivery, but to be brought, in one way or another, to the attention of the important persons (Theodosius and the imperial commissioners) for whose eyes they were intended or, in the case of *Oration* 23, to be read out before select groups.[4] While some of them contain clearly fictitious matter, the circumstantial detail in which they abound is invaluable for reconstructing what actually happened. There are striking parallels between the

---

[1] *Ad pop. Antioch. hom.* 1.4-5 (*PG* 49.22).
[2] The fullest, most up-to-date study, both of the events and of John's homilies, is F. van de Paverd, *St John Chrysostom: the Homilies on the Statues* (Rome 1991), which contains a full bibliography. His chronology has been followed here.
[3] P. Petit, 'Recherches sur la publication et la diffusion des discours de Libanius', *Historia* 5 (1956), 479-509.
[4] P. Petit, *Libanios: Discours* (Paris 1979) I, 272-3.

accounts given by the two men, and in the past Libanios has been unfairly accused of cribbing from John for his own purposes.[5] The sensible verdict, however, is that of A.F. Norman, that 'the coincidences of content and form are to be explained by the common subject-matter and the common rhetorical store of topic and rule, which made any account with pretensions to accuracy and to plausibility inescapably similar to another'.[6]

II

The insurrection[7] was triggered off by the reading out, in the court-house (*dikasterion*) on the island, of a government decree which imposed, without previous notice, a new, exorbitant tax. Its exact nature, which has been endlessly but inconclusively debated by historians, is irrelevant to this book, but it apparently affected all social classes. Its announcement provoked the city councillors (or decurions) and other prominent citizens crowding the hall to address tearful protests to the provincial governor (*consularis Syriae*), who was present.[8] When these proved unavailing and news of the levy spread to the populace, a crowd rushed to Flavian's house, doubtless hoping that a bishop held in high esteem at court would be able to do something to have the impost withdrawn; but he (as Libanios reports with satisfaction)[9] could not be found. At this point the mob took over, instigated by a small group plausibly identified as the theatrical claque,[10] a paid body which at Antioch and elsewhere had come to assume a political role, but consistently referred to by John as 'strangers, men of mixed race' or 'strangers and foreigners'.[11] First, they attacked the governor's residence, and then, having failed to break in, vandalised the nearby public baths.[12] Finally, they set about jeering at, pulling down, even breaking to pieces, the painted portraits and bronze statues of the emperor and his family set up before the palace and in public places.[13] When they had burned down the house of a citizen who had defended the tax and there was talk of setting fire to the palace, a company of archers acting as police intervened; then troops led by the count of Oriens in person moved in.[14]

The whole disturbance was over by noon.[15] Even before that, when the mob started maltreating the imperial effigies, the authorities had dis-

[5] R. Goebel, *De J. Chrysostomi et Libanii orationibus* (Göttingen 1910).
[6] *Libanius: Selected Works* (Loeb 1979) 2, 232.
[7] For a fuller account see F. van de Paverd, op. cit., ch. 2.
[8] Libanios, *Or.* 19.15-26.
[9] *Or.* 19.28.
[10] R. Browning, *JRS* 42 (1952), 13-21. For criticism of his thesis see F. van de Paverd, op. cit., 27-33.
[11] E.g. *Hom.* 2.3; 3.1 (*PG* 49.38; 48).
[12] Libanios, *Or.* 20.3; 22.6.
[13] Libanios, *Or.* 22.7-8.
[14] Libanios, *Or.* 22.9; 19.34-6.
[15] Libanios, *Or.* 22.9.

patched mounted messengers to Constantinople to report the outrage to the emperor.[16] The count of Oriens lost no time in rounding up such of the rioters as he could lay hands on, and having them summarily tried and, when found guilty, ruthlessly executed.[17] Meanwhile the citizens were filled with chill foreboding as the heinousness of what had been done sank in. Everyone knew that to insult or show disrespect to the images of the reigning emperor was equivalent to insulting him personally, and therefore counted as high treason.[18] Both John and Libanios[19] vividly record the rumours which circulated about the terrible punishment the angry emperor was likely to inflict. The city was likely, it was whispered, to be given over to plunder and devastation: it might even be razed off the face of the earth. It is scarcely surprising that there was a wholesale exodus, with people of all classes (including, to his chagrin, most of Libanios' students)[20] seeking refuge in the countryside or the mountains; the authorities, significantly, took steps to prevent the city councillors from joining the mad rush.[21] In contrast, Bishop Flavian, notwithstanding his advanced years, bravely set out on 22 February on the long journey to Constantinople to plead with Theodosius in an effort to 'rescue so great a people from the imperial wrath'.[22]

After more than a fortnight of anguished waiting, on 15 March, two commissioners nominated by Theodosius to investigate the affair, Caesarios, master of the offices, and the general Ellebichos, arrived at Antioch from the capital. They had, John was later to report,[23] passed Flavian as he travelled north, and had communicated to him the gist of their mandate. The choice of Ellebichos must have seemed a hopeful omen, for as military commander for Oriens he was a familiar figure in the city, where he had his headquarters.[24] They got down to business immediately, next day arresting all the city councillors; it was these whom the government seems to have held primarily responsible.[25] Their alleged crime did not consist, apparently, in having themselves done violence to the imperial images, nor even (as Libanios implies[26] in one of his Orations and some modern scholars accept)[27] in having failed to check the riot. Rather it lay in the fact that, whereas as subjects they should have welcomed the tax imposed by their

---

[16] Libanios, *Or.* 20.4.
[17] Libanios, *Or.* 21.9; John, *Hom.* 3.6 (*PG* 49.56).
[18] E.g. Ambrose, *Expos. in ps.* 118, 25 (*CSEL* 62.219).
[19] E.g. *Or.* 20.5; 23.12; *Hom.* 2.3-4; 6.7 (*PG* 49.36-8; 91).
[20] *Or.* 23.20-8.
[21] Libanios, *Or.* 22.11.
[22] *Hom.* 3.1 (*PG* 49.47).
[23] *Hom.* 21.2 (*PG* 49.213).
[24] For his career see *PLRE* 1.178.
[25] Libanios, *Or.* 21.7; 23.25.
[26] *Or.* 19.25-8.
[27] E.g. P. Petit, *Libanius et la vie municipale à Antioche au ivme siècle* (Paris 1955), 238-9.

generous emperor,[28] they had had the effrontery to voice disloyal complaints against it when it was announced – complaints which, taken up by the mob outside, had led to their seditious misconduct.[29] Then on the following day, 17 March, the commissioners presided as judges over the 'fearsome tribunal', as John calls it,[30] at which the councillors were interrogated and tried. Libanios, it is interesting to note, sat with them as an assessor.[31] A dramatic incident was the appearance in the city, very early in the morning as the commissioners were riding to the court-house, of some monks who had come down from their mountain retreats to plead for the accused, and who in fact persuaded the commissioners to agree to submit any decision they might reach to the emperor for his final ratification.[32]

It was towards evening that the judges announced the sentences. First, the emperor had decreed that Antioch was to be stripped of its status as a metropolis, that rank being transferred to its neighbour Laodikeia;[33] that its theatres, racecourse, and baths be shut down;[34] and that the free distribution of bread to the poor be suspended.[35] Military law was also imposed, with troops taking over the maintenance of order from the civic authorities.[36] Then came their verdict on the convicted city councillors. Some were sentenced to banishment, others to death; we do not know the criteria by which the different degrees of criminality were assessed. The carrying out of the death sentences, however, as the monks had demanded, was deferred until the emperor reached a final decision. In the meantime those so sentenced were to be kept in gaol. Next day, as darkness fell, Caesarios set off at high speed for Constantinople to report the results of the investigation to Theodosius.

III

Throughout these and the following weeks until Easter John went ahead with his planned programme of Lenten discourses. Because the events arising out of the riot and his concern to raise the morale of his stricken flock are prominent in all but two of them (the ninth and tenth), they are traditionally known as the Homilies on the Statues.[37] By conventional reckoning they number twenty-one. The first, however, cited in the first paragraph of this chapter, was preached before the outbreak of the insurrection. On the other hand, a strong case has been made out for including

---

[28] Libanios, *Or.* 22.4-6 (his considered view, as against that expressed in *Or.* 19).

[29] For a full discussion see Paverd, op. cit., 82-107.

[30] *Hom.* 17.1: cf. 13.1 (*PG* 49.172; 135).

[31] Libanios, *Or.* 22.23.

[32] *Hom.* 17.1-2 (*PG* 49.172; 174).

[33] *Hom.* 17.2 (*PG* 49.176; 179); Libanios, *Or.* 20.6.

[34] *Hom.* 14.6; 17.2; 18.4 (*PG* 49.151; 176; 187); Libanios *Or.* 23.26-7; 20.6.

[35] Libanios, *Or.* 20.7 and 38.

[36] Libanios, *Or.* 23.26.

[37] *Ad populum Antiochenum hom.* 21 (*PG* 49.15-222). A critical edition is urgently needed.

in the series an address which has commonly been treated as a baptismal instruction (*catechesis*).[38] Not only is it so included in the great majority of MSS, but it is demonstrably not a catechesis, being addressed largely to baptised Christians; while it makes pointed references back to other homilies on the Statues. As it is now generally accepted[39] that Antioch followed the Alexandrian calendar, according to which Easter in 387 fell on 25 April, and that the Antiochene Lent lasted for eight weeks,[40] it has become possible to establish, as F. van de Paverd has convincingly shown,[41] the order and, in most cases, precise dates of the homilies.

Page after page of these addresses is taken up with what at first sight seems routine religious or moral instruction; John was not the man to be distracted from this by a transitory political crisis, however alarming. So he carries on doggedly expounding Genesis (the book prescribed for Lenten meditation) to his congregation, or attempting to clear up for them the problems it raises.[42] Again, he lashes out at their follies and vices – the ostentatious luxury of the rich,[43] compared with which poverty borne with a humble spirit is a 'treasure inviolable', or the wickedness of malicious gossip.[44] His sharpest, most persistent attacks are reserved for the practice of swearing oaths. He regarded Jesus' ban on them (Matt. 5.21) as absolute, and had made the eradication of the habit in Antioch his principal objective for this Lent. It would be a great error, however, to be taken in by appearances. John presents his themes in the setting of the anguished plight of the city and its inhabitants, and so gives them enhanced relevance and urgency; he also stresses that the exposition of scripture is always the richest source of consolation.[45] With the hippodrome and theatres, even the factories, shut down, his church was thronged with worried people, like a harbour (as he graphically puts it)[46] packed with shipping in foul weather. The question on everyone's lips was 'What has the emperor decided? Will he really bring himself to annihilate such a great and populous city?'[47] The question was a reasonable one: Theodosius was a man of ungovernable temper, and in 390 was to order the slaughter of several thousand citizens at Thessalonica after an uprising.

The homilies mirror, in vivid and often poignant flashes, the drama as it unfolded week by week and John strove to set what was happening in a

[38] *Ad illuminandos cat.* 2 (*PG* 49.231-40): for the argument see F. van de Paverd, op. cit., 216-30.
[39] E.g. V. Grumel, *La chronologie* (Paris 1958), 267; Lietzmann-Aland, *Zeitrechnung der römischen Kaiserzeit* (Berlin 1984), 22.
[40] A. Baumstark, *Comparative Liturgy* (ET: London 1958).
[41] Op. cit., 205-364.
[42] E.g. *Hom.* 7-9.
[43] *Hom.* 2.5-8 (*PG* 49.41-6).
[44] *Hom.* 3.5 (*PG* 49.53-5).
[45] *Hom.* 7.1 (*PG* 49.92).
[46] *Hom.* 4.1; 15.1 (*PG* 49.59; 153-5).
[47] *Hom.* 6.7 (*PG* 49.91).

Christian perspective. In the second, for example, delivered a day or so after the riot, he depicts the desolate aspect of the city after its display of shameful, uncharacteristic violence.[48] Normally as crowded with busy citizens as a hive with bees, its main streets are deserted and everyone who has not abandoned it is shut up indoors, terrifiedly asking who is the latest person to be rounded up and executed. If only people had heeded his recent sermon urging them to deal severely with blasphemers,[49] the grievous insult to the emperor would never have been perpetrated. Even so, it is up to Christians to demonstrate their difference from unbelievers by the courage and reliance on God with which they face disaster. They at least are aware that he has permitted these things to happen so that they may be brought by their sufferings to a healthier frame of mind.

In the third (Sunday 28 February),[50] pointing dramatically to Flavian's empty throne in the apse, he encourages his congregation to take heart from their bishop's bravery in travelling, crippled as he is with age and ill-health, to the capital, and lists the pleas he will confidently present to 'our humane emperor', including the reminder that the paschal season, at which Christ obtained redemption for all mankind, is ideally suited for the exercise of forgiveness.[51] He will also press the point that the crimes committed were not the work of Antiochene citizens but (did John really believe this?) of 'foreigners and immigrants' for whose misdeeds it would be unjust to punish innocent people. In the sixth (Wednesday 3 March) he adds further reasons for confidence, especially the news just received that the horses of the messengers sent post-haste to Constantinople had broken down, so that there was a good chance that Flavian would catch up with them.[52] He adds that Flavian was carrying with him a copy of the Easter amnesty releasing prisoners from gaol which Theodosius had circulated at the beginning of Lent. Notwithstanding this upbeat message, however, he continues to urge his listeners to reflect earnestly on the moral instruction he has been giving them, for this will enable them to rise above 'the great despondency which weighs heavily upon us'.[53]

The atmosphere of despondency was evidently real. He begins his fifteenth homily (Saturday 6 March) by explaining that he is not going to give a lecture on fasting, as might have been expected on a Saturday.[54] With 'the dread of impending calamity' stalking the streets and the city itself threatened with destruction, no one is in the mood for excessive indulgence,

[48] *Hom.* 2.1-3 (*PG* 49.33-8).
[49] See above, p. 72.
[50] For the date see Paverd, op. cit., 48. For the dates of other homilies mentioned below see ch. iv with table on pp. 363f.
[51] *Hom.* 3.1-2 (*PG* 49.47-9).
[52] *Hom.* 6.2-3 (*PG* 49.83-4).
[53] *Hom.* 6.7 (*PG* 49.90-1).
[54] *Hom.* 15.1 (*PG* 49.153-4).

which shows, indeed, what a salutary emotion fear is. In the sixteenth,[55] however, delivered on 13 or 14 March, a day or two before the commissioners' arrival, he is distinctly upset, expressing indignation and shame that the governor, a pagan, had found it necessary to stand up in the church and address soothing words to the distracted congregation. Apparently a rumour that Antioch was surrounded by troops and was about to be sacked had induced widespread panic; it had perhaps been fomented by alarmist reports of the commissioners' approach. After grudgingly commending the governor's solicitude, he gives vent to his disgust that, after all the instruction he has given them about putting their entire trust in God, they have had to turn to a pagan to teach them how to bear adversity.

When the judges' sentence proved less harsh than anyone, himself included, had expected, John changes his tone, and in successive homilies urges his people to be continually thanking God for their deliverance. Indeed, they should keep the memory of their sufferings alive, and report them to their children, recalling that it was God from whom they had sought help, and God who had given it them.[56] To highlight the horrors from which God had saved them he sketches heart-rending pictures,[57] first, of the trial itself, with soldiers armed with clubs and swords standing guard and the relatives of the accused crowding outside in agonised silence pierced only by the shrieks of witnesses as they were scourged, and then of those sentenced to death being led away in chains, their property seized by the state and their wives and children left without a roof above their heads. As an eye-witness the spectacle had moved him to ask himself, and now to ask his congregation, 'If here on earth, when men are judges, neither mother, sister, father, nor any other person, though guiltless of the deeds perpetrated, can do anything to rescue the criminals, who will stand by us when we are judged at the dread tribunal of Christ?' On the Sunday following (28 March), in a more petulant mood, he contrasts the hermits who, at the hour of greatest terror, had come down from their mountain retreats to bring succour to the afflicted city, with the irresponsible rabble who, the public baths having been shut for weeks, 'in their eagerness for bathing rush to the Orontes, disporting themselves in it, leaping about and dancing indecently, dragging women in with them' – all this at a time when their chief magistrate and many leading citizens were still in prison, under sentence of death, with the emperor's final decision uncertain.[58]

Only the day before (Saturday 27 March) he had made light of the emperor's orders for the theatres and baths to be closed down and for Antioch to be stripped of its status as a metropolis.[59] The closures, he

[55] *Hom.* 16.1 (*PG* 49.161-3).
[56] E.g. *Hom.* 12.1: given Tues. 23 March (*PG* 49.128).
[57] *Hom.* 13.1: given on Wed. 24 March (*PG* 49.47-9).
[58] *Hom.* 18.4 (*PG* 49.186-8).
[59] *Hom.* 17.2 (*PG* 49.175-6).

claimed, are in fact blessings for which the emperor deserves gratitude. The theatres, which John prays may never be reopened, are the seed-bed of the city's depravity, while bath-houses only encourage softness and effeminacy. As for Antioch, what option had Theodosius but to downgrade its status? Did people expect him to thank them for their insults? The penalty he had imposed was a wise and salutary one, not least because it reminds the citizens that the true greatness of their city resides in 'the virtue and religious zeal of its inhabitants'. All this is of a piece with the message which echoes insistently throughout the homilies, that the present troubles are to be viewed as a penance for one's sins, and that it is by deepening one's spiritual union with God that one may hope to win his forgiveness.[60] John seems to have no doubt that the riot was a criminal outrage which, even though the work of a handful of good-for-nothing foreigners (as he regularly, against all likelihood, describes them[61] – no doubt in an attempt to save his congregation embarrassment), had justly brought down the emperor's wrath upon the entire city. Nowhere does he question Theodosius' moral right to levy whatever taxes he deems fit, or to resort to the most savage, indiscriminate punishments. For John he is always 'our humane', 'most mild and merciful' and 'godly' sovereign.[62]

IV

Fortunately the end was not far off. The degradation and other penalties inflicted on the city were real, and the commissioners, personally decent and well-disposed men, had pursued their interrogations reluctantly but with rigour. It was their duty to impress on the civil population that resistance to government tax demands was not to be tolerated. But they had decided to refer the death sentences to the emperor for final confirmation, and to recommend the convicted generally to his clemency. They had even leaked this hopeful news in appropriate quarters.[63] Caesarios had personally carried their report and recommendations at top speed to Constantinople, and it is very probable that Flavian, who, although travelling much more slowly than a great state official, had set out some nineteen days before him, had reached the capital shortly before he arrived there and had had an audience with the emperor. Very soon Theodosius published a decree which both granted a free pardon to all the councillors and announced the restoration to Antioch of all its previous privileges and, best of all, of the imperial favour.

Our two contemporary witnesses differ markedly in their accounts of how this happy outcome was achieved. Libanios gives all the credit for both

---

[60] E.g. *Hom.* 3.7; 4.2; 5.4; 6.1; 6.4; 7.1; 20.1 (*PG* 49.57-8; 61-2; 74-5; 81-3; 85-7; 91-3; 197-9).
[61] See above, p. 73.
[62] E.g. *Hom.* 3.2; 4.4 (*PG* 49.49; 65-6); see also *Hom.* 21 throughout.
[63] E.g. to Libanios: see his *Or.* 21.8; 10-11.

these decisions to Caesarios,[64] John to Flavian. Libanios, who nowhere mentions Flavian's mission, was clearly determined to ignore his role in the settlement, while for John it had been a triumph exclusively for the church. Both men were being selective with the truth, for while it is impossible now to reconstruct in detail what happened,[65] it seems reasonable to conclude that both the bishop and the master of the offices played their parts. Flavian knew nothing about the judges' sentences, or of their suspension, but he must have learned about the fate in store for the city when he met the commissioners on his way north; his plea is therefore likely to have been a general one for leniency to a great community only a handful of whose members had been culpable. Caesarios alone could have reported the results of the trial and the judges' recommendations. There are other discrepancies (for example, John suggests that the decree was entrusted to Flavian, Libanios to Caesarios),[66] but in any case the royal letters announcing pardon for the councillors and reconciliation for the city seem to have reached Antioch just before mid-April. Their arrival gave the signal for rapturous festivities, with the main square festooned with garlands and lit by night with torches.[67] Flavian himself was back in the city in the last days of holy week, and on Easter Sunday (25 April) John delivered the last, exultant homily of the series.

This was one of his most accomplished, and also most tendentious, orations. It opened with fulsome tributes, first to Flavian for having undertaken the risky, inconvenient journey to the capital and for having, while there, 'in only a few days' rescued the city and its citizens from impending calamity, and then to the emperor for having so swiftly and with such largeness of heart laid aside his wrath, making it 'plain that he would grant to the clergy what he would grant to no one else'.[68] It then reproduces at length what purports to be the tearful but carefully argued address in which the bishop, in audience with Theodosius, pleaded with him to spare the city from utter destruction, to pardon the councillors in spite of 'their having committed unforgivable sins'[69] and, finally, abandoning his fully justified anger, to restore Antioch to the favour it had previously enjoyed with him. Flavian even added, if we are to believe John, that if Theodosius turned down this last petition and decided to reject the city completely, he himself would never set foot in it again, 'for God forbid that I should ever account myself the citizen of a country with which you, the most humane and merciful of men, had refused to be peacefully reconciled'.[70] The emperor, John goes on, was himself close to tears, but held them back because

---

[64] *Or.* 21.12-23.
[65] The most thorough discussion available is by Paverd, op. cit., 135-49.
[66] *Hom.* 21.4 (*PG* 49.220); *Or.* 21.23.
[67] *Hom.* 21.4 (*PG* 49.220).
[68] *Hom.* 21.2 (*PG* 49.213).
[69] *Hom.* 21.3 (*PG* 49.218-19).
[70] *Hom.* 21.3 (*PG* 49.219).

of the bystanders. His response was a model one for a Christian ruler: 'Why should it be thought wonderful or magnificent that we should forgo our anger against the men who have insulted us, we who are ourselves only men, seeing that he who is Lord of the world, having come as he did to earth and having been made a servant for our sakes, and having been crucified by those to whom he had done kindness, besought the Father on their behalf, praying, "Forgive them, for they do not know what they are doing"?'[71]

John had explained to his congregation that the account he was about to give of Flavian's powerful and effective plea to Theodosius, as of the conference between the two men, had not been derived from the bishop himself, who had been much too modest to talk about his own noble achievements, but from one of the courtiers present.[72] While there can be no doubt that Flavian interceded with the emperor at a personal audience, it would be naive to regard John's seemingly verbatim report of his address, which completely ignores the part played by anyone other than the bishop in appeasing Theodosius, and also the emperor's exemplary reply, as other than a brilliant propaganda set-piece in which the speeches attributed to both parties were largely the product of the preacher's imagination. At this moment of civic jubilation John had a much nobler objective, as he would have considered it, than giving an accurately researched history lecture. So far as the vast audience cramming the church was concerned, he wanted to impress on it the salutary message he had set down in his opening paragraph,[73] that 'our city has become famous just because, when this appalling calamity overtook us, it bypassed all those in powerful positions or loaded with wealth, all those wielding great influence with the emperor, and turned for refuge to the church and to God's priest, and with supreme confidence placed all its reliance on the hope which is from above'. But he was also setting his sights on the educated pagans in Antioch, many of whom during the past anxious weeks had turned up in his congregation.[74] The resolution of the city's crisis, as he had delineated it in his homily, through the co-operation of a godly, humane emperor and a devoted bishop, should open their eyes to 'the power of Christianity' and persuade them to abandon their error and accept 'our philosophy'.[75]

V

The Homilies on the Statues have often been acclaimed as among the finest examples of John's pulpit oratory. They certainly illustrate his skill, so admired by scholars ancient and modern,[76] at composing Greek of near-

---

[71] *Hom.* 21.4 (*PG* 49.219-20).
[72] *Hom.* 21.2 (*PG* 49.213).
[73] *Hom.* 21.1 (*PG* 49.211).
[74] *Hom.* 15.1 (*PG* 49.153-4): cf. *De Anna* 1.1 (*PG* 54.684).
[75] *Hom.* 21.4 (*PG* 49.220).
[76] See above, p. 7.

Attic quality. His prose is, of course, strongly influenced, in vocabulary and phraseology, by the very unclassical language of the Septuagint and New Testament. Apart from this, the differences between his Greek usage and that of the best classical orators are confined largely to matters of detail – the use of words in a post-classical or Christian sense, the preference for a word-order characteristic of late writers, small points of syntax, etc.[77] John had acquired this mastery from the thorough literary training Libanios had given him, and from the remarkable continuity of the Greek educational system, which for hundreds of years focused attention on the same great texts. It would be a mistake, however, to find in it alone the clue to his success as a popular preacher, since relatively few in his avid audiences can have been literary connoisseurs. What must have counted much more with them were the extraordinary clarity of his diction (a clarity which Isidore of Pelusion, himself a stylist of grace, described as unequalled by any other writer he knew),[78] the simplicity and picturesqueness of his imagery, and, above all, the sureness with which he, as a speaker of rare charisma, was able instinctively to touch their hearts and consciences. To modern students his sermons, including several of these, often seem unbearably long (it has become a cliché to contrast John's *makrologia*, or long-windedness, with Augustine's *breviloquium*),[79] lacking in logical arrangement, disjointed in the way they pass from one idea to another. But they cannot listen to the preacher himself. The crowds which hung on his lips seem not to have been put off by such technical defects, for they were magnetised by the conviction and passion which pulsated through every paragraph.

With even pagans flocking to hear them, these homilies amply confirmed John's position as Antioch's leading preacher. From now, as a German scholar well expressed it,[80] he had the hearts and ears of the entire population wide open for him. It is likely, too, that they helped to bring him, just over a year in priest's orders, to the notice of the wider world outside the Syrian capital.[81] It is also clear from them, especially from the twenty-first, with its eloquent but misleading presentation of the settlement of the crisis as a transaction exclusively between Theodosius and Flavian, that the novice preacher was already master of the art of the political sermon.

---

[77] In reaching this conclusion the writer is indebted to discussions with his friend N.G. Wilson. For a detailed treatment see M. Soffray, *Recherches sur la syntaxe de saint Jean Chrysostome d'après les homélies sur les statues* (Paris 1939).

[78] *Ep.* 2.42 (*PG* 78.484), where he links his clarity with the Attic quality of his prose.

[79] E.g. O. Bardenhewer, *Geschichte der altkirchlichen Literatur* (Freiburg i. Br. 1912), 353.

[80] O. Bardenhewer, op. cit., 343.

[81] See below, p.105.

7

Decade of Development

I

The ten years from 387 to 397 were very busy ones for John, and they also had a formative impact on his career. It is therefore disappointing that, with one or two significant exceptions, we are completely in the dark about his personal life during the decade, and also about the major events in which he must have been involved from time to time. Fortunately substantial portions of his work as an author and preacher have been preserved, and these enable us to form some idea of the issues which chiefly interested him as a pastor and, in much more shadowy outline, of his steadily growing stature in the community.

It was in the first half of the decade, between 387 and 393, that he published his most famous and widely studied treatise, *Priesthood*.[1] Sokrates, indeed, assigned it to his diaconate,[2] but this seems excluded by the fact that John himself, in a homily preached almost certainly in 388, makes an unmistakable reference to it as a work he plans to produce 'at some future date'.[3] It cannot, however, be later than 393, for in that year Jerome, living at Bethlehem, noted that he had read it;[4] it was indeed the only work of John's he had read so far. As we must allow time for it to reach him, a date around 390/91, when John had had several years' practical experience as a working priest, would seem in order.

As was argued earlier,[5] *Priesthood* is really a *pièce justificative* designed to show, probably in view of doubts still persisting in certain circles in Antioch but also of his own desire to put out a personal statement,[6] that his refusal to be coerced into ordination almost twenty years earlier had been motivated solely by his deep sense of unworthiness for the priestly office. It shows many points of contact with, and has been strongly influenced by, the discourse *On His Flight*[7] which his older contemporary

---

[1] *De sacerdotio*: for text and critical edition see p. 26 n. 7 above. It is cited here by the pages of *SC* 272.

[2] 6.2.

[3] *In illud, Vidi hom.* 5.1 (*PG* 56.131). For the date see J. Dumortier, *Homélies sur Ozias* (*SC* 277, Paris 1981), 185 n. 1.

[4] *De vir. ill.* 129. For the date 393 see P. Nautin, *RHE* 56 (1961), 33-5.

[5] See above, pp. 26-8.

[6] So J.A. Nairn, *De sacerdotio* (Cambridge 1906), xv.

[7] *Or. 2 De fuga* (*PG* 35.408-513) (critical ed. by J. Bernardi in *SC* 247, Paris 1978).

Gregory of Nazianzos (who had himself been forcibly ordained by his father, and in dismay had temporarily withdrawn to solitude) had circulated in 362, but John's originality and the impress of his personality are obvious on every page. Cast in the form of a dialogue between himself and his boyhood comrade Basil, it is stylistically the most accomplished of his non-oratorical works, although its astonishing prolixity makes it heavy going for modern readers. The first of its six books is taken up with autobiographical reminiscences. In the remaining five he describes, in a series of elaborate developments, the awesome dignity and terrifying responsibilities of a priest or bishop, privileged as he is (for example) to baptise, to absolve sinners, even to make Christ present on the altar, but also liable to be held to account in the life to come for the misdeeds any of his charges may have committed.

As the essay draws to its close, John reflects that ordained clerics, being exposed to the busy world with its sensual allurements, face much greater temptations than 'monks dwelling in the desert, far removed from the city and the market-place'. Unlike these, he is in daily contact with women, and some of them deliberately set out to ensnare the hapless male.[8] A bishop, for example, cannot concentrate exclusively on the men in his congregation, but must be constantly visiting its female members pastorally – 'and it is not just a loose woman's glance, but a chaste woman's equally, which can upset and trouble a man's soul'.[9] Leaving aside temptations like these, and the no less insidious ones of ambition, the cleric shoulders a range of responsibilities unknown to the recluse. He has oversight of his charges' moral and spiritual welfare, and if things go wrong can never plead ignorance or inexperience. Mixing with men who have wives and children, own property and occupy public positions, he must have a certain know-how in worldly affairs, an ability to be understanding or critical as circumstances require. He is no seafarer idling in port, but has to steer his ship safely through every kind of weather.[10] He also has to deal with constant attacks on himself, however unjustified and from whatever quarter they come, calmly and constructively, 'forgiving irrational onslaughts, without making a fuss and losing his temper'.[11] Compared with his life, that of the recluse is easy; there is no need to lavish excessive admiration on him for falling so rarely into sin, and even then relatively minor sin, since he has only himself to cope with and little to excite his passions.[12]

Texts like these might seem to imply that John has lost the enthusiasm for monasticism evident, for example, in his earlier attacks on its detractors,[13] but such an inference would be misplaced. It was inevitable, in a

[8] *De sac.* 6.2-3 (306-10).
[9] *De sac.* 6.8 (332).
[10] *De sac.* 6.4; 6.9 (272; 318-20).
[11] *De sac.* 6.9 (334-6).
[12] *De sac.* 6.6 (324).
[13] See above, pp. 51-4.

work aimed at explaining how daunting as a young man living in quasi-monastic seclusion he had found the prospect of priesthood, that he should highlight the contrast between the two vocations. As a corrective we should note that in one of these very texts[14] he makes a point of insisting that, when selecting candidates for ordination, one should look for men who, while able to mix confidently in society, possess and seem likely to maintain all those qualities (serenity, inner strength, deep spirituality, continence, etc.) 'which distinctively belong to the monk'. We should also recall that those lyrical descriptions of monks as 'beacons who give light to the entire world'[15] which we recorded earlier were composed by him within a year at most of *Priesthood*. The fact is that, while always impatient of the recluse who cultivated cloistered virtue in the vain hope of saving himself,[16] John never ceased to regard the monk, whether layman or priest, as representing authentic Christianity. What he consistently demanded, with a seriousness which his own experience of clerical office greatly intensified, was that the monk should always be ready to place himself at the service of the community, since 'there is nothing chillier than a Christian who is not trying to save others'.[17]

II

Another work dating from this decade, one briefly mentioned earlier,[18] is the cumbrously, and misleadingly, named *On Vain Glory and How Parents Should Bring up Children*.[19] Surviving in only two MSS and first published in 1656 by the Dominican F. Combefis under the more apposite title (in Latin) *St John Chrysostom's Golden Book on Bringing Up Children*, its authenticity, and also its unity, have often been questioned, the latter on the ground of the apparent difference of subject-matter between the prologue and the body of the work. In recent years both have become generally accepted, largely as a result of studies by S. Haidacher and B.K. Exarchos demonstrating the book's linguistic and stylistic kinship and literary contacts with John's acknowledged writings.[20]

It opens with a stinging exposure of the absurd lengths to which people will go in their craving for popular esteem.[21] A very rich man will throw away his entire fortune putting on lavish shows in the theatre for the entertainment of the public (this was a service, or *leitourgia*, expected of wealthy city councillors).[22] Even if he is doomed to end up begging in the

---

[14] *De sac.* 6.8 (330).
[15] *In Matt. hom.* 72.4 (*PG* 58.672).
[16] E.g. *In 1 Tim. hom.* 14.1 (*PG* 62.571). See also J.M. Leroux, 'Monachisme et communauté chrétienne d'après s. J. Chrysostome', *Théologie de la vie monastique*, 1961, 168-72.
[17] *In Act. hom.* 20.4 (*PG* 60.162).
[18] See above, p. 53.
[19] *De inani gloria et de educandis liberis*: not in *PG*, but critically edited by A.M. Malingrey, *SC* 188 (Paris 1972): she provides full discussions of authenticity, date, etc.
[20] S. Haidacher, *Des hl. Johannes Chrysostomus über Hoffart und Kindererziehung* (Freiburg i. Br. 1907); B.K. Exarchos, *Johannes Chrysostomos über Hoffart und Kindererziehung* (Munich 1954) – developing three important articles in *Theologia* 19 (1941-8).
[21] *De inani gloria* 1-15 (*SC* 188.64-96).
[22] A.H.M. Jones, *The Later Roman Empire* (Oxford 1964), 2.736-7.

city square, he is desperate to bask for a day or two in his fellow-citizens' applause. Ordinary people, too, sometimes very poor people, will indulge in crippling extravagances, such as buying ostentatious silver, fine clothes or a servant they don't really need, just to attract compliments or to 'keep up their dignity'. The church itself, John laments, is being rent asunder by just such a fever of 'vain glory' (*kenodoxia*). In his second, much longer section he seems to change tack,[23] and argues that giving children a thorough moral and spiritual training calls for at least as much care as having them taught liberal arts at school. This is a task, moreover, which parents should undertake personally; much as he would like them to become monks, he does not advise sending them off to the monks' retreats.[24] He then outlines a detailed programme, based on scripture and Christian morality, for bringing up a boy from infancy to his engagement; he should marry young, before joining the army or the public service, for a youthful love-match will prevent him from getting interested in other women.[25] In a final paragraph he gives advice about bringing up girls.[26] Just as boys get excited by sex, so their sisters find pretty clothes and expensive jewellery irresistible; their mothers should keep these temptations well out of their way.

John makes a neat transition from his original theme, the wickedness and sheer folly of vain glory, to the seemingly unrelated one of education.[27] He does this by, first, protesting that a man's true dignity does not lie in ostentatious display but in contempt of riches, even in embracing poverty, and then asking how such an inversion of values has come about. Surely because parents, instead of caring for their children's true welfare, insist on surrounding them with meretricious luxuries. He thus slips naturally into an informal talk to parents[28] (this explains its repetitiveness and occasionally slipshod style) which reveals, incidentally, how greatly his ideas have changed since the days when he dreamed unrealistically of packing boys off to monasteries.[29] Although one suspects young people may have found his prescriptions for training them as 'athletes for Christ'[30] somewhat cramping, the book is the earliest surviving manual setting out a comprehensive programme for the moral and spiritual formation of young Christians at home, in addition to the education they received at school. John's complaint in his first paragraph[31] that the church itself is being split asunder by vain glory, coupled with his sharp question, 'Hasn't anyone done

---

[23] *De inani gloria* 16-90 (*SC* 188.94-196).
[24] *De inani gloria* 18-19 (*SC* 188.100-4).
[25] *De inani gloria* 81 (*SC* 188.186-8).
[26] *De inani gloria* 90 (*SC* 188.196).
[27] *De inani gloria* 15-16 (*SC* 188.94-100).
[28] *De inani gloria* 22 (*SC* 188.106): 'Well then, each of you fathers and mothers ...'
[29] See above, p. 53
[30] *De inani gloria* 19 (*SC* 188.102).
[31] *De inani gloria* 1 (*SC* 188.64-8.

what I demanded?', provides a clue to its date, for it is only in his tenth homily on Ephesians (as Haidacher first pointed out)[32] that he makes such a demand in the context of the church's divisions. As we shall shortly see, the reference there is almost certainly to an embittered struggle among members of the hard-line Nicene group in Antioch to find a successor to Evagrios, who had taken over its leadership on the death of Paulinos in 388, when he too died *c.* 393. This would place John's 'golden book' in the middle or even late 380s.

III

Priesthood and *Educating Children* form only a small fraction of John's literary *oeuvre* during this decade. Much the greater portion consists of either miscellaneous sermons or homilies expounding scripture (mostly in the form of continuous courses). Judging by the hundreds of these which have been preserved, and the many which one suspects may have perished, his output must have been enormous. It greatly exceeded his later output at Constantinople, even allowing for his having been resident there for only six years. There is nothing surprising in this, since as bishop, as the ninth-century patriarch Photios observed,[33] he was deeply involved with public business. Preoccupation with this, Photios also claimed, gives the clue to which homilies were composed at Antioch, which at Constantinople: the latter were perforce less finished in style. Here we shall pass his preaching activity during these ten years in selective review; questions of the dates, or provenance in the Syrian capital, of individual sermons or sermon courses will only be touched on when there is no general agreement about them.[34]

John's occasional sermons covered a wide range of topics. On 1 January 388, for example, we find him denouncing the ways in which pagans celebrated New Year, with night-long dancing and toasts in neat wine at dawn.[35] His eloquence was not, apparently, wholly successful for, preaching on the following day on one of the gospel parables,[36] he reproaches critics who sneered that, notwithstanding his rebukes, the pubs had been crammed with revellers. Yes, he retorted, but they were blushing with shame in their consciences. On 24 January he delivered a panegyric on Babylas,[37] on 4 February another on two local soldier-martyrs, Juventinos and Maximinos.[38] The former combines a eulogy of the saintly bishop with

---

[32] Op. cit., 20-3. Cf. *In Eph. hom.* 10.3 (*PG* 62.80).
[33] *Bibliotheca* 172-4 (P. Henry 2.170).
[34] On both questions M. von Bonsdorf, *Zur Predigttätigkeit des J. Chrysostomus* (Helsingfors 1922), remains reliable in general, and has been largely followed here.
[35] *In kalendas hom.* (*PG* 48.953-62).
[36] *De Lazaro concio* 1.2 (*PG* 48.964-5).
[37] *PG* 50.527-34: crit. ed. in *SC* 362 (Paris 1990), 279-313.
[38] *PG* 50.571-8.

a ferocious attack on Julian the Apostate and a tribute to Meletios; the latter, as well as graphically describing the young officers' beheading on Julian's orders, highlights the emperor's policy of facing Christians with the choice of either abandoning their faith or losing their jobs.

Among sermons for holy days two Good Friday addresses stand out:[39] one, delivered in the cemetery north of the city, proclaims that since the crucifixion death has become only a sleep for Christians (he is playing on 'cemetery', which in Greek means a place for sleep); in the other he recalls the penitent thief to whom Jesus promised entrance to paradise, and exhorts his hearers to pray earnestly for their enemies. In two other sermons,[40] given perhaps in 388 and 395/396, he strives to give fresh heart to the citizens after earthquakes, natural disasters which occurred frequently at Antioch. In the first he explains that the quake is a sign of God's anger, a warning too of the much more terrible judgment to come; in the second he congratulates his audience on the salutary change of conduct which the shock of the calamity has produced in them. Others could be cited, such as the seven on the parable of the Rich Man and Lazarus (Luke 16.19-31),[41] in which he argues again and again that the poor man is precious in God's sight while anyone who is rich is no better than a robber if he does not share his wealth with those who have none.[42] Pride of place, perhaps, should be given to seven enthusiastic eulogies of the Apostle Paul;[43] their first Latin translator, Anianus of Celeda (a Pelagian: fl. 400), commented that in them John had not so much drawn a portrait of his hero as brought him back to life again.[44]

One of John's responsibilities was, along with his brother clergy, to prepare candidates for baptism, and among his more noteworthy addresses are 'catecheses', i.e. lectures on Christian faith and morals given to them between their enrolment early in Lent and their baptism during the night of Easter, and then in Easter week. Two sets of these have survived, one of four catecheses[45] (three pre-baptismal, one post-baptismal) delivered apparently in 388, the other[46] of eight (three pre-baptismal, five post-baptismal) dating probably from 391.[47] They have exceptional interest, not least because we can compare them with two other fourth-century sets of

[39] *PG* 49.393-8; 399-408.
[40] *PG* 48.1027-43; 50.713-16. For the dates see A. Cameron, *Chiron* 17.354.
[41] *PG* 48.963-1054.
[42] E.g. *De Lazaro* 1.12; 2.4-5 (*PG* 48.980-1; 987-9).
[43] *De laudibus s. Pauli apostoli* (*PG* 50.473-514): crit. ed. by A. Piédagnel in *SC* 300 (Paris 1982).
[44] *PG* 50.471.
[45] *Cat.* 1 (*PG* 49.223-32); *Cat.* 2-4 in A. Papadopoulos-Kerameus, *Varia Graeca sacra* (St Petersburg 1909), 154-83 (I have not had access to this work).
[46] Discovered in a MS at Mt Athos in 1955 by A. Wenger and published in *Jean Chrysostome: Huit catéchèses baptismales* (*SC* 50bis, Paris 1970).
[47] For this date see F. van de Paverd, *John Chrysostom: the Homilies on the Statues* (Rome 1991), 291-3.

catecheses, twenty-four[48] given by Cyril of Jerusalem in 347/348, and sixteen[49] given (possibly at Antioch) by John's friend Theodore of Mopsuestia at some date between 388 and 392. Two points about them deserve notice. First, John's address to the newly baptised given at dawn on Easter Sunday (cat. 4 in the first cycle, cat. 3 in the second: identical in both), in which he exultantly salutes them as stars brighter than any in the sky, welcomes them at last as brothers, braces them for their combat with the devil, and warns them against backsliding ('just as there is no second cross, there is no second remission of sins by regenerative washing'), stands out as an exceptionally vibrant example of his oratory. Secondly, it is noteworthy that the post-baptismal addresses in his second series are not 'mystagogical', i.e. devoted to explaining the sacraments, as they are in Cyril's and Theodore's courses. That task was probably carried out by one of the other priests he mentions as collaborating in the course of instruction.[50] His message to the newly baptised is that, reborn as they now are in Christ, they must dazzle people by their exemplary conduct, avoiding for example excess in food and drink, keeping well clear of the distractions of horse-racing and the theatre, visiting the shrines of martyrs to obtain the healing of body and soul their relics bestow, resolutely adopting a routine which includes daily prayer in church before getting down to the day's business, and returning in the evening to implore God's forgiveness for any sins they may have committed.[51]

IV

Ten or twelve years earlier, as a solitary in his cave outside Antioch, John had acquired an exceptional mastery of the bible.[52] He now seems to have decided that it was his vocation to make this available to the general public. He therefore embarked on the great series of sermon commentaries, in most cases covering whole books of scripture, which is his chief literary legacy from this decade. Earliest in date are sixty-seven homilies expounding Genesis verse by verse, from beginning to end.[53] It seems clear from what he himself says in the opening paragraph of the twenty-third, that he delivered the first thirty-two during Lent (the season favoured for reading from Genesis),[54] the remaining thirty-five after Whitsunday of the same year, probably 389.[55] Photios, while recognising in them John's characteristic clarity and richness of ideas, was disappointed by their common-

---

[48] *PG* 33.331-1180.
[49] *ST* 145 (photocopies of the Syriac MS with French translation).
[50] *Cat.* 8.1 (*SC* 50bis.246).
[51] Each of the foregoing clauses summarises the content of *Cat.* 4, 5, 6, 7, and 8.
[52] See above, p. 32.
[53] *PG* 53.21-54.580.
[54] See above, p. 58.
[55] For the year, still debated, see Bonsdorf, op. cit., 9-13.

place diction, and for this reason, in obedience to the criterion mentioned above,[56] assigned them to his period as bishop.[57] But internal evidence (e.g. hints in the homilies that there are Syriac-speakers in the congregation, and a reference to 'infirm brothers ... nominally attached to us' who are in fact Judaizers)[58] make it certain that they originated in Antioch.

Along with these we may list his Explanations (*hermeneiai*: they are not described as homilies) of fifty-eight selected Psalms[59] (numbered in the Septuagint 4-12; 43-9; 108-17, 119-50). Photios considered them so thorough and so stylistically polished that John could only have composed them when he had some leisure from business; he implied, probably correctly, that they were prepared at Antioch.[60] Externally they present the appearance of a running commentary, and that is what the majority of critics since the days of Tillemont have taken them to be. Numerous passages, however, leave a strong impression of being addressed directly to a congregation,[61] and most of them end with the ascription of praise customary in a homily. The solution may well be that what were originally homilies have been grouped together as a continuous commentary. For Old Testament scholars they have a special interest: whereas John normally relies exclusively on the text of the Septuagint, here he occasionally refers to the translations of 'others' (in fact, Symmachus, Aquila, and Theodotion).[62]

Other examples of John's exposition of the Old Testament from this period could be mentioned, such as four homilies on Isaiah 6 dating from 386/387,[63] but he seems to have concentrated his main effort on the New Testament. Thus he delivered ninety homilies on Matthew[64] (the earliest and most extensive patristic commentary on the first gospel) in 390, eighty-eight on John[65] in 391. Internal evidence suggests that both courses were spread over their respective years. Bypassing Acts (he had preached on its beginning at Eastertide 388,[66] and was to tackle the entire book at Constantinople), he then threw himself into the exposition of Paul's letters. His thirty-two homilies on Romans,[67] since earliest times considered one of his most finished productions,[68] are plausibly assigned to 392. That they originated in Antioch, not Constantinople, seems confirmed not only by his

---

[56] See above, p. 87.
[57] *Bibliotheca* 172-4 (P. Henry 169).
[58] *In Gen. hom.* 4.4; 12.1 (*PG* 53.43; 98).
[59] *PG* 55.39-498.
[60] *Bibliotheca* 172-4 (P. Henry 2.169-70).
[61] E.g. *Expos. in ps.* 4.2; 7.1; 44.1; 140.1 (*PG* 55.41; 80; 183; 426-7).
[62] *Expos. in ps.* 4.9 (*PG* 55.53).
[63] *In illud, Vidi dominum* 2, 3, 5, 6 (*PG* 56.107-19; 129-42: see also *SC* 277).
[64] *PG* 57-8.
[65] *PG* 59.
[66] *PG* 51.65-112.
[67] *PG* 60.391-682.
[68] E.g. Isidore of Pelusion (*Ep.* 5.32: *PG* 78.1348) applauds their depth of thought and classical perfection of language.

statement that he and his congregation are subject to one and the same bishop,[69] but by the complete absence, from his discussion of 'the supreme authority' (Rom. 13.1ff.),[70] of any mention of the emperor. In 392/3 he followed these with fourteen homilies on 1 Corinthians,[71] and then thirty on 2 Corinthians.[72] It was probably in the same year, or perhaps in 394, that he prepared a course on Galatians,[73] but what has come down is a verse-by-verse commentary. In several passages,[74] however, John appears to be addressing an audience before him, and the conjecture of most critics[75] is that what was originally a set of homilies has been rearranged, probably but not necessarily by himself, as a single, unbroken exposition.

Four further sermon courses remain: eighteen homilies on 1 Timothy[76] and ten on 2 Timothy,[77] six on Titus,[78] and twenty-four on Ephesians.[79] That those on the Pastorals were given at Antioch seems proved both by repeated references to local features (e.g. to the monks settled near the city)[80] and by the fact that John discusses Timothy's position as bishop in ways which would have been impossible had he held the office himself.[81] In the Ephesians homilies too, sometimes assigned to Constantinople (on the basis of Photios' criterion) because of their generally careless composition, John speaks[82] enthusiastically of monks who have taken to the harsh mountains, a sure pointer to Antioch, and in the tenth and, more specifically, the eleventh refers to a schism in the community in which the dissident party is fully orthodox in belief.[83] There can be little doubt, as we shall later confirm,[84] that this is the protracted split between the main orthodox community presided over by Flavian and the small hard-line group headed for many years by Paulinos and then, after his death in (probably) 388, by Evagrios.

Since John's plan so far seems to have been to treat the New Testament books in their canonical order, one might have expected the homilies on the Pastorals, generally dated c. 394, to be later than those on Ephesians, but in fact they are earlier. This is brought out by the marked difference in tone

[69] *In Rom. hom.* 8.7 (*PG* 60.464).
[70] *In Rom. hom.* 23.2 (*PG* 60.617-19).
[71] *PG* 61.11-382).
[72] *PG* 61.381-610).
[73] *PG* 61.611-82).
[74] E.g. *In Gal. comm.* 9 (*PG* 61.627).
[75] E.g. H. Lietzmann, PW IX.1818.
[76] *PG* 62.501-660.
[77] *PG* 62.559-662.
[78] *PG* 62.663-700.
[79] *PG* 62.9-174.
[80] *In 1 Tim. hom.* 14.3-5 (*PG* 62.574-7).
[81] E.g. *In 1 Tim. hom.* 5.1; 10.1 (*PG* 62; 525-7; 547-9).
[82] *In Eph. hom.* 6.4; 13.4 (*PG* 62.47-8; 97).
[83] *In Eph. hom.* 10.3; 11.5 (*PG* 62.78-80; 87).
[84] See below, pp. 101f.

of their respective references to wars with barbarians threatening the empire. In the homilies on 1 Timothy John discusses with almost armchair detachment the effects of wars between Romans and barbarians, and the cruel treatment the latter inflict when victorious.[85] In the Ephesians homilies these speculative possibilities have become a horrendous reality, and John warns his listeners to wake up to their peril.[86] 'There are countless disasters everywhere now, and no one is alarmed. Let us at last be afraid. God is accustomed to punish the just along with the unjust ... Do you not see these wars? Do you not hear of the calamities? Do you not learn the lesson from what is happening? Nations, entire cities, are being engulfed and have perished. Tens of thousands are now being reduced to slavery to the barbarians. If the fear of hell does not bring us to our senses, let these appalling events bring that about.' This emotional appeal conjures up the alarms and anxieties of 395 and the years immediately following, when hordes of trans-Caucasian Huns poured through the Caspian gates and roved pillaging through the length and breadth of Syria, threatening Antioch itself.[87] The inescapable inference is that we should date the Ephesian homilies to 395-7, probably even as late as 396-7; and this would be confirmed if the disaster referred to in the tenth was the widespread earthquake of 396.[88]

These commentaries, if we can so designate them, differ greatly from one another. While some (e.g. those on Romans and Galatians) have always been acclaimed for their stylistic finish, others (e.g. those on the Pastorals and Ephesians) reveal what seems to be great carelessness in their composition. Again, the sprawling Matthew commentary (almost 800 columns in Migne), full of moral and ascetical exhortation shot through (it may be remarked) with Stoic presuppositions,[89] stands in marked contrast with the shorter, but theologically much more polemical, commentary on John. While the explanations of selected Psalms and of Galatians have come down in the guise of running commentaries, all the rest are in the form of homilies. John's biographer Baur, however, raised the question whether these homilies are in fact what they purport to be. Starting from the premiss that what chiefly identifies a spoken address by John as such is the presence in it of spontaneous interjections – e.g. comments on the weather or the reaction of the audience – he went on to claim that these tell-tale signs of actual delivery are wholly, or almost wholly, lacking in the great homiletic commentaries. This makes it plain, he argued, that they were not originally real sermons, but were composed by John in the

---

[85] *In 1 Tim. hom.* 7.1; 18.2 (*PG* 62.533-5; 589).

[86] *In Eph. hom.* 6.4 (*PG* 62.48-9).

[87] See esp. Jerome, *Letters* 60.16 (where he speaks of Antioch as being besieged); 78.8 (*CSEL* 54.570-1; 55.45-6).

[88] *PG* 62.79. For the quake see G. Downey, *Speculum* 30 (1955), 597.

[89] See esp. A. Uleyn, 'La doctrine morale de s. J. Chrysostome dans le commentaire sur s. Matthieu', *Revue de l'université d'Ottawa* 27.2 (1957).

artificial form of homilies with a view to publication. From this he drew 'the surprising conclusion that Chrysostom, considering everything, must have written more than he preached'.[90]

Few students have accepted, or even discussed, the case Baur made out. It seems particularly implausible when we study the homilies on Genesis, which he used as one of its main props. In the first of these we find John proclaiming how glad he is to see God's church packed with cheerful worshippers; in the sixth he expresses shame that they have neglected their Lenten duties to be present at games; in the thirty-third he recalls that the approach of Easter caused him to interrupt his course, and surveys his preaching activities in the meantime.[91] But Baur's case seems scarcely more plausible when we turn to the homilies on the gospels and the epistles. In them we even come across several instances of John breaking away from his argument to comment on the applause or laughter of the congregation.[92] But the debate should not be confined to spontaneous remarks of this kind, the absence of which in no way proves that what looks like a homily is not in fact one. These texts abound in passages which show John dealing directly with his audience in a way which makes it clear that they are, or are based on, spoken addresses. Sometimes it is a reference back, as when he exclaims, 'Come, let us resume today the discussion we were having three days ago about kindness, but left unfinished.'[93] Sometimes it is a lively sketch he draws of the crowd pushing and shoving to find a place in the church from which his voice can be heard.[94] Sometimes it is a rhetorical question which he throws at his auditors: 'Did you not think yesterday that I had said great, even extravagant things about Paul's love for Christ? ... Even I thought they could not have been surpassed, but what we have heard today is even more glorious than that.'[95]

This brings us to the related problem of the marked difference in literary finish between different series of homilies. Photios' famous solution of it was a brilliant guess, but had to be abandoned as evidence accumulated that some of the most carelessly composed courses originated at Antioch. An alternative explanation advanced recently[96] suggests that, where a sermon course has come down in a stylistically defective form, this may be due to the fact that the surviving text rests on an uncorrected transcription of the original notes of the stenographers who took it down. This proposal has great plausibility, and although it was based on a close examination of

---

[90] 1, 220-3.

[91] *In Gen. hom.* 1.1; 6.1; 33.1 (*PG* 53.21; 54-5; 305-6).

[92] E.g. *In Matt. hom.* 17.7; *In 1 Cor. hom.* 4.6; 26.8; *In 2 Cor. hom.* 5.5 (*PG* 57.264; 61.30; 224; 434).

[93] *In Matt. hom.* 52.3 (*PG* 58.522).

[94] *In Ioh. hom.* 3.1 (*PG* 59.37).

[95] *In Rom. hom.* 16.1 (*PG* 60.517-18).

[96] See B. Goodall, *The Homilies of St John Chrysostom on the Letters of St Paul to Titus and Philemon* (Univ. of California Press 1979), esp. ch. v.

only the homilies on Titus and Philemon (preached at Constantinople), it seems likely that it would be corroborated if an equally searching scrutiny were extended to other series. If accepted, the results of this experiment throw valuable light on John's procedures. His favoured practice, it would seem, was, before publishing a set of sermons, to edit carefully the notes supplied by stenographers and so produce a polished version; an excellent example would be the Homilies on the Statues. Sometimes, as in the case of the Romans homilies, he might subject the notes to a rather more thorough revision, or even, as with the homilies on Galatians, make it so drastic as to eliminate almost all the signs of their having been originally preached. On the other hand, several of his courses, for reasons about which we can only speculate, escaped all editing and have survived only in transcriptions of the stenographers' notes. That this is not guesswork is confirmed by the eloquent little note prefixed to the (later) homilies on Hebrews, which describes them as having been 'published after his [i.e. John's] falling asleep by Constantinos, presbyter of Antioch, on the basis of stenographers' notes' (*semeion*).[97]

An important, perhaps startling, corollary of this argument is that it is precisely these transcriptions, rough and unpolished as they are, which bring us closest (even allowing for the stenographers' inevitable mistakes) to the words which the great orator actually spoke. As the scholar cited above neatly expressed it, 'If we do not have the final revision of the master writer, we have something equally valuable – a very close approximation to the live oratory of the master preacher.'[98]

V

John's sermon-commentaries (they fill nine or ten folios if we include the ones he was to prepare later at Constantinople) form the most impressive, and also most readable, collection of patristic expositions of scripture. To modern students their chief value lies, not in his elucidation of the texts reviewed, but in the light they throw, first, on his exegetical methods, secondly and more importantly, on his understanding of Christian faith and morals. Neither John, nor any Christian teacher for centuries to come, was properly equipped to carry out exegesis as we have come to understand it. He could not be expected to understand the nature of the Old Testament writings, still less the complex issues raised by the study of the gospels. (The Pauline letters, it is worth noting, being actual letters, presented him with fewer problems; since he felt an empathy with the apostle, his explanations of them tend to be somewhat more in line with what modern critics look for.) Like other Christian expositors of that age he also believed that the true author of scripture (not remotely but directly) was the Holy

---

[97] *PG* 63.9.
[98] B. Goodall, op. cit., 78.

Spirit. Even though he recognised the human writer's personal involvement (which, he claimed, accounted for 'the discrepancy between the evangelists in small matters'),[99] this assumption effectively blocked any open-minded examination of the bible.

On the other hand, the commentaries reveal him as an effective, if slightly independent, exponent of Antiochene exegesis. This comes out in his frequently expressed determination to explain scripture in the plain, historical sense, without resort to the arbitrary allegorising fashionable in much of the contemporary church. Like his boyhood friend Theodore, he had learned this approach at the feet of their teacher Diodore of Tarsos.[100] Like Theodore, too, he was prepared (probably more freely than he), so long as the literal sense was safeguarded, to admit a further, even more important spiritual sense. To give but two examples, while confident that the stories of Noah and the Ark, and of Abraham's sacrifice of Isaac, recorded actual historical events, he held that in addition the former prefigured Christ and his church, the latter the cross.[101] Of these two outstanding pupils of Diodore, it may be remarked, Theodore was the more rigorous and probing, often producing insights well ahead of his age,[102] John was an equally conscientious disciple of the master, but was able to exploit his methods more effectively on the popular stage.

VI

Theodore, who a few years later was also to produce a commentary on John's gospel, remarks in his introduction that, while the exegete's task is to clear up obscure passages as succinctly as possible (only resorting to long-winded explanations when demolishing heretical interpretations), the preacher's is to spread himself to his heart's content (presumably in the interest of edification) on passages which are already perfectly clear.[103] As one who was primarily a preacher, John freely availed himself of this licence. As a result one of the most attractive and informative features of his commentaries is his readiness to go beyond strict comment on the text and draw out whatever useful lessons he thinks he can discern in it.

Sometimes these lessons are spiritual or religious, as when, expounding the Psalter, he manages to extract from Psalm 7 directions on the kinds of prayer Christians should use,[104] from Psalm 44 (45) an assurance that virginity is the becoming garment of the church,[105] and from Psalm 133

[99] *In Matt. hom.* 1.1 (*PG* 57.16).
[100] See above, p. 19.
[101] *Hom. de Lazaro* 6.7; *in Ps.* 46 (*PG* 48.1037; 55.209).
[102] On Theodore as an exegete see M.F. Wiles, *The Cambridge History of the Bible* (Cambridge 1970) 1, 489-510.
[103] *Theodori Mops. in evangelium Iohannis Praef.* (*CSCO* 115.6 – Syriac text; 116.2 – Latin trans.: Louvain 1940).
[104] *PG* 55.385-6.
[105] *PG* 55.202.

(134) a warning of the special purity one should aim at when receiving communion.[106] At other times they take the form of attacks on heretics, especially the Arians. Indeed, although their name is not mentioned in it, his commentary on John becomes a running debate with them, the reason being that while the Fourth Gospel abounds in passages suggestive of Christ's transcendence (on which the orthodox seized eagerly), it also contains many which seem to stress his human weaknesses (which equally delighted Arianizers). The Manichees, too, are frequent targets. In one lengthy tirade he pours scorn on them for tracing all wickedness to an increate principle of evil, whereas in fact (he argues) it originates in the negligence and perverse choices of human beings themselves.[107] In another he castigates them for picking out Paul's phrase 'the present evil age' (Gal. 1.4) as confirming their pessimistic vision of existence in this world.[108] After again insisting that the evils we deplore arise not from the natural order but from ill-directed human wills, he triumphantly concludes with the question, 'Can this life really be evil, in which we have come to know God, meditate on the world to come, have become angels instead of men, and take our part with the choirs of heaven?'

More often these homiletical excursuses are moral or social in import. So when expounding 1 Corinthians and Ephesians we find him not only discussing the questions of marriage and sex which they raise, but putting forward somewhat more positive views than he had earlier held.[109] He stresses, for example, the equality of man and wife in sexual relations, insisting that neither must deprive the other of intercourse without his or her consent – 'What is the advantage of abstinence and continence if love is disrupted?'[110] He upholds the Pauline principle that 'the husband is the head of the wife' (Eph. 5.23), interpreting it as meaning that the man's role is that of leader and provider, the woman's that of submission. But he is adamant that no relationship in human life is so close as that between them, for 'there is nothing that so welds our life together as the love (*eros*) of a man and his wife'.[111] Indeed, 'there is nothing in the world sweeter for a man than having children and a wife' – provided, he adds cautiously, he lives chastely.[112] Again, the apostle's promise (1 Tim. 2.15) that women will be saved through child-bearing prompts him to deliver a little lecture[113] on bringing up sons and daughters which, in its emphasis on the importance of implanting good habits from the start and on early marriages in the interest of sexual purity, bears a remarkable resemblance to the advice he

---

[106] *PG* 55.386.
[107] *In Matt. hom.* 59.2-3 (*PG* 58.576-7).
[108] *In Gal. comm.* 1.4 (*PG* 61.618-19).
[109] See above, p. 46.
[110] *In 1 Cor. hom.* 19.1-2 (*PG* 61.152-4).
[111] *In Eph. hom.* 20.1 (*PG* 62.135-6).
[112] *In Matt. hom.* 37.7 (*PG* 57.428).
[113] *In 1 Tim. hom.* 9.2 (*PG* 62.546-8).

had given in *On Vain Glory*.[114] But a favourite theme, to which he constantly returns irrespective of its relevance to the scripture he is explaining, is the corrupting influence of theatrical shows, in which young men dress up as girls, old men play degrading roles, unveiled women unblushingly deliver indecent speeches, and everything (the actors' words and gestures, their clothes and suggestive glances, the dissolute music, the very plots of the dramas) conspires to undermine moral standards, make men discontented with their wives and break up homes.[115]

What is perhaps most remarkable about these commentaries is the way they mirror John's indignation against conspicuous affluence and the selfishness of the rich, and his passionate championship of the poor, the exploited and the helpless. He pours contempt, for example, on the luxurious mansions of the wealthy, with their lofty columns crowned with gold capitals, their marble-encrusted walls and their fountains of running water, their exotically carpeted floors, and the cohorts of gold-liveried eunuchs who attend their owners' pleasure.[116] A man's true glory, he protests, does not consist in things like these, but in gentleness, humility, unfeigned charity. He is even more derisive of Christian women, especially those supposedly consecrated to virginity, who come to church flaunting extravagant hair-styles, decked out with gold and pearls, and trailing expensive dresses.[117] It is as if they were actresses, or even street walkers; they only succeed in making themselves laughing-stocks to pagans. He vents his fury, equally, on the sumptuous banquets which such people put on, at which the tables are laden with all kinds of luxurious meats, fowls, costly fish, pastries, and wine from Thasos, the guests reclining on ornate, softly draped couches while flute-players, dancers and buffoons are brought in to add to the fun.[118]

Such scathing descriptions are matched by heart-rending ones of impoverished outcasts stretched out all night, not on silver couches, but on dank straw in the colonnaded entrances to the public baths, frozen stiff with cold and racked with hunger;[119] of the beggar who, while warmly clad citizens saunter home from the baths to well-prepared dinners, hangs about the narrow lanes like a famished dog in the mud and the dark, head bowed and hand outstretched, starving but with nothing to eat;[120] or of convicts in prison, some of them lying there in squalor, chained and in rags, cowering like dogs at the visitor's feet and showing the still bleeding scars received from scourging, others who have been let out for the day, still in chains, to beg for sustenance in the city square, obliged when they return in the

---

[114] See above, p. 86.
[115] *In Matt. hom.* 37.6 (*PG* 57.426-7).
[116] *In Ps.* 48.8 (*PG* 55.510).
[117] *In 1 Tim. hom.* 8.1-3 (*PG* 62.541-4).
[118] *In Matt. hom.* 48.5-6; 70.4 (*PG* 58.492-5; 659-60).
[119] *De Lazaro conc.* 1.8 (*PG* 48.973).
[120] *In 1 Cor. hom.* 11.5 (*PG* 61.94-5).

evening to surrender the miserable sums they have received to their gaolers.[121]

John's indignation against the selfish rich reaches boiling-point when he declaims against their criminal madness in cramming whole wardrobes with expensive clothes while allowing human beings created in God's image to stand outside in the street naked, shivering with cold, scarcely able to hold themselves upright.[122] He then draws a terrifying picture of how, in the effort to soften people's hearts and make their appeals for alms more effective, some have been driven to stick sharp nails into their own heads so that they can present a laughable spectacle, or even to blind their children at an early age. 'As for you,' he concludes, 'you would let out your own children for your circus charioteers, you would throw away your very souls for your pantomime dancers, but to Christ when he is starving you would not hand over the smallest piece of money. If you do give a few pence, it is as if you had given away your entire fortune ... But when we have to give an account of ourselves, when we hear Christ saying, "You saw me hungry, and gave me nothing to eat, naked and you did not clothe me", what shall we say, and what shall we plead in our defence?'

John's appeal here to the key verses (Matt. 25.31-46) in which Jesus identifies himself with everyone who is needy and afflicted and warns that men will be judged by the way they treat such people, is significant. For him 'this most sweet passage', as he calls it,[123] provides the supreme motive for social action,[124] and he constantly strives to impress on his congregation that, when confronted with anyone in want or distress, they are in fact dealing with Christ himself, who when the reckoning comes will be their judge.[125] As for wealth, John's commentaries show that he was no political or economic theorist, but took a sharply critical view of it – a much more critical one than that of most of the fathers – based on his naive reading of the bible. It is obvious, he explains, that in the beginning God did not make one man rich and another poor.[126] Hence differences in wealth can only have been brought about by injustice, the strong defrauding the weak just as big fish gobble up the small ones.[127] So it has been down the ages since Adam. Even if a particular rich man has not acted improperly himself, the wealth he possesses must have been acquired somewhere far back by theft from others. In the end its true owner is the Lord, and if so it belongs equally to all since he dispenses his blessings (the sun, the air, the earth, water, etc.) to everyone without discrimination. In so doing he puts mankind to shame, for it is men who appropriate particular things to themselves and have

---

[121] *In Ioh. hom.* 60.4 (*PG* 59.333).
[122] *In 1 Cor. hom.* 21.5 (*PG* 61.176-9).
[123] *In Matt. hom* 79.1 (*PG* 58.717).
[124] See esp. R. Brändle, *Matt. 25.31-46 im Werk des Johannes Chrysostomos* (Tübingen 1979).
[125] From scores of passages see esp. *In Rom. hom.* 16.6 (*PG* 60.547-8).
[126] *In 1 Tim. hom.* 12.4 (*PG* 62.562-4).
[127] *In Ps.* 110.3 (*PG* 55.281).

introduced 'those chilly words (*to psuchron touto rema*) "mine" and "yours" '. The moral he draws repeated in sermon after sermon, is that anyone who has money should be generous in alms-giving: 'a rich man is good when he distributes his wealth ... but he is not good so long as he keeps it to himself.' And he should be generous without the patronising probing to which the comfortably-off like to subject the wretched applicant in the effort to expose him as an impostor. God pours his sunshine and rain on all of us alike without asking any questions, in spite of our wilful misbehaviour. If he were to make such searching inquiries about us when the day of judgment comes, we should never qualify for pardon, much less mercy.[128]

John's critique of slavery in these commentaries is much less radical than of wealth and the exploitation of the poor. The church, we should remember, showed little or no interest in reforming an institution so firmly built into the fabric of Roman society. The ordination of slaves, for example, was prohibited, while the council of Gangra in Paphlagonia had recently (c. 355)[129] anathematised those who, on religious grounds, encouraged slaves to resist or break free from their masters.[130] What weighed even more with John was Paul's advice to slaves to accept their status and serve their masters 'with fear and trembling' (1 Cor. 7.20-1; Eph. 6.5). His theoretical position,[131] often stated in these homilies, is that the origin of slavery is to be traced, far back in human history, to sin – more specifically, the sin of Noah's youngest son Ham (Gen. 9.24-7).[132] He is convinced that, if only the world heeded the commandment 'Love your neighbour as yourself ', there would be no slaves and no free men;[133] and he is sure that the first Christians in Jerusalem must have set their slaves free.[134] In practice, however, leaving theorising apart, he accepts the presence of slaves in households as a fact of life, reserving his rebukes for those who keep excessive numbers of them or inflict on them savage or humiliating punishments.[135] Commenting on Eph. 6.5-9, he argues that Paul's words 'be obedient to your earthly masters' imply that the master-slave relationship is purely temporary and slavery only a name, and that if the slave follows the apostle's further advice and serves his master 'with a good will, as to the Lord and not to men', 'slavery is divested of its indignity' (*dusgeneia*).[136] He clearly felt uneasy about slavery, arguing that we do not need domestic help since God has given us hands and feet to look after ourselves;[137] if

---

[128] *De eleemosyna* 6 (*PG* 51.269-71).
[129] T.D. Barnes, *JTS* NS 40 (1980) 121-4.
[130] Canon 3: Hefele-Leclercq, *Histoire des conciles* (Paris 1907) 1 (2), 1034.
[131] *In 1 Cor. hom.* 40.5; *in Eph. hom.* 22.2; *in 1 Tim. hom.* 16.2 (*PG* 61.353-4; 62.157; 590).
[132] *De Lazaro conc.* 6.7 (*PG* 48.1037-8).
[133] *In 1 Cor. hom.* 32.6 (*PG* 61.272).
[134] *In Act. hom.* 11.3 (*PG* 60.97): preached in Constantinople.
[135] E.g. *In 1 Cor. hom.* 40.5; *In Eph. hom.* 15.34 (*PG* 6.355; 62.109-10).
[136] *In Eph. hom.* 22.1-2 (*PG* 62.155-7).
[137] *In 1 Cor. hom.* 40.5 (*PG* 61.353-4).

slavery had been necessary, God would have created a slave to serve Adam. So we find him in his impatience urging anyone who has too many slaves to set those free who are superfluous to his needs, after having them taught a useful trade.[138] His objections, however, are more to the self-indulgence and ostentatious extravagance of keeping slaves than to the institution itself. Commenting on Rom. 13.1 he clearly recognises that slavery is a lawful state of life appointed by providence, analogous to the subjection of wife to husband and son to parent.[139]

<h2 style="text-align:center">VII</h2>

At first sight these homilies seem tantalisingly reticent about John himself and about current events in Antioch. He had been a prominent actor in the drama which paralysed the city during Lent 387, but once the curtain had dropped on it his figure seems to retreat into the shadows for a decade. While this is in general true, a close examination of the commentaries yields one or two valuable insights into his personal development, and also, even more revealingly, although only in haziest outline, into his attempts to grapple with a worrying crisis.

In the first place, it seems clear that, when studied in chronological order they convey the unmistakable impression of a man steadily growing in self-assurance and in confidence in his authority as a church leader.[140] In his early days as a preacher, as we have occasionally noted,[141] John regularly makes a great display of diffidence, of self-effacement, especially when Flavian is present, but by 390, when he prepared his Matthew commentary, no trace of this is left. Instead we find him ordering deacons to repel an unworthy would-be communicant, however exalted, from the altar, adding peremptorily, 'If you dare not do this yourself, bring him to me, for I shall not tolerate such impudence.'[142] From his imperious tone some earlier scholars[143] inferred that he must have been a bishop when he preached this homily; we know on other grounds that he was not, but he was clearly becoming a priest who expected his words to be heeded. When a few years later he lays it down that presbyters possess all the powers of bishops except that of ordaining,[144] he seems to be giving a strong hint that he is Flavian's co-equal collaborator in his other duties as bishop, viz. teaching and presiding over the church. A further pointer in the same direction is the way in which, when championing bishops against malicious charges brought by members of their flocks, he slips instinctively into the

---

[138] *In 1 Cor.* 40.5 (*PG* 61.353-4).
[139] *In Rom. hom.* 23.1 (*PG* 60.615).
[140] For this paragraph see Bonsdorf, op. cit., 52, 57-8, etc.
[141] See above, pp. 57 and 60.
[142] *In Matt. hom.* 82.6 (*PG* 58.744-6).
[143] Including his greatest editor, Sir Henry Savile (1610-13).
[144] *In 1 Tim. hom.* 11.1 (*PG* 62.553).

first person and exclaims, 'We don't dare avenge ...'[145] More generally, the progressive sharpening of his attacks on critics of the church's rulers (*archontes*) observable in these commentaries[146] may be fairly interpreted as evidence of his increasingly confident identification with the leadership. It is no accident that this growing self-assertiveness dates from the time when he was completing *Priesthood*, an essay in self-vindication which exalts the priest's authoritative position in the church.

The Ephesians homilies not only reinforce these impressions, but supply a graphic picture of John wrestling with a particular crisis. In the sixth he voices distress at the slackness which has gripped the church, from the clergy at the top downwards, and which results in scandalous behaviour, with no one stepping in to rebuke and offenders going unpunished.[147] There is a general break-down of order. In the tenth and eleventh he becomes more explicit:[148] the church's unity is threatened by the craving for power (*philarchia*), and the tyranny of ambition has kindled a blaze which, even if put out once, soon flares up again. In the eleventh he identifies the trouble as a split in the community in which the rebellious party professes the same orthodox faith, but is defective as regards ordination.[149] What amusement this must cause to pagans! You can hear them jeering, 'If they have the same doctrines, the same sacraments, why does another leader place himself in charge of another church?' John concludes with a challenge to the dissidents: 'At least let the church remain undivided. If we have been canonically appointed, persuade those who have mounted the throne un-canonically to step down ... If you cannot produce a just reason for separating yourselves from us, I entreat you to do your best to stand firmly yourselves from now on and to bring back those who have seceded.'[150]

While the reference here is clearly to the Antiochene schism, it is not so clear which of its many twists and turns John was dealing with. Paulinos, almost a hundred years old, died around 388, but on his deathbed had consecrated Evagrios,[151] a nobly born Antiochene of his congregation who had earlier been the young Jerome's patron and protector, as his successor. The consecration was irregular, having been carried out in Paulinos' lifetime without any other participating bishop.[152] Several scholars[153] have therefore concluded that Evagrios must have been John's target. This must remain a possibility, not least because we know[154] that Evagrios and his

---

[145] *In Tit. hom.* 1.4 (*PG* 62.669).
[146] *In Gal. comm.* 1.6-7; *In 2 Tim. hom.* 2.2-4; *In Eph. hom.* 10.2-3; 11.4-6 (*PG* 61.623-5; 62.609-12; 77-80; 85-8).
[147] *In Eph. hom.* 6.3-4 (*PG* 62.47-8).
[148] *In Eph. hom.* 10.2-3; 11.4 (*PG* 62.77-8; 85-6).
[149] *In Eph. hom.* 11.4-5 (*PG* 62.85-6).
[150] *In Eph. hom.* 11.6 (*PG* 62.88).
[151] *DHGE* 16.102-7 (M. Spanneut): see also J.N.D. Kelly, *Jerome* (London 1975), index.
[152] Theodoret, *HE* 5.23 (Parmentier 322-3).
[153] Notably Tillemont, *Mémoires* (1693-1712), xi. 269.
[154] Theodoret, loc. cit.

supporters maintained an energetic campaign against Flavian, seeking to poison the emperor's mind against him; but the theory has its difficulties. Flavian was remarkably tolerant of Paulinos, however much he may have been irritated by his opposition, and is not likely to have sanctioned open attacks on him or his (however unwisely) chosen successor. Evagrios, too, was a widely respected figure, not least in the circle of John's admirers.[155] A further objection is that Evagrios' death should almost certainly be placed in 393-4, well before the date to which we have assigned the homilies on Ephesians. An attractive alternative explanation[156] is that what had stirred John into action was the attempt by some unknown presbyter to set himself up as bishop of the separatist sect on Evagrios' death, or at some time thereafter. It is perhaps possible to overhear a hint of this move in Sokrates' report[157] that when Evagrios died Flavian saw to it that no successor to him was appointed, since he was 'moving every stone' to attach his followers to his own community.

Whatever the exact nature of the crisis, there can be no denying the central part John played in dealing with it. It was he, clearly, who was in charge of the campaign to bring the dissidents to order. There is no mention of Flavian, although it is likely that John was acting with his approval. The closing sections of Homily 11,[158] with their mixture of argument and pleading, illustrate the methods he employed. First, he forcibly makes the point that, on the analogy of the human body (Eph. 1.16), members of the church must stick together, no one of them trespassing on the position of another; where Christians hold the same doctrines, separatism can only be caused by the craving for power (*philarchia*); to make schism in the church is no less evil than lapsing into heresy. At the same time he insists that he is not bossing them: 'My job is to counsel and advise you.' He makes this point, he assures his audience, so that none of them may plead that he has not been warned of the sinfulness of schism. As he proceeds, however, his tone becomes more personal, and he implores them to desist if they think that in splitting the church they are getting their own back on him. By all means let them punish him, 'a person of no importance whatsoever', but they should do so by striking him or spitting on him – anything rather than by inflicting pain on Christ by sundering his body. Indeed, if it will do any good, he is prepared to step down from his office. He warns them, however, that they should not place all the blame on himself (*eph' hemas*). Each one of them is of full age, and like himself will in the end have to give an account of his conduct.

Even a casual reader can sense the passion which, even more than usual, vibrates through John's words. There can be no doubt that they, coupled

[155] Cf. Palladios, *Dial.* 5 (*SC* 341.130-2).
[156] First put forward by J. Stilting, *AASS* IV.495.
[157] 5.15.
[158] 4-6 (*PG* 62.84-8).

with whatever other measures Flavian and he took, were effective; we know that no third bishop took charge of the little sect after Evagrios' death, although a determined rump of dissidents kept themselves apart for many years. For students of John's career, however, the incident has exceptional importance, not least as suggesting that in the closing stage of his presbyterate, partly no doubt as a result of Flavian's increasing age and enfeeblement, he was called upon to shoulder the responsibilities of acting bishop of the see.

8

Unexpected Promotion

I

One day in (probably) late October 397 John received an urgent summons from Asterios, count of the civil diocese of Oriens and governor of Antioch. He was to present himself immediately at the great martyrs' shrine outside the Romanesian gate,[1] so called because the road through it led northwards to Constantinople or New Rome. Having got there, he was driven some 25 km to Pagrae (Bagras), the first post-station on the trunk road to Tarsos and beyond; as they drove, the governor gave him the astonishing news that he was being taken, on imperial orders, to the capital to become its new bishop. The emperor's letter had insisted that the operation should be carried out as discreetly as possible; it was feared that the populace might be tempted to demonstrate if they learned that their adored preacher was being taken from them. Nevertheless bishop Flavian, it seemed, was informed in confidence of what was afoot. Once at Pagrae, Asterios handed him over to two government officials, a palace eunuch and a courier attached to the master of the offices, under whose protection he was conveyed by a coach of the imperial post to Constantinople.[2] The land-route, by Tarsos and then over the Taurus range, and so to Ankyra and then Nikomedia, covered almost 1200 km.[3] In an emergency, travelling by night and day, a special courier could complete the journey in six days, but John and his escorts were in no hurry and probably took about a fortnight.[4]

This dramatic change in John's fortunes had been triggered off by the death on 26 September of Nektarios, the greatly respected city praetor whom Theodosius I, to everyone's surprise (he was then a layman, still unbaptised), had nominated as bishop in 381. Actually, it had been an astute choice, for Constantinople was then a predominantly Arian city, and while the emperor was determined to bring it round to the Nicene orthodoxy to which he was attached, he rightly judged that a popular, diplomatic figure like Nektarios was more likely to achieve this than a no-turning-back

---

[1] See above, p. 3: it was probably the one marked Bridge Gate on the plan of Antioch.
[2] For this para. see Palladios, *Dial.* 5 (*SC* 341.112-14).
[3] See *Itinerarium Burdigalense* (*CSEL* 39.14-17), which gives the distance as 800 Roman miles (= about 736 m cr 1185 km).
[4] L. Casson, *Travel in the Ancient World* (2 ed. London 1979), 88.

dogmatist. As was to be expected, there was intense competition and unabashed lobbying for the succession.[5] In particular, Theophilos, the ambitious and powerful patriarch of Alexandria, coveted the position for Isidore, an octogenarian priest whom he had employed on confidential missions and who was now guest-master of the Alexandrian church. Nothing could have suited him more than to install a trusted friend of his own in the see of the imperial city. But, as in 381, while the canonical procedures had to be formally observed, the choice effectively lay with the emperor – or, since Arkadios was no Theodosius, with the eunuch Eutropios, superintendent of the sacred bedchamber, who was then masterminding imperial decisions.

There has been much discussion of the motives behind John's selection. Sokrates attributes it to his renown as an eloquent teacher;[6] according to Palladios, Eutropios had gained an insight into his character and abilities when visiting the east on state business.[7] This has the ring of truth, especially if his visit took him to Antioch and he noticed that John was to all intents and purposes acting bishop there. It is also not impossible, as Baur suggested,[8] that Caesarios, who had been one of the commissioners investigating the riot of 387, and who had recently been praetorian prefect and was now consul,[9] had given a favourable report on John's performance during that crisis. Another suggestion[10] meriting serious consideration is that, in its zeal for Nicene orthodoxy, the Theodosian house wanted more vigorous action against Arianism in the capital, and considered John the man for the job: so far from being suppressed, the Arian minority was in a distinctly militant mood.[11] It is equally possible that the authorities were looking for a bishop who would collaborate with them in what was clearly one of their political objectives at this time, to consolidate and extend the authority of the imperial see. Any one, or perhaps a combination of some, of these reasons may have been at work. In any case it was entirely natural that Constantinople should look to the Syrian metropolis for a new bishop. It had done so in the past, and would do so again in the not too distant future.[12]

Whatever the motive, it was on Eutropios' recommendation that Arkadios had ordered John to be brought to the capital. At the same time the emperor had taken the unusual step of summoning a special synod of leading bishops of the east to take part in the election and consecration of the new bishop. His object, according to Sokrates and Sozomen,[13] was to

[5] Sokrates 6.2; Sozomen 8.2.
[6] Loc. cit.
[7] *Dial.* 5 (*SC* 341.112).
[8] 2, 7.
[9] *PLRE* 1, 171.
[10] J.H.W.G. Liebeschuetz, *Barbarians and Bishops* (Oxford 1990), 166.
[11] See below, p. 138.
[12] See pp. 11; 289.
[13] 6.2; 8.2.

highlight the importance and solemnity of the occasion – in other words, to impress on the outside world the special status he wished to be accorded to the imperial see. Among the bishops responding to the summons was Theophilos of Alexandria. When he arrived and learned who the chosen candidate was (the authorities seem to have kept this dark until the last moment), he was furious and did his best to oppose the decision and smear John.[14] The synod, however, duly carried through John's election; even Theophilos, in spite of initially refusing to do so, gave his vote for him and, as senior bishop, presided at his consecration.[15] He had been coerced, or rather blackmailed, it was said,[16] by Eutropios, who had threatened that, if he held back, he would make public certain treasonable letters of the patriarch's which had come into his hands. Although Theophilos had no option but to yield, it was a humiliation he was never to forget.

John was the twelfth bishop of Constantinople. There is a discrepancy in our sources about the date of his consecration, the calender of Constantinople (or *synaxarion*)[17] giving 15 December 397 and Sokrates 26 February 398.[18] Sokrates' dating is characteristically precise, and most authorities nowadays accept it.[19] The lapse of five months since Nektarios' death has never been satisfactorily explained. John was just under fifty years of age. A description of his appearance which may well derive from authentic reminiscences has been handed down in the *menaia*, or office-books for feasts of saints in the eastern church.[20] According to this, he was diminutive in stature, with a disproportionately big head on top of an emaciated body – which he was to describe as being as frail as a spider's web.[21] His nose was prominent, with the nostrils wide apart, and he had piercing eyes set deep in their sockets. His cheeks were pallid, withered as a result of rigorous fasting, and his lofty forehead was furrowed with wrinkles. He had big ears, and while his head was balding, he had a sparse, straggling beard. Although pleasant to look at, he tended to assume a severe expression.

II

John's promotion was almost certainly a surprise to him, but there is no reason to suppose (as has often been claimed)[22] that it was an unwelcome one. It made him chief pastor of a city which was even larger and more magnificent, and already more important ecclesiastically as well as politi-

[14] Palladios, *Dial.* 5 (*SC* 341.116); Sokrates, 6.2.

[15] So John addressed him as his father (Palladios, *Dial.* 7: *SC* 341.152).

[16] Sokrates 6.2.

[17] *Synaxarium ecclesiae Constantinopolitanae*: ed. H. Delehaye, *Propylaeum ad Acta SS. Novembris* (Brussels 1900), 312-13.

[18] 6.2.

[19] E.g. H. Lietzmann, PW IX (2), 1819; G. Dagron, *Naissance d'une capitale* (Paris 1974), 464-5.

[20] *PG* 29.cccxc.i-ii.

[21] *Ep.* 4.4 (*PG* 52.595).

[22] E.g. A. Moulard, *S. Jean Chrysostome* (Paris 1974), 270.

cally, than Antioch.[23] When Constantine the Great inaugurated his 'new Rome' in May 330, it covered an area four times as extensive (some 700 hectares) as old Byzantium. The walls he built, protecting its land-facing flank and linking the Golden Horn to the Sea of Marmara, stood more than two kilometres beyond the walls of the earlier city. He seems to have envisaged a capital of between 100,000 and 150,000 inhabitants. With the rapid growth of its population this total had certainly been reached by 380, and in 384 there was already talk of new walls that would be needed further to the west than the original ones.[24] These new walls, which remain one of the most impressive defensive systems of the ancient world, were in fact constructed in 412-13 more than a kilometre west of Constantine's, virtually doubling the area of the city to some 14,000 hectares (excluding the suburbs north of the Golden Horn). This would have sufficed for a population of 400,000-500,000 inhabitants, but in John's time the figure is likely to have been considerably less than that. The most recent estimates suggest that it may have been between 200,000 and 300,000.

If Constantinople was only slightly more populous than Antioch (although growing faster), by the time of John's appointment it had at last established precedence as the permanent seat of the eastern emperor and his government. For Constantine his new city, which he had deliberately modelled on the pattern of Rome and endowed with many of its privileges (including regular distributions of free bread – brought, however, not from North Africa but from Egypt), had been, after 330, his normal residence, but his immediate successors often preferred to set up their headquarters at Antioch.[25] All this changed with Theodosius I and his descendants: from 381 Constantinople was again the imperial capital of the east, rivalling Rome and Milan (later Ravenna) in the west. When John arrived there, he found himself living in close proximity to the emperor and his court. His cathedral, the Great Church (*Megale*), perhaps already becoming known as Sophia (Wisdom) or Hagia Sophia, a basilica with a wooden cupola (*xulotrullos*) which Constantius had started *c.* 346,[26] stood prominently to the north of the Augustaion, the vast porticoed piazza which Constantine had remodelled and renamed after his mother, the Augusta Helena, and which formed the political as well as the ecclesiastical hub of the city. To the east rose the senate-house, also an apse-ended basilica. On the south was the Chalke or Bronze House,[27] the principal entrance to the sacred palace which, with many changes and enlargements, was to remain the residence of eastern emperors for a thousand years. To the north-west the palace was bounded by the huge hippodrome, often to be the target of John's invectives; it was connected with the palace, and the emperors had a royal box

---

[23] For this section see G. Dagron, op. cit., 518-30.
[24] Themistios, orator and city praetor, *Or.* 18.223 (Downey 1.322).
[25] See above, pp. 2; 8f.
[26] Sokrates 2.16: cf. R. Janin, *Les églises et les monastères* (Paris 1965), 455-7; 469.
[27] See C. Mango, *The Brazen House* (Copenhagen 1959).

(*kathisma*) from which they could watch the chariot races and other excitements taking place in it.

Three other churches, within and outside the city, call for mention since they figure in this story. The first was Hagia Eirene (Holy Peace), only 150 metres from the Great Church. Often called the Old Church (*Palaia*), it had been there before Constantine, who (according to Sokrates)[28] had enlarged and beautified it, and given it its name. The general council of 381 was almost certainly held there. The second, the church of the Holy Apostles, stood far to the west, just inside the original walls that John knew. Much the most elaborately decorated, it had been begun by Constantine, who had erected on the site a circular mausoleum to be his own burying-place, and completed by Constantius II, who had built a large cruciform church, to be dedicated in 370, adjacent to it.[29] The street leading to it from the palace was the main thoroughfare of the capital, known as the *Mese*. This splendid ceremonial boulevard, the scene of state entrances by emperors into the city and of great ecclesiastical processions, started at the Augustaion and, after traversing the forums of Constantine and Theodosius, veered south-west, eventually reaching the old Golden Gate in the walls of Constantine, where it joined the Via Egnatia, the great highway linking the eastern with the western parts of the empire. From the Golden Gate it proceeded along the coast to Hebdomon (Bakirköy) seven Roman miles from Hagia Sophia, where there was an imperial palace and an extensive parade ground for military manoeuvres (the Campus Martius), and where emperors were proclaimed and part of their investiture carried out. Here, among others, stood our third church, an imposing circular sanctuary which Theodosius I had built in 391 to receive, and be the permanent shrine of, the head of John the Baptist when it arrived early next year.[30]

Although not yet a patriarchate, the see of Constantinople enjoyed in the 380s and 390s an increasingly important status. As Byzantium it had been a simple bishopric in the province of Thrace, with the bishop of Heraklea (Eregli) as its metropolitan, but as Constantinople, Constantine's official residence, it inevitably began to acquire an independent position. Its growing prestige is illustrated by the fact that a succession of ambitious prelates (e.g. Eusebios of Nikomedia in 339 and Eudoxios of Antioch in 360) were willing to exchange their metropolitan or even patriarchal sees for it. The council summoned by Theodosius I to Constantinople in summer 381 (to be recognised as the second ecumenical council) carried this process of advancement a decisive step further. In its third canon it decreed that 'the bishop of Constantinople shall have a precedence of honour next after the

---

[28] 1.16; 2.16 ('… enlarged and beautified').

[29] C. Mango, *BZ* 83 (1990), 51-62: this article supersedes R. Janin, op. cit., 42-8.

[30] Sozomen 7.21. For the church see R. Janin, op. cit., 413-14. No trace of it or of Holy Apostles (replaced in 1462-70 by the Mosque of Sultan Mehmet) survives. The present buildings of H. Eirene and H. Sophia (museum of Aya Sofya) were erected in the sixth century by Justinian.

bishop of Rome, since it is new Rome'. Behind this ruling we can discern not only the determination of the majority of bishops present to cut Alexandria, traditionally accepted as the senior eastern see, down to size, but even more the wish of the emperor to secure for the bishop of his capital a position superior to that of all other eastern bishops. The ruling did not, of course, assign him any specific jurisdiction over other churches. Nevertheless the fact that he was bishop of the capital, in close contact with the emperor and presiding *ex officio* over meetings of bishops resident or visiting there, could not fail to enhance his authority. As a matter of fact, there is evidence that, in the span between the council and John's accession, Nektarios intervened, or attempted to intervene, at least three times to settle difficult issues in churches outside his immediate jurisdiction (the civil dioceses of Pontica and Oriens), not however on his own initiative but in response to ecclesiastics who, without attributing to him any canonical oversight in those areas, recognised that the bishop of the imperial city was uniquely qualified to wield efficacious influence in them.[31]

III

John's installation as bishop gave him an entrée to the, to him, wholly new and not altogether congenial world of the imperial court; his life was to be closely, and tragically, bound up with it for the next six years. The emperor and empress, with their family and most of the high officials composing the government, were members of his flock. While normally attending the liturgy in the palace chapel, the imperial couple, both earnest Christians of strictly orthodox persuasion, were neighbours and came to his cathedral on great occasions. The emperor, Arkadios, was only about twenty years old. Slight of build, with drooping eyes and halting speech, he was intellectually dim and ineffectual in character. Basically decent, he tended to be guided by stronger personalities, but on occasion could break out of his habitual lethargy and show independence. Created Augustus in 383, he had been left as regent of the eastern part of the empire by his father, Theodosius I, when he marched west against the usurper Eugenius in 394; the praetorian prefect Rufinus, Theodosius' powerful minister, was in effective charge.[32] When Theodosius, after crushing Eugenius, died at Milan on 17 January 395, Arkadios had succeeded to the eastern throne (with Rufinus still guiding his policies), while his younger brother Honorius, then a boy of 10, whom his father had named Augustus in 393 and had taken with him to Italy, inherited the western one. Theodosius had already, probably in October 394, appointed Stilicho, the distinguished Vandal commander to whom he had given his favourite niece Serena in marriage, as regent for the youthful Honorius. On his deathbed, according

---

[31] See J. Hajjar, *Le synode permanent* (*OCA* 164: Rome 1962), 56-60; G. Dagron, op. cit., 461-7.
[32] Zosimos 4.51.4 (ed. F. Paschoud: see his n. 209).

to Stilicho himself, the emperor had named him guardian to both his sons, the 18-year-old Arkadios (legally of full age since 14) as well as Honorius. Although historians have questioned it,[33] this was a claim which Stilicho was to press in coming years, but which was to be strongly resisted by the eastern authorities, and which was bound to create a steadily widening rift between east and west.

The empress, Aelia Eudoxia, was intelligent, vivacious and strong-willed – the complete antithesis of her husband, over whom she soon established an ascendancy.[34] Daughter of a successful Frankish general, Bauto, she had been brought up in Constantinople in the household of one of the sons of Promotos, a bitter enemy and probable victim of Rufinus, but always retained a 'strong vein of barbarian high-spiritedness'.[35] A woman of exceptional beauty (*kallei lampousan exaisioi*), Arkadios, a man of sensual proclivities, had been induced to marry her in 395 by his chief chamberlain Eutropios, who had shown him her portrait[36] – thereby foiling a scheme of Rufinus to marry his own daughter to the young emperor and thus ensure imperial rank for himself. An ambitious intriguer, she was impulsive and volatile, much under the influence of palace eunuchs and, even more, of a camarilla of court ladies, especially Marsa, the widow of Promotos, and her confederates Castricia and Eugraphia. One of her intimates was a courtier described as count John, with whom gossip alleged she had sexual relations.[37] She was an enthusiastic, deeply superstitious Christian.

The sovereigns apart, much the most powerful figure in the court, or for that matter in Constantinople, was (as has been hinted) Eutropios,[38] superintendent of the bedchamber or head of the imperial household. Born on the Assyrian frontier, this extraordinary man had been castrated in infancy and sold into slavery. He had served several masters in menial, often degrading roles, had inevitably been the victim of physical abuse, but had at last, when already old (*c.* 379) been granted his freedom. His fortunes now underwent a remarkable change, for he entered the service of the imperial palace as a chamberlain, an office which gave him unique access to the emperor's person and the power to control the access of others. He quickly won the trust of Theodosius I, who *c.* 393, when preparing for his campaign against the usurper Eugenius, sent him as his personal emissary to Egypt to consult a renowned solitary, John, whose predictions had earlier proved accurate, about its likely result.[39] By 395, now chief of the bedchamber, he had become a strong rival to the generally hated praetorian prefect

---

[33] Notably A. Cameron, *Claudian* (Oxford 1970), 38-40.
[34] For her see K.G. Holum, *Theodosian Empresses* (California 1982), 48-78.
[35] Philostorgios, *HE* 11.6 (*GCS* 21.136: *barbarikou thrasous ouk oligon*).
[36] Zosimos 5.3.2-3 (indirectly confirmed by the Roman poet Claudian, *De nuptiis Honorii Augusti* 23-5).
[37] Zosimos 5.16.8: cf. *PLRE* 2.593-4.
[38] For his career see *PLRE* 2.440-1.
[39] Sozomen 7.22.

Rufinus, and later in the year almost certainly collaborated with Stilicho in his murder.[40] Persuaded by Rufinus, Arkadios had ordered Stilicho, then in Thessaly, to dispatch the eastern army which Theodosius had taken to the west, and which he had with him, back to Constantinople. Stilicho obeyed, placing it under the command of Gainas, a Gothic general who had risen from the ranks under Theodosius,[41] and with whom he had reached an understanding about Rufinus' fate. Gainas and his troops marched eastwards along the Via Egnatia; when they reached the outskirts of the city, Arkadios, in accordance with custom, came to meet them at the Campus Martius at Hebdomon. Rufinus accompanied the emperor, but as the praetorian prefect was carrying out an informal walk-about, greeting officers and men, they fell on him with drawn swords and he was cut to pieces (27 November 395).

Eutropios at once stepped into the dead minister's shoes and, as well as seizing much of his immense fortune, for the next four years took over his role as the emperor's all-powerful adviser, virtually in control of the eastern government. As the arranger of his marriage, with the insight and skill to exploit his weaknesses, he had enormous influence with Arkadios, who was genuinely fond of him, and also for a time with Eudoxia. In 396 he demonstrated his contempt for the army establishment by bringing about the downfall of two leading generals whose wealth he coveted, and in 398, to everyone's surprise and chagrin, personally conducted a successful military campaign against marauding Huns who had penetrated deep into the provinces of Asia Minor. In gratitude for his victory the emperor nominated him eastern consul for 399, and in the same year honoured him with the exceptional title of 'patrician'. Thus, when he selected John as bishop of the capital, although socially despised as a eunuch and former slave, hated for his shameless rapacity and cynical sale of offices, Eutropios was at the height of his power.

IV

John's new residence (the *episkopeion*), where he and the clergy closely associated with him lived and where he received visitors and conducted business, stood to the south-east of the Great Church, having direct access to it. Burnt down in 388 by Arian mobs rioting because of a false report that the orthodox Theodosius I had been defeated in battle by the usurper Maximus in N. Italy,[42] its rebuilding had been undertaken by Nektarios, but the work had not been completed.

Close to the house, adjoining the south portico of Hagia Sophia and communicating with its narthex by a staircase, was a sprawling convent

[40] Zosimos 5.8.1.
[41] Sozomen 8.14.
[42] Sokrates 5.13.

which had been founded, and was now presided over, by the deaconess Olympias,[43] a woman of remarkable intelligence, determination of character and outspokenness (some, in the sexist language of the time, declared that she was more a man than a woman).[44] Of aristocratic lineage, granddaughter of Constantine's praetorian prefect Ablabios, she was fabulously wealthy, with estates in Thrace, Galatia, Cappadocia and Bithynia, as well as numerous properties in Constantinople itself. In 385 Theodosius, eager to build connections between his Spanish relatives and the affluent élite of the capital, had arranged her marriage with one of them, Nebridios, city praetor in 386. When he died less than two years later, he pressed her to marry another kinsman, Elpidios. A Christian committed to the ascetic ideal, she refused, bluntly retorting that, if her king, Jesus Christ, had intended her to live with a man, he would not have taken her husband away. The emperor was furious; it was against the public interest for such riches as she possessed to remain in the keeping of a widow, and a downright waste if she were to lavish them on pious charities. He ordered her fortune to be impounded until she was thirty, but four years later, before she had reached that age, he relented and restored it to her, having been assured (we are told) of the sincerity and high quality of her ascetic devotion.[45]

Henceforth she gave herself wholly to the service of God and his church, especially the care of the sick and poor. According to Palladios,[46] a great admirer, she deliberately modelled herself, in her spiritual exercises and charitable works, on Melania the Elder, the wealthy Roman aristocrat who in 378, with Rufinus of Aquileia as her adviser, had founded a double monastery at Jerusalem, and whose relatives, years later when she herself had moved back to Rome, were to extend hospitality to John's supporters seeking refuge there.[47] This report has prompted the speculation (unprovable but not improbable) that Olympias herself may at some point have made a pilgrimage to the Holy Land and got to know the great lady personally.[48] At this time her main task was the supervision of her convent, which she had built on property belonging to herself and which, beginning with about fifty of her own maidservants, soon increased to the amazing total of some two hundred and fifty inmates, all virgins.[49] In addition, she kept open house for visiting ecclesiastics and Christian travellers in need

---

[43] For her see Palladios, *Dial.* 10, 16, 17; *Lausiac History* 56; also the anonymous *Life* written in the first half of the fifth century by a contemporary who knew her and her sisters (ed. by A.M. Malingrey, *SC* 13bis: Paris 1968). Much of this and the next paragraph is drawn from this. See also *BSS* IX.1154-8 (R. Janin).
[44] Palladios, *Dial.* 16 (*SC* 341.318).
[45] *Life* 2-4 (*SC* 13bis.408-14).
[46] *Lausiac History* 56 (Butler, 149-50).
[47] See below, p. 275.
[48] E.D. Hunt, *JTS* 24 (1973), 477.
[49] *Life* 6 (*SC* 13bis.418-20).

of hospitality. It is intriguing to note that, among the numerous guests she thus entertained, and freely loaded with gifts when they departed, were several (e.g. Epiphanios of Cyprus and Theophilos of Alexandria) who were to become John's irreconcilable foes.[50] Highly educated, well grounded in the scriptures, she had placed her services at the disposal of bishop Nektarios. The courtly old man so valued her charitable generosity, and found her advice on church affairs so helpful, that he ordained her a deaconess when she was still in her early thirties, notwithstanding the ban imposed by St Paul, and quite recently reaffirmed by Theodosius, on consecrating widows under the age of sixty.[51]

As the leading deaconess attached to his cathedral, John must have made the acquaintance of Olympias almost immediately after his arrival in the capital . From the start there seems to have developed between them a deep and, as events were to show, lasting friendship founded on an affinity which was both spiritual and intellectual. Like him, she was devoted to the bible, reading its books over and over again. Both practised similar austerities. Like him, she had ruined her digestive system by excessive fasting and an injudicious diet. While he needed warm baths because of his wretched physical condition, she on a similar principle shunned them except for urgent reasons of health. Even when she allowed herself one, she was careful not to remove her undergarment, thus avoiding the sight of her naked body or permitting her maids to see it.[52] Her convent was separated from his palace by a single wall, and he was the only outsider, man or woman, who had leave to cross the threshold. Indeed, he took over the spiritual direction of her community; his inspired talks, her unknown biographer records,[53] by means of the divine charity with which they overflowed, set ablaze the love of God in its inmates. In return Olympias made herself responsible for taking care of his clothes and for preparing his simple meals, which she sent across each day to the *episkopeion*. There was no one in Constantinople with whom he was to have a deeper or more sympathetic understanding, no one with whom he was to feel more at ease or to whom he was to pour out his heart more unreservedly, than this independent, strong-willed but also intensely emotional woman.

Modern students, influenced by the post-Freudian atmosphere in which they have been brought up, are bound to discern a sexual element in this close and strong relationship. They are entirely correct in so doing. It would be a mistake, however, to suppose that John and Olympias were unaware of this factor. The temptations to which relations between the sexes can give rise were never far from the thoughts of committed Christians of that epoch, least of all from John's. But while acutely alive to the sexual

---

[50] *Life* 14 (*SC* 13bis.436-9).
[51] 1 Tim. 5.9; CT 16.2.27 (21 June 390).
[52] *Life* 13 (*SC* 13bis.434-6).
[53] *Life* 8 (*SC* 13bis.422).

dimension, they viewed it with a profound repugnance which modern people usually find it hard to understand. Hence they employed a well-organised self-discipline (including, for example, the elaborate formal courtesy by which they distanced themselves from one another) to keep it at arm's length. What their heroic efforts cost them we can only surmise, but if their effects on John were relatively slight, on Olympias they were to be deeply damaging.

9

Diplomat and Rough Reformer

I

John took up the reins of his new office with resolution, and also with an assured conviction of his authority. From the start, however, he set himself to woo the common people, using language which strikes modern readers as extravagant, but which was in fact characteristic of his populist approach. In his second sermon in Constantinople (a tirade against rationalist Arianism) he exclaimed, 'I have already addressed you once, but from that day I have come to love you as if I had grown up among you from childhood. The chains of affection which bind me to you are as strong as if I had enjoyed your most pleasant company for time past counting. And this has come about, not because I am especially given to friendship and love, but because you are of all people the most desirable, the most lovable. For who would not admire and marvel at your zeal tested in the flames, your unfeigned love, your warm regard for your teachers, the unity you maintain among yourselves?'[1] He went on to assure his audience that he now felt no less attached to the church in Constantinople than to that of his birth and upbringing. Indeed, if the church at Antioch had been earlier in its foundation, that of the capital was even more fervent in its faith. If the congregation there was larger (was this a hint that the situation in Constantinople must be improved?) and the theatre more brilliant, the endurance of Christians here had been more severely tested by the ravaging wolves of Arianism.

As he spoke, John was, almost instinctively, building up a constituency which he would never lose. He was prepared also, as we shall see, when the occasion seemed appropriate, to address the emperor and empress with fulsome flattery. Towards both, especially the emperor, his public stance had all the respect, even obsequious deference which we should expect of an eastern prelate of that epoch, and which has often been contrasted with the commanding manner of a western bishop like Ambrose of Milan.[2] His sermons abound in colourful descriptions of the imperial regalia, as of the

---

[1] *C. Anomoeos hom.* 1.1-2 (*PG* 48.796-7). He recalls that in his first sermon (now lost), comparing himself to David facing Goliath, he had promised to counter the rationalism of the Anomoeans with the simpler weapons provided by scripture.

[2] E.g. F. Homes Dudden, *The Life and Times of St Ambrose* (Oxford 1935), 1.370.

majestic ritual of court and palace[3] – although a note of deprecation can almost always be detected in them. He was also studiously careful (considerations of personal safety must also have played their part) never to breathe a word of criticism of Arkadios himself. Nevertheless he stands out among contemporaries for his boldness in asserting the pre-eminence of the bishop over the temporal ruler, however august. Years before at Antioch, while assuring his congregation that 'the emperor is crown and head of all who dwell on earth',[4] he had been equally insistent that the bishop too was a prince, a prince moreover of greater honour and dignity than the emperor.[5] The divine laws, he went on to claim, made the emperor subject to the bishop since he had to resort to the bishop for every blessing from above. The bishop's panoply, too, was more splendid than the emperor's and his power much more effective, since the breastplate and belt he wore were of righteousness and truth, while he wielded a sword not of steel but of the Holy Spirit.

While his utterances on the subject at Constantinople are fewer, exactly the same principles inspire them. He is emphatic, for example, that the wrath of emperors can be arbitrary and cruel; when that happens, their power is thoroughly evil, as corrupting to the soul as disease to the body.[6] On the other hand, the basis of the bishop's authority is the fact that he is Christ's ambassador; his office is a spiritual one in which the grace of God operates. 'So long as I sit on this throne and possess this presidency (*proedria*), however unworthy I may be, I have the dignity and power' which belong to Christ's envoy.[7] Some years after his installation, lecturing on the book of Acts, he was to give a stern warning that if anyone were to disobey his spiritual admonitions, no matter how exalted his office, no matter if he were the wearer of the imperial diadem itself, he would have no hesitation in excommunicating him: 'So long as I sit on this throne, I shall not surrender any of the rights belonging to it.'[8] In thus proclaiming the bishop's independence of the state John was repudiating in advance the caesaropapism which was to be everywhere taken for granted in the churches of the east in contrast to that of the west, and which even he had found it convenient to accept in his Homilies on the Statues.[9]

II

John lost no time, as we shall see, in impressing the stamp of his authority on the church of the capital. For the moment, however, there was an urgent task transcending local problems which the new-found status of Constan-

---

[3] E.g. *De perfecta caritate* 6-7 (*PG* 56.286-7).
[4] *Ad pop. Antioch. hom.* 2.2 (*PG* 49.36).
[5] *Ad pop. Antioch hom.* 3.2 (*PG* 49.50): cf. *De Anna hom.* 2.4 (*PG* 54.648).
[6] *In Col. hom.* 7.3 (*PG* 62.547-8).
[7] *In Col. hom.* 3.5 (*PG* 62.323-4).
[8] *In Act. hom.* 8.3 (*PG* 60.74-6).
[9] See above, pp. 79-82.

tinople as a pre-eminent see laid upon him. It was customary for patriarchs and metropolitans to send formal notice of their appointment to their opposite numbers, accompanying it with a statement of their belief, and to expect in return an acknowledgment implying fellowship. Without delay, therefore, John dispatched a delegation to Rome to announce his election and consecration to the pope, Siricius (384-99). Not surprisingly, however, he decided to use this exchange of courtesies to achieve another objective close to his heart, the ending of Antioch's ecclesiastical isolation from Rome and the west. As we have often noted,[10] Rome had steadfastly cold-shouldered Meletios and Flavian, along with Alexandria recognising only Paulinos, and after him Evagrios, as lawful bishop of the Syrian metropolis. In 393 a representative eastern council had been held at Caesarea in Palestine to settle the Antiochene affair, and had come out in favour of Flavian's legitimacy. Although the council had received advice from the pope which effectively ruled out Evagrios on the ground that his ordination had been irregular,[11] the holy see had taken no action to break the deadlock.

John's two objectives, obtaining letters of fellowship from the pope and healing the schism, were by no means distinct, as often seems to be supposed.[12] If Siricius was still minded to distance himself from Flavian, he could scarcely accord recognition to one who had been his trusted associate for so long. So John selected the members of his delegation with diplomatic shrewdness. They were Akakios, a white-haired champion of orthodoxy who was bishop of Beroea (Haleb), an important see close to Antioch, and Isidore, none other than Theophilos' passed-over candidate for Constantinople. Akakios was a venerable ascetic who inspired trust and could report reliably on the situation in Antioch. Isidore was a clever negotiator who was well known in Rome from previous business visits, and who could vouch that the embassy had the full support of Alexandria. It appears that he had agreed these names with Theophilos, whom, according to Sozomen,[13] he had persuaded to support his efforts to secure the recognition of Flavian by the holy see as well as by Alexandria. Theophilos' readiness to co-operate with John is not really surprising, for, although he had not taken part in the council at Caesarea, he was fully aware that Flavian's legitimacy was now generally acknowledged in the east; but it shows him in an unexpectedly attractive light, since he is unlikely at this time to have been personally well-disposed to John.

The mission was doubly successful. Backed as John was by Alexandria, on which Rome relied for information about and guidance on eastern church affairs, the elderly pope, who was probably not wholly clear about the game

---

[10] See above, pp. 12; 37.
[11] E.W. Brooks, *The Sixth Book of the Select Letters of Severus, Patriarch of Antioch* (Oxford 1903) 2 (2), 223 (Letter 2.3).
[12] E.g. by Baur, 2.19.
[13] 8.3.

'new Rome' was playing with him,[14] had no qualms about recognising him and sending him letters of communion, notwithstanding his long association with Flavian. Equally he was persuaded by Akakios and Theophilos' agent Isidore to grant full recognition to Flavian. Thus when Akakios, after sailing first to Egypt, returned to Syria, he carried with him to Flavian letters of fellowship both from Alexandria and, after almost twenty years, from the holy see itself.[15] As for John, he could congratulate himself on having done a good deed both for the church of his native city and for his revered former bishop. His great disappointment must have been that, in spite of the recognition of Flavian by Rome, a tiny but obdurate rump of Eustathians continued to hold aloof from him.[16]

III

Having dispatched his delegation to Rome, John carried out what would nowadays be called a visitation of his diocese. He had not been idle, one suspects, during the weeks between his consecration and enthronement, but had spent time briefing himself on the current state of the church in the capital. His conclusion was that reform was urgently needed, and he soon made it plain that he was going to be a bishop with both standards and a style radically different from those of his easy-going predecessor. He also revealed, in more ways than one, that he had, perhaps unexpectedly, a shrewd eye for business and an appreciation of the value of money – although he himself, it is ironical to note, was later to be accused of being somewhat cavalier about disclosing the income and expenditure of the church.[17]

He made a start with the finances both of the see and, more particularly, of his own palace.[18] He carefully scrutinised the accounts, and ruthlessly cut out any expenditure which did not seem of benefit to the church. He was especially shocked by the palace accounts, from which he discovered that sums he considered excessive were being squandered on hospitality. As was normal for a bishop of a great city, Nektarios had entertained on a large scale and had kept a generous table. John was prepared to provide accommodation and board for visiting ecclesiastics, but on a modest scale. Lavish banqueting and glittering receptions, however, amounted in his eyes to robbing the church and the poor. He himself refused to offer official or private dinners in his palace, and regularly turned down invitations to such functions. Indeed, it was his practice to take his meals alone, the main reasons being (as his defenders never tired of pointing out) either that his

---

[14] So Ch. Pietri, who gives an admirable summary of the affair, with full references, in *Roma Christiana* (Rome 1976) 2, 1282-8.

[15] Sozomen 8.3.

[16] See below, pp. 286f.; 290.

[17] See below, p. 222.

[18] Palladios, *Dial.* 5 (*SC* 341.122).

lifelong asceticism had ruined his digestive system, or that his absorption in pastoral duties obliged him to defer his meals to unsocial hours.[19] It is clear, however, that this mean and kill-joy attitude (as they judged it) dismayed influential circles in the capital, and created a great deal not only of resentment against him but also of libellous gossip. This is confirmed by the painstaking lengths to which Palladios goes to defend his hero, filling page after page with arguments, often strained and even bizarre, to demonstrate that, quite apart from the evils to which lavish hospitality can give rise (sickness, quarrelling, sexual licence), being a good teacher is far superior to being a generous host.[20] He was walking on a tightrope, for Paul had ruled (1 Tim. 3.2) that a bishop should be 'given to hospitality' as well as 'apt to teach'.

Several years later, when he was standing his trial, it was to be alleged of John that he had appropriated and sold valuable marble slabs which Nektarios had assembled with a view to cladding the walls of the church of Anastasia with them.[21] This was the small, highly revered oratory (originally a private house) in which in 379-80, in the difficult days of Arian domination in the city, Gregory of Nazianzos had held forth to the orthodox minority and sustained their spirits. It had been the policy of subsequent emperors to enlarge it greatly, and also to embellish it.[22] It is more than likely that, so far as the facts were concerned, the accusation was correct, but that this was just another example of his impatience with wasteful extravagance. We can easily envisage John, in his zeal for frugality and concern for the efficient use of church funds, suspending a programme of what he regarded as unnecessary decoration. It is also probable that the related charge of having sold off a large number of precious objects belonging to the church provides a further example of his converting treasures he thought unsuitable for the church to hoard to useful purposes.[23]

These drastic economies and high-handed disposals, although making him unpopular in smart society and suspect to critics eager to catch him out, resulted in substantial savings as well as a useful inflow of fresh money. These assets John devoted, Palladios reports,[24] 'to the hospital'; the expression suggests that there was already one attached to the see. Palladios adds that, because the need for such institutions was pressing, he founded several more. The compressed narrative gives no indication when he did this, but the probability is that these foundations were spread over several years. His most striking, and certainly most controversial, initiative of this kind was the establishment, in the countryside outside the city

---

[19] Palladios, *Dial.* 12 (*SC* 341.230-2): cf. Sokrates 6.4; Sozomen 8.9.
[20] *Dial.* 12-13 (*SC* 341.220-66).
[21] See below, p. 222.
[22] Sokrates 5.7; Sozomen 7.5. See R. Janin, *Les églises et les monastères* (Paris 1965), 22-5.
[23] See below, p. 222.
[24] *Dial.* 5 (*SC* 341.122).

walls close to the river Lykos, of a hospital for lepers. Almost all our knowledge of this enterprise (again it should be dated somewhat later than his reform of the palace expenses) comes from a panegyric pronounced by an admirer conventionally known as 'Martyrios'[25] immediately after the news of John's death reached Constantinople in late 407. This contains a vivid description of his sympathy for the victims of the dread disease, his purchase of the land required, the start of the building works, and the furious indignation of the wealthy owners of property in the neighbour-hood.[26]

It would be a mistake to assume that John was a pioneer in this field. It is likely that he was inspired by the example of Basil of Caesarea, who in the early 370s, in the suburbs of his see city, had founded a multipurpose complex, popularly likened to a new town, providing accommodation for sick people, including lepers, and their doctors and ancillary staff.[27] In Constantinople itself Makedonios, semi-Arian bishop in the early 340s and again 350-360, had established a number of poor-houses which almost certainly took in the sick,[28] while in the early 380s, well before John's arrival, we hear of hospices (*xenones*) for the sick attached to the churches and have a vivid picture of the empress Flacilla, Theodosius' first wife, going her rounds of them and personally giving the patients their meals.[29] These settlements seem to have been in the charge of monks, and John's originality, it has been suggested,[30] may be detected in the steps he took to withdraw them from monastic influences and attach them to the central administration of the see. At any rate Palladios hints that he kept the control of his new foundations firmly in his own hands, placing two of his trusted clergy in charge of them and nominating the necessary doctors, cooks, and other staff (he insisted that they should be unmarried).[31]

IV

Next, John turned his attention to his clergy.[32] His object was ostensibly to impose his own high standards on their day-to-day conduct, eradicating any trace of worldliness, self-indulgence, and money-grubbing, but also, it seems clear, to bring them more effectively under his personal control. Sokrates, it is significant, speaks of them as his 'subjects' (*hupekooi*), an expression unusual in this context which is eloquent of his authoritarian style of leadership. His scrutiny, according to Sozomen and Palladios alike,

[25] F. van Ommeslaeghe, *Studia Patristica* XII (*TU* 115), 478-83. See Appendix A.
[26] P 491b-495b; 499a-b.
[27] See esp. Gregory of Nazianzos, *Or.* 43.63 (*PG* 36.577-80).
[28] Sozomen 4.20: cf. 4.27 ('communities of sick and poor').
[29] Theodoret, *HE* 5.19.2-3 (*GCS* 44.314).
[30] G. Dagron, *Naissance d'une capitale* (Paris 1974), 511.
[31] *Dial.* 5 (*SC* 341.122).
[32] For this para. see Sokrates 6.3-4; Sozomen 8.3; Palladios, *Dial.* 5 (*SC* 341.118-20).

covered every facet of their behaviour, from their deportment in public to their meals, which he insisted should be as simple as possible, avoiding both luxury and excess. It is evident that many of them had fallen into indulgent habits, but Sokrates' comment that his criticism was harsher and more violently expressed than was appropriate deserves note. Even Palladios admits that, while he sometimes used 'the flute of reason' in carrying out the investigation of his clergy, he could also resort to 'the cudgel of reprimand'. He was assisted, and enthusiastically abetted, in his inquiries by his archdeacon Sarapion. An Egyptian, rough-spoken, hot-tempered, and a bully, he had been chosen by John himself, who left much of the day-to-day administration of the see in his hands. On one occasion, when most of the clergy were within earshot, he is reported to have said to John in an audible voice, 'You will never, bishop, be able to get control of this lot unless you drive them all with a rod.'[33] As a result of his investigation, and no doubt on Sarapion's advice, John carried out a drastic purge and sacked a number of his clergy for a variety of reasons. These included two deacons (one of them also named John) who had been found guilty, according to Palladios,[34] of murder and fornication respectively.

A practice to which he particularly objected was that of men vowed to celibacy sharing their homes with spiritual sisters (*suneisaktoi*: unmarried women supposedly consecrated to God). Long ago, as a deacon at Antioch, he had published two treatises deploring, with sometimes coarse realism, the moral dangers to which it could too easily give rise.[35] Now he seems to have been informed that numbers of clerics in the capital were given to it, and rushed out a pastoral inveighing against 'the pretence of living together as brothers and sisters'.[36] The general view[37] nowadays is that this was, in all probability, a revised edition of the former of his two Antiochene pamphlets. This evidently caused deep resentment – so deep that he was later to be accused of grossly insulting the reputation of his clergy.[38] Such a charge could scarcely have been made with any plausibility if it had been common knowledge that the ménages to which he objected had in fact been widespread at the time.[39] One is left with the uneasy suspicion that, misled perhaps by exaggerated or even malicious rumours, he may have misjudged the situation and weighed in with unnecessary severity. At the same time John was turning a critical eye on what Palladios calls 'the brigade (*tagma*) of widows' in Constantinople.[40] Although some have thought that these were widows in general,[41] Palladios' use of the military term *tagma*, and

---

[33] Sokrates 1.4.
[34] *Dial.* 8 (*SC* 341.162).
[35] See above pp. 48-51.
[36] Palladios, *Dial.* 5 (*SC* 341.118).
[37] See J. Dumortier, *S. Jean Chrysostome: les cohabitations suspectes* (Paris 1955), 24.
[38] See below, p. 222: also Appendix C.
[39] Cf. J. Dumortier, *JTS* 6 (1955), 101.
[40] *Dial.* (*SC* 341.122-4).
[41] E.g. A.M. Malingrey, *SC* 341.123 n. 4.

the fact that John was able to 'summon' them, suggests that the reference is to the official or 'canonical' widows of the church. From the earliest times widows had had a special status in the Christian community, forming a kind of order, and from the fourth century deaconesses were largely recruited from them. As official widows consecrated to God's service John felt entitled to expect them to observe the strictest standards. He called them before him, carried out a searching review of their behaviour, and when he came across any whose lives he considered worldly or sensual, confronted them with a stark alternative. Either they must take up regular fasting, eschew the indulgence of baths and give up wearing attractive clothes: or they should have done with the fiction of consecrated widowhood and settle as quickly as possible for a second marriage (a state permissible in his eyes, but vastly inferior to the one they were forsaking).

Even his close neighbour and regular attendant, the rich widow and deaconess Olympias, did not escape his scrutiny, but in her case it was for very different reasons and resulted in his giving her rather different advice. He quickly discovered, Sozomen informs us,[42] that while she was disposing of her enormous wealth exclusively for the benefit of Christians and the Christian religion, she was doing so quite indiscriminately, giving to everyone who asked regardless of whether he was in genuine need. Courteously but firmly he called her to order, pointing out that handing money to people who were already well off was like pouring it into the sea. She would benefit a greater number of God's poor, and herself receive a greater spiritual reward, if she planned her charity more selectively. The state, understandably, viewed the fortunes of widows with a jealous eye, and even the devout Theodosius I had authorised legislation declaring null and void the wills of widows or deaconesses leaving money or property to clerics.[43] There is evidence that, under Arkadios, the powerful eunuch Eutropios tried hard to ensure that this legislation was properly applied.[44] It did not, however, preclude benefactions to the church itself, even though, as in this case, they were being placed in effect at the disposal of the bishop. Already under John's spell, the strong-willed aristocrat accepted his counsel, and in due course the bulk of her property, including a huge amount of real estate in Constantinople, was handed over to him for the benefit of the Great Church.[45] We need not doubt that he administered the funds thus placed at his disposal as wisely as he could; it was his considered view[46] that the church, by absorbing the surplus wealth of the rich, should be the divinely appointed agent for its redistribution to the needy. But we can also understand that his success in securing exclusive control of Olympias'

[42] 8.9.
[43] CT 16.2.27 and 28.
[44] G. Dagron, op. cit., 500-1.
[45] *Life of Olympias* 5-7 (*SC* 13bis.416-20).
[46] E.g. *In Act. hom.* 11.3 (*PG* 60.96-8).

entire inheritance aroused, as Sozomen reports, feelings of envy and hostility among the clergy, and perhaps in other quarters as well.

V

Even more intriguing, although at first sight surprising in view of the esteem with which he normally regarded monasticism, was the hostile stance John adopted soon after his installation to the great majority of monks in the capital. 'He had', according to Sozomen,[47] 'a dispute with a large number of the monks [in the city], and especially with Isaac. For while he greatly commended followers of this vocation who lived quietly in their monasteries, and indeed took every care to prevent them suffering injustice and to see that they were provided with whatever they needed, he abused and castigated those who went out of doors and showed themselves in the streets, arguing that by doing so they brought their vocation into disrepute.' Palladios does not dwell on John's attitude to the monks in general, but launches a terse, personal attack on their leader, sneering at 'Isaac, the little Syrian, the layabout, troop-leader of bogus monks, who has worn himself out with incessant slander of bishops'.[48]

To understand these two comments, the one detached and factual and the other bitterly prejudiced, two things must be remembered. First, while the origins of monasticism in Constantinople[49] are obscure (largely because the earliest communities had been founded by semi-Arian bishops[50] whose initiative the orthodox preferred to overlook once they had taken over), it clearly developed after 380 certain highly distinctive features which marked it off from the more usual forms with which John was familiar and of which he approved. In contrast to Antioch, for example, where the monks dwelt in the nearby mountains and only made exceptional appearances in the city, in Constantinople it was an urban phenomenon, with an increasing number of monastic houses within the walls. In organisation, moreover, it seems to have been extremely loose and informal, with the minimum of discipline and little, if any, recognition of episcopal oversight. In this last respect it stood in glaring contrast to the situation in Alexandria, where the vast army of monks was mobilised to be at the bishop's beck and call. Further, the monks of the capital refused to be confined to their monasteries, but roamed freely about the streets and had no hesitation about visiting friends in private houses. They had strong social and, on occasion, political concerns, were frequently fomenters of and participants in street demonstrations, and since they were very numerous were liable to form a powerful

[47] 8.9.
[48] *Dial.* 6 (*SC* 341.126-8).
[49] See esp. J. Pargoire, 'Les débuts du monachisme à Constantinople', *Revue des questions historiques* 65 (1899), 67-143; G. Dagron, 'Le monachisme à Constantinople jusqu'au concile de Chalcédoine', *TM* 4 (1970), 229-76.
[50] Sozomen 4.20.

pressure rabble. They were to cause trouble to the authorities for decades, and even the measures which the council of Chalkedon (451) took to curb them were only partly successful.

Secondly, there can be no doubt that the Isaac mentioned in the two sources quoted is to be identified with the revered figure[51] of that name who, in the orthodox tradition, came to be venerated, with his disciple Dalmatios (an officer of the imperial guard converted to the religious life), as the true founder of monasticism in the capital. Originally a hermit of the Syrian desert, he had come to Constantinople in response to a divine call to do battle with Arianism and had settled in a cell just outside the city. In 378, when the Arian emperor Valens was setting out for his disastrous campaign against the Goths, Isaac had publicly rebuked him and had (correctly, as it turned out) prophesied that, unless he restored the churches to the orthodox, he would not return in safety.[52] Gaoled for his treasonable insolence, he had been freed by Theodosius I, and two high-ranking officers, Saturninos and Victor, had persuaded him to remain in the capital, building him a cell outside the (Constantinian) walls, close to the Xerolophos gate, where the pious emperor often visited him. A colony of monks settled around him, and in 282-3 he and Dalmatios got the first (orthodox) monastery going. Before long he had become the charismatic spiritual leader of the great army of monks in the city.

It is little wonder that John had a dispute, a pretty acrimonious one as it appears, with the multitude of monks he found in the capital. Wandering about the streets singly or in groups, apparently completely undisciplined and visiting their friends in tenements or mansions, they shattered his cherished vision of monastic life as separated from city life by an unbridgeable gulf. Genuine monks, he liked to think,[53] were 'liberated from the market-place and the turmoil that goes on there, with their huts set up in the wilderness, where they have no dealings with anyone but converse with God in the tranquillity of isolation'. Worst of all, they acknowledged no allegiance to himself as their bishop, but gave their entire loyalty to Isaac. As one who knew the situation well has recorded,[54] Isaac visited and supervised the various monastic communities in the city 'as if they were his own children'; when he had ascertained their needs he persuaded comfortably-off people to supply them, and in return 'he was honoured by all the monks, and they paid him their obedience as their father'. It was impossible for John to have patience with monks of this kind ('bogus monks', as his admirer Palladios called them), and he had no hesitation in taking repressive measures to bring them to heel. It is not at all clear what

[51] *AASS* May VII (the Greek *Vita Isaacii* with Latin translation). For his identification with the Isaac mentioned by Sozomen and Palladios see most recently G. Dagron, art. cit., 245.
[52] Sozomen 6.40; Theodoret, *HE* 4.34 (*GCS* 44.272).
[53] *De Lazaro conc.* 3.1 (*PG* 48.932).
[54] Kallinikos (prior c. 406-46 of the Rufinianai monastery near Chalkedon), *Vita Hypatii* 11.4 (ed. G.J.M. Bartelink 1971: *SC* 177.110).

form these took, but there are hints that he tried to force them to accept ordination;[55] there is a story that one of them showed his reluctance by biting his finger when he laid hands on him. His object, clearly, was to reduce what he considered a disorderly rabble to canonical obedience to himself.

John's clash with Isaac, whose hold over the monks he begrudged as trespassing on his own authority, seems (to judge by the language of Sozomen and even more of Palladios) to have been sharper and more personalised. It was to cause deep embarrassment to their admirers, in ancient and also modern times, since both came to be venerated as saints; they preferred to pass it over, as far as possible, in silence.[56] Again, we have no clue to the measures John took to discipline Isaac and limit his activities, but they left 'the little Syrian' with a burning sense of resentment which led him, years later when John was standing his trial, to volunteer a whole sheaf of additional charges against him, including the claim that he himself had suffered much at his hands.[57]

VI

At one level John's reforming efforts were directed, high-mindedly but perhaps unrealistically, at imposing on his clerical and near-clerical subordinates the same rigorous moral standards and life style as he observed himself. At another level a rather different motive can be detected in them: a centralising, authoritarian bishop, he was determined, 'so long as' he 'sat on this throne', to bring every group of churchmen in his diocese under his personal control. It must therefore have been particularly exasperating to him that there was one important group, the so-called Novatians, to which, however much it irked him, he found himself obliged to concede independence.

The Novatians[58] were a rigorist sect which traced its origins to the learned Roman presbyter Novatianus who, in 251, had broken with the new pope, Cornelius, because of his lenient policy in readmitting to communion Christians who had 'lapsed' under persecution. With others who shared his view, he had himself set up as antipope, and with them moved into schism. Completely orthodox in other respects, the Novatians differed from the catholic church only in their insistence that there could be no forgiveness, not only for apostasy but also for the major sins; they called themselves 'the pure' (*katharoi*) or 'the assembly of saints' in contrast to the church, which offered pardon for post-baptismal sin through its penitential system. The sect spread rapidly throughout the empire, and in the

---

[55] Kallinikos, op. cit., 11.8 (*SC* 177.114).
[56] There is no mention of it, for example, in either the *Vita Isaacii* printed in *AASS* May VII or the entry for Isaac (by R. Janin) in *BSS* VII.920-1.
[57] Photios, *Bibliotheca* cod. 59 (Henry 1.56; *SC* 342.112).
[58] See esp. H.J. Vogt, *Coetus sanctorum* (Bonn 1968).

fourth century had a bishop and several churches in Constantinople. Because of their strict adherence to Nicene orthodoxy the Novatians shared to the full with catholics in the persecutions imposed by the official Arianizing bishops, and could point to their confessors and martyrs. As recently as June 383, when Theodosius I was considering measures to end religious divisions, his bishop, Nektarios, had sought the advice of his Novatian colleague, Agelios, and it was the solution proposed by Agelios' reader, Sisinnios, which was accepted. As a result, when the emperor placed a ban, under severe penalties, on all sectarian worship, the Novatians were specifically exempted because of their loyalty to the Nicene faith, being permitted to function freely and hold public services, while their churches were granted the same privileges as those of the catholic church.[59]

This was the situation confronting John when he became bishop of the capital; for all his centralising zeal, there was nothing that even he could do about it. The Novatian bishop was Sisinnios, Agelios' reader and now his successor. As well as being intellectually able and a fine preacher, he was a wit with a flair for mordant repartee.[60] He had been the theological confidant of John's predecessor, Nektarios, and was greatly liked and admired by leading members of the senate. That relations between John and him were not easy is understandable, and John's frustration is vividly portrayed in a confrontation between the two men described by Sokrates.[61] In characteristic fashion John took occasion to rebuke Sisinnios, insisting that the city could not have two bishops. Sisinnios replied that in fact it did not. When John angrily retorted that he seemed to be wanting to be sole bishop, Sisinnios explained that what he had been trying to say was that it was only John in whose eyes he was not a bishop. By this point the interchange was becoming acrimonious, with John threatening that he would prevent Sisinnios from preaching. Fortunately Sisinnios had a sense of humour and quipped, 'I'll richly reward you if you relieve me of such a chore.' This seemed to mollify the stern John, who assured him that he would not silence him if he really found preaching such a burden.[62]

The Novatians were clearly a special case. As a reforming bishop, resolved to assert his authority, he had a much freer hand with clergy and monks belonging to the catholic church, and did everything in his power to make them conform to his ideals. Whatever his success, his uncompromising methods certainly alienated, and made bitter enemies of most of them. As Sokrates, a sharp-eyed observer living in the city, remarked, 'At the very start of his episcopate he appeared so harsh (*trachus*) to churchmen that

---

[59] Sokrates 5.10.
[60] See esp. the picture of him in Sokrates, 6.22; he was particularly well informed about the Novatians.
[61] 6.22.
[62] The suggestions that the anecdote shows that Sisinnios viewed John as his rival as a pulpit orator (R. Janin, *Échos d'Orient* 28 (129), 397), or that John was jealous of him as a preacher (H.J. Vogt, op. cit., 258), seem equally improbable.

they began to hate him, while many felt a revulsion from him and began avoiding him because he was so ill-tempered (*orgilos*).'[63] Even the more sympathetic Sozomen admitted that his natural proneness to be critical of misconduct was compounded when he became a bishop; the acquisition of power made his tongue readier in condemnation and incited him to more violent outbursts against wrongdoers.[64] He added that, as a result of the stern measures he took, 'the clergy and great numbers of the monks became hostile to John, calling him severe, irascible, cruel, and imperious'.[65] Both historians agree that, because of his high-handed and violent treatment of them, his clergy began a whispering campaign to undermine his authority, disseminating (for example) damaging innuendoes about his habit of taking his meals alone. Thus any honeymoon period he may have enjoyed in the first few months after his enthronement was swiftly replaced by deep and widespread unpopularity in circles from which a bishop would normally expect to find loyal backing.

[63] 6.4.
[64] 8.3.
[65] 8.9.

10

The Bishop at Work

I

As bishop of the imperial city John faced a range of responsibilities and opportunities extending far beyond anything that had come his way at Antioch. In this chapter we shall pass in quick review, without regard for strict chronology, the chief areas of his activity and concern, dwelling on one or two of them in greater detail. In passing it should be noted that he was known simply as bishop. The titles of archbishop and patriarch, often mistakenly attributed to him, are not attested for the see of Constantinople until the council of Chalkedon (451).

In the first place, his office gave him an altogether unique status in the capital. In an illuminating aside he recalls that, when visiting the mansions of the great, even the imperial palace itself, the bishop is received with greater deference and honour than prefects or governors.[1] Quite apart from social precedence, however, he now assumed the role of counsellor and ecclesiastical confidant of the emperor and his family. Since Constantine the Great became a Christian, the emperors had relied for advice, on matters of faith and on church affairs generally, on the bishop of the city in which they from time to time resided. Now that the court was permanently settled at Constantinople, that function naturally devolved on its bishop. This meant that John was in frequent and regular contact, except when some really serious break-down of relations occurred, with the palace, and also with the ministers and state officials who continually gathered there. In this and the following chapters we shall be able to observe his relations, usually cordial, sometimes cool, on occasion completely disrupted, with Arkadios and Eudoxia, and to catch occasional glimpses of his dealings with the powerful superintendent of the bedchamber, Eutropios, and other leading personalities of the capital.

Closely connected with, indeed arising out of, this special relationship with the emperor, was the presidency which John now took over, as bishop of Constantinople, of what was coming to be called the 'resident synod' (*sunodos endemousa*).[2] This was a new type of synod, unexemplified else-

---

[1] *In Act. hom.* 3.5 (*PG* 60.41).
[2] Cf. J. Hajjar, *Le synode permanent dans l'église Byzantine des origines au xi siècle* (*OCA* 164, Rome 1962).

where, which seems to have come into existence quite recently, probably during Nektarios' episcopate (381-97). It was composed of the bishops resident in or temporarily visiting the capital, and it met, with the emperor's encouragement and under the chairmanship of the bishop of the see, to discuss and settle matters of ecclesiastical business, great or small, referred to it. There was no shortage of members, for now that the emperor, whose influence could be decisive in church affairs, was settled in Constantinople, many bishops liked to reside there for prolonged spells, while many more flocked there from all corners of the eastern empire to seek solutions to their local problems, or even simply to advance their personal interests or those of their friends. It was natural that the emperor, with his wider responsibilities, should delegate all this multifarious business to the bishop of the capital sitting in conclave with such other bishops as were available. As Anatolios, one of John's successors, was to explain to the council of Chalkedon some sixty years later, 'It is a time-honoured custom that the reverend bishops visiting our famous city should meet together when occasion demands to resolve ecclesiastical disputes and causes, and to give answers to petitioners.'[3] When John assumed this new role, he became effectively the intermediary between the court and the eastern episcopate, and inevitably exercised an influence on the discussion and settlement of its disputes.

Thirdly, there can be little doubt that John's jurisdiction as bishop extended, *de facto* if not yet *de jure*, far beyond the imperial city and the surrounding territory. In 451 the council of Chalkedon was to enact, in its 28th canon,[4] that the 'archbishop' of Constantinople should have authority to consecrate the metropolitans of the three civil dioceses of Pontus, Asiana and Thrace, as well as the bishops of sees in barbarian territories. This effectively transformed Constantinople into a patriarchate, for although ecclesiastical oversight over the dioceses and other regions specified was not mentioned, it was, in the thinking of the times, implied in the right to consecrate the metropolitans.[5] To a large extent, as several bishops present when the canon was discussed testified, this legislation merely gave canonical recognition to existing practice. It is impossible now to trace the precise stages by which the jurisdiction of the imperial see was progressively extended, but it is clear that John played a noteworthy part in the process. Theodoret's statement,[6] made c. 420, that he had exercised oversight over the six provinces of Thrace, the eleven of Asiana, and the eleven of Pontus, is, from the canonical point of view, a palpable error, for the primacy of honour assigned to Constantinople by the council of 381[7] had

---

[3] *ACO* II.i.465-6.
[4] *ACO* II.i.3.88-9.
[5] A. Grillmeier and H. Bacht, *Das Konzil von Chalkedon* (Würzburg 1953), II.472-4 (E. Herman).
[6] *HE* 5.28 (*GCS* 44.329).
[7] See above, pp. 108ff.

not carried with it the right to intervene in the affairs of other churches. Nevertheless John, as we shall discover, never showed any hesitation, when the opportunity offered, about asserting such a right on behalf of his see.

II

Apart from presiding at the liturgy, John's most conspicuous function as bishop was preaching. At special seasons, such as Lent and the festival days following Easter, he might preach daily, but this would have been highly exceptional; his normal practice seems to have been to preach every Sunday and feast-day when not taken on business outside the capital. In one passage he remarks that he has been expounding the scriptures 'twice a week',[8] but this cannot be taken as a rigid rule. Most of his sermons were given in Hagia Sophia, his cathedral, but many others, as occasion demanded, in Hagia Irene (the oldest church in the city), in the basilica of the Holy Apostles, in the little Anastasia church, or in other churches or martyrs' shrines. A bishop customarily preached from his throne at the far end of the apse well behind the altar (in those days not concealed from the congregation, as today in the east, by an icon-bearing screen), but John preferred normally to address the people at closer range, seated at the ambo or pulpit-like lectern just west of the chancel from which the scripture lessons were chanted.[9] The explanation usually given, that his voice was not strong enough to carry from the distant apse, has the support of Sokrates,[10] but it is also likely that he wished to establish a close personal rapport with his hearers, looking them in the eyes as he spoke.

John's preaching proved immensely popular. The people were so excited by it, Sozomen reports,[11] so insatiable in their appetite for it, that there was a real danger of their injuring one another as they jostled and shoved to get closer to him so as to hear more distinctly what he was saying. A less friendly witness, the pagan historian Zosimos, paid him the backhanded compliment, 'The fellow was quite clever at bringing the ignorant masses under his spell.'[12] The surviving sermons themselves confirm their rapturous reception, containing (as we saw his earlier ones at Antioch do) frequent references to the applause which greeted them. As always, John was sceptical of this, and in one passage confesses that when he heard his words clapped, his instinctive reaction was delight, but that this human feeling turned to despondency when he got home and reflected that the cheering crowd had derived no benefit from his teaching.[13] So he tried to lay down

---

[8] *In Act. hom.* 29.3 (*PG* 60.127).
[9] Sozomen 8.5.
[10] 6.5.
[11] 8.5.
[12] 5.23.4.
[13] *In Act. hom.* 30.4 (*PG* 60.226-7).

the rule that his words should be listened to and, if necessary, admired in silence. At this point the cheering broke out afresh. Having rebuked it, he reminded his audience that both the pagan philosophers and the apostles, even Christ himself delivering the Sermon on the Mount, had been listened to without interruption. Much better than noisy applause, the proper place for which was the theatre or the public baths, was the secret approbation of the heart as one reflects, at home or in the market place, on the words spoken.

Notwithstanding the magnetism of his eloquence, John sometimes had occasion to express disappointment at the sparseness of his congregation.[14] Sozomen, however, speaks of great crowds, including many heretics and even pagans, flocking to hear him.[15] Some, he admits, came out of curiosity, attracted by his reputation as an orator. But the attachment of the people, it is evident from an episode he relates,[16] was all too obviously to him personally. One Sunday, when to their surprise he had, out of customary hospitality and respect for his age, invited an elderly bishop from Galatia to preach in his place, the huge congregation expressed their disappointment by streaming out of the church with loud complaints. Even he, however, for all their devotion to him, could not draw them to Hagia Sophia when alternative excitements like the theatre and horse-racing were available. This particularly exasperated him, and one of his most colourful and brilliant addresses is a tirade, delivered on Sunday 3 July 399, denouncing the shamelessness of the crowds which had forsaken the church on the two previous days, preferring to watch the races in the nearby hippodrome on the Friday (when they should have been contemplating the Lord's supreme sacrifice on the cross), and on the Saturday (when they should have been preparing penitentially for Sunday) to succumb to the seductions of the theatre.[17] It is a reasonable surmise[18] that the law[19] published on 27 August 399 banning the holding of theatrical shows, horse-races, and other spectacles 'designed to make people effeminate', on the Lord's day (unless, of course, it coincided with the emperor's birthday) was inspired by him.

John's output of sermons was much smaller at Constantinople than at Antioch, but it included some interesting new types. In addition to homilies given at festivals or other church celebrations, quite a number of his addresses were prompted by circumstances in his own life or political happenings; we shall consider some of the more important of these in later chapters. An entirely fresh category is the sermon on a state occasion, a

---

[14] *Hom. 4 in eos qui non adfuerunt* 1; *Hom. 5 de studio praesentium* 1; *Hom. 7 in templo s. Anastasiae (PG* 63.477; 485; 493).
[15] 8.5.
[16] *In illud, Pater meus (PG* 63.511-12).
[17] *C. ludos et theatra (PG* 56.263-70). For its date see J. Pargoire, *Échos d'Orient* 3 (1899-1900), 151-62.
[18] Baur, 2.89.
[19] CT 2.8.23.

noteworthy example being the short panegyric[20] he delivered in the church of the Holy Apostles, in the presence of Arkadios and Eudoxia, on 17 January 399, the anniversary of the death of Theodosius I (whose body lay in the adjacent mausoleum). The message he impressed on the imperial couple was the novel one that the dead emperor deserved respect, not because he had been sovereign and had worn the purple mantle, but because he had been a devout Christian who had clothed himself with Christ in baptism. His armour had been the breastplate of righteousness, the sword of the Spirit, and the shield of faith. It was with these, and these alone, that he had overcome the usurper Maximus (in August 385), and then the puppet emperor Eugenius (on 5/6 September 394 at the river Frigidus). With a dramatic flourish John recalls how, on the latter occasion, when the conflict was at its height and his own forces looked like being defeated, Theodosius had jumped from his horse, cast away his shield and, kneeling on the ground, implored God's help.[21] Miraculously the wind changed, the tide of battle turned, and Eugenius' troops were forced to surrender and hail Theodosius as their emperor. He had emerged as glorious not simply because of his victory, but because he had won it by reliance on God. To savour to the full John's eulogy we should remember that the battle was the final encounter between a Christian emperor and traditional paganism, for Eugenius, himself a Christian, was backed by prominent pagans determined to rescue the ancient cults. Christians regarded its result as clear evidence of divine intervention.[22]

As at Antioch, a large proportion of John's sermons were scripture homilies. Notwithstanding the distractions of episcopal office, he quickly resumed the systematic exposition of the Pauline epistles, and several courses spread irregularly over his years as bishop have come down. The earliest seem to have been fifteen homilies on Philippians and five on Colossians,[23] given in spring-summer and early autumn 399 respectively. Next came fifty-five homilies on Acts;[24] it will be argued later that these were started soon after 12 July 400 and were continued, with breaks, into early 401. They were followed, probably after a prolonged interval, by eleven homilies on 1 Thessalonians, five on 2 Thessalonians.[25] That the latter series came directly after the former is suggested both by the close similarity of subject-matter and by the explanation John gives in its first paragraph[26] of Paul's reasons for writing a second epistle. A plausible dating would be 402, after his return in April from the journey he made to

---

[20] *PG* 63.491-2. It seems to be a fragment of a larger whole now lost.
[21] Cf. Rufinus, *HE* 2 (11).33 (*PL* 539-40). For the battle see Ambrose, *Explan. in psalm.* 36.25.2-4 (*CSEL* 64.91).
[22] See J. Straub, 'Eugenius', *RAC* 6.869-72.
[23] *PG* 62.173-299; 299-392.
[24] *PG* 60.13-384. For the date see below pp. 166-8.
[25] *PG* 62.391-468; 467-500.
[26] *In 2 Thess. hom.* 1.1 (*PG* 62.467-9).

Asia Minor in the early months of that year.[27] The three homilies on Philemon[28] cannot be placed very long after these, since in the third he claims[29] to be fulfilling a promise (viz. that he would explain how God's mercifulness can be squared with his sending people to hell) which he had 'recently' (*proen*) made to the congregation, in fact in his eighth homily on 1 Thessalonians. Finally, we have thirty-four homilies on Hebrews,[30] the last of John's great series of commentaries, published (as the heading in the MSS records) after his death by the presbyter Constantinos on the basis of surviving shorthand notes. They were probably preached in the winter of 402-3.

The relative order of these courses, and their approximate dates, have been worked out largely from internal evidence.[31] For example, John's sombre comment,[32] in Homily 2 on Philippians, that, 'while many paupers lead lives free from care, government ministers, wealthy people, grandees have suffered more miserable fates than criminals, bandits, and grave-robbers' has been widely taken as a veiled allusion to Eutropios' arbitrary rule, under which such reversals of fortune were regular occurrences. If this is correct, the homily must predate the powerful eunuch's downfall in July 399.[33] On the other hand, in his seventh homily on Colossians John illustrates the futility of earthly power by citing an example from 'present-day affairs', an exalted official who only yesterday sat on a raised-up tribunal, with heralds announcing his approach and clearing the streets before him, but who now cowers abject and alone, bereft of everything.[34] The wretched man can only be Eutropios; and since, though disgraced he is still alive, the homily must have been preached in autumn or early winter 399. Again, hints in the 2 Thessalonians homilies[35] that John's congregation is split into factions, awash with ugly rumours against himself, suggest a relatively late stage in his episcopate, while the mention of someone else having been temporarily responsible for baptising the catechumens points unmistakably to Severian of Gabala, who was to carry out his episcopal functions during his absence in Asia during the early months of 402, including Easter.[36] Finally, while everyone agrees that the Hebrews homilies belong to the closing stages of John's ministry in Constantinople, they nowhere betray any sign of strained relations between him and the imperial couple. They might conceivably be fitted into the period of resumed friend-

---

[27] See below, pp. 173-7; 181.
[28] *PG* 62.701-20.
[29] *In Philem. hom.* 3.2; *in 1 Thess. hom.* 8.4 (*PG* 62.716-18; 445-6).
[30] *PG* 63.9-236.
[31] See esp. M. von Bonsdorf, *Zur Predigttätigkeit des J. Chrysostomus* (Helsingfors 1922), 76-117.
[32] *PG* 62.198.
[33] See below, p. 147.
[34] *In Col. hom.* 7.3 (*PG* 62.346-7).
[35] *In 2 Thess. hom.* 2.1-2; 4.4 (*PG* 62.473-4; 491-2).
[36] See below, p. 173.

ship after his return from his first exile in early October 403,[37] but it seems much preferable to place them well before that troubled autumn, indeed in the preceding winter, since in the eleventh he speaks of the extreme cold and chides his listeners for neglecting the poor who are exposed to it.[38]

III

The subject-matter of John's sermons and homilies in the capital is broadly identical with that of his Antiochene ones, although less space is devoted to theological polemics. There are, for example, virtually no serious critiques of Manichaeism; on Syrian soil he had come face to face with it at every turn, but probably met it very rarely at Constantinople. He occasionally delivers carefully argued attacks on Arianism, e.g. in two sermons given on 17 and 24 July 399, the one claiming that the words 'My Father is working still, and I am working' (John 5.17) indicate the Son's perfect equality with the Father, the other seeking to refute Anomoean misinterpretations of the text 'The Son can do nothing of his own accord but only what he sees the Father doing' (John 5.19).[39] But there are no set-piece courses directed against it; he preferred, as we shall see, to conduct his anti-Arian campaign in a populist manner in the streets.

On the other hand, on the theme of marriage, which he seems to have constantly pondered, it is interesting to observe a small but significant extension of the relaxed, positive approach which, no doubt as a result of pastoral experience, he had been coming to adopt at Antioch.[40] Tackling in Homily 12 on Colossians the question how a man and his wife become 'one flesh', he explains that, just as when one takes the purest gold and fuses it with other gold, so in sexual intercourse the woman receives from her husband 'the rich, fecund element' (*to piotaton*: he chooses this periphrasis rather than *sperma*, i.e. semen), nourishes and warms it, and then, when she has contributed something of her own substance, gives back a child, which is a sort of bridge linking the three as one flesh.[41] It is the pleasure involved in the act, he emphasises, which welds the two spouses together; and even if no child results, the two still become one flesh, for their intercourse (*mixis*) accomplishes their union, fusing and commingling their two bodies just as when we pour myrrh into olive oil. Evidently many in his audience were embarrassed by his frank speaking. The reason for this, he retorts, is their own loose, indeed prurient attitude to marriage, only too glaringly betokened by the licentious behaviour they accept at weddings. They should recognise that marriage is the gift of God, the very root of our existence. There is no need to blush when talking openly about marriage,

---

[37] See below, p. 235.
[38] *In Heb. hom.* 11.3 (*PG* 63.94).
[39] *PG* 63.511-16; 56.247-56. For their dates see J. Pargoire, art. cit., 157-9.
[40] See above, pp. 96f.
[41] *In Col. hom.* 12.5-6 (*PG* 62.388).

which is an honourable state (Heb. 13.4) and an image of the presence of Christ.

In the moral and social fields, again, the ground covered is much the same, but John's tone becomes sharper. He had always, for example, condemned the seductions of the racecourse and the theatre, but nowhere with such violence (or, for that matter, such psychological insight) as in the sermon of 13 July 399 mentioned in the previous section. First, he graphically recalls how, on the preceding Friday, when he heard from his palace the shouting of the fans in the nearby hippodrome, he had held his head in shame for them.[42] Instead of reflecting on Christ's sacrifice, these so-called Christians were leaping up and down and screaming themselves hoarse, their souls in degrading bondage to their passions. To make matters worse, they had next day crowded into an even viler den of perdition, the theatre, old men disgracing their white hair, young men tossing their youth to destruction, fathers to all intents and purposes murdering their children.[43] Even in the street a man's self-control can be knocked off balance when he passes a pretty woman, but in the theatre his eyes are fixed on a slut shamelessly parading her charms, singing lewd songs, making suggestive movements and gestures. Of course he falls under her spell, for his body is only flesh and blood, and in his imagination he slips into having sex with her. Nor is that all: when the theatre shuts its doors and he returns home, he in effect takes her with him, for he cannot get her glances, the swaying of her body, her provocative poses out of his mind. So besotted is he with these sexual fantasies that his wife and family seem dull and commonplace by comparison and, as the blaze the temptress has kindled spreads, the stability of his home and the happiness of his marriage go up in smoke.

John's denunciation of the rich, above all of the vulgar display of their wealth, also reached fresh heights. Palladios singled this out for special mention, reporting that 'he brandished the sword of rebuke against the wealthy', urging them to show humility and avoid condescension.[44] No doubt the capital offered even more glaring examples of the abuse of riches than Antioch. So we find him railing at the luxurious banquets, the silver and gold dinner-services, the beautiful, richly clad servants of the well-off, or at the expensive clothes and elaborate ornaments favoured by upper-class ladies. Flaunting such attire is more dishonourable and shameful than if they were completely naked, as Eve had been in Paradise before her sin. What is the point of all this extravagance if the soul within is polluted?[45] What chiefly scandalises him, as we should expect, is the stark contrast between conspicuous affluence and the appalling lot of the poor. His indignation reaches a crescendo when he savages rich ladies who, while the

[42] *C. ludos et theatra* 1 (*PG* 56.263-5).
[43] *C. ludos et theatra* 2 (*PG* 56.265-7).
[44] *Dial.* 5 (*SC* 341.124).
[45] E.g. *In Act. hom.* 35.5 (*PG* 60.252).

poor (also made in God's image) are shivering with cold, insist on having toilet utensils made for them of solid silver, as if they thought their excrement merited privileged treatment.[46] 'What senselessness, what madness is this! The church has so many poor standing around it, and has also so many children who are rich; yet she is unable to give relief to one poor person. "One man is hungry, another gets drunk" (1 Cor. 11.21); one man defecates in a silver pot, another has not so much as a crust of bread.'

This particular sally caused great offence. He admitted as much in his next homily a few days later, and begged forgiveness. He had no wish, he explained, to violate the canons of decency, but felt obliged to speak out on the interest of his hearers' salvation.[47] In an address given (probably) in spring 400 he freely acknowledged that his incessant diatribes against the rich aroused angry protests – 'Will you never stop sharpening your tongue against the well-off?'[48] They go far to explain the dislike in which he was coming to be held among the propertied classes, as well as his growing popularity with the common people, who felt sure that he was their champion. No amount of criticism, however, could deter him from proclaiming, for example, how much better it is to sit down at table with the poor than with the rich, notwithstanding the unbridgeable gulf between the simplicity of the one and the luxurious style of the other, since at the poor man's table one comes face to face with Christ.[49] Nor can he resist reminding his congregation, again and again, that the Lord makes not the slightest difference between a ragged old man, filthy and with his nose dribbling, and the handsome young man who wears the diadem and the purple, but invites both to his spiritual banquet to receive exactly the same benefits.[50] The rich should never be repelled by the wretched poor, but should assist them, share their food with them, give them shelter in their homes.[51] Above all, they should use their wealth to help them: the man who denies alms to the starving is as much his brother's murderer as was Cain.[52]

John even floats, in a passage[53] which is tantalising for other reasons (for example, are the population figures accurate, or mere guesses?), a utopian scheme for solving the problem of poverty for Christians; it is inspired by the report in Acts 4.32-4 that the earliest believers in Jerusalem 'had everything in common', with the result that 'there was not a needy person among them'. Let us suppose, he suggests, that there are 100,000 Christians in Constantinople, and that in the entire city there are not more than 50,000 poor people. If all the citizens above the poverty line sold their

---

[46] *In Col. hom.* 7.4-5 (*PG* 62.349-52).
[47] *In Col. hom.* 8.1 (*PG* 62.351).
[48] *Cum Saturninus et Aurelianus* 2 (*PG* 52.415-16). For its date see below, pp.153f.
[49] *In Col. hom.* 1.4 (*PG* 62.304-5).
[50] *In 1 Thess. hom.* 11.4-5 (*PG* 62.466-7).
[51] *In Act. hom.* 45.3-6 (*PG* 60.318-19).
[52] *In 1 Thess. hom.* 8.4 (*PG* 62.444).
[53] *In Act. hom.* 11.3 (*PG* 60.97-8).

land, houses, movable goods, everything in fact of which they are possessed, and pooled the proceeds, they would realise a million pounds weight of gold, perhaps two or even three times as much. If this were shared out, the whole population would be able to live comfortably, especially if, since living separately is more expensive, they saved money by living in community like monks. As a bonus, such a mutually beneficial rearrangement of community finances would convert the pagans. Up to a point John was teasing his auditors. The poor should not get excited, he assured them, nor the rich alarmed; there was no prospect of his idyllic project being carried out. Yet he remained convinced that, if it were, both rich and poor would be happier. What is interesting to modern students is that he always envisaged the voluntary charity of individuals as being the agent of such a redistribution. It never occurred to him, although often described as 'almost a socialist',[54] that central government should have any responsibility for it.[55]

IV

The new bishop did not confine his efforts to promote Christian faith and morals to sermons. He was well aware of the dramatic impact of the liturgy, religious ceremonial, solemn processions, and the like, and exploited it to the full. An example which Palladios records[56] was the encouragement he gave to men (women he advised to stay at home at such dangerous hours)[57] to attend night services; they could in fact last throughout the night, and so were called *pannuchides*. He had been used to, and greatly valued, nocturnal devotions at Antioch,[58] and may have been disappointed not to find them in vogue at Constantinople. He seems to have had some success, for about three years later we find him rhapsodising, with haunting eloquence, on the spiritual benefits such vigils bestow.[59] When darkness and silence enfold everything, our minds are purer, lighter, more spiritually alert, and we are brought to a true contrition when we gaze up at the sky spangled with stars as with ten thousand eyes, and experience to the full the joy of contemplating our Creator. Palladios comments acidly that some of John's clergy were not so thrilled at having to get out of bed and work at such unsocial hours.

Sometimes confused with this initiative,[60] but in fact quite distinct, was another which John took, this time with the object of foiling Arian propa-

---

[54] So, e.g., J.B. Bury, *History of the Later Roman Empire* (London 1923), 1.139.
[55] Cf. S. Giet, 'La doctrine de l'appropriation des biens chez quelques-uns des pères', *Recherches de science religieuse* 35 (1948), 55-91.
[56] *Dial.* 5 (*SC* 341.124).
[57] See *De sacerdotio* 3.3 (*SC* 272.216).
[58] *In Oziam hom.* 1.1; *Comm. in ps.* 133.1 (*SC* 277.44; *PG* 55.386-7).
[59] *In Act. hom.* 26.3 (*PG* 60.202).
[60] E.g. (apparently) by A.M. Malingrey, *SC* 341.124 n. 2.

ganda. Whatever the truth of the suggestion that he had been specifically appointed to consolidate the Nicene orthodoxy dear to the imperial family,[61] it was inevitable that he should be disturbed to discover a significant, aggressive Arian minority in the capital. Theodosius I, it is true, had ejected them from the churches of the city,[62] but they continued to hold regular services just outside the walls. Their practice was to assemble, during the night between Saturday and Sunday and on the eves of great festivals, in public porticoes just within the gates, and then chant Arian-slanted hymns antiphonally throughout the night.[63] When dawn broke, they would proc-ess, still chanting their hymns, through the centre of the city, march out through the gates, and then celebrate the liturgy at their customary meeting-places. As well as proclaiming the specifically Arian teachings, their hymns regularly caricatured or taunted the orthodox doctrine, one popular refrain provocatively asking, 'Where are the people who declare the Three to be but one single power?'

These colourful propagandist manifestations seem to have been effec-tive, sufficiently so at any rate to worry John that simple folk might be enticed from their allegiance to orthodoxy by them. To counter them he therefore set himself to organise rival nocturnal processions involving his own congregation, with antiphonal choirs intoning the dogmas of Nicaea. Indeed, he contrived that these processions of his were more elaborate and spectacular than the Arian ones, carrying as they did silver crosses with blazing tapers fixed to them. What is of especial interest is that, in setting up these religious diversions, he had the enthusiastic support and co-op-eration of the empress Eudoxia, who not only met the cost of the silver crosses, but lent John a favourite chamberlain, the eunuch Brison,[64] a skilled musician, to train and lead the choirs. As was to be expected, the Arians were furious at having their brilliant propaganda weapon copied, and were determined to exact their revenge. By design or accident, the rival processions clashed one night, a vicious street battle broke out, there were casualties (some fatal) on both sides, and Brison himself was gashed on the forehead by a stone. The disastrous affray gave the government a pretext, which it no doubt welcomed, for banning all such public hymn-singing by the Arians, although Sozomen reports that the orthodox kept up the practice started by John 'right down to the present day', i.e. the 440s.

Another field in which John as bishop sought to stimulate faith and devotion by magnificent liturgical improvisations was the public venera-tion of saints and martyrs. An example of the veneration of saints was the day-long excursion in honour of the apostles Peter and Paul of which we are given a snapshot glimpse in the sermon denouncing theatrical shows

---

[61] See above, p. 105.
[62] e.g. CT 16.5.6 (10 Jan. 381).
[63] For this and the following paragraph see Sokrates 6, and Sozomen 8.8.
[64] He was to remain a valued friend of John's: see *PLRE* 2, 242.

already cited. John recalls how, on the previous Wednesday, he and his congregation, 'our entire city' in fact, had crowded into the church of the Apostles, where they spent some time praising Peter and his brother Andrew, Paul and his aide Timothy.[65] Their original intention, apparently, had been to cross the Bosporus to The Oak (Drys) or Rufinianai[66] (now Caddebostani), 4 km south-east of Chalkedon, where Rufinus, the former prefect, had erected a splendid mansion and a church enriched with relics of the two apostles, and pay tribute to them there. A violent storm with pelting rain had at first frustrated the plan and forced them to seek refuge in Holy Apostles, which contained relics of Andrew and Timothy but not, alas, of Peter and Paul. At last, however, the wind and the rain ceased; John and his flock went down to the shore, boarded boats and braved the sea-passage. After a few hours they were holding 'a spiritual festival' in Rufinus' church, proclaiming the struggles and triumphs of the two apostles.

In the fourth century, as we have noted earlier,[67] the cult of martyrs was in full swing among Christians, but Constantinople, having been founded after the cessation of persecution, unfortunately could not boast of martyrs of its own. From 381 onwards, if not earlier, the authorities had been diligent in importing sacred relics, some from places which had a surplus of them and others of special relevance to the city, and installing them in shrines where they could be venerated. Theodosius I, for example, had had the remains of Paul the Confessor, an early orthodox bishop of Constantinople who had been exiled to Cucusos in Armenia and, it was supposed,[68] strangled there, brought back in 381 and solemnly placed in the church which his Arian successor Makedonios had erected.[69] John seems to have entered into the good work with enthusiasm, and we have graphic accounts of two splendid occasions when he presided over the reception of relics of hallowed persons. Both have generally been taken to date from 398-9, the honeymoon period of his relations with the imperial family, largely because they represent the emperor and the empress, particularly the latter, as eagerly collaborating with their bishop, but it has been persuasively argued[70] that the second should be placed after 9 January 400, when Eudoxia was proclaimed Augusta, on the ground that she is depicted as wearing the diadem, a part of the imperial insignia which was reserved exclusively to a reigning Augustus or Augusta.

The first occasion was the arrival in Constantinople, from Sinope (Sinop) on the southern shores of the Black Sea, of certain relics of the martyr

---

[65] *PG* 56.265. For this paragraph see J. Pargoire, art. cit., 153-5.
[66] Cf. J. Pargoire, 'Rufinianes', *BZ* 8 (1899), 429-77.
[67] See above, pp. 66f.
[68] For doubts about his murder see W. Telfer, *HTR* 43 (1950), 88.
[69] Sozomen 7.10; Sokrates 5.9.
[70] K.G. Holum, *Theodosian Empresses* (California 1982), 56.

Phokas,[71] a gardener who was to become patron of sailors. The ship transporting them docked on a Saturday, when John delivered an address which has been lost. In his sermon next day he recalled how the martyr had yesterday been carried in triumph through the main square of the city, and encouraged the eager congregation to escort him today by sea, with lighted torches which would set the waves ablaze, to his final resting-place.[72] No one, not even a girl or a married woman, had any excuse for absenting himself, since the emperor and empress had themselves left the palace to join them in escorting the holy man to the shrine in which they planned to place him. As they had to make the journey by boat, it seems likely that this was in Ortaköy, on the European shore of the Bosporus about 4 km north of the Golden Horn, where Basil I (867-86) was to establish a monastery in honour of Phokas in the ninth century and where a Greek Orthodox church bearing his name can be seen today.[73]

The second was, if anything, a more spectacular celebration. Relics of three martyrs had arrived in Constantinople, and now had to be taken to the shrine prepared for them. The martyrs' names are not given, but there is a strong case[74] for identifying them with Sisinnius, Martyrius and Alexander,[75] who had been brutally done to death in Anaunia (Val di Non), in the Tridentine region of north Italy, in 397; bishop Vigilius of Trent had written to John promising to send him some relics.[76] These were now borne by night, in a vast torchlight procession which emptied the city, along the sea-shore to the church of St Thomas at Drypia, more than 13 km west of the city centre. John himself marched in front, and at dawn preached the festival sermon in the *martyrion*.[77] Claiming to be 'drunk with spiritual joy', he rapturously described how the enormous crowd, comprising every rank from courtiers and state officials to the humble poor, had trudged the entire way, the rich abandoning their chariots. Their torches had given the sea, alongside which they had marched, the appearance of being on fire. The Christ-loving empress, he exulted, throwing away her diadem and purple robe, had herself followed the veiled casket on foot like a handmaid, repeatedly touching it and so drawing spiritual power from its hallowed contents and encouraging ordinary folk to do likewise. In an extended climax he apostrophised Eudoxia personally, assuring her that not only the present but all future generations would proclaim her blessed for her unparalleled devotion to the holy martyrs and for the humility with which, casting aside all pomp and circumstance and mingling on equal terms with the common people, she had accompanied them to their shrine.

[71] His relics were widely distributed, his head being kept at Rome: Asterios of Amasea, *PG* 40.309.
[72] *PG* 50.699-706.
[73] *AB* 30 (1911), 256-7.
[74] J. Vanderspoel, *CQ* 36 (1986), 239-55.
[75] *BSS* XI. 1251-4 (Igino Rogger).
[76] *Ep.* 2 (*PL* 13.552-8).
[77] *PG* 63.467-72.

Arkadios had not followed the reliquary on the long journey to Drypia, nor been present at John's address. On the empress's prudent advice, the preacher explained, he had stayed at home in case his cavalry escort should endanger the milling crowds of devotees. But Eudoxia had promised, John assured the congregation, that he would attend the liturgy on the following day. The indolent but devout sovereign duly arrived, with his full military bodyguard, and, having doffed his diadem and ordered his soldiers to lay down their arms, did respectful obeisance to the heroic martyrs; but he was careful to take his departure before John got started on his second sermon.[78] His premature leave-taking, however, should be attributed to temperamental lethargy rather than any lack of confidence in his bishop. Indeed, the whole episode, as well as being a remarkable illustration of John's propagandist methods – perhaps, too, of his skill at arranging colourful diversions as exciting as, but much more edifying than, the theatre and the hippodrome – provides vivid proof of the cordial relations he enjoyed, certainly at the start of his episcopate but also for prolonged periods before the final break, with the imperial couple. His first sermon, too, with its astonishing build-up of flattery, demonstrates that the stern bishop, normally so ready to find fault with great persons, was quite ready, when the occasion demanded, to be as extravagantly fulsome in his tributes to royalty as any Byzantine court prelate.

V

Among John's responsibilities as bishop was oversight of all the charitable institutions in and around the city. In addition to hospitals for the sick,[79] these included numerous poor-houses (*ptocheia*); some of them dated back to the Arian bishop Makedonios, and they were usually attached to churches. Although detailed information is lacking, it seems reasonable to suppose that, when John assumed control, he centralised their administration and brought them under his personal supervision.[80] Outside the city itself and in a rather different field, we hear of his efforts to evangelise the peasants of Thrace, and to encourage landed proprietors in rural districts to build churches on their estates rather than, as many were prone to do, shopping-centres, baths, and taverns, which would only make country folk as decadent as town dwellers.[81] They should also maintain clergy to man the church and ensure that regular services would be held and the holy sacrifice offered each Sunday. How satisfying they would find it to be carried in a litter to the house of God, knowing that they had built it themselves, and after attending the morning and evening hymns invite the

[78] *PG* 63.473-8.
[79] For these see above, pp. 119f.
[80] See G. Dagron, *Naissance d'une capitale* (Paris 1974), 510-11.
[81] *In Act. hom.* 18.4 (*PG* 60.147-8).

priest home as a guest at their table. With all these local preoccupations it seems remarkable that he found time and energy to organise campaigns, outside Constantinople and in areas remote from its jurisdiction, both to eradicate the lingering remains of paganism and near-pagan heresy, and to promote missionary work among barbarians. These campaigns provide evidence not only of his zeal for evangelism, but also of the enhanced role he was determined to give to the see of the capital.

Thus John was responsible, with government authority and help, for securing the closure of the pagan temples still in use at Gaza, the important, obstinately pagan port on the coast of Palestine, and later their complete destruction (including that of the world-famous Marneion, or temple of Marnas, the Cretan Zeus), and the settlement of Christian missionaries in the area. In his *Life* of his bishop, Porphyrios of Gaza (395-420), Mark the Deacon relates how Porphyrios had sent him to Constantinople in 398 to beg the emperor to suppress these temples; he had also furnished him with a personal letter to John.[82] This John had shown to Eutropios, and as a result of the eunuch's intervention an edict was shortly after published shutting the temples down. Although doubt has been thrown on large portions of Mark's narrative, there is no reason to suspect the authenticity of this section. A couple of years later, however, John was upset to learn that the Marneion was still functioning, and again used his influence at court to obtain a further edict ordering its complete destruction.[83] According to Theodoret,[84] he also dispatched a group of monks to Gaza; and the historian adds that the money required to pay the workmen was not defrayed by the imperial treasury but by John himself, who persuaded certain wealthy, devout ladies to make liberal contributions. Theodoret also reports[85] that John wrote to the then bishop of Kyrrhos (some 100 km north-east of Antioch), urging him to take severe measures against adherents of the Marcionite heresy,[86] and promising him government support in these worthy endeavours.

John's main field of missionary work was among the Goths, the great majority of whom were Arians of the radical Anomoean brand.[87] By an accident of history Christianity had originally been brought to the Goths north of the Danube by Ulfila (c. 311-83), who had been consecrated when this was the official orthodoxy. In spite of his seven-year mission, ending in 347-8, the main body of Goths remained heathen, but when Valens allowed them to settle in the empire south of the Danube in 376, a condition

[82] Ch. 26 (ed. H. Grégoire and M.A. Kugener, Paris 1960: pp. 22-3).
[83] See below, pp. 168f.
[84] *HE* 5.29 (*GCS* 44.329-30).
[85] *HE* 5.31 (*GCS* 44.330-1).
[86] A dualist heresy which contrasted the NT God of love with the OT God of justice.
[87] See above, p.11.

had been their conversion to the faith,[88] naturally in the Arianizing form professed by the emperor. John found numbers of Goths settled in Constantinople, and assigned a church, almost certainly that of Paul the Confessor mentioned in the previous section, for their use, appointing priests, deacons, and readers proficient in the Gothic language to service it.[89] The services were, of course, orthodox, and he himself on occasion preached in it, using an interpreter. In this way 'he rescued many from their error' (Theodoret). There survives, in fact, one of the sermons he delivered there, an enormously long homily[90] somewhat patronising in tone, in which John, recalling that a Gothic preacher had preceded him, insists that there is nothing disgraceful in his arranging for barbarians to stand up and speak in church. Had not Isaiah prophesied (65.25) that wolves and lambs would feed together? He had not been talking about mere animals but predicting that 'the savage part of mankind' would be brought to gentleness by the gospel message. This happy situation, he claims, has been realised today, when we see 'the most barbarous of humans standing alongside the sheep of the church, sharing with them a common pasture and a single fold, with the same table set before all'. Since Abraham had been a barbarian who received his call in what is now Persia, Moses had grown up in a barbarian home and the Magi had come from barbarian Persia, no one should be surprised or dismayed to hear barbarians proclaiming the word in church. He was careful to slip in a firm rebuttal of the Arian position:[91] 'Even when the Son was in the virgin's womb, he was with the Father. Don't inquire how, or demand proofs. When God is accomplishing his work, only faith, assent and confession are required.' He did so, however, unprovocatively, and it must quickly have got around that in the bishop the Goths had a friend who sympathised with them and whom they could trust.

In addition, to judge by two letters John was later to write in exile,[92] he set up a community of Gothic monks in Constantinople on property which had belonged to the general Promotos, i.e. just south of Holy Apostles. This may have served, among other things, as a training-school for Gothic clergy.[93] But his zeal for promoting orthodox Christianity ranged far beyond the capital and its resident Goths. On the one hand, he dispatched missionaries, probably monks, to work among the nomadic Goths along the lower Danube.[94] He also consecrated (when we do not know) a Goth named Unila, apparently a man of outstanding ability, to be bishop of Christian Goths

---

[88] P. Heather, 'The crossing of the Danube and the Gothic conversion', *GRBS* 27 (1986), 289-318.

[89] Theodoret, *HE* 5.30 (*GCS* 44.330).

[90] *PG* 63.499-511.

[91] *PG* 63.504.

[92] *Epp.* 14.5; 207 (*PG* 52.618; 726-7).

[93] G. Dagron, *Naissance d'une capitale* (Paris 1974), 466. For the location of *Ta Promotou* see R. Janin, *Les églises et les monastères* (Paris 1962), 229.

[94] Theodoret, *HE* 5.31 (*GCS* 44.330-1).

settled in the Crimea, where he seems to have accomplished a great deal in a relatively short time.[95] On the other hand, he would appear to have had a lively interest in the fortunes of Christianity in Persia. This comes out in a letter he was to write in 404 to Olympias, asking her to get in touch with, and give him the latest news of, Maruthas.[96] This was none other than Maruta,[97] bishop of the frontier town Mayferqaṭ (Martyropolis, in Mesopotamia), the physician cleric whom Arkadios sent as ambassador to Persia in 399, at the accession of Yazdegerd I, and who was able to induce the shah to adopt a more tolerant attitude to Christians in his realms, in contrast to the prolonged persecution they had had to endure under Sapor II (340-79). He was even granted permission to build churches wherever he pleased.[98] John is likely to have met him, if not before, on the occasion of his appointment as ambassador, when he must have been a frequent visitor at court, and to have concerned himself with his plans for assisting the Christian cause in Persia. Whether he was in touch with him again on his return in 400-1 we do not know, but before long Maruthas was to move into the camp of John's adversaries[99] and be one of his judges at The Oak. For the moment we should note that John's great interest in promoting Christianity among barbarians and outside the borders of the empire was at this time unusual, not to say unprecedented.

[95] *Ep.* 14.5 (*PG* 52.618).
[96] Ibid.
[97] For a concise summary see *BSS* VIII.1300-9 (J.M. Sauget).
[98] Sokrates 7.8.
[99] Sozomen 8.16.

11

Crises in the Capital

I

John had not to wait many months before being drawn into grave political crises. The first concerned the chief chamberlain Eutropios, Arkadios' all-powerful favourite, the patron to whom John owed his throne. In spring 399 his star seemed to be irreversibly in the ascendant. Not only were the reins of government of the eastern parts of the empire effectively in his hands, but in 397 he had shown his independence of Stilicho, as emperor Honorius' regent virtual ruler of the western parts, having him declared a public enemy by the senate of Constantinople.[1] His successful campaign in the following year against the Huns in Armenia[2] had given a great boost both to his prestige and to his own self-confidence. He enjoyed the full backing of Arkadios, who had rewarded him with exceptional honours and titles. It mattered little that the western government, disgusted at the bestowal of the consulship, the highest office open to a private citizen, had refused to include his name on the official list. Everywhere in the east he was being publicly fêted, with statues in his honour erected in front of the senate-house in Constantinople and in public squares and boulevards. His position seemed impregnable; but by early August he had been stripped of his offices, disgraced and (his life spared for a while as a result of John's eloquent pleadings) sent into ignominious exile.

The prime originator of Eutropios' downfall was Gainas, the ambitious but deeply frustrated Gothic general who had had the praetorian prefect Rufinus cut down before the emperor's eyes at Hebdomon in November 395.[3] In early 399 there had been a dangerous revolt, led by his kinsman Tribigild, of Goths whom Theodosius I had settled in Phrygia; they had taken part in Eutropios' campaign against the Huns, but both they and Tribigild himself had been outraged by the meanness of the rewards they had received. Eutropios dispatched two armies to put the rebellion down, one under Gainas to Thrace to protect the European side of the Hellespont, the other under a militarily incompetent friend of his own, Leo, to Asia to

---

[1] Zosimos 5.11.1.

[2] See above, p. 111.

[3] See above, p. 111. For the background history of this chapter see esp. G. Albert, *Goten in Constantinopel* (Paderborn 1984); J.H.W.G. Liebeschuetz, *Barbarians and Bishops* (Oxford 1990).

confront the mutineers. Both men were, it would seem,[4] given the rank of *magistri militum praesentales*, i.e. commanders-in-chief attached to the emperor's person. When Leo's army was disastrously defeated, Gainas was given full command, but did not engage Tribigild, with whom he was in fact in collusion. Instead he terrified the government in Constantinople by telling it that Tribigild was a formidable foe with whom it would be advisable to negotiate. He finally warned Arkadios that, if Tribigild and his mutineers were to return to their allegiance, the indispensable condition would have to be the liquidation of Eutropios.

Gainas' animosity[5] against Eutropios seems to have been mainly inspired by resentment that he himself had not been granted the rank and public status to which, as the most experienced general in the east who had also opened the door to the eunuch's rise to power, he felt he was entitled. In fact, he had been passed over as commanding officer when Eutropios chose himself to lead the campaign against the Huns, and had been kept as a military count (*comes rei militaris*), a high but by no means top-level army rank, until the crisis over Tribigild forced Eutropios to promote him to generalissimo. Coupled with this was jealousy at the exalted honours and enormous wealth which Eutropios was acquiring – particularly his wealth, for Gainas, in addition to the regular army under his command, had been building up a private army of his own people[6] which needed money for its upkeep. Further, he was probably afraid, not without reason, that he might before long share the fate of other Theodosian commanders whom Eutropios, always suspicious of soldiers of prominence, had eliminated.[7]

Unfortunately for Eutropios, Gainas' ultimatum arrived at a moment when, behind a façade of deferential congratulation, influential circles in Constantinople had decided that they had had enough of him. Loathed and feared by the military establishment, he was despised by the senatorial aristocracy as a eunuch, and hated for his arrogance and his flaunting of his power. Leo's crushing defeat had strengthened his adversaries' hands, since he had been personally responsible for choosing such an inept general. Even John, with whose measures to curb the relics of paganism and to promote missions he had fully co-operated,[8] had turned against him, angered by legislation he had pushed through checking abuses of the right to seek sanctuary in churches[9] and, in particular, limiting intervention on behalf of condemned persons to making an appeal to a higher tribunal.[10] What proved decisive, however, was the fact that the empress, once his friend but increasingly resentful of his influence over her husband, had

---

[4] See PW Supp. XII. 734-5 (A. Demandt); G. Albert, op. cit., 115.
[5] Zosimos 5.13; 17.
[6] Sokrates 6.5; Sozomen 8.4. Cf. G. Albert, op. cit., 112-14.
[7] See above, p. 111.
[8] See above, p. 142.
[9] Sokrates 6.5; Sozomen 8.7.
[10] CT 9.40.16; 9.45.3; 11.30.57; 16.2.32 and 33 (all of July 398).

joined the hostile camp. The crunch came, it is said,[11] when in his folly he sneered that he could have her ejected from the palace just as easily as, by arranging her marriage, he had brought her into it. Stung by the insult, she went to the emperor, holding their two little daughters in her arms, and bitterly complained of the eunuch's insolence. Arkadios exploded with anger (although normally sluggish, he was liable to violent outbursts of temper), ordered Eutropios into his presence, and summarily dismissed him from all his offices and dignities.

II

Eutropios' panic-stricken but also (as it turned out) tactically shrewd reaction, on hearing the emperor's sentence, was to make his way, as quickly and inconspicuously as possible, from the palace to nearby Hagia Sophia. It is perhaps ironic that, after legislating to limit the right to asylum in churches in an effort to control its abuse, he should himself have sought to take advantage of it, but in his desperate situation the move was an astute one. If anyone could be counted on to stand up for a suppliant seeking the protection of his altar, it was John. So in fact it proved. The news of the powerful minister's dismissal spread throughout the city like wild-fire, and the church was soon filled with an excited mob calling for him to be handed over. Eutropios had flung himself at the base of the holy table, but when government officers arrived to arrest him John refused to yield to their demands. Meanwhile units of the army assembled before the palace, loudly denouncing his crimes and calling for his summary execution. Eventually Arkadios himself appeared in public, addressed the crowd of soldiers at great length, begged them to take account not only of Eutropios' misdeeds but also of the valuable services he had rendered the state, declared that he himself was prepared as a fellow-human being to forgive him his wrong-doing, and, finally, visibly weeping (his affection for the favourite he had trusted so long could not be concealed), pleaded with them to respect the holy table at which he had sought sanctuary.[12]

For the moment the infuriated crowd dispersed. It was, apparently, a Saturday in late July 399. The following day, when John presided at the liturgy, Hagia Sophia was thronged with an enormous congregation; it was equalled only (as he observed with satisfaction) by the full house to be expected at Easter. The occasion had evidently been stage-managed to produce the maximum of dramatic effect. As the crowd pressed forward, women and girls as well as men, to catch a glimpse of the altar as the veil normally concealing it was withdrawn, they could see, with gloating eyes, grovelling beneath it and clutching one of its supporting pillars, white-faced

---

[11] Philostorgios, *HE* 11.6 (*GCS* 21.136): cf. Sozomen 8.7 ('he offended the empress').
[12] These scenes are reconstructed from John's remarks next day: *Hom. in Eutrop.* 3-4 (*PG* 52.393-5).

and with chattering teeth, the aged eunuch who a few hours earlier 'was shaking the whole world'. When the time came, John took his seat at the ambo and delivered what has always been considered, from that day to this, one of his most dazzling addresses.[13] Its stylistic finish, the elegance of its structure, the skilful blending of indignation, pathos and religious appeal, betoken the thought he had given to its preparation overnight, as well as the care with which he must have revised the stenographers' notes.

Its pervading message was one close to John's heart: 'Vanity of vanities, everything is vanity' (Eccl. 1.2). Poignantly illustrated in Eutropios' reversal of fortune, this text, he insists, should be inscribed in everyone's conscience. With its help and the pitiable example before them, the rich man should abandon pride in material possessions, the poor man be grateful for poverty as a refuge in which he can trust. But John's object, as he repeatedly emphasises, was to soften his hearers' hearts, to persuade them to spare Eutropios' life and be content with the punishment so far inflicted, remembering that God encourages the merciful and that they themselves will have to give an account of their own failures. To achieve this he first castigates the disgraced minister for surrounding himself with fair-weather friends and parasites, for throwing pretentious drinking-parties and banquets, for his flaunting (against all John's advice) of his wealth, for his extravagant staging (again against all advice) of theatrical shows and horse-races. In his hour of need these follies bring him no comfort; it is only the church, on which he waged war (*polemetheisa ekklesia*) and which he delighted to harry,[14] which comes to his aid. Then turning to the congregation, surprised and indignant that he was offering sanctuary to the man who had done his best to abolish the right to it, he pleaded that it was the church's glory to wrap her cloak, like an affectionate mother, around her erring son. As for its being disgraceful that 'the accused sinner, the extortioner, the robber' should be allowed to cling to the altar, people should remember the harlot who, in the gospel (Luke 7.36-50), took hold of the Lord's feet. So far from being rebuked, she had won his admiration and praise, and, impure though she was, had been rendered pure by touching him. Eutropios, too, by being the first to violate the law he himself enacted against asylum in churches, had triumphantly exposed its wickedness.[15]

Interspersed with these reproaches and pleadings are some brilliantly etched, sometimes cruel images highlighting the fallen eunuch's desperate plight. Only recently richer and more exalted than any subject, 'he has become more wretched than a chained convict, more pitiable than a menial slave, more indigent than a beggar wasting away with hunger, having every day a presentiment of sharpened swords, the criminal's grave, executioners

---

[13] *Hom. in Eutropium eunuchum, patricium, ac consulem* (PG 52.391-6). Although often translated (never worthily), there is no proper critical edition of this great work.
[14] *Hom. in Eutrop.* 1 (PG 52.392).
[15] *Hom. in Eutrop.* 3 (PG 52.394).

taking him away to death ... Though I should try my very best, I could never convey to you in words the agony he must be suffering, from hour to hour expecting to be butchered.' Or, again, John compares the cowering figure to a fearsome lion which has at last been tied up, or to a frog or a hare which has been galvanised by sheer terror. In a final sally he invites the congregation to look at 'the harlot-face which a few days back shone radiant (such is the prosperity derived from acts of extortion), but which now looks uglier than any wrinkled old hag, with its usual enamel and grease-paint make-up wiped off by the sponge of adversity.'[16]

Apart from denouncing his greed and rapacity, John nowhere touches on the political background of Eutropios' disgrace. Characteristically, he preferred to stand aloof from the clashes of rival groups or of individuals competing for power, and concentrate on the ambitions and passions inspiring them. Many contemporaries, however, according to Sokrates and Sozomen,[17] found the sermon objectionable because of its censorious tone; it was just another example (Sokrates evidently shared this view) of John's habit of lecturing the highly placed with excessive vehemence. Instead of showing compassion, they complained, he had been guilty of kicking a man when he was down (just the thing he had twice at least protested he had no intention of doing).[18] Their criticism suggests that they had missed the point. His granting sanctuary to Eutropios was being sharply criticised; he also realised that, if he was to deflect the wrath of the army and the mob, he had to combine a frank acknowledgement of the eunuch's misdeeds with as vivid a portrayal as possible of his present humiliation. The tactic succeeded, and as the address drew to its close he could exclaim that he detected many people's eyes streaming with tears. So in his peroration he implored them to show compassion. What kind of mercy will they deserve if, when the emperor, whom Eutropios had really injured, lays his anger aside, they persist in theirs? How can they presume to approach the altar, after repeating in the liturgy the Lord's Prayer with its petition for reciprocal forgiveness, if they have excluded it from their hearts?

John's eloquence had saved Eutropios from death, at least for a few months. According to the usual account, he was allowed to stay in the church, but some days later, mistrustful of his security there, he slipped out, only to be quickly rounded up. This implausible story, however, is based on a further address of John's[19] which, as we shall shortly see, probably refers to a very different asylum-seeker. What actually happened was that he was first banished to Cyprus, having been given a guarantee that his life would be spared in Constantinople.[20] On 17 August an edict[21]

---

[16] *Hom. in Eutrop.* 2; 4; 3 (*PG* 52.393; 395; 394).
[17] 6.5; 8.7.
[18] Cf. the opening words of paras. 2 and 3: *PG* 52.392.
[19] *Hom. de capto Eutropio* (*PG* 52.395-414). See below, pp. 154-6.
[20] Zosimos 5.18.2.
[21] CT 9.40.17.

was published (the first, so far as we know, addressed to the new praetorian prefect Aurelianos) setting out this sentence, and also annulling his acts, confiscating his entire property, and stripping him of all his dignities. But neither Gainas nor his other enemies in high places (including, we may suspect, the empress) were satisfied. So at their insistence, the wretched man was brought back from Cyprus three or four months later, tried before a court presided over by Aurelianos on a trumped-up charge of high treason, and beheaded.[22] The trial and execution took place at Chalkedon so that the promise given to him that he would be safe in the capital might be observed to the letter. He must have been dead before the end of the year, since Asterios of Amasea (d. *c.* 410) refers[23] to his fate in a sermon given in the first days of 400.

III

John's success in getting Eutropios' life temporarily spared can only have irritated the influential circles which were bent on, and (as we have seen) were soon able to bring about, his destruction. He made a pointed reference to them in a sermon[24] delivered (as he himself stated) scarcely thirty days after the eunuch's downfall, a reversal of fortune which, he characteristically argued, should shake his hearers out of their insane rapacity and trust in material riches. He drew a sombre picture of Eutropios' present plight: after spending sleepless nights and taking endless trouble indulging his extortionate greed, he now finds himself a fugitive, without home or city, without the bare necessities of life, haunted every hour by premonitions of the sword's blade, the executioner, the criminal's grave, dragging out an existence worse than a thousand deaths. By contrast other people gorge themselves with his possessions, and those who recently toadied to him now plot his extermination. Among these latter it is tempting to include the empress and her close circle of friends; one suspects, too, that their annoyance at his attitude to the fallen minister, so much more generous than theirs, may have created a rift between them and their bishop. All this is speculation, but if correct it would explain an extraordinary outburst in which John, contemptuously contrasting the gold ornaments favoured by wealthy ladies with the chains Paul as a prisoner had to wear, pointed a finger at Eudoxia herself. If the empress, he declared,[25] clad all in gold, and the Apostle Paul carrying his chains entered the church together, everyone present would turn his eyes – and rightly too – away from her to him. A man like Paul, more an angel than a man, was a more wonderful spectacle than a woman in her most exquisite finery. As a devout

[22] Philostorgios, *HE* 11.6 (*GCS* 40.136).
[23] *Hom.* 4 (*PG* 40.225).
[24] *Quod frequenter conveniendum* 1 (*PG* 63.461-2).
[25] *In Col. hom.* 10.4 (*PG* 62.371). This reference confirms the date proposed on p. 133 above.

Christian Eudoxia was bound to agree, but she is not likely to have thanked the preacher for making the comparison so publicly.

But Eudoxia had other things to think about at this time than such needling puritanical diatribes. In a matter of weeks, on 9 January 400,[26] she was to be raised to the rank of Augusta, with Arkadios himself no doubt presenting her with the purple chlamys, or military cloak fastened to the right shoulder, and the distinctive imperial diadem. For generations it had been usual for emperors to grant this courtesy title to their wives or close female relatives, and Eudoxia must have felt that the time had come for her to receive it. If she needed help in securing it, she could rely on the new praetorian prefect Aurelianos, grateful for his own elevation to office and for the part she had played in bringing about Eutropios' disgrace, or perhaps also on her intimate friend, the young count John, who, we are told,[27] was in a special degree in the emperor's confidence. While the title was honorific, conveying no executive powers, it is evident that from the date of its bestowal, in the vacuum after the removal of Eutropios, her influence over her ineffectual husband was greatly increased. If O. Seeck's remark[28] that she was now named 'co-ruler – Mitregentin' goes too far, this was the perception of her role which the coinage depicting her as Augusta and the whole apparatus of imperial propaganda aimed at disseminating.[29]

IV

Meanwhile a crisis far more damaging to the imperial city than the toppling of an over-mighty minister, a crisis in which its deeply non-political bishop would again find himself involved in one way or another, was building up. While aspects of it (e.g. chronology) are still debated, its broad outline is clear enough.[30] Important sources, though often difficult to interpret, are two works by Synesios of Cyrene (c. 370-413), in Libya, a cultivated Neoplatonist, later to be ordained bishop, who was in Constantinople as a special envoy from 397 to late 400. These are his speech *On Kingship* (*De regno*), which he delivered before a picked audience in 398, and his *Egyptian Tale*, or *De providentia*, composed in Constantinople in 400, which gives a

[26] *Chronicon Paschale* s.a. 400.
[27] Zosimos 5.13.8. For John see *PLRE* 2, 594-5, which states that he became *comes* in 401/3. In this book he is sometimes given the title by anticipation so as to distinguish him from the bishop.
[28] *Geschichte des Untergangs der antiken Welt* 5, 318.
[29] K.G. Holum, *Theodosian Empresses* (California 1982), 65-7.
[30] For the chronology and historical framework I am chiefly indebted to G. Albert, 'Zur Chronologie der Empörung des Gainas', *Historia* 29 (1980), 504-8; *Goten in Constantinopel* (Paderborn 1984). For Synesios we now have A. Cameron and J. Long, *Barbarians and Politics at the Court of Arkadios* (California and Oxford 1993), which includes an annotated ET of *De providentia*. It reached me too recently to take account of its wide-ranging, revisionist discussions.

first-hand account of events there during this critical period in the form of colourful, highly tendentious allegory.

Once again the threat came from Gainas. To start with there was no apparent breach between him and the new praetorian prefect Aurelianos. They had worked together to bring about the eunuch's fall, and it was Aurelianos who had presided at his trial. Behind the façade of co-operation, however, it was clear to the Gothic commander that Aurelianos, consul from the beginning of 400, was at least as great an obstacle to his ambitions as Eutropios. The earlier view[31] that he was leader of an 'anti-German' party set on reducing the role of barbarians in the empire has been generally discarded;[32] there was in fact no such 'party'. He undoubtedly represented, however, a deeply rooted conviction, widely held in the court and other important circles, that the growing influence of Germans and other barbarians in the state, especially in the army, must be resisted and reversed. Even if he did not inspire, he was in sympathy with the trenchant presentation of this policy in his friend Synesios' *De regno*, which called for the creation of a truly national army and the removal of barbarians from positions of command and the senatorial rank to which their holders were entitled, and included thinly veiled attacks on Gainas himself.[33] The Goth, who had been in Constantinople ostensibly negotiating an agreement between the government and Tribigild, decided to anticipate his enemies and strike first. Having concluded a treaty with Tribigild which seems to have allayed the fears of the capital, he moved to Thyatira and there, throwing off the mask, joined forces with him. The two then marched in early April with their armies, Tribigild to Lampsakos and Gainas to Chalkedon in Bithynia, looting wherever they went. With Tribigild watching the Hellespont, Gainas could threaten the capital, which was filled with alarm, with impunity. His position was in fact so strong that he was able to insist that the emperor should come in person to meet him at Chalkedon.

The two men met in the splendid, beautifully situated church of the martyr Euphemia, just outside Chalkedon[34] (in 431 to be the setting of the fourth general council). Although neither was in any doubt which had the whip hand, the discussions were conducted with elaborate courtesy and mutual expressions of non-aggression and friendship.[35] Gainas held Arkadios in deep respect and, provided his own position was secured, had no wish to upset the established order. His first demand was that three men whom he judged his most dangerous political adversaries in the emperor's entourage should be handed over as hostages, to be dealt with at his discretion. These were Aurelianos, the former consul (383) and

---

[31] See esp. O. Seeck, op. cit., 5, 314-18.
[32] See G. Albert, *Goten* passim; also A. Lippold's review in *BZ* 78 (1985), 398-9.
[33] E.g. *De regno* 20 (Terzaghi 2.46C).
[34] For an eloquent description see Evagrios Scholastikos, *HE* 2.3 (*PG* 86.2492-3). No vestige survives today.
[35] Sokrates 6.6; Sozomen 8.4.

high-ranking general Saturninos, and count John, Eudoxia's favourite (her lover too, gossips whispered), the emperor's confidant, and since Eutropios' removal the strongest political influence inside the palace. Arkadios had no option but to agree. He also had to comply with Gainas' further demands (a) that he should be confirmed in the office of generalissimo (*magister utriusque militiae*), and (b) that as such he should be empowered to take over military control of Constantinople and garrison his Gothic troops (including his private army) there. Because he wanted to be absolutely sure of his position, both parties bound themselves by solemn oaths. In addition Gainas forced the emperor to appoint Caesarios, brother and political foe of Aurelianos, as praetorian prefect in his place. It seems probable, too, that he obliged Arkadios to nominate him as consul for 401.[36]

John found himself drawn into the affair of the hostages from the start. Two of them at any rate (Sokrates and Sozomen mention only Saturninos and Aurelianos) had been conducted to Gainas' camp near Chalkedon under threat of execution. At this precise moment John was planning (as we shall see)[37] to travel to Asia Minor to settle a serious disciplinary problem, but on receiving an urgent message from the palace he cancelled the proposed trip. Arkadios and Eudoxia must have been aware of his interest in Goths,[38] and probably influence with them, and judged him the man to help them in the present crisis. At their request, therefore, he crossed over to Chalkedon to intercede with Gainas for the lives of the hostages. Our sole direct knowledge of this démarche comes from the sermon[39] he is commonly held to have delivered on his return to the capital; its ancient title, it should be noted, speaks only of Saturninos and Aurelianos. He apologises in this for his long absence from his congregation, but explains that, 'as the common father of you all', he has had to concern himself for members of his flock in desperate need. So he has expended immense time and trouble moving around, arguing, pleading, that 'these important people' might be spared their threatened fate. The rest of the address is, for the most part, an impassioned tirade against the lust for riches; his hearers should blame this, and the insane reliance on material prosperity of which it is the expression, both for the disaster which has befallen the hostages and for the pitiable, divided situation in which the city now finds itself. But his advocacy, long-drawn-out and difficult though it was, had eventually proved successful. Resisting Caesarios' demand for the hostages' execution, Gainas contented himself with some macabre play-acting, merely grazing their skin with a naked sword, and sentenced them to exile.[40] He even abstained from seizing their property,[41] much as

---

[36] Theodoret, *HE* 5.32.6 (*GCS* 44.333).
[37] See below, p. 164.
[38] See above, pp. 142-4.
[39] *Hom. cum Saturninus et Aurelianus acti essent in exsilium* etc. (*PG* 52.413-20).
[40] Zosimos 5.18.9.
[41] Synesios, *De prov.* 1.16 (Terzaghi 102).

he needed funds for the maintenance of his private army – an act of unexplained generosity which should also, in all probability, be attributed to John's persuasiveness.

Some historians[42] are sceptical about the whole incident. A visit to Chalkedon, just across the straits, near enough (as we have seen)[43] for John and his congregation to pay it a devotional visit one afternoon, would not have required a lengthy absence. So they would place the sermon some months later, to his return from the expedition he made in the summer to Thrace.[44] But this is to miss John's point. He wanted to impress on his auditors how arduous and time-consuming his negotiations had been; in any case, any separation from his flock, because of illness or whatever other reason, always seemed an eternity to him. Rhetoric apart, it is unrealistic to suppose that so ambitious and controversial a mission could have been carried to its conclusion in a brief span. There must have been a great deal of toing and froing, tough discussions, and confrontations with different persons, including the recently promoted Caesarios. John's proposals are likely to have been bitterly opposed by some Gothic commanders, and even more by their Greek supporters; Gainas himself seems to have been neither a strong nor a decisive leader. The haggling could have dragged on for a week or ten days; John's success in the end speaks volumes for his persuasiveness and commanding personality, but also for the respect which his known concern for Gothic Christians had engendered in Gainas and other Goths in his close circle.

This was not, it is clear, John's only involvement with the hostages. The eleventh of the charges to be brought against him some three years later[45] was that 'he informed against count John during the mutiny of the troops'. Since we know of no other military uprising in this period, the reference can only be to Gainas' coup. The likeliest explanation is that, in a desperate attempt to avoid being handed over to the Goth, the count had tried to conceal himself in a church, and that John was accused of betraying his whereabouts. The mystery is solved if we accept that, as has been convincingly argued,[46] the subject of the homily conventionally entitled 'On the arrest of Eutropios'[47] is not in fact the eunuch but the young courtier. In its opening paragraphs the preacher's concern is to repudiate the allegation that he had been responsible a few days before for the 'betrayal' of someone who had sought sanctuary; the fugitive, he claims, had had only himself to blame since he had left the church of his own volition. That the man, who is nowhere named, was Eutropios can be safely ruled out, if only for the

[42] E.g. J.H.W.G. Liebeschuetz, op. cit., 110.
[43] See above, p. 139.
[44] See below, pp. 160-3.
[45] See below, p. 222: also Appendix C.
[46] A. Cameron, *Nottingham Medieval Studies* 32 (1988), 34-48.
[47] *Hom. de capto Eutropio* (*PG* 52.395-414: only 395-402 are relevant, the remainder of the sermon being taken up with generally edifying themes).

reason that none of the personal allusions fits him. To give but one example, he is described[48] as having plotted against John and done him much harm, whereas however much John disapproved of Eutropios there was no personal animosity between them. But the fatal objection to the traditional identification is the improbable scenario it presupposes. It is hard to understand why Eutropios should have attempted to escape, since John had assured him of asylum, Arkadios had publicly announced his readiness to forgive him, and it was clear that his life at any rate was going to be spared. It is equally hard to reconcile the tumultuous violence on the part of the army, which apparently maltreated John and insulted the emperor, described in the homily,[49] with its noisy but loyal and respectful demonstration a few days earlier when Eutropios had fled to Hagia Sophia.[50]

An alternative reconstruction, which both explains how the charge came to be levelled against John and takes full account of the alarming situation depicted in the homily, may be proposed. Only two hostages were initially handed over to Gainas; they were (as Sokrates, Sozomen, and the sermon's title suggest) Saturninos and Aurelianos. Somehow count John had managed to lie low; it would indeed be surprising if one so intimate with both Arkadios and Eudoxia had not received, and acted on, a warning signal. When the Goths took over the city, however, one of their chief immediate objectives must have been to track down the third wanted man. Such a well-known figure could not long remain concealed, even though he tried to hide himself in a church. Soon it was crowded with Gothic troops searching for him and brandishing naked swords. 'The church was besieged,' John states,[51] but 'I withstood them; I was not afraid of their wrath.' The infuriated soldiers then carried him off by force to the palace; their rough usage convinced him that he faced death. When they got there, 'the diadem proved impotent, the purple was insulted': in other words, Arkadios' appeals for his friend were thrown rudely back at him and he could do nothing. The armed rabble eventually discovered and seized the count. We are not told the details of his arrest, but John is insistent that the fault lay with himself: had he clung to the altar he would have remained untouched.

Nothing in the homily actually requires us to identify the fugitive with the courtier, but there is also nothing in it which is inconsistent with this identification, which in the light of the accusation later brought against John is highly plausible. Indeed, some of John's remarks seem to point in the count's direction. For example, the hint that 'the wearer of the diadem' could do nothing to help the fugitive suggests that he was a close friend of Arkadios. Again, John seems to link him with Saturninos and Aurelianos, rebuking him in section 3 for pursuing 'wealth the runaway' in language

[48] Section 5 (*PG* 52.400).
[49] Section 3 (*PG* 52.399).
[50] See above, p. 147.
[51] Section 1 (*PG* 52.397).

almost identical with that he had used to rebuke them, and in sections 4 and 6 including him with 'those who have gone away ... whose careers are ended'.[52] Acceptance of the identification clears up several other points. Thus we now know that the homily was not preached, as generally assumed, in August 399, but in late April 400. The troops whose disorderly, insolent behaviour is highlighted were not the disciplined, loyal imperial guard, but Gothic soldiers on the rampage. Even more interesting, perhaps, is the discovery that the count, later to rank among John's bitterest foes, was already intriguing against him in 399.[53] In general, this re-reading of this usually neglected homily brings to light a hitherto unsuspected episode of some importance in the history of the capital and in the personal life of John.

V

Meanwhile, his demands met and the hostages (two for the moment) dealt with, Gainas had crossed the Bosporus and installed himself with his army in Constantinople. It was probably the end of April 400.[54] It is calculated[55] that he had some 35,000 troops with him, mostly Goths, although this total includes the Gothic soldiers' families. Even allowing for this, a much smaller force would have sufficed, since no military units were stationed in the capital – apart from the imperial guard (*scholae palatinae*). But Gainas had to satisfy his men's desire to plunder and enjoy the rich pickings of the splendid city.[56] They were billeted at scattered locations throughout it, to the great discomfort of the inhabitants, who had to put up as best they could with their rough behaviour, but also to their own danger, since they were living in widely separated groups amid a frightened and hostile population. Synesios, who was there at the time, reports[57] that they treated the city as if it were their camp. With sombre eloquence John, returning to Constantinople from his negotiations over the hostages, recaptures[58] the atmosphere of confusion, fear, mutual suspicion and mistrust he found there. He even speaks of a 'civil war' (*polemos emphulios*), a not inapt expression since the army of the state (for such it officially was) was oppressing its citizens, and since these were split by fierce political and, now that the Arian minority could raise its head, religious animosities.

Gainas was now effectively in control of the government as well as the capital. The mastery of the eastern parts of the empire was within his

---

[52] *PG* 52.398; 400 and 401.
[53] Sect. 5 ad init. (*PG* 52.400). It was A. Cameron (art. cit.) who first explained this text.
[54] This is G. Albert's chronology: some prefer late December 399 or early January 400.
[55] On the basis of Synesios, *De prov.* 2.2 (Terzaghi 2.115C); Zosimos 5.19.4. See G. Albert, op. cit., 131 n. 184.
[56] Synesios, *De prov.* 1.15 (Terzaghi 2.99A; 100).
[57] *De prov.* 2.1 (Terzaghi 2.109B).
[58] *Cum Saturninus et Aurelianus* 1 (*PG* 52.415).

grasp, with the emperor obliged to gratify his wishes and a highly placed citizen who backed him installed as praetorian prefect. But it was no part of his plan to overthrow a regime under which he had risen to the highest military rank, but rather to consolidate his own position within it. The dream he cherished, it is likely, was to build up a commanding role for himself in the eastern empire analogous to that conspicuously achieved by another (but far abler) barbarian general, the Vandal Stilicho, in the west. This bold, but strictly limited, ambition is well illustrated by the fact that, although now at the height of his power, he approached the emperor with the seemingly modest request that one of the city churches should be assigned to his Goths for Arian services. His ostensible plea, it is reported, was that it was unbecoming to his dignity, as a Roman officer of the highest rank, to be obliged to go outside the city walls, as the legislation of Theodosius I required of Arians, when he wanted to worship God. But his ulterior motive may have been, it has been suggested,[59] to secure for himself and his followers, dispersed as they were haphazardly throughout a resentful city, a convenient rallying-point where, in addition to holding services, they could meet to formulate plans and affirm their national identity.

The incident is reported, cursorily by Sokrates[60] (who cites it merely as illustrating John's notorious 'outspokenness' (*parrhesia*)), but in circumstantial detail by Sozomen and Theodoret.[61] The last-mentioned relates a verbal exchange between John and Gainas which, although the historian was himself probably responsible for the phrasing, retains (as many have noted)[62] a remarkable flavour of verisimilitude. It seems that Arkadios, almost certainly advised by the new praetorian prefect Caesarios and in any case thoroughly afraid of what the Goth might do if he were thwarted, was at first inclined to yield to his demand, and asked John's co-operation in complying with it. Oblivious (as we should expect) of the political issues at stake, John indignantly refused and brushed his fears aside, and at his request the emperor arranged a meeting between the two men in his presence.

When Gainas repeated his demand, John, who was accompanied by several other bishops, retorted[63] that the emperor, as an adherent of the true religion, could not act so sacrilegiously. In reply Gainas urged that he too, as a man of faith, needed a house of prayer. John's rejoinder was that every church in the city was open to him. Gainas countered this by arguing that this was no use to him since he belonged to a different denomination; his request for a place where he could worship was fully justified by the long years of military service he had rendered to the Roman empire. With

---

[59] G. Albert, op. cit., 132.
[60] 6.6.
[61] Sozomen 8.4; Theodoret *HE* 5.32.2-8 (*GCS* 44.332-3). Their accounts agree in substance.
[62] E.g. É. Demougeot, *De l'unité à la division de l'empire romain* (Paris 1951), 254.
[63] This summary is a conflation of Sozomen and Theodoret.

astonishing frankness John insisted that the rewards he had received
greatly exceeded any labour he had expended. He reminded him that, when
he had crossed the Danube to join the Roman army as a common soldier,
he had been a rough-clad, penniless barbarian, whereas he was now
commander-in-chief and had been deemed worthy of a consul's robe of
office. He had sworn allegiance to Theodosius the Great, and was now guilty
of great ingratitude when he sought to persuade Arkadios to violate his
father's law banning the holding of heretical services in the city. At one
point he turned to the emperor and, with a rhetorical flourish, exclaimed
that it would be nobler to step down from his throne than to hand over the
house of God to infidels.

Without saying so explicitly, Theodoret seems to imply that John's
intervention was successful, while Sozomen states that, by his outspoken
protest, he prevented the introduction of any innovation in church practice
in Constantinople. Synesios, it is true, is often cited as evidence[64] that
Caesarios was able, in spite of everything, to get a church in the city handed
over for Arian worship, but this interpretation is based on what is probably
a mistaken translation of his text, which in fact suggests that this was what
he set himself to bring about without implying that he was successful in
his efforts. John's speech, as reproduced by the historians, gives some
readers an impression of hauteur, even harshness, but it is unlikely to have
struck Gainas as a hostile rebuke. A Christian himself, he revered John as
a holy man, and was aware of his pastoral concern for Goths; he was also
under the spell of his forceful personality. We can readily understand that
he was reduced to silence, and felt he had no option but to drop his project.

VI

Reports of John's successful confrontation with Gainas got around the city
immediately. There were many bystanders who witnessed it. Apart from
the bishops forming his escort, there must have been courtiers and servants
present; several of these had an interest in spreading the news. His prestige
in the city received an enormous boost. The flagging spirits of the citizens,
the great majority of whom were keenly orthodox, were cheered when they
learned how boldly and effectively their bishop had defied the Arian
generalissimo. For Gainas himself the episode was an irretrievable setback. The more its significance sank in, the more his standing with the
palace and with the faction supporting him, even with his own followers,
must have been weakened. Not surprisingly, it is to this moment that the
break-down of his control of the city, and also of his own barbarian troops
occupying it, can be traced. There are reports[65] of an abortive attempt to

---

[64] *De prov.* 1.18 (Terzaghi 2.108-9). For the correct interpretation of the text see G. Albert,
op. cit., 157 n. 41.

[65] Sokrates 6.6; Sozomen 8.4; Philostorgios, *HE* 11.8 (*GCS* 21.139).

plunder the cash-tables of the bankers, even of soldiers being sent to set fire to the imperial palace. It is difficult to believe that, as the ancient historians allege and some modern ones accept, these outrages were carried out on his orders in an effort to terrorise his enemies and so restore his position. It is more plausible to attribute them to arbitrary action by groups of barbarian soldiers stationed in the city, and to see them as evidence of the growing disregard for his authority among them. Whatever the truth, these excesses inevitably increased the apprehensions of the populace, already raised to fever-pitch by the appearance some weeks earlier of a comet[66] of unprecedented size which was taken as the harbinger of dreadful calamities.

In the second week of July, disturbed by the deteriorating situation, worried perhaps also by the hostility of the population and the threat it posed to his men and their families, Gainas left the capital, accompanied by trusted units of his army, and made for Hebdomon about 10 km to the west. The pretext he gave out, according to Sokrates and Sozomen,[67] was that he was possessed by a demon and wished to pray at the great church there in which the head of John the Baptist was venerated. That he was confused and troubled is likely, but there is plausibility in the suggestion[68] that, being resolved to quit Constantinople, he was planning to regroup his forces, dispersed and becoming more and more unmanageable, at the parade ground and barracks at Hebdomon. His orders, however, for the gradual, unostentatious evacuation of the main army were misunderstood or at any rate disregarded. In their haste and panic the soldiers drew attention to their movements, and made things worse by looting their billets.[69] In the resulting confusion violent incidents between them and the exasperated citizens were unavoidable. There was a popular rising against them, the gates were eventually shut, there was bitter street fighting, and 7,000 barbarians (so it is said, but the number must be exaggerated) crowded into a church near the palace, probably the one which John had assigned to Goths for orthodox worship. They expected to find sanctuary there, but the emperor ordered their destruction. The roof of the building was torn off, blazing torches were flung in, and the packed masses of soldiers were burned or stoned to death.[70] The date was 12 July 400.[71]

In the months following his confrontation with Gainas John's position in the capital was probably more influential than it had ever been, or would ever be again. It is far-fetched, however, to claim[72] that the mass of the

---

[66] This was the comet first seen in China on 19 March 400 and visible there during April-May: Ho Peng Yoke, 'Ancient and Mediaeval Observations of Comets and Novae in Chinese Sources', *Vistas in Astronomy* (ed. A. Beer) 5 (1962), 161 no. 183.

[67] 6.6; 8.4.

[68] G. Albert, op. cit., 135-6.

[69] See esp. Synesios, *De prov.* 2.1; 2.2 (Terzaghi 2.111; 112).

[70] Sokrates 6.6; Sozomen 8.4; Synesios, *De prov.* 2.3 (Terzaghi 2.118); Zosimos 5.19.4.

[71] *Chronicon paschale* s.a. 400.

[72] E.g. S. Mazzarino, *Stilicone* (Rome 1942), 215-16.

citizens looked to him personally, after his refusal of a church to the Goth, as the leader around whom they could rally and who could unleash their pent-up fury against the hated occupiers of their city. John's interest in the affair was exclusively religious; he had no hostility to Goths as such but was in general well disposed towards them, demanding only their conversion to orthodoxy. If he was glad to see them ejected from Constantinople, as some have argued on the basis of his 37th *Homily on Acts*,[73] this implied (as his later missionary activities were to show) no alteration in his support for their assimilation in society. The rising of the citizenry against them was in fact an entirely spontaneous explosion which, as the catastrophic course it took demonstrated only too clearly, owed nothing to his inspiration. It is even more misleading to speak[74] of him as 'tolerating the massacre' of the Goths. The historian Zosimos, himself a pagan, remarked[75] that seriously committed Christians (among whom John was surely pre-eminent, and cannot have been far from his thoughts) viewed the burning of the church and the extermination of the barbarians inside it as 'an enormous sacrilege'. One's surmise is that John would resign himself to the butchery of the soldiers as a mysterious judgment of providence, the penalty no doubt for their sins, but that he would have been horrified by the gross violation of the right to sanctuary.

VII

John was to have one more meeting with Gainas. After the success of the popular insurrection against the Goths, the emperor had declared their commander a public enemy,[76] and the gates of Constantinople had been closed against him. He nevertheless still had a large part of the imperial army at his disposal, and with it marched into Thrace, pillaging and ravaging as he went. Meanwhile confusion reigned in the capital. The unexpected turn of events had been a severe setback for the praetorian prefect Caesarios and his supporters, but equally an immense encouragement for their opponents, who included Eudoxia and her close circle. There were loud demands for the return of Aurelianos and the other exiles. But Caesarios continued in office; indeed, the situation was too menacing to allow of changes at the top. Everyone, according to Theodoret,[77] rulers and ruled alike, was paralysed with dread of the Goth, without an army to march against him, at first too divided even to parley with him. Eventually, Theodoret continues, they persuaded John, who was utterly fearless,

---

[73] *PG* 60.267. See A. Cameron, *Chiron* 17 (1987), 346-9.
[74] É. Demougeot, op. cit., 298.
[75] 5.19.5.
[76] Sokrates 6.6; Sozomen 8.4.
[77] *HE* 5.32-3 (*GCS* 44.333-4).

unworried by his recent clash with Gainas or any resentment it might have engendered in him, to go as the city's ambassador to Thrace and negotiate with him. When Gainas learned of his approach, he went out to meet him, received him with every mark of deference, and even got him to bless his children.

The incident illustrates in a remarkable way John's standing at the time, both with the authorities in the capital (whatever they thought of him personally) and with Gainas. He was apparently the only person with whom the now embittered and hostile barbarian was prepared to enter into discussions. But Theodoret provides no clue to the object of the mission, although the abrupt termination of his narrative may indicate that it ended in failure. Fortunately we are able to supplement his account with the help of the thinly veiled, tendentious description of the situation in Constantinople at the time given by Synesios in his *Egyptian Tale*. This suggests[78] that, in the first place, after the massacre and the enforced withdrawal of the main body of Goths, the emperor was persuaded by Caesarios that the net result of his supposed victory over the barbarians was the loss of the best part of the army. It might therefore be in his interest to induce this to return, however unpalatable this might be to the local population. Messengers were therefore dispatched, with urgent petitions and even gifts, in an effort to bring about some mutually acceptable accommodation. In the light of language like this it seems probable that one part at any rate of John's mission, undertaken at the behest of Caesarios (who apparently tried to bribe him), was to use his influence to persuade Gainas to return and resume his position as commander-in-chief. But in the same passage Synesios also records the holding of a solemn service of thanksgiving presided over by 'the high priest', presumably John, at which thanks were offered for recent events and the people called for the return of Aurelianos and the other hostages. The high priest, we are told, assured them that, if heaven were well disposed, this would indeed be brought about. It seems likely,[79] therefore, that, included in the petitions which John carried to Gainas on this final visit to him, was an urgent plea for the restoration of the exiles.

If this reconstruction is correct, when John set forth for Thrace in summer 400 he was the envoy both of Caesarios and his partisans and of the friends and supporters of Aurelianos. This dual role illustrates not only the dominant part he was playing at this critical juncture in the political life of the capital, but also, intriguingly, what has been aptly called[80] his 'versatility', even his 'dangerous independence'. So far from being a political

---

[78] *De prov.* 2.3 (Terzaghi 2.118-19). It was O. Seeck (*Untergang* 5.324) who first linked the accounts of Theodoret and Synesios.

[79] On this see C. Zakrzewski, 'Le parti théodosien et son antithèse', *Eus Supplementa* 18 (Lemburg 1931), 119.

[80] É. Demougeot, op. cit., 298.

bishop serving one or other of the factions in the state, he remained supremely detached from the political struggles of the time, prepared when he thought fit to take up the causes of mutually opposed groups. His overriding concern was always with his pastoral responsibilities and with the defence and promotion of orthodoxy. It is ironic that, while the rival parties had little option but to accept his services, the efforts he made on their behalf brought him, from Eudoxia and the hostages at any rate, more hostility than gratitude.[81] It is no less ironic that, in spite of having successfully resisted Gainas' demand for a church, his relations with the Goth and readiness to negotiate with him should have induced some of his enemies to whisper that he had been willing to sacrifice the interests both of church and empire to him.[82]

On this occasion, notwithstanding the obsequious reception the Gothic commander gave him, his mission proved unsuccessful. Gainas had no reason to place any faith in the proposed reconciliation, and in any case was fully occupied with pillaging. Still less, we must suppose, could he see any reason to order the return of the hostages, even if he were in a position to do so. The rest of his story scarcely concerns us here, although it is worth recording that the government was eventually able to muster an army to send against him, led by another barbarian general, Fravitta (a pagan this time), and that this defeated him ignominiously as he was trying to cross the Hellespont into Asia. Escaping northwards across the Danube, as Zosimos reports,[83] or (as seems more probable) returning to upper Thrace,[84] he found himself confronted by the Hunnish chieftain Uldin, was engaged by him in battle, and was killed. According to the *Paschal Chronicle*,[85] the fatal battle took place on 23 December 400. Uldin sent his head as a grateful tribute to Arkadios, who had it paraded in the streets of Constantinople in early 401.

---

[81] See below, pp. 171f.
[82] So 'Martyrios', P 486a: *AB* 97 (1979), 152.
[83] 5.21.6.
[84] Philostorgios, *HE* 11.8 (*GCS* 21.139): cf. Sokrates 6.6; Sozomen 8.4, who both attribute his final defeat and death to Roman troops.
[85] *Chronica minora* 2.66.

12

Intervention in Asia

I

In April 400, when the crisis over Gainas and his Goths was coming to the boil, John found himself drawn into an affair which, with a protracted gap between its two phases, was to occupy him for two full years, and lead him into exercising quasi-patriarchal authority far beyond the confines of the imperial city. Because of its far-reaching ecclesiastical implications, and also because it provides eye-witness glimpses of his style of leadership, the story deserves examination in some detail. Our principal source is Palladios,[1] who was personally present at the key incidents.

One Sunday morning, before the start of divine service, John was in his palace conferring with some twenty-two bishops. The majority were from Asia, the province on the western seaboard of Asia Minor; headed by Antoninos, metropolitan of its capital Ephesos, they were staying in the palace, having come to Constantinople on urgent business. Among others present were three elderly metropolitans from Scythia, Thrace and Galatia respectively. Palladios, who was also present, more than once calls their meeting a 'synod', and there can be no doubt that this was the 'resident synod' mentioned earlier.[2] All unexpectedly, Eusebios, bishop of Valentinopolis and one of Antoninos' suffragans, joined the gathering and produced a formal dossier of accusations against him. Keeping his annoyance in check, John begged him to desist, but the excited man was not to be silenced. John therefore called on Paul, bishop of Heraklea, to mediate between Antoninos and his enraged suffragan, and himself led the other bishops into the Great Church to begin the liturgy. Almost immediately, however, Eusebios burst into the sanctuary and, in full view of the bewildered congregation, thrust a copy of the charge-sheet into his hands. To calm him down and avoid alarming the people further, John took it but, feeling too upset to offer the holy sacrifice himself, delegated this responsibility to another bishop and withdrew after the scripture readings.

When the mass was over, John reconvened the resident synod in the baptistery, and summoned Eusebios. First, he warned him that he had

---

[1] *Dial.* 13-16 (*SC* 341.273-303). There are brief references to John's activities in Asia Minor in Sokrates 6.15 and Sozomen 8.6.

[2] See above, pp. 128f.

better be sure he had proof of his allegations; once they had been made public and entered in minutes, the process would be irreversible. Since Eusebios insisted, his seven charges were read out. Antoninos, he claimed, had melted down sacred vessels and given the silver ingots to his son. He had appropriated slabs of marble taken from the baptistery of his church and converted them into baths for his personal use. He had decorated his dining-room with marble columns which he had found lying around in churches. He had retained in his employ a servant who was guilty of murder. He had sold real estate bequeathed to the church and pocketed the proceeds. He had taken back, and resumed sexual relations with, the wife from whom he had separated when made a bishop. Worst of all, it was his regular practice to demand a fee proportionate to the revenues of the prospective see from anyone he consecrated bishop. Men who had paid for their offices, Eusebios declared, as well as the agents who had handled the cash, were present in the baptistery; he had the necessary proofs.

On the advice of the most elderly bishops present it was agreed that, while all the charges were shocking, it would be sensible to concentrate on the most heinous, selling holy orders, believed to be bestowed by the Holy Spirit, for money (technically known as simony). John therefore formally asked, first, Antoninos, and then certain bishops alleged to have paid him to ordain them, what they had to say. Both he and they firmly repudiated the accusations. The debate dragged on until the afternoon, but reached a deadlock when Eusebios failed, in spite of his assurances, to produce witnesses who could swear that they had seen money changing hands. At this point John, who was determined to have the scandal cleared up, announced his intention to travel to Asia himself and personally carry out an investigation there. It is not recorded that anyone objected that, from the strictly canonical point of view, this might be *ultra vires*. Antoninos, however, was so alarmed at the prospect of such a visitation that he privately persuaded a powerful friend (a man, in fact, whose estates in Asia he managed) to use his influence at court to block John's projected journey. The palace, we may surmise, was taken aback to hear of it. John had taken his decision on the spur of the moment, but it had its own reasons for wanting his presence in the capital. So he received a peremptory order:[3] 'It is unthinkable that you, our bishop and the protector of our souls, should absent yourself from the city and undertake a journey to Asia at a time when great trouble is expected. The witnesses can easily be fetched.'

The great trouble, as Palladios explains, was the threat offered by Gainas, who was camped at Chalkedon just across the straits. John was urgently needed, as we have seen,[4] to negotiate with him on behalf of the hostages. He therefore had no option but to comply. Rather than wait, however, for the witnesses to find their way to Constantinople, or risk their

[3] Palladios, *Dial.* 14 (*SC* 341.282).
[4] See above, pp. 152f.

being tampered with in the meantime, he reassembled the synod and got it to agree to send, in his place, three of its members to Asia to examine the witnesses. The three chosen were Synkletios of Traianopolis (Thrace), Hesychios of Parion (Hellespont) and John's friend and biographer Palladios of Helenopolis (Bithynia), only the second being from the civil diocese of Asiana, of which the province of Asia was part. They were to carry out their interrogations at Hupaipa, a small town at the foot of the Tmolos mountains on the road between Ephesos and Sardes, chosen as being conveniently placed for all parties. Anyone they summoned who failed to present himself within two months would be liable to excommunication.

From this point onwards the affair assumed the air of a black comedy. Setting out while the city was occupied by the Goths, Synkletios and Palladios duly landed at Smyrna and found their way to Hupaipa, but without Hesychios; a friend of Antoninos, he had excused himself on grounds of ill health. Letters were dispatched summoning the interested parties, and eventually Antoninos and Eusebios turned up – but not a single witness. Antoninos, we are told, had in the meantime bought off both his accuser and the witnesses, and Eusebios was reduced to pleading unconvincingly that these were detained by pressing business. Asked by the exasperated commissioners when he expected to produce them, he swore to do so within forty days; it was his private hope, and expectation, that, as the summer heat was reaching its extreme intensity (middle to end of July),[5] the two would not relish sticking it out so long at Hupaipa. They did stick it out, however, and when neither Eusebios nor his witnesses put in an appearance after forty days, they notified the bishops of Asia that he had been excommunicated. For good measure they then waited thirty days more, and when there was still no sign of the witnesses, they packed their bags and returned to Constantinople. Here, according to Palladios,[6] they had a chance encounter with Eusebios; but when they reproached him, he pleaded sickness, but promised to produce the witnesses without fail.

Thus ended the first act of the bizarre drama. The second and final act, which opened with the death of Antoninos at some unknown date and an urgent plea to John to come in person to Asia to sort out the confused situation, is held both by Baur[7] and by some present-day students[8] to have followed almost immediately, with John setting sail from the capital shortly after Epiphany (6 January) 401 and returning in triumph soon after Easter (14 April). But there are strong grounds for rejecting this chronology. A decisive one is that Palladios, who was closely involved in the affair from start to finish and had access to the minutes, insists twice over[9] that

---

[5] G. Albert, *Historia* 29 (1980), 507 with nn. 22 and 23.

[6] *Dial.* 14 (*SC* 341.286).

[7] 2.145; 152 n. 13.

[8] E.g. J.H.W.G. Liebeschuetz, *Nottingham Medieval Studies* 29 (1985), 5: he later abandoned this view.

[9] *Dial.* 15 (*SC* 341.290 and 296).

it dragged on for two years, i.e. until Easter 402 (6 April). No less compelling, however, are certain pieces of evidence, relating to John's known activities or to events in which he played a part, which cannot be reconciled with such a programme but point, quite independently, to his continued presence in Constantinople in the early months of 401 at any rate. The older view, which has recently been convincingly reargued,[10] that John's Asian journey took place about a year later, from late 401 or, more probably, early 402 to spring 402, makes full allowance for these as well as cohering admirably with Palladios' timetable. In the following two sections, which form an extended entr'acte, we shall review some of this evidence before recounting, in the fourth and fifth, the saga of John's activities in Asia Minor.

II

One of John's best-known, but also (in the form in which they have been handed down) stylistically least satisfactory, sermon-courses is the series of 55 homilies on the Acts of the Apostles.[11] Long ago M. von Bonsdorff established[12] that he delivered them in Constantinople, and went on to argue that he began the course shortly after the collapse of the Gothic occupation on 12 July 400 and continued it, with occasional interruptions (e.g. when absent on his embassy to Thrace),[13] well into 401. As regards their starting-point, he maintained that the homilies must post-date (a) the synod at which Antoninos was accused since they contain covert but unmistakable warnings[14] against the kinds of misconduct with which he was charged, and (b) the Gothic occupation since there is no trace in them of the alarm and confusion which paralysed the city during it. Indeed, the only reference to the Goths comes in Homily 37,[15] where John uses the expulsion of foreigners from a city as an illustration of the need to purge the human soul of the alien, vicious elements which exist in it side by side with natural, healthy ones. It seems clear[16] that it was the expulsion of the Goths which inspired his imagery, but equally clear, not least from the detached tone of his discussion, that the expulsion was no recent event, but lay some months back in the past. The inference must be that the homily was preached some months after 12 July 400, probably late in 400 or even early in 401.

It is Homily 44, however, which provides clinching proof that the course

---

[10] A. Cameron, *Chiron* 17 (1987), 350-1. For older scholars see, e.g., O. Seeck, *Untergang der antiken Welt* (Stuttgart 1920), 5.577.

[11] See above, p. 132.

[12] *Zur Predigttätigkeit des Johannes Chrysostomus* (Helsingfors 1922), 90-9.

[13] See above, pp. 160f.

[14] See esp. *hom.* 3.4-5; *hom.* 12.1-2 (*PG* 60.40-1; 101-2).

[15] 37.3 (*PG* 60.267).

[16] Cf. A. Cameron's examination in art. cit., 346-7.

was still in progress in the early months of 401. In this he dramatically exclaims,[17] 'By God's grace I too have spent three years (*trietia*), not indeed exhorting you day and night, but often every three or every seven days.' Taken literally, this would suggest that the homily was preached in late February 401, since he had been consecrated bishop and had started his career as a preacher in Constantinople on 26 February 398. It may be argued that we should not press him too strictly, since he was clearly echoing Paul's speech to the elders of Miletus in Acts 20.31 (on which he was commenting), in which the apostle reminded his auditors that he had been admonishing them 'night and day for three years' (the same word *trietia*). In any case it was his habit to round off numbers. Even so, he could scarcely have made the claim with any plausibility unless he and his congregation were already some weeks into 401. But the argument against taking his words too literally cuts both ways: the sermon could have been given somewhat later than 26 February. Moreover, on either interpretation there were eleven more homilies to follow, and they must have occupied at least a full month, possibly more.

Interesting confirmation that the course on Acts was in full swing in 401 is furnished by John's reference in it in two passages[18] to an impressive earthquake. The second of these is relevant for dating; it is also worth quoting in its own right as a trenchant example of John's pulpit style. Lamenting the proneness of human beings to forget almost immediately any benefits they receive, he cries: 'Tell me, did not God last year (*perusin*) shake our entire city with an earthquake? Did not everyone rush to be baptised? Did not fornicators, homosexuals, and depraved people forsake their homes and their familiar lairs, alter their practices, and turn religious? But when just three days had passed, they reverted to their habitual misbehaviour. How did this come about? Through their downright laziness!' Hitherto there has been great uncertainty about the earthquake in question, but a strong case was recently made[19] for identifying it with the earthquake which Synesios of Cyrene, writing to a friend, describes[20] as having taken place on the very day on which he was leaving Constantinople after his three-year stay there: 'God shook the earth repeatedly during the day.' In the same letter he expresses regret that he has not been able to say goodbye to Aurelianos, 'dear friend and consul', which must date it to late 400 when Aurelianos, whose consular year was 400, had returned with his fellow-hostages from exile. On other grounds it seems certain[21] that Synesios' stay in the capital lasted from 397-8 until late 400, probably until just before the end of the sailing season in early November. If the earthquake took place about that time and John could refer to it as an event of 'last

[17] 44.4 (*PG* 60.312).
[18] *Hom.* 7.2; 41.2 (*PG* 60.66; 291).
[19] See A. Cameron, art. cit.
[20] *Ep.* 61 (*PG* 66.1404-5).
[21] See esp. T.D. Barnes, *GRBS* 27 (1986), 93-118.

year', without any hint that it was of very recent occurrence, he must have been speaking at a date some way into 401.

III

An incident which, as well as confirming John's continued presence in Constantinople in early 401, throws an intriguing light on his relations at that time with both Arkadios and Eudoxia, is an interview he is reported to have given, possibly as late as February or even March of that year, to Porphyrios, bishop of Gaza, in Palestine. Our knowledge of it comes exclusively from the so-called *Life*[22] of Porphyrios by his deacon Mark. The underlying original of this fascinating little work in all probability goes back to its supposed author, but in its present form it has undergone far-reaching, tendentious revision in the sixth, possibly seventh, century and abounds in strongly fictional elements.[23] Although scepticism about it has deterred scholars from drawing on its evidence, there can be little doubt that, used with discrimination, it remains a valuable historical source, and that it is astonishingly accurate about contemporary institutions and practices, and in particular recaptures much of the atmosphere and style of the Byzantine court.

As we saw earlier,[24] Porphyrios had managed in 398, after John's persuasive intervention with Eutropios, to obtain an imperial edict shutting down the pagan temples at Gaza. The most famous and important, however, the Marneion, had escaped closure, and in the meantime pagan worship had been resumed; in addition, the small Christian population was being subjected to increasing harassment. According to the *Life*,[25] Porphyrios therefore resolved personally to petition the emperor to have the offending temples once and for all destroyed, and so journeyed to Constantinople accompanied by Mark and also his metropolitan, bishop John of Caesarea (in Palestine). They travelled by sea, setting out in late September and spending some time in Rhodes with the anchorite Prokopios. Gifted with clairvoyance, the holy man at once recognised the episcopal rank of two of his guests, and prophesied in detail the way in which they would be received at court. On reaching the capital, their first call was on its bishop,[26] but while encouraging his project John warned Porphyrios that he would not be able himself to press his suit with Arkadios since the emperor was not on speaking terms with him: 'the empress has made him angry with me because I rebuked her on account of a property which she coveted and then appropriated.' He referred the matter, however, to Amantios, one of Eudoxia's principal eunuchs, a devoted Christian who had great influence

[22] *Vita Porphyrii* 32-54 (ed. H. Grégoire and M.A. Kugener, *Collection Byzantine*, Paris 1930).
[23] See esp. P. Peeters, *AB* 59 (1941), 65-216.
[24] See above, p. 142.
[25] Chs. 33-50.
[26] Ch. 37.

with her. Amantios took up the case with enthusiasm, and introduced the visitors to the empress, who received them with great courtesy and promised to put pressure on her husband. Porphyrios played his part adroitly, and at one interview, noticing that she was in an advanced state of pregnancy, disclosed a prophecy made by Prokopios that the child she would bear would be a son, and that he would one day ascend the throne. Not surprisingly, he was promised by the grateful Augusta all he had petitioned for. But he had to wait many months – indeed, until the baptism of the child at Epiphany 402 – for the promises to be fulfilled. Even then (as we shall see) he had to employ a cunning stratagem suggested by the empress, for Arkadios and his advisers had understandable objections to harassing such loyal subjects and reliable taxpayers as the pagan inhabitants of Gaza.[27]

Some features in this richly embroidered tale seem more plausible than others. For example, Porphyrios is not likely to have ventured on the long sea route to Constantinople, taking in Rhodes on the way, in the late autumn and early winter; from 24 September to 10 November the sea was considered dangerous for shipping, while there was a general shut-down of seaborne traffic from 11 November to 10 March.[28] The narrative here is redolent of miracle, and Mark's (or his reviser's) choice of seasons seems to have been motivated by the desire to highlight the triumph of faith over natural hazards rather than to record actual dates. We have in fact no reliable evidence when or how his hero travelled to the capital. On the other hand, there is no reason to question the substantial accuracy of his account of Porphyrios' interview with John, any more than of his success in at long last securing the destruction of the temples in Palestine, additional privileges for the Christians there, and, finally, the erection in 406 of a magnificent church, the Eudoxiana, on the site of the Marneion.[29] As has often been remarked,[30] his portrayal of the main personalities (Arkadios, Eudoxia, John himself) and his report of their conversations and behaviour have a striking air of verisimilitude. John in particular is drawn to the life, and the words put into his mouth are the very ones we should expect to hear from him. For example, his comment[31] that he was not in the least concerned about the sovereigns' wrath since by yielding to it they only did harm to themselves without injuring him exactly recaptures his style and attitude.

Two points in this ancient 'faction' call for special comment. First, when Porphyrios and his companions were first brought into Eudoxia's presence, she begged forgiveness because her pregnancy had prevented her from

[27] Ch. 41.
[28] J. Rougé, *L'organisation du commerce maritime en Méditerranée sous l'empire romain* (Paris 1966), 33.
[29] Ch. 92.
[30] E.g. Grégoire-Kugener, op. cit., lxiii-lxiv.
[31] Ch. 37.

getting up from her golden couch and greeting the holy men at the door with the reverence they deserved.[32] This detail provides a fairly firm date for the episode, and also for Porphyrios' encounter with John shortly before, for it was on 10 April 401 that Eudoxia gave birth to her only son, the future emperor Theodosios II.

Secondly, the existence of a serious quarrel at this time between John and the empress has been called in question on the ground that, when he made his trip to Asia Minor, he was acting with a decisive authority which implied that 'he enjoyed unlimited credit with the court'.[33] But this is to assume that the break was of long duration, whereas Eudoxia was an impulsive woman whose fits of temper could be transitory. There was time enough for her mood to change, for on our chronology John's Asian journey lay several months ahead. In any case, it is important to distinguish between personal quarrels, however explosive, and matters of government policy, with which they are not likely to have interfered. Needless doubts have also been cast on the empress's alleged seizure of a piece of property, an action which would certainly have brought her bishop's wrath down on her if he had reason to suspect injustice. We have, as it happens, an independent witness to her insatiable rapacity in the historian Zosimos.[34] Later biographers, like Theodore of Trimithos in Cyprus and Pseudo-George of Alexandria (both seventh-century), were to enlarge on Mark's terse statement.[35] They identify the victim as a poor widow and the property as a small vineyard, all that was left to her after the confiscation of the estate of her unjustly accused and exiled husband Theognostos. Eudoxia fancied it, and took advantage of an imperial law supposedly decreeing (no such law existed) that any land on which the emperor or empress had trodden should pass into their possession. Both elaborate on John's championship of the wronged woman, and on the crescendo of confrontation between bishop and sovereign.

In addition, both represent John as drawing a comparison between her action and that of Jezebel, king Ahab of Israel's queen, who, when her husband had set his heart on a nearby vineyard and its owner, Naboth, refused to surrender it, caused the poor man to be stoned to death on a false charge (1 Kings 21.5-16), and as dwelling on this comparison in a public address. Many of these picturesque details are plainly legendary, but doubts about the nucleus of the story, that it was a widow who was dispossessed and that John, as her bishop, leaped to her defence, are surely misplaced. There is nothing intrinsically improbable in it. Equally misplaced is the scepticism so often voiced[36] about his having likened her

[32] Ch. 39.
[33] Grégoire-Kugener, op. cit., 113n. 1.
[34] 5.24.1-2.
[35] For these texts see F. Halkin, *Douze récits byzantins sur Jean Chrysostome* (Brussels 1977), esp. 191-204 (Pseudo-George's version).
[36] See esp. F. van Ommeslaeghe, *AB* 97 (1979) 131-59.

conduct to that of Jezebel. It would indeed be surprising, assuming she had in fact appropriated a poor widow's land, if such a comparison had not occurred to him, and equally surprising if so forceful and fearless a pastor had refrained from reminding her, and his congregation, of the shameful precedent for such behaviour. Palladios himself, as we shall discover,[37] was later to report that he was charged with having treasonably called the empress Jezebel, a charge which makes it clear that it was he, not later writers, who first invoked the biblical parallel.[38]

This is, we should remark, the first recorded open break between John and the imperial couple. It is likely that there had been earlier brushes between the censorious bishop and the hot-tempered Augusta; indeed, we have already noted[39] one occasion of possible friction. But however provocative his pulpit sallies, a public rupture seems to have been avoided. It is tempting to connect Eudoxia's resort to openly expressed indignation with the return to Constantinople of the three hostages – Aurelianos, Saturninos, especially her favourite and intimate count John. This must have occurred at latest in the first weeks of 401, but most probably in the closing quarter of 400.[40] The historian Zosimos confirms this surmise, actually stating[41] that, while she had previously been irritated by her bishop because of his habit of lampooning her before his congregation, it was 'after the return of John and the others' that 'she began openly showing the hostility (*dusmeneia*) she felt for him'. It would seem that the hostages, especially John, instead of being grateful for his repeated efforts on their behalf, bore him a bitter grudge and (again especially John) incited her against him. One possible reason for this may have been lingering resentment at the tone of his sermon on returning from his only half-successful mission to Gainas. So far from protesting against their ill-treatment, he had indirectly suggested that the blame for it lay with their own exorbitant trust in riches – and had done so in language strikingly reminiscent of the language he had used about the despised, and to them odious, Eutropios.[42] More immediate and important, however, were their suspicions both of his attitude to Gainas and of the confidence which the hated Goth so evidently placed in him. Above all, perhaps, they were enraged by his collaboration, so clearly implied (as they saw it) in his mission to Thrace, with their enemy Caesarianos, who had replaced Aurelianos as praetorian prefect and, to their chagrin, still retained the office.[43] In addition, count John had a

[37] See below, p. 228.
[38] On this para. see G. Dagron, *Naissance d'une capitale* (Paris 1974), 498-504; K.G. Holum, *Theodosian Empresses* (California 1982), 72.
[39] See above, p.150.
[40] For this date see Synesios, *De prov.* 2.4 (Terzaghi 2.122); *ep.* 61 (*PG* 66.1404). See above, p. 167.
[41] 5.23.2.
[42] G. Albert, *Goten in Konstantinopel* (Paderborn 1984), 163-5.
[43] On this para. see G. Albert, op. cit., 167 and 192-3.

private grievance of his own, believing, rightly or wrongly, that the bishop had betrayed him in his hour of need.[44] It is significant that, from now onwards, he was to remain an influential figure at court, ready (we may believe) to seize every opportunity to fuel the empress's animosity against him.

IV

It is now time to resume the story of the see of Ephesos and its corrupt bishop Antoninos. We have no certain knowledge when the news of his death and the Ephesian church's invitation to John to come in person to its rescue reached Constantinople, but the date is likely to have been late autumn or, more probably, early winter 401. Had they arrived in the summer or early autumn, it is likely that John would have rushed off to Asia immediately; it was the best time for travelling and, so far as we know, he had no other urgent business to detain him. The church's invitation was indeed a pressing one; it took the form of a solemn resolution (*psephisma*), ratified by both the clergy of Ephesos and the bishops of the province, calling on John to assist it in choosing a successor to Antoninos and in restoring order to a community which had been led astray by greedy self-seekers.[45] As it happened, he was preoccupied (as we shall discover)[46] with a body of fugitive hermits from Egypt seeking his protection, but he was satisfied that he had their troubles well in hand. So far as the palace was concerned, there was this time no hint of a veto. On the contrary, everything suggests that his mission had the support and full co-operation of the government, which may not have shared to the full his concern for clearing up scandal, but was at least as interested as he in extending the influence of the imperial see.

John must have been eager to set out at the earliest possible moment, but an overridingly important task imposed delay. The christening of Eudoxia's infant son, the future emperor Theodosios II, had been arranged for Monday 6 January 402, the feast of Epiphany, a highly suitable day since it celebrated the Lord's baptism. No one but the bishop of the imperial see, if present in the capital, could fittingly preside at so solemn an occasion, and there was no reason why John should not. Notwithstanding earlier frictions, his relations with the court were sufficiently correct for him to have government backing for his projected Asian journey. As a matter of fact, Eudoxia herself, in a letter written eighteen months later begging him to return from his first exile, confirms that he did so, declaring that she reveres him as 'the baptiser (*mustagogon*) of her children'.[47] Earlier this

---

[44] See above, pp. 155f.
[45] For Palladios' paraphrase of it see *Dial.* 14 (*SC* 341.286).
[46] See below, pp. 191ff.
[47] Sozomen 8.18.5: he uses the verb *mustagogein* in the sense of 'baptise' in 8.21.1.

century a hitherto unknown fragment came to light of a sermon which John preached, almost certainly on the Tuesday following,[48] and which attests his presence in the city and his amicable relations with the emperor. In this he prays that Arkadios may live to enjoy many consulates, and may acclaim the child who is being baptised, and who shares with him the governance of the world (an allusion to his proclamation as Augustus on 10 January), as his well-loved son.

In passing we may note that, as he was present at the royal christening, John is likely to have witnessed (with what feeling we can only speculate) the ingenious trick by means of which Porphyrios, prompted by Eudoxia, at last, after so many months' delay, obtained the imperial consent to the destruction of the pagan temples at Gaza and relief for the local Christian population.[49] As the brilliant procession emerged from the baptistery, the bishop pressed a written petition asking that these pious requests of his be ratified into the hands of the courtier carrying the infant (was he the empress's favourite, count John?). A party to the plot, the courtier caused the child's head to bend forward in token of acquiescence, and cried out, 'His majesty commands that whatever the petition asks for shall be done.' However reluctant to harry the poor pagans of Gaza, the emperor had no option but to arrange for his newly baptised son's first command to be rigorously carried out.

It was immediately after 7 January, therefore, that John set sail from Constantinople, disregarding (as Palladios pointedly remarks)[50] both the wintry season and his own wretched state of health. He had entrusted the day-to-day administration of the see to his sharp-tongued, domineering archdeacon Sarapion,[51] who was also to keep him posted about current happenings in the capital. His episcopal functions, more particularly his preaching duties, he had delegated to Severian, bishop of the little sea-port of Gabala in Syria (Jeble, 25 km south of Laodikeia – Latakia), a popular pulpit orator with a fine command of scripture who, being an ambitious social climber, was trying his fortune in Constantinople. A date in very early January fits in neatly with the claim[52] he was to make on his return, two or three weeks (as we assume) after Easter (6 April), that he had been absent slightly more than 100 days. He took ship to cross the Propontis or Sea of Marmara to Apamea (Mudanya), on the north coast of Bithynia, a brief voyage which would shorten the journey to Ephesos and perhaps make up for lost time. It has often been objected that a sea trip was out of the question in early January, but this rests on a misunderstanding. While there was a general shut-down of shipping from 10 November to 10 March,

[48] A. Wenger, *REB* 10 (1952), 51-4: Greek text, French translation, and full discussion of date and circumstances.
[49] For the story see *Vita Porphyrii* 45.
[50] *Dial.* 14 (*SC* 341.288).
[51] See above, p. 121.
[52] *PG* 51.421.

it was by no means absolute; urgent voyages could be undertaken at any time in winter.[53] There was always a risk, of course, as Palladios emphasises, and in fact he and his party narrowly escaped being shipwrecked by a violent squall, but after a couple of days' delay put in safely at Apamea. There he was met, apparently by previous arrangement, by Palladios, bishop of nearby Helenopolis, Cyrinos, bishop of Chalkedon, and Paul, bishop of Heraklea. This rendezvous, incidentally, confirms our chronology:[54] if John had left Constantinople in early January 401, Palladios would not have had time to travel to Helenopolis, do what business he had there, and then go to Apamea to meet him. With these three as his companions, he travelled south by road to Ephesos.

V

Although not a patriarchal see (and never to become one), Ephesos was a leading ecclesiastical centre, and seems to have claimed some sort of primacy over the provinces adjacent to Asia itself; John's mandate, Palladios expressly states,[55] was 'to restore to health the deeply disordered affairs of the entire civil diocese of Asiana'. When he got there, he set about his task with characteristic energy and decisiveness. First, a successor to Antoninos had to be elected. He therefore summoned a council of seventy bishops from Lydia, Asia and Caria, the more western of the eleven provinces making up the civil diocese (the only ones, apparently, which came directly under the authority of the see, whatever its grander pretensions). Several bishops from Phrygia also attended voluntarily, from their keenness, Palladios loyally observes,[56] to profit from the great man's wisdom and eloquence. As the deadlock between rival aspirants to the vacant throne remained unresolved, John broke it by proposing, and pushing through, the election of an outsider, Herakleides, a Cypriot who had spent years in the Egyptian desert as a disciple of Evagrios Pontikos (345-99), the widely influential exponent of Origenistic spirituality, but for the past three years had served him as a deacon at Constantinople.[57] It seems more than likely that, anticipating the impasse, John had brought him with him. Before many months his association with Evagrios was to bring Herakleides into great trouble.[58] In the meantime his election (which Palladios, significantly, passes over in silence) proved extremely unpopular, and aroused a storm of protest on the score of his unsuitability. We even hear of rioting, which must have led to the intervention of the civil

---

[53] See E. de Saint-Denis, 'Mare Clausum', *REL* 25 (1947), 196-214; J. Rougé, 'La navigation hivernale sous l'empire Romain', *REA* 54 (1952), 316-17.
[54] A. Cameron, art, cit., 350 n. 38.
[55] *Dial.* 14 (*SC* 341.288).
[56] *Dial.* 14 (*SC* 341.290).
[57] Sozomen 8.6. Cf. E. Honigmann, *ST* 173 (1953), 120-1.
[58] See below, p. 223.

authorities in John's support, and it is reported that the general dissatisfaction was so great that he was obliged to prolong his stay in Ephesos well
beyond his original intentions.[59]

Next, the unfinished business of the damaging allegations against
Antoninos called for completion.[60] Indeed, of all the abuses John was
expected to sort out this was on every count the most urgent and important.
Antoninos' accuser, Eusebios, had in any case turned up, and was demanding a place on the council. Objections were raised to this, but he pointed
out that the inquiry, now two years old, had only been adjourned because
of the non-appearance of the witnesses; Antoninos might be dead, but six
bishops who had purchased their consecration from him were still in office.
The objection having been overruled, the minutes of the earlier proceedings
were produced and noted, and John instituted a thorough investigation.

This time the hitherto elusive witnesses, some of them clergy, others lay
folk (including some women), came forward. The six bishops who figured
on Eusebios' charge-sheet were also present; presumably they were there
as members of the council. At first they categorically denied the allegations,
but the witnesses were able to supply particulars of the payments made –
the dates, the places, the exact amounts. With the evidence looking blacker
and blacker, the defendants at last caved in and acknowledged their guilt.
In mitigation they pleaded that their only motive for paying Antoninos to
consecrate them had been to secure exemption from the often burdensome
municipal charges for which they, as members of their city councils (membership was in practice hereditary), had been liable, but from which, under
legislation going back to Constantine the Great,[61] they would be freed if
they were made bishops. Notwithstanding a recent ban on the ordination
of councillors[62] (not in fact rigorously enforced), they had considered this a
fairly innocuous form of tax-avoidance, and therefore begged either to be
allowed to continue as bishops or to have their money refunded; some of
them had handed over personal belongings of their wives to Antoninos.

It is at first sight puzzling that John apparently took this unblushing
avowal in his stride. Penalties against simony, as selling ordination for
money was called, were normally severe in the early church; here the
offence was compounded by the lesser one of continuing after consecration
to enjoy the comforts of married life. But if simony of this kind was, as it
seems to have been, widespread in Asia Minor, John perhaps reckoned that
it could be more effectively flushed out if those who confessed voluntarily
were treated mildly. At all events he was prepared in the present case, with
the agreement of his council, to take what seems an extraordinarily lenient
line. The guilty six were, of course, to be stripped of episcopal rank and

---

[59] Sokrates 6.11, supplemented by a revealing fragment from his first edition printed in *PG*
67.732, which alone mentions the rioting and the prolongation of John's stay.
[60] For the following see Palladios, *Dial.* 15 (*SC* 341.294-6).
[61] CT 16.2.2 (21 Oct. 319): cf. Eusebios, *HE* 10.7 (*SC* 55.112).
[62] CT 9.45.3 (27 July 398 – enacted probably under the influence of Eutropios).

office. Surprisingly, however, they were to be allowed, at divine service, to occupy places and receive communion within the sanctuary of the church, from which the laity were excluded. The heirs of Antoninos were to pay them back the money and goods he had received from them. Even more surprisingly, John undertook to obtain from the emperor permission for them to be permanently exempt both from membership of their councils and from the financial and other burdens attaching to it. This last promise provides eloquent confirmation (if confirmation is required) that, throughout this entire expedition, he was acting with the full backing of the emperor and his advisers.

Six new bishops were consecrated and installed in place of the six he had dethroned. They had, presumably, been vetted and approved by John himself; Palladios assures us that they were all men of exemplary life and teaching, and all dedicated celibates.[63] But the drastic purge he had carried out at Ephesos was not the end of John's activities in Asia Minor. Sozomen reports that he deposed thirteen bishops on grounds of simony, 'some in Lycia and Phrygia, others in Asia itself', and nominated replacements.[64] His accuracy has sometimes been questioned in view of Palladios' indignant insistence that he deposed only six;[65] he was rebutting the charge Theophilos was later to bring that, in his 'passion for domination' (*philarchias pathos*), John had unseated sixteen in a single day.[66] But there is in fact no discrepancy: Palladios was referring exclusively, as his reference to the minutes of the proceedings makes plain, to the depositions carried out in the province of Asia as a result of the decisions taken at the council held at Ephesos. It is reasonable to conclude that, perhaps on the basis of information received there, John afterwards moved south to Lycia and then east to Phrygia, and carried out similar purges in those provinces too. It is worth recording that, at the council of Chalkedon in 451, a priest from Constantinople was to affirm, without anyone contradicting him, that John had gone to Asia (Asiana?), and had there deposed and replaced fifteen bishops.[67]

One final step which, before leaving Asiana, John took in the interest of religious uniformity was, according to Sokrates,[68] to seize and close down numerous churches of the Novatians, Quartodecimans and other heretics. The Novatians belonged to the rigorist but otherwise orthodox sect which John had, with great reluctance, been obliged to tolerate at Constantinople.[69] The Quartodecimans celebrated Easter on the 14 Nisan, the day of the Jewish passover; it is possible that these Quartodecimans were Nova-

[63] *Dial.* 15 (*SC* 341.296).
[64] 8.6.
[65] *Dial.* 15 (*SC* 341.300-2).
[66] *Dial.* 13 (*SC* 341.272).
[67] *ACO* II.i.453-8.
[68] 6.19.
[69] See above, pp. 125f.

tians who had adopted this practice, as many of them seem to have done.[70] Some scholars[71] have questioned whether John could have carried out this purge, since the Novatians at any rate still enjoyed the protection of the law granted them by Theodosius I.[72] But Sokrates' evidence is not to be dismissed lightly; he was keenly interested in the Novatians, and carefully collected information about them. He also reports[73] that Leontios of Ankyra, before long to be one of John's bitterest enemies, had similarly deprived a Novatian community in Galatia of their church. John was certainly acting with a harshness which he could not have got away with at Constantinople, where the Novatians were respected and their bishop, Sisinnios, a popular figure and in good standing with court circles.[74] But where he was convinced the good of the church was at stake, he was not the man to shrink (as his behaviour at Ephesos had shown) from taking matters into his own hands. In any case it seems likely that the existing legislation favouring the Novatians, to which sticklers for orthodoxy strongly objected, was already beginning to crumble, for Theodosios II seems to have had no difficulty in replacing it in 423 with a law[75] which placed Novatians on exactly the same footing as other sectarians.[76] John's harassment of the Novatians, it is worth noting, caused resentment back in the capital, where Sisinnios (who had tried to persuade Leontios to reverse his policy) is likely to have protested; and when John himself was deposed, there were some who argued that because of it he deserved his fate.[77]

His business in the civil diocese of Asiana successfully concluded, John and his party made their way back to the capital. As it was March, when the sea-lanes were officially closed to all but the most venturesome,[78] they travelled the entire distance by road. This meant that they passed through Nikomedia (Izmit), the leading city of Bithynia and of the civil diocese of Pontica, a favourite imperial residence. Here John summarily dismissed the bishop, Gerontios.[79] Originally a deacon at Milan, this man had incurred the displeasure of its masterful bishop, Ambrose, who had ordered him to remain within doors for a year in penitential seclusion. Ignoring this sentence, he had betaken himself to Constantinople, where his proficiency as a physician, agreeable social manners and facility in public speaking

[70] E.g. Sokrates 4.28; 5.21. Cf. E. Amann, *DTC* 13.1446-7 (citing Theodoret, *Haeret. fabul. compend.* 3.4: *PG* 83.405).
[71] E.g. Baur, 2,150.
[72] See above, p. 126.
[73] 6.22.
[74] See above, p. 126.
[75] CT 16.5.59 (9 April 423).
[76] For this suggestion, and the whole incident, see H.J. Vogt, *Coetus sanctorum* (Bonn 1968), 257-8.
[77] Sokrates 6.19.
[78] J. Rougé, op. cit. (1966), 33.
[79] Sozomen 8.6 (the only source for this episode).

won him favour everywhere, especially at court. As a result he had been promoted bishop of Nikomedia, a metropolitan see. Ambrose's demands to John's easy-going predecessor Nektarios to have him sacked had had no effect whatever. Gerontios was the kind of prelate of whom John intensely disapproved, and he seized this opportunity of getting rid of him. In his place he consecrated Pansophios, a mild and upright man who had earlier been tutor to Eudoxia herself.

We can readily believe that John considered Pansophios the right man for the job. It is intriguing to note, however, that it was an appointment which was likely to give pleasure to the empress. For that very reason it was also a politically astute one: it was not likely to be overturned by the authorities however much local opposition it aroused. In fact, the people of Nikomedia were outraged by both John's moves. Gerontios was a highly popular bishop, all the more so as he had unsparingly placed his medical skills at the service of rich and poor alike. As for Pansophios, they received him 'with a mixture of aversion and fear' (Sozomen). There were demonstrations and riots, deputations of protest were sent to Constantinople, and indignant crowds paraded the streets chanting litanies as at a time of calamity; the universal plea was that Gerontios should continue as their bishop. As we should expect, John remained entirely unmoved. While in Bithynia, he also concerned himself with the vacant see of Basilinopolis, just west of the great lake on which Nicaea stands, filling it with a devoted disciple of his own named Alexander.[80] Born into a senatorial family at Cyrene, in North Africa, he had embraced the monastic life as a teenager, and had later been ordained priest. He had made John's acquaintance when visiting Constantinople on business, and in the dark days following his patron's downfall was to remain unswervingly loyal to him.

VI

John's Asian tour had all the appearances of a triumphal success. In modern times there has been endless debate[81] among historians and canonists about the constitutional propriety of the programme he carried out. Had not the council of Constantinople (381), in its second canon, decreed that in the civil dioceses of the eastern empire the bishops of one should not interfere in the affairs of another unless specifically invited to do so? Yet John had been busily unseating bishops, first, in Asiana, then in Pontica, and consecrating new men, in some cases nominees of his own who were locally resented, in their places. The council had also, in its third canon, assigned the see of Constantinople a primacy second only to that of Old Rome, but that had been a primacy of honour, not of executive action. It has often been remarked that there was little or no disposition, among

---

[80] For him see Synesios, *Ep.* 66 (*PG* 66.148-10).
[81] For a useful summary see P.J. Hajjar, *Le synode permanent*, *OCA* 164 (Rome 1962), 60-8.

contemporaries, to criticise John's behaviour. Antoninos himself, when Eusebios first brandished his charge-sheet, seems to have raised no objection,[82] on grounds of legal competence, to either John himself or, as was eventually decided, a three-man commission going to Asia to investigate the charges. Even at John's trial, two years later, when his enemies were scraping around for indiscretions with which to blacken him, only one of the numerous indictments brought against him denounced him for encroaching on other men's territory and ordaining bishops there, and this was apparently not deemed important enough to be discussed. Against this, there is an often overlooked remark of Sozomen's,[83] made years after John's death, that, following on his sacking of Gerontios, both the victims of his purges and their associates began complaining that he was behaving like a revolutionary, overturning the traditional rights of consecration in the churches.

So far as church law is concerned, a balanced verdict, modelled on that pronounced earlier this century by Pierre Batiffol,[84] seems in order. However high-handed some of his actions at Ephesos (e.g. his imposition of his protégé Herakleides), John's intervention there was entirely in conformity with the council of Constantinople. Asia lay outside his jurisdiction as bishop of the capital, but he had been expressly requested by the local church to sort out its problems; this explains Palladios' emphasis on the formal resolution it had passed.[85] By contrast, his earlier decision to adjudicate on Antoninos' conduct and his dispatch of a commission to Asia to act for him were seriously open to question. The 'resident synod' with whose assent he took it was still, to the best of our knowledge, a largely consultative gathering without judicial teeth. His deposition of Gerontios was an even more blatant infringement of accepted procedures; Nikomedia was a metropolitan see in the civil diocese of Pontica, and he was behaving as if he had primatial responsibility for it.

But there are wider considerations which a strictly juridical analysis tends to ignore, and in so doing obscures what was really happening. For one thing, both church institutions and church law were still developing, in some areas more rapidly than in others. For another, the influence of the Christian emperor, often arbitrary but always a force to be reckoned with in the east, could cut across canonical conventions. The 'resident synod', for example, was to become an important organ in the later Byzantine church; when John decided to investigate Antoninos' conduct, we can observe it taking a big step in that direction. Its status was still undefined, however, and we may question whether that step would have been taken if John had been a less forceful character, or if Antoninos had not had a

[82] See above, p. 164.
[83] 8.6.
[84] *Le siège apostolique (359-451)* (Paris 1924), 291; 296.
[85] See above, p. 172.

guilty conscience and had resisted. Again, John's expedition to Asia clearly had, and could never have been carried through without, the imperial government's approval and active co-operation. This goes far to explain why criticism of his actions was so muted, and why the single protest at his trial was quickly swept under the carpet. Government backing, too, explains how he got away with his brutal deposition of Gerontios.

More generally, John's Asian journey vividly shows him, sometimes within established conventions but quite as often in defiance of them, always however with the blessing of the state, firmly extending the authority of his see. He was setting a pattern which his successors were quick to follow. It is scarcely surprising that, just half a century later, the council of Chalkedon (451), in its 28th canon,[86] was to decree, as if it were merely spelling out the 'primacy of honour' conferred by the council of Constantinople, that the bishop of New Rome should consecrate all metropolitans in the three vast civil dioceses of Thrace, Pontica and Asiana. John's contribution to the recognition of Constantinople as the patriarchate of the eastern empire was not insignificant.[87]

---

[86] *ACO* II.i.447-8.
[87] V. Grumel, in *Les regestes des actes du patriarchat de Constantinople* I.1.14-26, actually lists (nos. 20 and 23) John's deposition of six bishops at Ephesos and others in Lycia and Phrygia as fully canonical enactments.

Dispute with Severian

I

Returning from Bithynia, John crossed the Bosporus and entered Constantinople some two or three weeks after Easter 402 (6 April). It was a triumphal homecoming, and he was greeted by an enormous, cheering crowd. It seems to have escorted him from the harbour to the square adjacent to his palace, transforming the city, as he was shortly to exclaim with delight, into a church ringing with God's praises. On the day following, back again in his own cathedral, he delivered one of his warmest, most pastorally sensitive addresses,[1] thanking the people both for their steadfastness during his absence from them and for their rapturous welcome.

Moses, he exulted, when he had been communing with God on the holy mountain, had been away from the Israelites for only forty days, and when he came down had found them given over to idolatry and sedition.[2] 'I have been away, not forty days, but fifty, a hundred, indeed more, and I have found you well behaved, practising our holy religion with enhanced devotion.' He had no need, therefore, to regret his lengthy absence; his confidence in their affection, in their faith, in the chastity of his spiritual spouse had been fully justified. Their ecstatic welcome had made him abundantly happy to return to his paradise – a paradise far superior to Eden, where there had been a scheming serpent, an Eve who proved a temptress, an Adam who had been led astray. Here to his delight he found a people worshipping God, confuting heretics and celebrating Christ's mysteries. If any vines or olives in this garden were deteriorating, he would soon restore them to a healthy condition. It had grieved him, it had grieved them too, that he had been prevented from keeping Easter with them. But this was no occasion for worry; he and they could keep the feast together today, since Christians proclaim the Lord's death and resurrection every time they celebrate the eucharist. No need to be distressed either that he had not officiated at the baptisms on the eve of Easter. Although he had been absent, Christ himself had been present, guiding the officiant's hand. It is not the human minister, but the Holy Spirit, who bestows the grace. All

---

[1] *PG* 52.421-4 gives only the ancient Latin version in a defective text. For the Greek original, discovered in 1958 in a Moscow codex, see A. Wenger, *REB* 19 (1961), 114-23; he also prints the excellent Latin text of Vaticanus 3.836.

[2] Exodus 24.18; 32.1-29.

the time he had been away, correcting abuses in the Asian churches, he had been linked to them by the bond of love, praying for the church God had entrusted to him. Their prayers, too, had sustained him whenever he boarded a ship, or entered a town or an inn. Most love withers with time, but separation had made theirs more intense. He begged them to continue loving him; their prayers were his bulwark and protection, their love his treasure beyond price.

It was a masterly performance, an eloquent illustration of his skill at exploiting the affectionate ties between himself and his flock – and also at seizing every opportunity to slip in useful morsels of theological instruction. He spoke with passion and conviction, all the more so perhaps because he was all the time angrily aware that, while he could rely unreservedly on the huge audience before him, there were other circles in the city of whose loyalty he could not be so sure. There was bitter irony in several passages of the address, obvious today to anyone who cares to read between the lines, but far more obvious to his listeners, who could watch every gesture, every facial expression, and interpret every inflection of his voice. They must immediately have sensed that he did not expect them to believe that his paradise regained harboured no scheming serpent, no Eve leading the innocent astray, no Adam whose seduction was planned. They must have had shrewd ideas as to whom he was pointing to when he spoke of wild vines or olive trees in need of corrective treatment if they were to bear fruit. They would quickly guess whom he had in mind when, having expressed his joy that his sheep were in good heart and that no wolf could be seen anywhere, he darkly added that, whenever one did put in an appearance, it soon disguised itself as a sheep so as not to seem to lag behind them in love. What they probably did not all know was that, while John was in Asia Minor, his archdeacon Sarapion, in obedience to his instructions, had been feeding him with information of what was going on in Constantinople,[3] and that these reports had alarmed and depressed him. Their gist was that bishop Severian,[4] the fellow-Syrian whom he had welcomed in the capital, had encouraged to preach, and had introduced at court, whom he had even invited to stand in for himself as cathedral preacher and had installed in his palace, had been exploiting this position to promote himself at his patron's expense. He had, Sarapion suggested, been undermining, systematically and with considerable success, John's standing both with the palace and with influential clerical and lay circles.

It is not difficult for us to reconstruct, in very broad outline, what had actually been happening. There was clearly no love lost between Sarapion and Severian, and it is more than likely that the archdeacon's reports to John were heavily prejudiced. There is no reason to suppose that, at the

[3] Sokrates 6.11.
[4] M. Aubineau, *Un traité inédit de christologie de Sevérien de Gabala* (Geneva 1983), gives an excellent summary of his career and relations with John.

early stages of their relationship at any rate, Severian was out to damage John, who from his great position had been extremely helpful to him; in Sozomen's words,[5] he had found John 'well disposed' to him. He was an ambitious man, however, with an eye to the main chance. A first-rate biblical scholar, he was an accomplished preacher whose sermons[6] (quite a few survive – many of them handed down, ironically, under John's name) have often been underrated by critics. They reveal that one of his strong points was the exposition of scripture. Although he had a harsh voice and spoke with a strong Syrian accent, they evidently went down well with popular audiences. Even before John's departure for Asia, he was becoming a favourite preacher with Arkadios and Eudoxia, and it is scarcely surprising that, with the stage left to himself, he made it his business to enhance his reputation, even striving (to Sarapion's annoyance)[7] to outshine John himself. As acting bishop he had the entrée to the court, and the surmise of historians that the empress and her intimate coterie of ladies found him a much more easy-going and acceptable spiritual mentor than the ever censorious John has much plausibility.

This was a critical juncture in John's career. His split with the imperial family over Eudoxia's appropriation of the widow's vineyard had clearly been patched up by the time he presided in early January at the infant Theodosios' baptism. His relations with the sovereigns must then have been correct, if not cordial, and it is evident that his Asian mission had government backing throughout. It was all too easy, however, for things to come unstuck, and for him to turn his back on the capital for more than three months was a risky venture. The danger was all the greater since the caretaker bishop he had nominated was a character so different from himself, a man well able, and only too eager, to ingratiate himself with influential people at court. Although the evidence is difficult to piece together, there can be little doubt that the various individuals and groups hostile to him took advantage of his prolonged absence, and of Severian's presence, to get together and form something like an organised opposition. He was not the first, and certainly not the last, confident leader to undertake a lengthy mission far from his home base, only to discover on his return that the political atmosphere there had changed significantly.

II

From the moment of John's departure there seems to have been tension, not to say hostility, between the two men he had left in charge of his affairs. Sarapion was convinced that the plausible, popular Syrian bishop was seeking to upstage, in the end to undermine, his master. It irked Severian

---

[5] 8.10.
[6] See esp. J. Zellinger, *Studien zu Severian von Gabala* (Münster 1926); H.D. Altendorf, *Untersuchungen zu Severian von Gabala* (Diss. Tübingen 1957 – typescript).
[7] Sokrates in *PG* 67.733 (a fragment from the first edition of his History).

that the role he had been assigned was a largely public relations one, preaching and presiding at the liturgy, while the real management of the diocese had been entrusted to the archdeacon (in whose hands John, blind to his adjutant's character, had in fact always been glad to leave it). Their mutual animosity came to a head in an incident which, trivial in itself, was quickly blown up out of all proportion to its importance. It is intriguing to note that two very different accounts of it and its repercussions have come down from the pen of Sokrates, one in a fragment[8] of the first edition of his History (now almost entirely lost), the other[9] in the second, revised edition.

Both versions agree that one day, when Severian walked past the place where Sarapion was seated, the archdeacon conspicuously failed to rise respectfully as courtesy to his senior required. God only knew, Sokrates confessed in his first edition, whether he had simply not noticed the bishop (as he was later to affirm on oath), or was arrogantly showing his contempt for him. According to his revised account, Severian, who had no doubt that the latter was the true explanation of his casual behaviour, indignantly exclaimed, 'If Sarapion dies a Christian, then Christ did not become man.' His earlier version had not mentioned this outburst, but had gone on to relate that Severian was so infuriated by Sarapion's apparent rudeness that he summarily, without awaiting the verdict of a formal investigation, degraded him from the diaconate and excluded him from communion. It is extremely unlikely, as is generally agreed,[10] that he in fact imposed these drastic penalties, for such an action would have gone far beyond any authority he had as John's stand-in preacher.

It was thus a troubled situation, heavy with petty bickerings, that John found on his return home. He had not to look far for material for the veiled expressions of disenchantment evident in his sermon. In addition, as Sokrates (in his final version) and Sozomen emphasise,[11] he was already nursing a grievance of his own against Severian. No more immune from vanity than other brilliant orators, he had been stung to the quick by the reports he had received of his locum's pulpit successes. The incident of Sarapion's apparent rudeness to Severian must have been the talk of the town, but when the archdeacon gave his personal report of it to John, he repeated Severian's angry exclamation but dishonestly omitted (according to Sokrates in his revised edition) the conditional clause, 'If Sarapion dies a Christian', thereby transforming it into a crude denial by the bishop of the Lord's incarnation. He even got friends to swear that that was what Severian had actually said. John was naturally shocked, but instead of setting up a tribunal to investigate what was obviously a preposterous charge immediately went over the top, and ordered the bishop to remove

---

[8] *PG* 67.732-6. For this earlier edition see Appendix A.
[9] 8.11 (*PG* 67.696-700).
[10] E.g. Baur, 2.159; Moulard, 409.
[11] 6.11; 8.10. Sokrates speaks of John's 'jealousy' (*zelotupia*), while Sozomen employs the verb derived from the noun.

himself from the city because of his insolence and his 'blasphemy against God'.[12]

In his first edition, which (as we noted) omitted Severian's outburst altogether, Sokrates had given a rather different account. According to this, John held a court of inquiry which looked into the allegation of rudeness on Sarapion's part, and acquitted him of intentional disrespect. To induce Severian to accept Sarapion's apology John even suspended the archdeacon from his duties for a week. It was only when the bishop refused to accept this verdict and insisted on Sarapion's demotion and excommunication that John, put out by his obstinacy, indicated to him, through a third party, that it was high time he returned to his diocese in Syria, which he had so long neglected. This is a pleasant story, presenting John and Sarapion as behaving sensibly and fairly and Severian as unreasonable inflexible. Indeed, the degree of inflexibility it attributes to Severian seems incredible since (if the rest of the story is true) he had been offered a generous settlement. It is not surprising that Sokrates omitted this entire feature, as well as his earlier report of Severian's action against Sarapion, from his revised edition, when he had clearly been more fully briefed on what had happened. Palladios seems to have been equally keen to protect his hero, for while normally profuse in his references to Severian, he nowhere refers to his expulsion from the city by John on a charge of blasphemy, something we should have expected him to exploit if it had not been so embarrassing.

John was, we may suspect, enjoying the euphoria of his successful Asian expedition; he was also intensely irritated by what he considered Severian's disloyalty. It is hard otherwise to explain his acting in such an impetuous and high-handed manner. He was evidently in an angry mood; the accusation later to be brought against him[13] that he had set loose his *dekanoi* (i.e. ushers or bailiffs attached to his household) to hound Severian suggests that he took rough measures to hasten the troublesome Syrian's departure from the city. But he had reckoned without the empress, who had conceived a liking for Severian as well as admiring his sermons. She was deeply upset by the news that he had been sent packing, and that he had already quitted Constantinople. In fact, he had only crossed the Bosporus and was at the moment staying at Chalkedon, almost certainly with its bishop Cyrinos, waiting probably to see whether the wind would veer in his favour. (Cyrinos, we recall,[14] had very recently been John's trusted friend, but was soon to become an implacable enemy. If, as seems likely, he had already turned against John, his hostility can only have been strengthened by the tales of his harshness which his guest poured into his ears.) Eudoxia at once sharply reprimanded John, and ordered that Severian should be

---

[12] Sokrates 6.11; Sozomen 8.10. Sokrates implies Severian's expulsion, while Sozomen (largely but not exclusively dependent on him) spells it out.
[13] The seventh of the first list of charges brought against him at The Oak: see below, p. 222.
[14] See above, p. 174.

immediately recalled.[15] John had no option but to acquiesce, and Severian returned, taking up residence again, it is generally assumed, in the bishop's palace. But John stubbornly refused to hold any intercourse with him, still less would he listen to well-wishers urging him to lay aside his disdainful aloofness. It was humiliating for him that the empress should have countermanded his instructions and openly taken sides with the upstart who was flagrantly abusing the kindness shown him.

The rupture between the bishop and his stand-in preacher became public knowledge immediately, and as John was the idol of the people there were violent demonstrations, with his supporters going on the rampage. This is clear not only from the evident alarm of the authorities, but from his own sermon of reconciliation some days later, in which he repeatedly urged his listeners to restrain their anger and desist from rioting.[16] There is no reason to suppose that he had instigated the mob to demonstrate on his behalf, but he was fully alive to the political usefulness of crowds and was a master at managing them.[17]

III

It was the empress herself who, in her impulsive but shrewd fashion, took the initiative and brought the ugly situation which had developed to an end.[18] Quite apart from the desirability of restoring calm to the disorderly city, she still stood in superstitious awe of her bishop. She knew that her flare-up of temper on hearing of Severian's expulsion had angered him, and she must have been reluctant to incur his further wrath. So, with a characteristically theatrical gesture, she sought John out in the church of the Holy Apostles, and, placing her year-old son in his lap, implored him, in the name of her dear child, to be reconciled with Severian. It was only with great difficulty that she prevailed upon him, and with many misgivings that John gave his consent. But the restoration of amity could not be a private transaction. The mob violence which had convulsed the city demanded that it be given the fullest publicity, and so a spectacular liturgical celebration lasting two days was arranged, presumably in the Great Church, at which the two bishops pledged themselves to unity and harmony. In his address Severian was to evoke[19] eloquently the practice of fine artists who, in order to emphasise that 'two emperors or two brothers who are also magistrates', though physically separate, are one in heart, like to paint the female figure of Concordia (*Homonoia*) standing behind them and enfolding them both in her arms. This was no conventional comparison, but a pointedly topical reference, intended to flatter the imperial family, to

[15] Sokrates 6.11.
[16] *De recipiendo Severiano* (*PG* 52.426).
[17] See, e.g., p. 208 below for his ominous message to Epiphanios.
[18] Sokrates 6.11.
[19] *Sermo ipsius Severiani de pace* (*PG* 52.426-7; Papadopulos-Kerameus, 17-18).

the concord which had been achieved between Arkadios and Honorius in 402, when the two brothers (whose governments were so often at odds with each other) assumed the consulate together, and which, for reasons of imperial propaganda, was celebrated by images on coins and public monuments depicting them as standing together as united comrades (none, alas, survives with an actual representation of Concordia).[20] Severian's apt rhetorical flourish tempts one to speculate (it is probably only a fanciful guess) whether John and he may not have stood side by side in token of unity, in full view of the congregation, at some stage in the stately ritual.

John addressed the crowded church on the first day; it is likely that Eudoxia, if not Arkadios himself, was present. The Greek text of his sermon has, unfortunately, not survived; all we have is a Latin translation[21] of what, from its relative shortness and compression, reads like an abbreviation of the original. As the occasion required, it was an appeal for peace and reconciliation, but one which John seems to make in a cool, even grudging spirit, clearly in deference to the imperial command. It opens with an elaborate plea to the people to show obedience to him. The church owes obedience to its bishop, just as subjects do to their ruler; as their father, a father excessively fretting for his children, and ready to lay down his life for them, he has a right to their obedience. Then he comes to his point. He is an ambassador pleading for peace; nothing could be more appropriate for a bishop to ask from his flock than peace, since it was to reconcile men that Christ became incarnate and died on the cross. So let them not shame him or frustrate his embassy. Dreadful things have been done in the church, but he could never give his approval to violence or sedition. So let them calm down, control their excited feelings, and put a curb on their indignation – indignation, presumably, at Severian's presumption. A cessation of strife is both God's will and the will of their devoutly Christian emperor. It is right that princes should be obeyed, especially when they themselves comply with the church's laws. 'If then I have prepared your minds to accept my petition as an ambassador, receive back our brother Severian.' There was a burst of cheering at this point, and he went on: 'Even as I spoke, you expelled all your anger from your minds. So receive him back with full hearts and open minds. Overlook and forget the wretched events of the past; when the moment of peace has arrived, there should be no remembrance of divisions.'

On the day following it was the rehabilitated Severian's turn. A truncated Latin version of his address has traditionally been printed alongside John's, but the complete Greek text[22] came to light in the 1880s (although

---

[20] See R. Grigg's remarkable article in *The Art Bulletin* (New York) 59 (1977) no. 4, 469-82. Also now A. Cameron, *Barbarians and Politics at the Court of Arkadios* (California University Press 1993), 246-9; 407-8.

[21] *PG* 52.423-6.

[22] A. Padadopulos-Kerameus, *Analekta Hierosolumitikes Stakhuologias* (St Petersburg 1891) 1.16-26. The Latin text is to be found in *PG* 52.425-8.

historians have made little use of it). It is a fine example of his oratorical style, highlighting its simplicity and repetitiveness, his liking for a succession of short, balanced clauses linked by assonance or rhyme, and the variety and originality of his imagery. He starts off by announcing, like the heavenly choir at Christ's birth, tidings of great joy: today the church's ship is in peaceful waters, only the heretics are storm-tossed. Is there a hint here that, although a charge of heresy had been the pretext for his expulsion, he had no truck with it? Here and there he inserts tactful references to John; twice he salutes him as 'our common father', i.e. 'mine as well as yours', once as 'the divine trumpet'. The body of the sermon in an extended paean of peace which would have been tedious if it had not been developed so ingeniously and flexibly. It is Christ himself, 'who is our peace and who has made both of us one' (Eph. 2.14), who has restored it. There has been, he emphasises, no division of heart or mind, of faith or doctrine, between the two; their rift has been entirely the insidious work of the devil. So today, as he with open arms accepts yesterday's invitation to renewed friendship, it is the devil and his allies who are weeping and lamenting, while the angels are rejoicing.

In his closing section[23] Severian attempted to allay the worries which he implied must be troubling many good Christian souls. In doing so he made full use of his renowned exegetical skills, but also displayed a measure of confidence, even of provocation, which must have raised many eyebrows, and which explains the omission of the entire passage from the Latin text. 'Let no one', he pleaded, 'be upset, or ask, "Should Christ's high-priests have yielded to petty-mindedness (*mikropsuchia*)?" ' He answered the question by avowing that bishops were only human, and for their comfort referred doubters to the example of the apostles. He then proceeded to a detailed analysis of the 'sharp contention' between Paul and Barnabas narrated in Acts 15.36-41 which, because Paul was not happy with the evangelist Mark, had led to their parting and going their separate ways. That again had been an instance of 'human petty-mindedness', but it had not been a case of the one party honouring justice, the other injustice, but of both seeking to advance true religion in their different ways. Paul's rejection of Mark had had the effect of spurring the younger man on to greater endeavour, and in the end this had led to a reconciliation between Paul and Barnabas. 'Let this ancient precedent', Severian concluded, 'be an encouragement to us in our situation. If there was petty-mindedness between Paul and Barnabas, why should people be surprised if it should arise between us two? ... So let us beseech our common father to seal the word of peace between us in Christ Jesus our Lord.'

<hr>

[23] Papadopulos-Kerameus, op. cit., 25-6.

IV

John's clash with Severian, in its origins a trivial affair, but one which he managed clumsily and with headstrong brutality, was to prove a turning-point in his career. The solemnly celebrated reconciliation was, of course, a political comedy played to appease public opinion – and, not least, to bring the rioting mobs to order. As Sokrates noted,[24] beneath the façade of amity the two men preserved their festering antipathy for each other. For Severian this meant little or nothing. He was free to continue living in Constantinople, he enjoyed access to the court and retained the friendship of the imperial family, and he had nothing to fear from the bishop beyond his frown and cold shoulder. In contrast to John's, his sermon had exhaled an air of assurance and confidence. But for John it meant that he had gained an implacable adversary who was resolved never to give up. Whatever Severian's original attitude to John, he could not now forget, or forgive, his humiliating expulsion, without a trial or even a cursory investigation. From this point onwards, indeed until the drama reached its denouement with John's death, he was to be a key figure at the centre of all the intrigues and plots against him. While Theophilos, as we shall see, was to be the immediate architect of John's downfall, it was Severian who was to prepare the ground in Constantinople, assiduously fanning the flames of hostility against him among the clergy, at court, with government officials and with the sovereigns themselves. He had already been getting to work, as we noted,[25] on Cyrinos of Chalkedon.

To outward appearances, of course, John had emerged as victor in the petty squabble. The empress herself, who had at first rebuked him for banishing her favourite preacher, had thought better of her anger, had thrown herself on his Christian charity, and had begged him, in her humblest manner, to reach an accommodation with his despised rival. If peace had been restored to the church and calm to the streets of the capital, the credit lay with him; it was he who had, however grudgingly, held out the hand of friendship to Severian and ordered the unruly crowds to desist from violence and go home. But the reality was rather different. For once John had been clearly in the wrong and, as a result, had publicly lost face. For once, yielding to vanity and extreme irascibility, he had allowed himself to make an egregious mistake which no one could pretend was anything other than that. Although the empress still retained, and would until the end retain, her awe and almost superstitious respect for him, his standing with her, and with many others, must have been seriously diminished.

We cannot tell how far John, always resilient and optimistic, was aware of this, but he seems to have realised that radical adjustments would have to be made in his administrative arrangements. A major step he took was

[24] 6.11.
[25] See above, p. 185.

to ordain Sarapion, from the start his indispensable man of confidence but hated by most of his clergy and now the instigator of his ill-judged attack on Severian, to the priesthood. That he did so at this juncture is evident from the fact that one of the accusations to be levied against him at his trial was that he had ordained Sarapion when he still had a serious charge hanging over him[26] – presumably that of having shown disrespect to Bishop Severian. This is often represented[27] as a concession which John made in the interests of conciliation. It may have been, but John did not make concessions easily; we are also entitled to view his action, which he must have taken with a heavy heart since he had by no means lost confidence in Sarapion, as a sign of his awareness of his weakened position. As a result he had to find a replacement for the all-important position of archdeacon and steward of his household. Choosing men was never John's strong suit, and the deacon he now appointed, a man of whose name and background we know nothing, was to prove a traitor to him in his darkest hour, disloyally persuading his clergy to renounce their allegiance to their bishop.[28]

---

[26] See below, p. 222; also 299.
[27] E.g. Baur, 2.161.
[28] So John himself reports in his first letter to Pope Innocent I: *SC* 342.72-4. See below, p. 216.

14

The Affair of the Long Brothers

I

A few months before John set out for Asia, probably in late autumn 401, there had suddenly appeared in the streets of Constantinople some fifty travel-worn monks of Egyptian origin,[1] headed by four – Dioskoros, Ammonios, Eusebios, and Euthymios – who were conspicuous for their height and therefore known as the Long Brothers (*makroi adelphoi*). The eldest of the four, Dioskoros, had been bishop of Hermopolis (Damanshur), a tiny see some 60 km south-east of Alexandria created to provide for their spiritual needs. They had originally been settled at Kellia ('the cells'), not far from Nitria (Wadi el Natrun) in the desert south-west of the Nile Delta, and had been prominent members of the group of monks whom Evagrios Pontikos (345-99),[2] spiritual author and founder of monastic mysticism, had gathered round him during his fourteen years' stay there. Ammonios indeed seems to have shared with Evagrios the leadership of the community[3] (to which Palladios tells us[4] he too had belonged for nine years). They had a great reputation for holiness and courageous endurance for the orthodox faith. More than a year before, however, the three younger brothers had been excommunicated, and all four of them hounded out of Egypt, then out of Palestine, by Theophilos, patriarch of Alexandria, ostensibly on the charge of being Origenists, i.e. followers of the teaching of Origen, the remarkable third-century Alexandrian biblical scholar, theologian, and spiritual writer. Origen's influence had been widely pervasive in the eastern churches, but in the later fourth century his ideas were increasingly becoming the subject of attack, notably by Epiphanios, the aged, immensely venerated bishop of Constantia (formerly Salamis) in Cyprus (367-403), who as early as the mid-370s had set himself in the vanguard of opposition to him.

Like other cultivated eastern Christians, like Theophilos himself until a year or so back,[5] the Long Brothers and their adherents enthusiastically

---

[1] See above, p. 172.
[2] See above, p. 174.
[3] Palladios, *Hist. Laus.* 24 (Butler 78).
[4] *Hist. Laus.* 18 (Butler 47).
[5] For Theophilos' attitude to Origen (and a detailed discussion of all the issues), see E.A. Clark, *The Origenist Controversy* (Princeton 1992).

agreed with Origen that the divine nature is wholly spiritual and incorpo-
real. After all, their spiritual mentor had been the fervently Origenist
Evagrios, whom Theophilos too had so much admired that he had wanted
to make him a bishop.[6] By contrast the great majority of simple Egyptian
monks, uneducated and fanatical, clung tenaciously to the naive view
('anthropomorphism') that, since the bible declares that God had made man
in his own image, he too must have all the corporeal attributes that men
have (eyes, hands, feet, mouth, etc.) – and which, indeed, scripture constantly appears to represent him as possessing. But if on the matter of God's
incorporeality the Long Brothers were certainly Origenists, there is no
evidence that they endorsed any of the great theologian's more daring
speculations which were now being called into question and which later
orthodoxy was to condemn. Hitherto they had basked in Theophilos' favour,
and it was out of his great regard for them that he had not only consecrated
Dioskoros as bishop, but had forcibly constrained Eusebios and Euthymios
to settle in Alexandria, accept ordination, and share the administration of
the church with him.[7] Suddenly, however, he had turned implacably
against them. The reasons for his decision to persecute them are not wholly
clear, but can be reconstructed in broad outline.

What initially turned him against them was the decision of Eusebios and
Euthymios to abandon his service and return to the desert. At first, while
irritated, he was not unduly upset, believing their motive to be their longing
to resume the contemplative life. Annoyance, however, turned to anger
when he discovered that the real cause of their dissatisfaction was disgust
at his absorption in money-making; they even feared for their souls if they
continued being associated with such activities.[8] But this alone does not
provide the full explanation of his bitter hostility. This is to be found in the
fact that he had broken irrevocably with his guest-master Isidore, the once
trusted agent whom he had earlier backed for the see of Constantinople,
and that he, disgraced and excommunicated by his master, had been given
shelter and active support by the Long Brothers.[9]

Theophilos' squalid quarrel with Isidore has been variously reported.
Sokrates[10] traces the rift to a row he had with Peter, archpriest of Alexandria, whom he wanted to get rid of anyway, in which Isidore had supported
Peter. For Palladios,[11] whose account is echoed by Sozomen,[12] its main-
spring was the patriarch's cupidity. A rich widow, it seems, had given
Isidore 1,000 gold staters with instructions to spend them on clothing for
the poor, but to keep this secret from Theophilos since she feared he would

[6] Sokrates 4.23.
[7] Sokrates 6.7.
[8] Sokrates 6.7.
[9] Sozomen 8.12.2.
[10] 6.9.
[11] *Dial.* 6 (*SC* 341.130-6).
[12] 8.12.

squander the money on the costly building projects for which he was notorious.[13] Isidore did as she had requested, to the extreme annoyance of Theophilos, who was kept informed by his spies. Whichever of these stories is true (it is quite probable they both are), Theophilos was outraged by Isidore's insubordination, and was determined to destroy him. He recalled that eighteen years previously he had received a letter accusing Isidore of buggery with a young sailor. He had done nothing about it at the time as he was too busy (and Isidore then stood high in his favour), but he had filed the letter in case it should some day come in useful. He now brought it out, dragged Isidore before the assembled clergy, and, although neither the sailor nor any supporting evidence could be produced, had him excluded from church fellowship. He had, if we can trust Palladios,[14] got over the embarrassing lack of hard evidence by bribing another young man with fifteen gold pieces (which he dutifully handed over to his widowed mother!) to accuse Isidore of sexual misconduct with him. In his despair, and fearing for his life, Isidore fled to the monastic community in the Nitrian desert of which he had been an inmate in his youth, the very community to which Ammonios and the other Long Brothers belonged. They welcomed the wretched octogenarian, and boldly took up his cause, making a powerful plea to Theophilos to restore him to communion.[15]

Theophilos was infuriated that Ammonios and his brethren had given Isidore shelter, and still more that they had dared to become his champions. He therefore thought up an ingenious scheme for exacting his revenge. As it happened, he had recently decided that, outspoken Origenist though he had hitherto been, the time had come when it would suit his interest to make his peace with the simple-minded 'anthropomorphist' monks. In his pastoral letter of early 399 announcing the date of Easter, which was circulated throughout Egypt but is now lost,[16] he had denounced anthropomorphism and come out unambiguously in favour of the incorporeality of God taught by Origen. He had been thoroughly alarmed, however, by the hostility which this had aroused among anthropomorphist monks, who descended in force on Alexandria and demonstrated menacingly. He had managed temporarily to appease them by tactfully exclaiming,[17] 'When I look at you, I am sure I am seeing the face of God', but from this moment he carried out a cynical *volte-face* and declared a holy war on Origenism and its adherents. He was thus enabled, at a stroke, both to enlist the formidable army of crudely literalist monks as his storm-troopers and, on

[13] For his passion for building (*lithomania*) and worship of money see Isidore of Pelusion, *Ep.* 152 (*PG* 78.285).
[14] Loc. cit. Theophilos confirms the charge of immorality and his condemnation of Isidore in a garbled, tendentious account given in his synodical letter to the bishops of Palestine and Cyprus: see Jerome, *Ep.* 92.3 (*CSEL* 55.150-1).
[15] Sozomen 8.12.
[16] Its argument in outline can be deduced from Sokrates 6.7.; Sozomen 8.11; Gennadius, *De vir. ill.* 33 (*PL* 58.1077-8).
[17] Sokrates 6.7.

the pretext of their being Origenists, to order the expulsion of the leaders of the intellectually-minded ascetics of Nitria. When a number of these went up to Alexandria with their priests to seek an explanation of their unexpected dismissal, he seized Ammonios by the throat, struck him on the face causing his nose to bleed, and shouted, 'Anathematise Origen, you heretic!'[18]

Shortly afterwards, to put the matter on a proper legal basis, he assembled a synod 'of bishops of the neighbourhood' and, in their absence, had the Long Brothers formally excommunicated, branding men (as Palladios lamented)[19] whom until recently he had been treating with exceptional honour, as impostors, all because they had loyally supported his fallen guest-master. Relying exclusively on Palladios' report, scholars[20] have generally assumed that this synod was held in Alexandria in 400. There is a strong case,[21] however, for identifying it with the synod of anti-Origenist bishops from the vicinity of Nitria which Theophilos, by his own account,[22] convened in a church of one of the monasteries there, and which fulminated against Origenism. But Theophilos' real object was to rid himself of the Long Brothers altogether. He therefore lodged incriminating charges against them with the Augustalis, or prefect of Egypt, demanding their expulsion by military force. He backed his own indictment with another of similar content (he was responsible for its wording) which he had suborned five Nitrian monks to sign publicly; as a reward he ordained one of them bishop, another priest, and the remaining three deacons.[23]

Having received the authorisation he needed, Theophilos personally, in spring 400, with a handful of government soldiers provided by the Augustalis and a drunken rabble of his own, supervised a night attack on the Nitrian settlements which culminated in the ejection of the Long Brothers and their monks, the deposition of Dioskoros from his bishopric, and the plundering and burning of the monks' cells.[24] The Long Brothers, who had managed to conceal themselves while the brutal assault was in progress, had no option but to take to the road. Even then they could not escape the despotic patriarch's fury. When he learned that the fugitives were being kindly received in various places, he addressed a circular letter[25] to the bishops of Palestine (he was later to send it on to those of Cyprus),[26] reminding them of his condemnation of Origen's teaching, giving a shamelessly distorted account of what had happened at Nitria, and sternly

---

[18] For the order, and his challenge to Ammonios, see Palladios, *Dial.* 6 (*SC* 341.138).
[19] *Dial.* 7 (*SC* 341.140).
[20] E.g. Baur 2, 204 n. 11.
[21] See A. Favale, *Teofilo d'Alessandria* (Turin 1958), 106-7.
[22] Cf. his synodical letter: Jerome, *Ep.* 92.1 (*CSEL* 55.147-8).
[23] Palladios, *Dial.* 7 (*SC* 341.140-2).
[24] Palladios, *Dial.* 7 (*SC* 341.142-6); also Sokrates 6.7.
[25] Jerome, *Ep.* 92 (*CSEL* 55.147-50: as usual, Jerome was his translator).
[26] See below, p. 197.

warning them to shield their flocks from the misguided monks' teaching. Palladios, in what seems a selective citation of this letter, represents[27] him as requesting them not to grant them admission to either a church or a private house.

II

Harassed and hustled along wherever they went, the Long Brothers and their companions, originally more than three hundred, made their way to Jerusalem, and thence to Scythopolis (Bethshan, on the west side of the Jordan valley). Here the abundance of palm-trees attracted them; they fancied they could scrape a living by making matting with their leaves. But wherever they went, they found that doors were slammed in their faces; Theophilos and his emissaries had seen to that. Their number was steadily dwindling as the faint-hearted dropped out. Eventually, after many months of wandering, they conceived the idea of sailing to Constantinople, taking Isidore with them, and there, according to Sokrates and Sozomen,[28] submitting their case to the emperor and the bishop of the imperial see. The likelihood is, however, that it was John on whom they mainly pinned their hopes, renowned as he was for his years-long sojourn in the Syrian mountains as a hermit, although they must also have been fully aware of the influence he could use in official circles in their favour. They had no inkling that taking up their cause might be liable to embroil him with adversaries who would be only too eager to undermine him.

On arriving in the capital the refugees made their way straight to John's palace, fell on their knees before him, and poured out the story of their tribulations. Although Sokrates states[29] that John was in the dark about the whole affair, this was plainly not the case. The Origenistic controversy had been raging for some years and must have been talked about everywhere; nothing interested people more than theological wrangles. More importantly, Theophilos' circular to the bishops of Palestine and then those of Cyprus can hardly have escaped him, and it is likely that (as we shall see)[30] he had recently received a letter from Epiphanios of Cyprus warning him to abstain from studying Origen's writings and urging him to convene a synod to condemn their teaching. What was true was that he had so far kept himself aloof from the controversy, having no wish to be forced to adopt a public stance on the issues at stake. As we have seen, he was by nature much more a practical than a dogmatic theologian. All his life he had been convinced that to rack one's brains about the being of God, which in the

---

[27] *Dial.* 7 (*SC* 341.148).
[28] Sokrates 6.9.; Sozomen 8.13. Palladios (*Dial.* 7: *SC* 341.148) speaks only of their having recourse to John.
[29] 6.7 ad fin.
[30] See below, p. 198.

last resort transcends human comprehension, was one of the most presumptuous sins of heretics.[31]

In fact, when the refugees appeared[32] before him, begging for his help
and threatening that, if he could do nothing for them, the only course left
to them would be to resort to the emperor, he was painfully conscious of
the awkwardness of his position. However shocked he was by their ill-
treatment, he knew that they were canonically subject to the bishop of
Alexandria, and that they lay under his ban. No one was more aware than
he of Theophilos' extreme touchiness, or recalled more vividly how annoyed
he had been when John had been appointed bishop of the imperial see
instead of his own nominee. He was anxious, too, we may suspect, to do
nothing to endanger the fragile co-operation he had established with him
in ending the schism of Antioch.[33] He took every care, therefore, to observe
all the proprieties, and to avoid giving the Egyptian Pharaoh the least
ground for complaint. Thus he declined to put even the monks' leaders up
in his palace as official guests, a courtesy which in normal circumstances would
have been expected of a bishop, but lodged the party in a hospice attached to
the church of Hagia Anastasia.[34] Again, so as to avoid the charge of expending
church funds on their maintenance, he arranged for this to be looked after by
Olympias and her deaconesses. Some of the more able-bodied were encouraged
to contribute to the upkeep of the group by taking jobs.

John knew that Theophilos had agents resident in the capital whose
business it was to ensure, by the tactful distribution of bribes, that the
persons appointed to government posts in Egypt were likely to meet with
their master's approval. These he now summoned, and inquired of them
what they knew about the fugitives, and also what should be done about
them. Although it seems surprising that they should have dared speak so
frankly, we have Palladios' word that they honestly admitted that the
monks had been violently treated. Their advice was that, while it was his
duty as a bishop to show them kindness, it would be highly imprudent to
admit them to communion, since this would enrage Theophilos beyond
measure. John was careful to follow this advice: while permitting them to
attend public prayers, he refused to allow them to receive communion. In
fact, if we can trust Palladios, he seems at first to have imagined, with his
customary optimism, that if he handled the matter discreetly, he stood a
good chance of persuading Theophilos to lay aside his embittered feelings
towards them. So he took two important steps (the importance of the former
has not usually been sufficiently noticed). First, he forbade them to talk
publicly about the injustice they had suffered, insisting that they keep
silent about the reasons for their flight to the capital. They must have been
taken aback by this ban, but he explained that the success of the negotia-

---

[31] See, e.g., his sermons 'On God's Incomprehensibility' delivered in 386: see above, pp. 61f.
[32] Palladios, *Dial.* 7 (SC 341.148-52), is the source of much of the rest of this section.
[33] See above, p. 117.
[34] See above, p. 119.

tions he planned to undertake with Theophilos on their behalf depended on their observing it.

Secondly, he sent a personal letter to the patriarch, couched in warm and conciliatory terms, begging him to receive them back. The summary preserved by Palladios[35] runs: 'Please do me a courtesy – me, who am your son as well as your brother – and take these people back under your protection' (the reference to his being his son was a reminder to Theophilos that he had, albeit reluctantly, been John's consecrator). Sozomen's version[36] of this letter is somewhat more circumstantial. According to it, John requested Theophilos to restore the monks to communion since their belief concerning God was, as far as he could discover, entirely correct. If he considered that their case should be judicially investigated, he should send someone to Constantinople to charge them formally.

III

Theophilos himself had not been idle in the meantime. When news that the Long Brothers had set sail for Constantinople reached him, he at once realised the damage they could do there to him and his reputation. His first thought was to enlist Epiphanios of Cyprus, renowned as a heresy-hunter and the pioneer of anti-Origenism, as an ally; with his immense prestige he could be useful in swinging opinion in the capital against the fugitives. He therefore rushed off a personal letter to him,[37] at the same time dispatching to him and the other bishops of Cyprus the circular letter he had earlier addressed concerning the Nitrian affair to the bishops of Palestine.[38] In the personal note he urged Epiphanios to convoke a synod of the island's bishops, have Origen and his teaching formally condemned, and then send the minuted decisions to himself, to the bishop of Constantinople and to anyone else he deemed suitable, so that no one could be under any illusions about the perniciousness of the doctrines for which the Long Brothers had been appropriately punished. So that no time might be lost, he suggested that he send the documents by special courier to Constantinople. He had singled out Epiphanios, he tactfully added, as one who had been a doughty fighter in this field long before himself. The old man, needless to say, was flattered by the conversion to his own way of thinking of 'so great a pontiff', who only a year or two back had been rebuking him for anthropomorphism.[39] As requested, he at once assembled the Cypriot bishops in synod and had Origen and his works condemned. He then

[35] *Dial.* 7 (*SC* 341.152).
[36] 8.13.
[37] Letter 90 in Jerome's correspondence (*CSEL* 55.143-6).
[38] See above, p. 194.
[39] Sokrates 6.10. For his satisfaction see his letter to Jerome (*Ep.* 91 in Jerome's correspondence: *CSEL* 55.145-6).

communicated these decisions to John, and exhorted him to summon a synod in Thrace which would likewise proceed to outlaw Origenism.[40]

Meanwhile Theophilos himself, as he informed Epiphanios in his letter, had sent to Constantinople several hermits and clerics to act for him there. He had astutely arranged that the hermits should be drawn from the Nitrian settlements themselves (they probably included the five he had suborned to denounce the Long Brothers to the Augustalis),[41] and that all the members of the group should be dignified men of austere bearing, likely to inspire respect. Their mandate was to rebut any propaganda the Long Brothers might disseminate, and to present their eviction from Nitria and Palestine in the most favourable light.

Having thus prepared the ground, Theophilos was in no mood to respond positively to John's conciliatory letter. His mood had in fact become distinctly hostile, for completely unfounded rumours were circulating Alexandria that John was offering communion to the refugees and was prepared to rally to their defence.[42] More importantly, he seems to have begun to suspect that John's espousal (as he took it to be) of the Long Brothers in a dispute which was the exclusive concern of the Alexandrian church was all part of a deliberate policy of extending the authority of the imperial see. John was at this time carrying out his visitation of the Asian churches, and the reports which Theophilos received of his activities there can only have confirmed his worst suspicions. The Alexandrian church had never been slow, at least until 381, to intervene in the controversies of the eastern churches, not least Constantinople, but similar pretensions by New Rome were not to be tolerated. It was inevitable, he saw clearly, that what had begun as an irritating dispute with a pack of insubordinate monks should from now onwards take on a wider, political dimension. John being absent from the capital, there was no point in calling him to order for interference for the moment. He decided, however, that since the Long Brothers had apparently found such a powerful protector in the capital, the agents he had earlier sent there needed reinforcement. According to Palladios,[43] he therefore dispatched to Constantinople a further delegation, this time composed of men chosen for their skill in controversial debate, and armed them with damaging dossiers which he had personally drafted.

One of his objects, Palladios adds, was through these agents to spread the impression, especially in the palace, that the fugitives were nothing but impostors. In this he seems to have had considerable success, for the monks were forced back on the defensive and found it necessary to send him

[40] Sokrates 6.10.

[41] Palladios, *Dial.* 7 (*SC* 341.152) refers only to Theophilos' second delegation (see below); but this consisted of trained dialecticians, not simple monks.

[42] Sozomen 8.13.

[43] *Dial.* 7 (*SC* 341.152). It is tempting to identify the two sets of emissaries, but the sources are positive that the first set were sent immediately after Theophilos learned of the sailing of the monks for Constantinople, the second after he had received John's letter.

written assurances that they abjured any form of erroneous doctrine. As these apparently failed to specify Origenism, they only increased his exasperation. The monks then decided that the time had come for a counter-attack. For the first time, therefore, they drafted for presentation to John a formal petition giving a detailed statement of the violence of which they had been victims and a catalogue of their charges against Theophilos. Palladios was careful to call their submission a 'petition' (*libellous enteuktikous*)[44] since he knew that John could not properly receive a formal accusation against the patriarch of another province. The refugees' grievances against Theophilos were, apparently, so serious, and expressed in such outspoken terms that Palladios, who was not normally backward in reporting matters prejudicial to him, coyly excused himself from reproducing them in case he should upset the faith of younger and less mature Christians.

Once again, therefore, John, probably on his return from Asia, found himself in an acutely embarrassing position.[45] As we have seen, the last thing he wanted was for the affair to become an open scandal. First, he made a fresh attempt, getting other bishops to add their voices to his own, to persuade the refugees to abandon their incriminating charges against Theophilos. Only mischief, he argued, could result from pressing them in a formal way. Whatever Theophilos imagined, he himself had no wish to provoke a clash between the sees of Constantinople and Alexandria, still less to be drawn himself into confrontation with the Egyptian patriarch. Then, when his request was met with a stubborn refusal, he sent Theophilos a second letter informing him that the refugees had lodged a written indictment against him. He enclosed a copy of it, and begged him to respond to it as he judged best. He had done everything he could to induce them to leave the capital, but they had paid no attention to his plea.

Theophilos' reaction was immediate, and explosive. First, in a fit of temper he excommunicated bishop Dioskoros, eldest of the Long Brothers. At the time of his night raid on the Nitrian settlement he had had him manhandled and had deposed him from his modest bishopric (Hermopolis Parva), but had been careful not to include him when he excommunicated his three brothers. Then he dashed off a truculent note to John, in effect bidding him mind his own business. As summarised by Palladios,[46] it runs: 'I think you are not unaware of the ordinance of the Nicene canons forbidding a bishop to adjudicate a case which falls outside his ecclesiastical area. If however you were unaware, now that you have been informed refrain from meddling with accusations brought against me. If it were necessary for me to be put on trial, it would be before Egyptian judges and

---

[44] *Dial.* 7 (*SC* 341.154).
[45] Palladios, *Dial.* 7 (*SC* 341.152-4) is the source of this and the following paragraph.
[46] *Dial.* 7 (*SC* 341.154), the sole source for the letter. Theophilos refers to canon 5 of the council of Nicaea (325), reaffirmed in a fuller form in canon 2 of the council of Constantinople (381).

not before you, who live more than seventy-five days' journey away.' This was a shot across John's bows, a sharp warning that if the see of Constantinople had got away successfully with unwarranted intervention in Asia, it must not expect to do so in Egypt. What the letter did not reveal was that for Theophilos the misdeeds of the Nitrian refugees were becoming an issue of secondary importance in comparison with the threat which John himself seemed to pose to his authority and prestige.

IV

If our chronology is correct, the agony of the refugees had been dragged out for several months, the delay being caused in part by John's insistence that they should on no account ventilate their grievances officially, in part by his absence in Asia Minor for more than three months in early 402. A further factor contributing to it undoubtedly was the distrust and suspicion of them which Theophilos' two groups of agents had, it would seem, successfully sown. It may be remarked that the alternative chronology favoured by many scholars,[47] which places the Asian trip in early 401, makes the prolonged delay much harder to understand. The long impasse, however, was abruptly broken in mid-summer 402. On receiving Theophilos' letter John decided that there was nothing more he could do in the affair.[48] Keeping the contents of the letter to himself, he summoned both the Nitrian monks and the Egyptian patriarch's agents, and urged them to make peace with one another. His well-intentioned mediation, however, only had the effect of making both parties stick more obstinately to their entrenched positions. The Nitrian monks, in particular, after waiting two-thirds of a year with no prospect of vindication, had reached the end of their patience. Driven to despair at being let down by the man they had confidently expected to be their champion, they resolved to emerge from their enforced silence, bypass John, and make a direct appeal to the emperor and empress. With this object they drafted two petitions addressed to them personally. One was directed against Theophilos' agents, and charged them with having made scandalously defamatory statements about them. The other was a detailed catalogue of highly damaging accusations against Theophilos himself.

Their opportunity came, it seems certain, on 24 June 402. This was the feast of John the Baptist, and on it, according to Palladios,[49] they contrived to waylay the emperor and empress at the Baptist's shrine at Hebdomon – the shrine hallowed by its possession of the Precursor's head, to which Gainas had gone to pray two years previously.[50] The royal couple, one would

---

[47] See above, p. 165.
[48] Palladios, *Dial.* 8 (*SC* 341.154-6).
[49] *Dial.* 8 (*SC* 341.156).
[50] See above, p. 159.

guess, had gone there to make their devotions on the holy day, and the monks seized the chance to present their petitions to them. In particular, they begged the empress that their complaints against Theophilos' agents might be investigated by the civil courts, and that the patriarch himself should be brought to stand his trial before John. Sozomen, who makes no mention of either the emperor or the Baptist's shrine, gives a somewhat more colourful picture of the encounter.[51] According to him, Ammonios and his companions poured out their grievances against Theophilos to Eudoxia as she was driving in her carriage. As she already had some knowledge of their troubles, and respected the men personally, she had ordered her coachman to stop when she saw they wanted to speak with her, and then leaned out of the carriage, and begged them to bless her and to pray for the emperor, for herself and their children, and for the empire. When she had heard their story, she promised that she would make it her business to see that a council before which Theophilos would have to appear was speedily convened.

Whatever we make of Sozomen's picturesque additions, his report of the meeting and that of Palladios supplement each other without introducing any disturbing discrepancies. What is interesting is that both stress the role of Eudoxia; both make it plain that it was to her that the refugees wished to present their petitions, and that they were confident that they could rely on her support. It is tempting to suspect that their dramatic encounter with her was not wholly accidental. We should dearly like to know what comings and goings (if any) there had been behind the scenes, and in any event how her sympathies had been enlisted. There can be little doubt, however, that it was as a result of pressure from Eudoxia that the government now at last decided to act in the refugees' interest. On the authority of the master of the offices (head of the central administration) an imperial order[52] was issued requiring Theophilos, whether willing or unwilling, to present himself before a court presided over by John. As befitted such an important mission, a high official, Elaphios,[53] chief of the imperial couriers (*agentes in rebus*), was dispatched to Alexandria to convey the order to Theophilos and conduct him to the capital. At the same time the agents he had been employing to destroy the Nitrian refugees' reputation were arrested, taken to court, and confronted with the alternative of either substantiating the defamatory statements they had made or undergoing the harsh penalties imposed by law for slander.[54]

Thus what John had dreaded, and had striven by every means at his disposal to prevent, had been brought about. He cannot have been con-

[51] 8.13.
[52] This is summarised by Palladios, *Dial.* 8 (*SC* 341.156-8).
[53] *PLRE* 2, 387.
[54] Ten laws dating from 319 to 406 and dealing with defamation (*De famosis libellis*) are listed in CT 9.34. In certain circumstances death could be the penalty.

sulted by the authorities, or if he was they must have ignored his advice. His position, we recall, was much weakened at the time; his public reconciliation with Severian, with its embarrassing loss of face to himself, had been forced on him by the empress only a few weeks back. Officially, of course, his relations with the court continued correct; the fact that it was before him that Theophilos was to be arraigned confirms that he retained the authorities' confidence. It is interesting, however, that they were prepared to brush aside his scruples about intervening in Egyptian church affairs. They probably took it for granted that the imperial see was fully entitled to do so. Altogether John cannot have regarded his dealings with the Nitrian refugees with much satisfaction. Although his pastoral sympathies lay with them, he had felt obliged, out of regard for canonical order and to avoid a collision with Theophilos, to abandon them to their fate. If their prospects for the moment looked brighter, this was not due to any action on his part, but to the Augusta having taken up their cause and having persuaded the emperor and his ministers to act on their behalf.

15

Epiphanios to the Rescue

I

It is not difficult to imagine Theophilos' indignation and disgust when Elaphios handed him the imperial rescript summoning him to Constantinople. It was an insult for the bishop of Alexandria, acknowledged until quite recently as the premier see among the eastern churches and still their link with the holy see in the west, to be peremptorily called to answer charges concerning his treatment of persons wholly under his own jurisdiction. It was a further shock that the investigating judge was to be the bishop of the upstart see of Constantinople, a man whom the government had appointed in preference to his own favoured candidate, and whom only Eutropios' blackmail had induced him to consecrate. The summons, he must have inferred, was one more move in the step-by-step advancement of the imperial see, and there can be little doubt that he detected John's hand behind it.

There is also likely, some have claimed, to have been an element of fear in his reaction. Fear is not an emotion one would normally attribute to Theophilos, but we can agree that the omens probably looked threatening to him. About the same time, or not much later, the news must have reached him that his envoys in Constantinople had been brought to trial on charges of slandering the Nitrian refugees. The case had gone against them, a sentence of death seemed certain, but since the terrified plaintiffs had put the entire blame for the libels they had been putting about on Theophilos himself, it had been deferred pending his arrival for the synod. In the meantime they had been flung into gaol; because of his delay in reaching the capital, one or two of them died there.[1]

II

Theophilos had, of course, no option but to obey the imperial order, but he was determined to do so, as far as possible, at the time and in the manner best suited to his interests. In particular, before setting out he wanted to organise a counter-offensive. It was clear to him that the moment was now

---

[1] Palladios, *Dial.* 8 (*SC* 341.158).

come when he might usefully revive a plan he had first conceived when John was consecrated. It was precisely then, according to Sokrates,[2] that he had begun considering how he might bring about his deposition; he had discussed the matter secretly with some friends by word of mouth, with others by correspondence. Since John clearly had full government backing, he had had to put the plan into cold storage at the time, and indeed (as we have seen)[3] he had agreed to co-operate with him in finding a solution to the schism at Antioch. Everything he heard, however, about John's reception of the Long Brothers, especially the malicious rumours reaching him that he was admitting them to communion, had brought these long dormant ideas back to life again. His resolve to act on them must have been finally confirmed when he learned that John had been chosen to sit in judgment on him. He must have taken it for granted that, in spite of his warnings against interfering in a field outside his jurisdiction,[4] he had consented to play this role.

So Theophilos devised an ingenious strategy which, if he kept his nerve, might enable him not only to extricate himself from his present predicament but also, with luck, to turn the tables on his adversary. First, he delayed his departure as long as he decently could, and when he eventually set out chose the lengthy land-route[5] through Palestine and Asia Minor rather than the obvious and expeditious sea-passage (only 17-20 days).[6] His object, as we shall see,[7] was not to spin out time, but to muster support for his cause.

Secondly, he seems to have made contact with bishops Akakios, Antiochos and Severian, and the monk Isaac, four of John's most determined enemies in the capital, and arranged with them to have a thorough investigation of his conduct as a young man carried out at Antioch. Our information about this comes from Palladios,[8] who however represents the four Syrians as themselves instituting the inquiries and only turning to Theophilos for advice when these proved fruitless. The unlikelihood of relatively minor figures like them having done so on their own has long been recognised, although it is agreed that an outsider in Constantinople observing them at work might well have drawn that conclusion. There was, in fact, no point in raking over John's past until his possible deposition became an issue, i.e. until Theophilos received the news that he was to be tried by him, and then it was Theophilos himself, not the Syrians, who had a powerful motive for collecting material (if any could be found) likely to

[2] 6.5.
[3] See above, p. 117.
[4] See above, p. 199.
[5] Sozomen 8.14.
[6] So L. Casson, *TAPA* 82 (1951), 145.
[7] See below, p. 213.
[8] *Dial.* 6 (*SC* 341.128).

damage him. It was he, therefore, who was likely, as part of his carefully concerted counter-attack, to have set the Syrians to work to unearth it.

A third step he took was to get in touch, as he had done[9] the previous year on learning that the Nitrian refugees had set sail for the capital, with Epiphanios of Cyprus. On that earlier occasion he had stopped short of voicing any overt criticism of John or of his theological stance, referring to him neutrally as 'the reverend bishop of Constantinople'.[10] Now he seems to have gone over the top, accusing him of taking the excommunicated monks under his protection, probably also of admitting them to communion, and of being tainted with Origenism himself. The gist of his message was that Epiphanios should hasten in person to the capital since the orthodox faith was in dire peril there. The letter itself has not survived, but we can safely infer that its contents were along these lines from Epiphanios' subsequent behaviour. It is fruitless to ask whether or not Theophilos actually thought that John was an Origenist. It seems unlikely, for he was aware that as a theologian John belonged to the non-speculative Antiochene school. But there were no limits to the fantasies which a man of his violent, passionate temperament could bring himself to believe. His cynical object was, by involving John in the current wave of hostility to Origenism, to undermine his credibility, first, as judge of himself, and then, he must have hoped, as bishop. The fiery old champion of orthodoxy, for years notorious as the hammer of Origenism, seemed to him to be ideally cut out to be his ally in achieving this aim.

III

The reconstruction of events set out above, it is fair to warn the reader, while generally accepted, has not satisfied some students. Their preferred version,[11] which would date Epiphanios' visit to Constantinople several months earlier, is that he went there on his own initiative immediately after holding the synod in Cyprus condemning Origen and, instead of sending them by special courier, took its decrees with him. It is difficult to see, however, why he should have done so, still less why, when he got to the capital, he should have treated John (as we shall find him doing) with aloofness and plain distrust as out-and-out heretic, since in his original letter Theophilos had cast no doubts on John's orthodoxy. In addition, we have Sokrates' explicit statement[12] that it was in response to Theophilos' promptings (*tais hupothekais Theophilou peistheis*) that he went to the capital, which surely implies a second letter, this time denigrating John and calling on Epiphanios to rally to the defence of the faith.

On receiving this letter Epiphanios, characteristically, leaped into ac-

[9] See above, p. 197.
[10] *Ep.* 90 in Jerome's correspondence (*CSEL* 55.143-5).
[11] See, e.g., P. Nautin's article 'Épiphane (saint) de Salamine' in *DHGE* 15.624.
[12] 6.12 (*PG* 67.701A).

tion. He had long had his suspicions of John. Had he not for years been the devoted adjutant of Flavian, whom to his disgust the council of Constantinople (381) had appointed bishop of Antioch, over the head of Paulinos, the rightful claimant (as he saw it) to the see on the death of Meletios? More recently, had he not been dragging his feet when challenged to convene a synod in Thrace to condemn Origen and his writings?[13] Theophilos' revelation that he was now offering hospitality, even church fellowship, to the Nitrian heretics made hesitation out of the question. At the first opportunity, presumably just so soon as the festivities of Easter 403 (28 March) were concluded, he set sail from Cyprus armed with the synodical decisions condemning Origenism.

In early or mid-April his ship docked, not at one of the harbours close to the centre of Constantinople, but at Hebdomon, some 10 km from it. Having stepped ashore, Epiphanios with his escorting clergy marched to the church of John the Baptist, none other than the shrine at which the Nitrian monks had poured out their woes to Eudoxia almost a year previously. Here, according to Sokrates,[14] he proceeded, first, to celebrate mass, and then to ordain a deacon, in neither case seeking the permission of the local bishop (John). This was a gross violation of canonical order, but it was not the first time that Epiphanios had chosen to flout it. Almost a decade before, at Besanduc in Palestine, he had ordained Jerome's younger brother Paulinian to both diaconate and priesthood successively, despite the fact that John, bishop of Jerusalem, had refused to do so.[15] Although Besanduc lay outside his jurisdiction, John expostulated vehemently since Paulinian was to serve Jerome's community at Bethlehem, which lay within it; he even excommunicated Jerome and his monks. In defence of Epiphanios some[16] have pleaded that, misled by the identity of the two bishops' names, Sokrates must have transferred to Constantinople an incident which actually took place at Jerusalem years before. Quite apart, however, from the detail that the two stories were quite different, Sokrates was a young man living in the capital at the time and was not likely to have slipped up about an event which must have been much talked about. From our knowledge of Epiphanios' character there was in any case nothing implausible in his acting a second time in this high-handed fashion.

His gesture was in fact a deliberate signal of the grave doubts he felt about John's legitimacy as bishop. It was to be quickly followed by others conveying the same message. Meanwhile John, who had received no advance notice of Epiphanios' projected visit, had been informed of his arrival at Hebdomon. He immediately dispatched a special delegation of his clergy to welcome the great man and invite him, as a matter of course, to take up residence with his entourage at his palace. Epiphanios met them as he

[13] See above, p. 198.
[14] 6.12 and 14.
[15] See J.N.D. Kelly, *Jerome* (London 1975), 200f.
[16] E.g. Cesare Baronius, *Annales ecclesiastici* ad ann. 402 (Lucae 1740), vi.384.

approached the city gates and, in compliance with Theophilos' advice,[17] disdainfully rejected the proffered invitation. Instead he insisted, as John must have learned with consternation, on putting up in private lodgings. As if this were not a sufficient rebuff, he went on to declare that he would not stay under the same roof with John or join him at divine service until he had expelled Dioskoros and his companions from the city, and had signed with his own hand the condemnation of Origen's writings he had brought with him.[18] The demand was an unreasonable one, since John had already taken steps to satisfy himself about the refugees' orthodoxy. But Epiphanios was acting, in his naive and impetuous way, as the agent of Theophilos, who shrewdly calculated that if John declined to comply with the demand, he might be judged a heretic by right-thinking people and his credibility as a judge at the forthcoming synod might be compromised.

IV

Once established in his private lodgings, Epiphanios set in motion his planned anti-Origenistic campaign aimed at exposing John. His first step was, on his own authority and of course without reference to his intended victim, to make contact with all the bishops staying in Constantinople at the time and invite them to a meeting. When they were assembled, he read out to them the condemnation of Origen's writings which had been ratified by the previous year's special synod at Cyprus, perhaps also that agreed by Theophilos' earlier synod at Alexandria. He then called on everyone present to add his signature to these censures. Out of respect for the venerable champion of orthodoxy, several agreed to do so; it is probable that two or three did so less out of regard for him than out of hostility towards John. But the majority flatly refused to acquiesce. The most resolute and outspoken of these was Theotimos, since 392 bishop of Tomi (Constantza), capital of Scythia Minor, whom we recall[19] as having been present at the 'resident synod' at which Antoninos of Ephesos was denounced, a man respected for his learning, ascetic life and supernatural powers. He stood up boldly and declaimed against the indecency of insulting the memory of one who was long dead, and with whose teaching no one had hitherto found fault. In support of his plea he produced one of Origen's books, read out a number of passages from it, and showed how valuable they were, and then exclaimed that people who cast aspersions on such teaching were acting absurdly.[20]

This was an unexpected setback for Epiphanios, but he was apparently not in the least dismayed. On the contrary, he allowed himself to be

[17] Sokrates 6.12.
[18] Sokrates 6.14.
[19] See above, p. 163.
[20] Sozomen 8.14.

persuaded by some of John's enemies to plan a much more direct and public attack on him. (It is intriguing to reflect that, if he had been able to carry it out, it would have been a repeat performance of a similar attack he had launched on John of Jerusalem, whom he had also suspected of Origenism, in the church of the Resurrection in September 393.)[21] His plan was to go to the church of the Holy Apostles and, as divine service was beginning, to take his place at the ambo and, in the full hearing of the packed congregation, first, to denounce Origen's writings as heretical, then to declare Dioskoros and the other desert monks excommunicate, and finally to upbraid John himself for his sympathetic attitude to them.

So far John, whatever exasperation he may have privately felt or expressed to his close circle, had shown what for him was quite remarkable restraint in face of Epiphanios' provocative behaviour. What had held him back, it is likely, was partly respect for him personally, but partly too awareness of the immense veneration the public generally felt for him. The furthest he had gone was to counter his demand for Origen to be publicly condemned by pleading that such a drastic step would not be proper without a general council. When alerted, however, to Epiphanios' latest scheme, he decided that it was time to call a halt to the dangerous drama. On the following morning, when Epiphanios, braced for action, was entering the church of the Holy Apostles, he found himself confronted at the door by the priest Sarapion, John's former archdeacon and still, apparently, his hatchet man, bearing a stern message from his master. This pointed out that, in carrying out an ordination and celebrating mass without the authority of the bishop of the see, he had been violating the canons of the church. In the past he had declined invitations to come to Constantinople; now he had come without any invitation. The concluding sentence had an ominous ring: Epiphanios had better look out, for if popular demonstrations were to break out, he might find himself in grave danger.[22] There was no mistaking the warning these words contained, and Epiphanios turned back and left the church. He was as well aware as anyone of the power a populist bishop like John could wield through excitable mobs.

V

Epiphanios' stay in the imperial city was, it is generally agreed, extremely short, a matter of days rather than weeks. Even so, it would have been extraordinary if a visitor so eminent, so admired, and whose business so directly affected people whom the empress had taken under her protection, had not been received at court. In fact, Sokrates reports that John was to be greatly upset, after his departure, by rumours that Eudoxia had incited

---

[21] For the story see J.N.D. Kelly, op. cit., 198-9.
[22] Sokrates 6.14; Sozomen 8.14.

Epiphanios against him.[23] These rumours, if they existed at all, were wildly off the mark, but the report clearly implies that she and the Cypriot bishop had met and talked together. Sozomen gives a fuller, much more circumstantial account of exchanges between them. According to him,[24] the infant heir to the throne, Theodosios, was sick, and Eudoxia summoned Epiphanios, who was reputed to have remarkable powers in such cases, and begged him to pray for his recovery. Exploiting the situation, he promised that the little boy would live provided she withdrew her support from Dioskoros and his heretical monks. This apparently upset the empress, but she recalled, or was reminded, that a highly valued archdeacon of the bishop's had recently died. So she coldly replied that if God wished to take her son's life she was content to bow to his will. Then she added, with a touch of asperity, that if Epiphanios had possessed the power to raise the dead to life, he would have saved his archdeacon.

Sozomen has a further report that, with Eudoxia's encouragement, the Long Brothers sought an interview with Epiphanios and he held a conference with them. This took place, it would seem, in an atmosphere of cordiality, and Ammonios was able to extract an admission from him that he had never had contact with their followers, much less examined anything they had written. In fact, he confessed, he had condemned them on the basis of hearsay alone. In return they professed themselves regular readers and admirers of his writings, including his *Ancoratus*, a work he had written as long ago as 374 and which contains sections critical of Origenism. They declared they had always defended his opinions when attacked. Understandably flattered by their compliments, the old man allowed himself to be persuaded that they were not such outrageous heretics after all.

Because they rest on the authority of Sozomen alone, these stories are often played down or even dismissed as later gossip, but this is a mistake. They may have undergone some 'amplification postérieure',[25] but much of the detail in them has the ring of authenticity. For example, both Eudoxia's appeal on behalf of her child, and her quick stiffening of attitude when the wily bishop made abandonment of the refugees a condition of his intercession, seem lifelike and entirely in character. Epiphanios' realisation all too late that he might have been wrong in his wholesale condemnation of the Long Brothers reminds us of a similar, equally sudden change of heart in his earlier quarrel with John of Jerusalem.[26] So far as our John is concerned, the incident of the empress's appeal on her child's behalf indirectly confirms that, at this stage at any rate, she bore him no special animosity. It is hardly conceivable that, when urging her to throw over the Nitrian

---

[23] 6.15 (ad init.).
[24] 8.15.
[25] So P. Nautin, *DHGE* 15.625.
[26] See J.N.D. Kelly, op. cit., 200.

monks, Epiphanios refrained from voicing bitter criticism of the bishop he regarded as shielding them and sharing their objectionable views. Yet the confidence of the court in John, and its determination that he should preside at the forthcoming trial, seem to have remained undisturbed.

VI

Epiphanios' mission, as he must have known, had ended in failure. He had not obtained anything like the number of signatures condemning Origen he had expected; despite a show of embarrassed deference, he had encountered firm opposition from the majority of bishops. So far from bringing the empress over to his side, he had only succeeded in irritating her. He had become confident that he would teach John a sharp lesson, but the message conveyed by Sarapion had been a stinging public rebuke to himself. As he contemplated the futility of his too hastily undertaken journey, did it perhaps occur to him that Theophilos had been cynically using him for his own purposes? His decision to return home, so soon after he had arrived, is scarcely surprising. His bitterness and disillusionment were vividly expressed in a sentence he is said[27] to have uttered to the bishops seeing him off at the quay: 'I am glad to leave you with the city, the court, the whole wretched show. I am off home as fast as I can.'

Another story[28] which was later bandied about in the capital alleged that, before boarding his ship, Epiphanios sent John a note expressing the unkindly wish, 'I hope you will be no longer a bishop when you die.' John's riposte was, so it was said, equally unfriendly: 'And I hope you will not set foot in your city again.' We need not take the anecdote literally, but it illustrates the intense rancour which public opinion assumed must exist between the two men – who, in fact, in an extraordinary way, resembled one another in passionate zeal for orthodoxy, inability to compromise with what they considered false or wrong, and fearless outspokenness. The wish attributed to John was the first to be fulfilled, for Epiphanios ended his days on the high seas on 12 May 403, well before Theophilos set out from Egypt. The supposed wish of Epiphanios was also to find fulfilment in due course. But while John had no responsibility for Epiphanios' death, reports that the octogenarian champion of orthodoxy, doubly revered now that he was dead, had refused to share communion with him, and that he had spoken slightingly of the old man, were to be brought forward at his trial as damning evidence against him.

[27] Sozomen 8.15.
[28] Ibid.

16

The Oak

I

With the collapse of Epiphanios' clumsy attempt to brand John as an Origenist heretic, Theophilos' first plan for destroying the credibility of his proposed judge had failed ignominiously. But he was already well advanced with a far more ambitious strategy which, if successful, would result in the reversal of their roles, in himself in fact being called upon to sit in judgment on John. It is ironical that John, although still apparently supported by the court, seemed bent on smoothing the path for him.

Not long after Epiphanios' departure in early May 403, he took it into his head to preach a sermon violently denouncing the weaknesses conventionally attributed to women. We have no idea what provoked this outburst. Sokrates (not followed by Sozomen) alleges[1] that it was irritation fired by reports that Eudoxia had incited Epiphanios against him. While not impossible, this seems unlikely: all the evidence is that the empress keenly supported the Long Brothers and that, while meeting Epiphanios, her relations with him had been cool. In fact, criticism of what sexist preachers considered feminine vanity or excessive influence had been a favourite theme of John's since his days at Antioch.[2] Following his normal practice, his diatribe on this occasion was in general terms, but the congregation at once jumped to the conclusion (probably correctly) that it was a thinly veiled attack on Eudoxia personally. Some have suggested that ill-disposed people may have tampered with the text so as to give this impression (they are said to have done this sometimes);[3] but Sokrates explicitly states that it was the people who, listening to his words, interpreted them as a satiric portrayal of the Augusta.

The sermon itself has long disappeared, but its impact on the court could not fail to be damaging to the preacher. Reports of it were rushed to Eudoxia; it must have infuriated her that the common people were in no doubt that she was the target. It wounded her on a sensitive spot, her natural self-esteem as a woman. Fuel must have been added to her

---

[1] 6.15 ad init.: cf. Sozomen 8.16.

[2] From many examples see *In Matt. hom.* 7.3; *In Joh. hom.* 61.4 (*PG* 57.257-9; 59.340-2); *De sacerdotio* 3.9 (*SC* 272.162-4).

[3] Palladios, *Dial.* 6 (*SC* 341.126).

indignation as she discussed the affair with her intimate circle, and she found an all too eager ally in Severian, still nursing bitter memories of John's harsh treatment of him the previous year. She hastened with her complaints to Arkadios, insisting that the insulting language was no less injurious to him than to herself. According to Sokrates and Sozomen,[4] it was at this point that the imperial couple began planning to have Theophilos brought as quickly as possible to Constantinople to preside over a council to try John, but this (as we shall discover) cannot be correct; however intense his annoyance, Arkadios was still sticking to the original idea agreed with his advisers of bringing Theophilos to trial. In their highly compressed narratives the historians have brought a somewhat later switch of plan forward. Nevertheless the sense of outrage and resentment in the palace was so great that some [5] have identified the crisis provoked by the tactless sermon as the fateful turning-point in John's fortunes.

II

In late August 403 it became known in the capital that Theophilos had at last arrived, more than a year after the imperial summons had been sent to him. From this point, in addition to our usual authorities, we have a fresh, exceptionally vivid source in a letter which John was to send,[6] some nine months later, to the Roman pope, Innocent I (401-17). Traditionally preserved as the second chapter of Palladios' *Dialogue*, it has been convincingly shown to have been no part of the original text of that work.[7] In it John, already doomed, in a desperate effort to enlist the pope's support, sets out his personal version of the key events leading to his downfall, starting with the Egyptian Pharaoh's arrival in the capital. Although his report is tantalisingly selective and charged, understandably, with deeply felt emotion, it clearly counts as evidence of primary importance, providing as it does information not available elsewhere.

For the moment Theophilos was at Chalkedon, on the Asiatic shore of the Bosporus, having made the entire journey from Egypt by land.[8] Significantly, he was staying with the local bishop, Cyrinos, an Egyptian like himself, who had accompanied John as a chosen colleague on his visit to Asia Minor, but had since become his uncompromising enemy; he kept telling the members of Theophilos' party that John was 'impious, haughty, and inexorable'.[9] Ostensibly summoned by Arkadios to stand his trial before John, Theophilos had made it clear, both before leaving Alexandria and while travelling north, that he was 'on his way to the court to depose

---

[4] Sokrates 6.15; Sozomen 8.16.
[5] E.g. Baur, 2.229.
[6] See below, p. 246. Critical edition by A.M. Malingrey in *SC* 342 (Paris 1988).
[7] *SC* 342.55-8.
[8] Sozomen, 8.14: confirmed by 'Martyrios': see *AB* 98 (1977), 402.
[9] Sokrates 6.15: the meaning of *agonatos*, here translated 'inexorable', is not wholly clear.

John'.[10] He had made his plans with elaborate thoroughness. Thus, to be sure of local support, he had sent ahead by sea some twenty-nine Egyptian bishops – causing John to complain to the pope that, although ordered to present himself alone, he had arrived with quite a crowd of fellow-country-men he had collected.[11] Again, his choice of the exhausting land-route rather than the more obvious sea one had a characteristic ulterior motive: in every church centre through which he passed he was at pains to mobilise the local clergy against John. When he reached Chalkedon, he was accom-panied by numerous bishops, some invited by himself, others responding to the emperor's summons (presumably for the council at which the Egyp-tian patriarch was to be tried). The motley band included the bishops John had deposed in Asia, who joined the party 'with the utmost alacrity', as well as several who were ill-disposed to him for other reasons.[12]

After a short interval, his plans completed, Theophilos and his entourage crossed the Bosporus, putting in at the great harbour of Eleutherios,[13] later of Theodosios, on the sea of Marmara (now reduced to the pretty little fishing port of Yenikapi). The harbour normally used by travellers from Chalkedon was (as is the case today) in the Golden Horn; there the Prosphorianos port had a special Scala Chalkedonensis reserved for them. His decision to break with normal practice was deliberate: he wanted to ensure a rousing send-off for his visit to the capital. It was in the harbour of Eleutherios, with its vast adjacent granaries, that the ships bringing from Alexandria the corn for the regular free distributions of bread docked, and he was aware that the fleet was already there, unloading its cargoes. Thus, when he stepped ashore one Thursday around noon, he was greeted by the thunderous cheers of the crews, proud to welcome their own patri-arch.[14] John had sent no delegation to meet him; it was common knowledge that he had come as an enemy.[15] He had nevertheless prepared accommo-dation and hospitality which he pressed him and his companions to accept. Theophilos, however, scorned the offer and refused to have anything to do with him. In John's own words, 'He did not enter the church, as custom and long-standing religious propriety required. He paid me no call, but rejected all conversation with me, and declined to take part in prayer or communion with me. Once disembarked from his boat, he rushed past the main porch of the church and, disregarding my entreaties that he and his companions would occupy the rooms we had been preparing for them, marched off and set up his camp somewhere outside the city.'[16] In fact, we know in precise

---

[10] Palladios, *Dial.* (SC 341.174).
[11] *Ep. 1 ad Innocentium* (SC 342.70).
[12] Sozomen 8.16 (the sole source for these interesting facts).
[13] R. Janin, *Constantinople byzantine* (Paris 1950), 218-20; 226 (Prosphorianos port).
[14] Palladios, *Dial.* 8 (SC 341.160); Sokrates 6.15; Sozomen 8.17.
[15] Sozomen 8.17.
[16] *Ep. 1 ad Innocentium* (SC 342.70-2).

terms from Sokrates, and more generally from Sozomen,[17] that Theophilos found lodging in a magnificent mansion, the Palatium Placidianum, normally assigned by the state to the reigning Augusta or one recently widowed, which stood in the First Region close to the imperial palace itself.[18] John's evasive reference to his camping 'somewhere outside the city' was probably prompted by his reluctance to have to tell the pope that his persecutor had been the empress's personal guest.

With this palace as his base Theophilos spent the next three weeks systematically lobbying anyone who had a grievance against John or for any reason disliked him, not scrupling (if we can trust Palladios)[19] to make lavish use of bribery or the persuasive power of sumptuous entertainment. For his headquarters he used the house of the rich widow Eugraphia, leader of a cabal of society ladies who hated John for his unsparing strictures on their avarice, extravagance, and vanity. A typical sally, which Palladios cites as reflecting credit on his hero, was the reproof: 'Time has made you old women: so why do you take forceful measures to rejuvenate your appearances, arranging kiss-curls above your foreheads as tarts do, shocking other decent women, all so as to give a false impression of youthfulness to the people you meet, whereas in fact you are widows?' In the same house he met and plotted with John's most determined adversaries, Severian of Gabala, another Syrian Antiochos of Ptolemais (also a popular preacher, nicknamed Golden Mouth in his lifetime),[20] and the venerable, widely respected Akakios of Beroea (Haleb), whom John had sent in 398 as a trusted envoy to pope Siricius.[21] For what it is worth, Palladios attributes the present bitterness of the last-mentioned against John to disgust at the mean accommodation provided for him when visiting the capital the previous year.[22] There is a suggestion in 'Martyrios', who also reports that these three worked together to ruin John, that Theophilos also held a private conference with the empress at which they reached a mutual compact assuring her of the elimination of her bishop and him of judicial immunity[23] (it is scarcely surprising that our other sources are silent about so delicate a matter). Meanwhile John, by his own frank admission to the pope,[24] was in a state of total embarrassment, at a loss to understand the motive for Theophilos' hostility, still less what he was up to. As he put it, 'I did everything that seemed proper. I repeatedly invited him to meet me, and to explain for what reason he had, from the moment of his arrival, set such a conflict ablaze and brought scandal to our great city.'

[17] Sokrates 6.15; Sozomen 8.17.
[18] R. Janin, op. cit., 135-6, with n. 1.
[19] *Dial.* 8 (*SC* 341.160-4).
[20] Sozomen 8.10.
[21] See above, p. 117.
[22] *Dial.* 6 (*SC* 341.126).
[23] P 480b-481a: see *AB* 95 (1977), 402-3. His reference to the three bishops is in P 483a-b.
[24] *Ep. 1 ad Innocentium* (*SC* 342.72).

True to character, Theophilos spurned these approaches. Until now the tide had been flowing wholly in his favour. Rapturously received in the city, installed in an imperial palace, he was intriguing with circles close to the court and, apparently, with the empress herself. If he had not yet discredited John, he would soon be well placed to do so, and also perhaps achieve his downfall. It was probably at this juncture that the plan, reported by Sokrates and Sozomen,[25] for getting Theophilos to preside over a synod which would impeach and condemn John began being canvassed in the palace. At this point, according to John's own account,[26] Theophilos' accusers, i.e. the Long Brothers and their companions, began applying fresh pressure to the emperor; presumably they were alarmed by the signs that their persecutor, supposedly summoned to stand his trial, was about to stage a triumphant come-back, with unforeseeable but certainly ruinous consequences to themselves. Their pleas seem to have recalled Arkadios to his senses. With a weak man's unpredictability he sent John a peremptory message ordering him to cross the Bosporus and present himself at the palace on the eastern side where he was temporarily residing.[27] This can only have been the Rufinianai, the sumptuous mansion three miles from Chalkedon which the praetorian prefect Rufinus had built for himself, but which had been seized by the state when he was disgraced.[28] Here he was to open the council convened to adjudicate the charges brought against Theophilos – charges which, John added, included violence, even murder. The abrupt change of course suggests that the court, always irresolute and vacillating, but still primarily concerned for the unhappy refugees, was also shot through with divisions which interested parties like them were quick to exploit.

This was John's great opportunity. Had he been a political realist, he would have seized it without hesitation. Had he done so, we can only speculate what the outcome would have been. But he did not. Without hesitation and in the strongest terms he refused to act as Theophilos' judge. His own report to the pope clearly explains his reasons for so deciding: 'Aware as I was of the laws of our fathers, respecting and honouring this man, having moreover in my hands a letter of his which demonstrated that judicial cases may not lawfully be tried outside the territory of their origin but that matters affecting each province should properly be settled within that province, I refused to act as his judge, indeed rejected the proposal with the utmost vehemence.'[29]

---

[25] See above, p. 212.

[26] *Ep. 1 ad Innocentium* (*SC* 342.72).

[27] Loc. cit., lines 44-5: we are indebted to A.M. Malingrey's restoration of what seems the correct text, substituting the infinitive *peran* suggested by the mss E and R for the adverb *péran* commonly accepted.

[28] R. Janin, op. cit., 150-1; 459-60.

[29] *Ep. 1 ad Innocentium* (*SC* 342.72). It is not clear whether the letter he refers to is the one he had received from Theophilos on his return from Asia (see above, p. 199) or a fresh warning shot.

III

This, as events were soon to prove, was in fact the critical turning-point which determined John's fate. However intense the indignation felt in the palace, by Eudoxia in particular, at his blistering denunciations, it is evident that the authorities were still, with whatever understandable hesitations, adhering to their original policy of bringing Theophilos to justice for his ill-treatment of the Long Brothers. They must have been astonished, mystified and finally infuriated by John's stubborn refusal to co-operate and implement the agreed plan. From this moment they seem to have decided to wash their hands of him, and to give the go-ahead to the alternative plan now being mooted in court circles of having John himself brought to trial before Theophilos. Arkadios and his advisers must have been strengthened in their decision by the evidence rapidly piling up of the bitter hostility which John aroused among great numbers of bishops and clergy in the capital, as well as in circles close to the court.

Theophilos, to whom the news of the emperor's summons to John to proceed with his trial must have come as an unexpected shock, must for his part have been equally amazed and delighted by his enemy's reluctance to act. Not only had the danger disappeared, but the initiative had clearly passed to himself. Most important, he could now count (as will soon emerge) on the co-operation, indeed support, of the authorities. With enthusiasm he redoubled his efforts to amass a dossier of plausible charges against John. Among those who eagerly supplied him with accusations, in return for a promise of reinstatement, were the two deacons whom John had sacked on criminal charges at the beginning of his reign.[30] Isaac also, revered leader of the monks of the capital, but burning with bitter resentment against its bishop,[31] was only too keen to provide compromising material. But in his present confident mood Theophilos felt the time had come for him to take a drastic initiative. 'Launching a fresh line of attack,' John was to write helplessly to the pope,[32] 'he summoned my archdeacon entirely on his own authority, as if the church were already widowed and no longer had a bishop, and with his collaboration won my entire clergy over to his side. From that moment the churches were in uproar, with the clergy in each being seduced from their allegiance, suborned to produce allegations against me, and encouraged to indict me.' Even allowing for the defections to be expected as the realisation of his beleaguered position spread, one is amazed by his frank admission of the fragile hold he apparently had on the loyalty of his clergy.

Soon Theophilos had not only compiled what he judged to be a plausible charge-sheet, but had mobilised a numerous, formidable opposition to

---

[30] Palladios, *Dial.* 8 (*SC* 341.162).
[31] See above, pp. 123-5.
[32] *Ep. 1 ad Innocentium* (*CS* 342.72-4).

John. With his bishops and other supporters he then recrossed the Bosporus to the eastern shore; it would be much less risky to mount his offensive against John there, in territory controlled by his ally bishop Cyrinos, than in Constantinople itself, where the populace was likely to demonstrate if they saw their beloved bishop threatened. The operation had been carefully planned, and he established himself in the suburb of Chalkedon known as The Oak (*Drus*) in the splendid Rufinianai palace mentioned in the previous section; close by it was a small port which, as we shall see, was to prove convenient. The fact that he had permission to use this imperial mansion as the setting of the proceedings he was planning to bring against John is itself proof that they had the approval, indeed authorisation, of the government.

One final but indispensable preparatory step he now took was to make peace with the Long Brothers. Sokrates,[33] followed by several modern scholars,[34] places his reconciliation with them soon after John's deposition, but Sozomen's statement,[35] backed by fairly circumstantial information, that it took place before the opening of John's trial, inspires greater confidence. This was a concession on which the imperial couple is likely to have insisted, and which in any case Theophilos knew it would be tactful to make in view of Eudoxia's personal concern for the Long Brothers. Sozomen indicates that he had them brought across the Bosporus to The Oak and housed in the monastery attached to Rufinianai. Here he invited them to reconsider their position, promising that if they did so he would bear no grudge against them; it was made clear that the whole issue of Origenism had been dropped. The wretched men, already stunned by John's refusal to sit in judgment on their persecutor, were easily persuaded to supplicate for pardon, and this the Egyptian Pharaoh graciously granted them, restoring them to communion with himself. Sozomen sardonically remarks that the settlement could hardly have been reached so easily had their more resolute leaders been available. Bishop Dioskoros, however, had died some time previously, and Ammonios was fatally ill and, although he had struggled to get to The Oak, died before John's trial opened. He won a tearful tribute from his former persecutor, who remarked that, although he had caused him a great deal of trouble, he had never known a monk to equal him in moral stature.[36]

[33] 6.16.
[34] Notably Lenain de Tillemont, *Mémoires pour servir à l'histoire ecclésiastique des premiers six siècles* (Venice 1732), XI.487 and 644 n. 15. See also Baur, 255.
[35] 8.17.
[36] Sozomen 8.17.

IV

It was probably in late September that Theophilos' court, henceforth to be known as the Synod of The Oak, opened.[37] Its actual members, according to Palladios,[38] numbered thirty-six; twenty-nine of these, he emphasises, had come from Egypt. Those from other regions included notorious enemies of John, like Severian, Antiochos, Akakios and Cyrinos of Chalkedon. Among others present who were not strictly members of the tribunal were the bishops John had deposed in Asia and prominent clergy he had quarrelled with or degraded in Constantinople, notably the abbot Isaac. Photios, later to be patriarch (857-67; 878-86), who had access to the archives of the see of Constantinople, published an invaluable resumé of the acts of the synod,[39] and these make it clear that while Theophilos, with Akakios, Antiochos, Severian, and Cyrinos as his coadjutors, effectively controlled its business (*huperchon katarchontes*), Paul, bishop of Heraklea, was its official president (*protos tes sunodou*).[40] This arrangement had been carefully thought out. It would not have done for Theophilos himself to be seen as presiding at any stage of the proceedings. Had he done so, he would have been guilty of the canonical impropriety against which he had sternly warned John. On the other hand, Heraklea was the senior see of Thrace next after Constantinople, and for its bishop to take the chair gave the tribunal a plausible air of legality. Paul, we recall,[41] had been a close confidant of John, accompanying him on his Asian visitation, but had evidently had second thoughts about his master. Reluctance to recognise this explains the insistence of some older scholars that Theophilos presided over at any rate the opening sessions.[42] Palladios, it is true, makes no mention of Paul's presidency, but he too had no wish to bring it into the open that John's old friend was now sitting in judgment on him. His references to 'the envoys of Theophilos' and to John's replies being sent to Theophilos imply nothing more than that the Alexandrian was in *de facto* charge of the agenda.

The court had before it a list of twenty-nine charges industriously compiled by the two deacons whom John had discharged soon after his own appointment; Theophilos had promised them reinstatement as their reward.[43] These were to be supplemented, as we shall see, by a further seventeen submitted by Isaac. The preliminaries concluded, the court

[37] P. Ubaldi, 'La sinodo *ad Quercum* dell'anno 403', *Memorie della Reale Accademia delle Scienze di Torino* ser. II, t. 52 (1903), 33-98 remains fundamental. See also F. van Ommeslaeghe, *AB* 95 (1977), 389-413. For the date see Baur, 2.257-8.
[38] *Dial.* 3 (*SC* 341.66).
[39] Critical edition by A.M. Malingrey, *SC* 342; ET in Appendix C.
[40] *SC* 342.100 and 112.
[41] See above, p. 174.
[42] See, e.g., the discussion by A. Favale in *Teofilo d'Alessandria* (Turin 1958), 136-7.
[43] Palladios, *Dial.* 8 (*SC* 341.162).

dispatched two young, recently consecrated bishops from Libya, accompanied by a secretary, to convey a formal summons to John to appear before it. According to Palladios,[44] the citation was addressed, with calculated insolence, 'to John', with no mention of his status as bishop. He was requested to bring Sarapion, his former archdeacon, and the priest Tigrios, a protégé of Sarapion's, with him. Sokrates adds that he was also asked to bring a reader named Paul.[45] John's own report to the pope was terser: 'He sent to fetch me, and cited me before his tribunal.'[46] But it had a sting in its tail: 'This he did notwithstanding the fact that he himself had not been cleared of the accusations brought against him – something grievously contrary to the canons and to every law.'

Meanwhile John seems to have been well aware of what was happening. Palladios, who claims to have been present, draws a graphic picture of him seated, in the reception hall of his palace, surrounded by and conversing with forty bishops;[47] they were probably bishops who had assembled in Constantinople in response to the emperor's summons, and had until now been expecting to sit in judgment on Theophilos. Some historians[48] have deduced from this, and from the message they were shortly to send to The Oak, that, provoked by Theophilos' challenge, John had revoked his earlier decision and had convened the council originally ordered by Arkadios. There is no hint of this either in Palladios' account or in John's letter to Innocent I, and such a move by him would have been inconceivable without the express authorisation of the emperor, who had now given his full support and encouragement to Theophilos' tribunal. In fact, Palladios' narrative, a set-piece richly charged with emotional overtones and recalling (possibly modelled on) the philosopher Sokrates' (d. 399 BC) last conversation with his friends set out in Plato's *Phaedo*,[49] depicts John consoling, encouraging, and exhorting his faithful brothers at what he believes must be his last hour. Palladios describes how John, with a characteristic gesture, thrust the index finger of his right hand into the palm of his left, and impressed on all present that they must not abandon their churches whatever happened to him. They must not, of course, sign any decree deposing him since he was not conscious of anything meriting such a sentence. That apart, they must do all in their power to maintain communion with his adversaries so as to avoid splitting the church.

When 'Theophilos' envoys', as they are called by Palladios, had arrived and had had the citation read out by the secretary, John's supporting bishops, according to Palladios,[50] sent the Alexandrian a sharp rejoinder

[44] *Dial.* 8 (*SC* 341.170).
[45] 6.15.
[46] *Ep. 1 ad Innocentium* (*SC* 342.74).
[47] *Dial.* 8 (*SC* 341.166-8).
[48] E.g. É. Demougeot, *De l'unité à la division de l'empire romain* (Paris 1951), 318.
[49] P. Ubaldi, art. cit., 68 n. 4.
[50] *Dial.* 8 (*SC* 341.170-4).

on their own account, protesting against the illegality, under canon 5 of the council of Nicaea, of his presuming to set up a court in a region outside his episcopal jurisdiction, and adding for good measure that, as they were a more numerous and representative assembly, armed with a full dossier of charges against him, it would make more sense for him to cross the Bosporus and come to be judged by them. John for his part declined to associate himself with this blunt challenge, but insisted on sending a personal reply. This amounted to a robust refusal to appear before a court manifestly packed with declared enemies; before he would recognise its jurisdiction at least Theophilos and Akakios, who had made no secret of their determination to destroy him, as well as Severian and Antiochos, must be removed from it. His own later, compressed report to the pope[51] makes no mention of a separate, more sharply worded reply sent by his colleagues to Theophilos, but confirms, in agreement with Palladios, that the proven hostility of several of the judges, together with the canonical impropriety of an Egyptian bishop setting up a court in Thrace, was the substance of his objection. From this report, as well as from Palladios' narrative and the excerpts of the official record preserved by Photios,[52] it is clear that he was fully prepared to answer accusations brought against him provided that those who were his sworn enemies were excluded from the tribunal.

The clergy carrying the two rejoinders back to the synod met with such a brutal reception that some of them, to save their skins, switched to Theophilos' camp, while others, intimidated, could only advise waiting to see how events unfolded.[53] Palladios records that scarcely had the ill-fated men set out from the reception hall than a notary, an official of the consistory, arrived from the palace bearing an imperial order instructing John, whatever his personal wishes in the matter, to present himself before the court. Sozomen gives further details,[54] speaking of 'a courier and a shorthand writer' and adding that their task included urging the tribunal to get on with its work with all speed. According to Palladios, a second delegation from The Oak was then announced, consisting of two of John's own priests, Eugenios and the monk Isaac. But John rebuffed them with the complaint that his enemies were still sitting among his accusers. But Palladios' information was not complete (he was not out to be an exhaustive chronicler), and can be supplemented from our other sources. First, these indicate that no fewer than four[55] citations were dispatched to John in rapid succession that day (a succession of boats must have been scurrying to and fro between the little harbour at Rufinianai and the port of Prosphorianos).

---

[51] *Ep. 1 ad Innocentium* (*SC* 342.74-6).

[52] See esp. Photios' excerpts: *SC* 342.106.

[53] Palladios, *Dial.* 8 (*SC* 341.176-8), supplemented by 'Martyrios', P 486b-489b, and Sozomen, 8.17.

[54] Loc. cit.

[55] On this the acts of the synod, 'Martyrios' (loc. cit.), and the historians are agreed.

Three was the prescribed number; but if the tribunal was prepared to exceed that, it failed to observe customary procedure in other important respects – notably in not submitting to the accused the list of accusations and the names of his judges, and in not allowing him to raise objections to any of the latter.[56] Secondly, 'Martyrios' suggests not one but repeated interventions by the palace. All vacillation had evidently disappeared, and the imperial couple were now openly taking sides with Theophilos. This makes one sceptical of the charge of illegality, as distinct from canonical irregularity, commonly alleged against the synod.[57] Finally, it is clear, both from the historians but most persuasively, of course, from John's own letter to the pope, that he was already appealing over the heads of his accusers to a general council to review and adjudicate the whole affair. It was to be his bitter protest that, 'although I had declared my readiness to refute their charges in the presence of a hundred, even a thousand, bishops ... in my absence, while I was calling for a synod and demanding a judgment', Theophilos had pressed shamelessly ahead with his illegally constituted court packed with prejudiced accusers and witnesses.[58]

V

While impatiently awaiting John's reaction to its successive summonses, the synod had before it, and was no doubt exchanging views on, the charge-sheet compiled by his two former deacons. For the reader's convenience all twenty-seven charges, along with the seventeen later submitted by the monk Isaac, are printed in Appendix C[59] in an English translation of the authoritative text preserved by Photios. Palladios, we should note, gives no account of the proceedings, but refers to two or three of all these charges in unrelated contexts; 'Martyrios' reproduces seven of them,[60] but the historians none. This highlights the difficulty we should have had in reconstructing the events of the synod had not Photios made his abstract of its acts. The charges in fact make an extraordinary medley, set out as they are haphazard and without regard to logical order. For convenience we may arrange them in several groups.

Three (2, 19, 27) fastened on acts of violence or cruelty attributed to John: e.g. he had had accusers of the Long Brothers imprisoned[61] and had then neglected them, and had given a bloody blow in the face to one Memnon before starting divine service. Four more (1, 9, 21, 26) blamed him for having had clergy unjustly suspended, accused, deposed, or even exiled. One (6) recalled that he had spoken of the recently deceased, everywhere

[56] F. van Ommeslaeghe, art. cit., 417.
[57] Cf., e.g., Photios' description of it as 'illegally (*paranomos*) assembled': *SC* 342.100.
[58] *Ep. 1 ad Innocentium* (*SC* 342.76).
[59] See below, pp. 299-301.
[60] Loc. cit. See F. van Ommeslaeghe, art. cit., 410-11.
[61] See above, p. 201.

revered Epiphanios as a crazed babbler; while others (5, 7, 8, 20, 22) claimed that he had treated his clergy with contempt, slandered them in his writings, or otherwise exposed them to embarrassment (his victims included Severian and Antiochos). Four (3, 4, 16, 17) cast doubts on the probity of his financial administration: he had sold precious objects and marble building material belonging to the church, as well as a bequest left to it, while no one had a clue to what he had done with the revenues of the see. Three more (15, 23, 25) held his private life up to question: he received visits from women with no one else present, reserved the palace bath for his exclusive use, and took his meals alone, gorging himself gluttonously. In five (10, 13, 14, 18, 24) he was alleged to have conducted ordinations irregularly (e.g. ordaining men still subject to charges, or without witnesses being present). Two (12, 28) referred to supposed liturgical omissions or improprieties (failing to say prayers when setting out for or leaving church, and changing his vestments at the throne and eating a piece of bread after communion), while another (29) insinuated that he gave money to bishops he consecrated so as to consolidate his hold over the clergy under him. One (11), incongruously but with the clear object of embarrassing him politically, dragged up from the past the allegation that he had betrayed[62] count John, Eudoxia's favourite, at the time of Gainas' military coup.

Sokrates was to brush these indictments aside as 'bizarre' (*atopous*),[63] and the modern student is puzzled what to make of them. Some seem merely frivolous. A bishop can hardly have merited deposition because he allowed an over-zealous minder to bar his bath to other users, still less because of his preference for robing in full view of the congregation rather than in the vestry. The complaints about John's shabby treatment of his former deacon, and of his demanding guest bishop Akakios, were no more than grouses put forward by these very persons. The innuendo about his receiving women alone was malicious tittle-tattle. Other charges bordered on the libellous. Whatever John's reasons for taking meals privately, they did not include gourmandise; while, however high-handed his sales of church property, most people must have known that they were not designed to enrich himself but to finance his charities. He may not have been as sympathetic as he should have been to the Long Brothers' slanderers, but it was the government, not he, which had gaoled them.[64]Admittedly, there is likely to have been an element of truth, perhaps a substantial one, in several of the charges. John was authoritarian and imperious; we can readily believe, for example, that when he was determined to ordain somebody, he may have pushed ahead with the ceremony without observing the usual conventions or scrutinising possible objections to the candidate. He could also be blunt-spoken, ill-tempered and harsh; from the start

[62] See above, pp. 154-6.
[63] 6.15. Cf. P. Ubaldi's remark about their showing 'una mancanza di serietà': art. cit., p. 76.
[64] Palladios, *Dial.* 8 (*SC* 341.158).

he had ruled his clergy with a firmness which brooked no opposition but created great resentment.[65] Even so, one may reasonably question whether the specific grievances voiced in the charge-sheet could have stood up to close judicial scrutiny. Sokrates' dismissal of them is significant, and hardly less so is the tribunal's own reluctance to spell them out when forwarding its verdict to the emperor.[66]

When it became apparent that, even after four citations, John was stubbornly refusing to appear before it unless his principal accusers were stood down, the synod (according to Photios' summary of its proceedings)[67] started its formal business, addressing itself to the first two charges. There was then an interruption; it had to turn its attention to the cases of Herakleides, whom John had consecrated bishop of Ephesos,[68] and of Palladios of Helenopolis, John's biographer. This diversion was caused by the monk John, whose complaint of victimisation by John the synod had begun considering. It would seem that, when giving his evidence, he had launched an attack on Herakleides (possibly on Palladios too), branding him as an Origenist, and also as having been guilty of petty theft when John ordained him. After dealing with these matters and other grievances put forward by the monk, the synod returned to the charge-sheet and, apparently deciding that it was too long for clause-by-clause scrutiny, concentrated on the ninth charge (John's public indictment of three of his deacons for theft) and the twenty-seventh (the punch he was alleged to have given Memnon – an ironical choice since the judges themselves had recently witnessed the beating-up of John's envoys). At this point Isaac stepped forward and, after adding fuel to the case against Herakleides by stating that Epiphanios had refused all fellowship with him because of his Origenist leanings, volunteered a fresh dossier of charges against John compiled by himself. One suspects he was prompted to do so by his own, perhaps the general, dissatisfaction with the official dossier.

This suspicion is borne out by the fact that, while several of his charges overlap with ones on the monk John's list, his revised version omits their implausible features and gives them a sharper edge. For example, he repeats (3) the complaint about John's taking his meals alone, but cuts out the absurd suggestion that he was privately indulging himself. The objection to the practice, he argues, was the discredit it brought on the duty of hospitality expected of a bishop. Again, he gave added weight to the allegation that John's ordinations could be irregular by claiming (14) that it was his habit to ordain men without proper synodical consultation or even contrary to the wishes of his clergy (an imputation modern students are likely to find credible). Most of the items on his dossier, however, were

[65] See above, pp. 125-7.
[66] See below, pp. 226; 228.
[67] *SC* 342.106-8.
[68] See above, p. 174.

fresh. In one (2), for example, he pointed out that Epiphanios had refused to hold fellowship with John, a statement which, in the atmosphere of veneration surrounding the holy man, came close to declaring him excommunicate. In another (8) he accused him of inciting the people to demonstrate against The Oak. It is hard to believe there was any truth in this, since John was fully aware that his trial had the emperor's blessing; but the thrust provides interesting evidence that his treatment by the authorities was already provoking popular indignation.[69] In others he attacked John for ordaining bishops in provinces outside his jurisdiction (10), for ordering bishops to be driven from his house without the customary letters of commendation (11), and for consecrating as bishops slaves who did not belong to him and had not been freed by their masters (16). The first is the only clear reference at the synod to his seemingly high-handed behaviour during his Asian tour; one might have expected to hear more of it, but the better-informed of his judges were probably anxious to play it down since they knew that it had imperial backing. The second reads like a modified version of the more violent account of his attempt to pack Severian off to his Syrian diocese[70] which figured as the seventh item in the official charge-sheet. The third gives us a sharp reminder that both church and state still excluded slaves from holy orders unless they had previously been granted freedom by their masters.[71]

Several of Isaac's imputations continue to baffle scholars, who can find no satisfactory explanation for them. In the ninth he criticises John for giving asylum in church to pagans (*Hellenas*) who have injured Christians, but no specific instance of his having done so has been produced. The suggestion[72] that Isaac was referring to Eutropios seems untenable since by all accounts the eunuch was a serious Christian. In two more (4 and 5) he demands an explanation of bizarre language he alleges John used in church, describing the altar as 'filled with Furies' and exclaiming 'I am beside myself with love'. No trace of such expressions can be found in John's surviving sermons; if the attribution is correct, it is conceivable that either the preacher or an editor erased them as inappropriate from the stenographer's draft.

Finally, two challenged John on important points of doctrine. The sixth accused him of giving *carte blanche* to sinners by teaching that, however often they sinned, so long as they repented and came to him, he would heal them; while the seventh alleged that he had blasphemed by asserting in church that, while Christ had prayed, he had not been heard because he had not prayed in the proper way. For the former charge, which was

---

[69] See below, p. 229.
[70] See above, p. 185.
[71] Cf. Arkadios' recent legislation in CT 9.45.3 (27 July 398).
[72] P. Ubaldi, art. cit., 80, who remarks (rather weakly) that 'his life was in truth more pagan than Christian'.

apparently widely believed and brought criticism from his friends,[73] John, we may suspect, had only himself to blame. The church in those days had a severe penitential discipline for dealing with sins committed after baptism, but it was a once-for-all exercise and subject to such demanding conditions that it was normally postponed until death's approach. In his eagerness to give fresh hope to troubled consciences, he often went over the top in extolling the efficacy of repentance (i.e. the humble outpouring of the contrite heart to God) in liberating them from their sins;[74] for example, he could say, 'You are a sinner? Don't give up. I keep on applying these ointments to you ... Even if you sin every day, every day repent.'[75] It is little wonder that such unqualified language upset puritan-minded people. But the thrust of the second charge escapes us, for it has proved impossible to identify any passage which exactly fits it. Perhaps it rests on a misunderstanding of John's exegesis of the unanswered prayer, 'Father, let this cup pass from me' (Matt.26.39), according to which it was in respect of his humanity that Jesus uttered the prayer, while in respect of his divine nature his will was in complete harmony with the Father's;[76] or on a misinterpretation of his routine teaching that, as Christ, Jesus had no need to pray since he and the Father were one in will.[77]

VI

The tribunal did not, apparently, investigate John's extra-territorial power-building. In fact, according to Photios' excerpts from its acts,[78] it examined only two items on Isaac's dossier: Epiphanios' refusal to hold communion with him (2), and his supposed blasphemy in the matter of Christ's unanswered prayers. It then turned back to the original dossier submitted by the deacon John, concentrating on the charges (3 and 4) that John had sold off precious objects and marble building material belonging to the church. Here the archpriest Arsakios, bishop Nektarios' brother who a year later was to succeed John, and the priest Attikos stood up as witnesses and testified against him. Photios interposes on his own account the tart question how these two could possibly have claimed to be witnesses of the affair. There was then a demand that the synod should conclude its proceedings and pronounce judgment. The president, Paul of Heraklea, agreed, and those present and entitled to do so voted one by one, Theophilos casting his vote last. When the turn of Akakios of Beroea came, he is reported to have remarked, 'If only I could be sure that, if we were to grant

---

[73] Sokrates 6.21.
[74] See esp. *in Heb. hom.* 9.2-4; 31.3 (*PG* 63.78-80; 215-17).
[75] *De poenit. hom.* 8.1 (*PG* 49.337).
[76] *In illud, Pater si possibile* (*PG* 51.35-7).
[77] E.g. *In Joh. hom.* 64.2 (*PG* 59.356-7).
[78] *SC* 342.112.

him pardon, John would reform himself and abandon his hardness and rudeness (*duritia et asperitate*), I would have interceded with you all on his behalf.'[79] We owe this reminiscence to no less a person than Theophilos' young nephew Cyril, destined to be his successor at Alexandria and a renowned if controversial theologian, whom his uncle had brought from Egypt with him. Akakios' comment is all the more significant because, although he was now hostile to John, he had formerly been a trusted confidant[80] and was himself a widely respected man.

The vote was for John's deposition, not apparently on the basis of the specific charges adduced (were they considered too loaded in the main with petty personal complaints?), but on the ground of his contumacious refusal to respond to the court's summons. 'Martyrios' sarcastically remarks that, after condemning John for non-appearance, his judges somewhat inconsistently produced a memorandum, to be circulated to the public as well as the clergy and official circles, listing the accusations on which their verdict had been based.[81] According to Photios' summary of the minutes,[82] forty-five voted. How the number had risen from around thirty-six is not immediately clear, but it is possible that some of the additional signatures were those of bishops deposed by John who had not originally been members of the court; others may even have been those of defectors from John's camp. Palladios is often said to have claimed that the synod carried through all its deliberations in a single day.[83] This is intrinsically unlikely, for the sending of the four citations and of the replies of John and his supporters must alone have consumed many hours, with boats ferrying their bearers to and fro across the straits. But at this point Palladios' narrative is exceptionally condensed; what in fact he seems to have been protesting about was that the judges had carried out their sentence of deposition in a single day, i.e. with the barest minimum of deliberation. 'Martyrios', we should note, simply remarks that the synod worked in great haste. Photios' abstract, however, categorically states that the proceedings occupied twelve sessions (*praxeis*), a thirteenth being assigned to the case of Herakleides of Ephesos. On the basis of this and a comparison with the general procedural practice of synods one of John's most learned biographers, J. Stilting, argued that the tribunal must have 'lasted three or four weeks'.[84] We get a distinct impression, however, that both the court and the synod itself were determined that it should dispatch its business

---

[79] Cyril of Alexandria, *Ep.* 33 (*PG* 77.159: only the Latin translation survives).
[80] See above, p. 117.
[81] P 498a-b.
[82] *SC* 342.112.
[83] *Dial.* 8 (*SC* 341.178). Cf. F. van Ommeslaeghe, art. cit., 406: 'toutes les sessions ... en un jour.'
[84] *AASS* Sept. IV 591C (Venice 1761).

with all speed, and the evidence of 'Martyrios' concurs with this. More recent conjectures that its duration was 'about a fortnight',[85] or even just 'eight or ten days',[86] have much to commend them, but they are only conjectures.

[85] J.B. Bury, *History of the Later Roman Empire* 1, 152 n. 1.
[86] Baur, 2,261 n. 49.

17

Between Two Exiles

I

The synod lost no time in sending Arkadios a formal report of its decisions. As summarised by Palladios,[1] this declared that various charges had been brought against John but that, although aware of his guilt, he had declined to appear in person to answer them. He had therefore been sentenced to deposition as the canons required. The report added that the indictments had included a charge of high treason, on which the synod admitted that it had no competence to adjudicate. No trace of this, we should note, appears in Photios' excerpts from the minutes. The report ended by expressing the hope that the emperor would issue an order for John's summary banishment, and would refer the charge of treason, which was a capital one, to the appropriate court. Notification of John's deposition was simultaneously sent to the clergy of Constantinople.

'The crime of high treason', Palladios went on, 'was the insult he had given the empress, according to the synod's report, in having called her Jezebel.' Only Palladios mentions the inclusion of the treason charge in the report to the emperor, but there is no reason to question his accuracy. It has been suggested,[2] however, that Palladios himself may not have believed that John had been guilty of such an indiscretion, but nothing in his language supports this. On the contrary, his expression of relief in the next sentence that, mercifully, God had softened the hearts of the royal couple indicates that he accepted that he had: there would have been no need for generosity had no prima facie offence been committed. It is more difficult to identify the occasion when John had ventured into such dangerous territory. A common view is that he may have brought Jezebel as a hate-figure into his notorious tirade against the female sex preached shortly after Epiphanios' departure, which was widely interpreted as a covert attack on Eudoxia,[3] and that must remain a distinct possibility. Alternatively, and perhaps more probably, the reference may be to a much earlier sermon in early 401, when he and the empress were estranged

---

[1] *Dial.* 8 (*SC* 341.178).

[2] F. van Ommeslaeghe, *AB* 97 (1979), 132-3: see K.G. Holum, *Theodosian Empresses* (California 1982), 74 n. 105.

[3] See above, p. 211.

because of her seizure of a widow's property.[4] That was a long time ago, and the authorities had taken no action then. But it would not have been untypical of the judges, with their ham-fisted methods of assembling their evidence, to have dragged up this incident from the past in their efforts finally to break John.

In any case the authorities were not prepared to do anything in regard to the allegation of treason. Whatever they may have thought of it, they were not interested in pressing a capital charge against their bishop. What they wanted was his removal, and the synod's sentence of deposition gave them that. The sentence was at once confirmed,[5] and an imperial order was issued for John's immediate banishment. In the view of some modern students[6] it was carried out that very day; this, they claim, is what John himself implies in his later letter to Innocent I. But the claim rests on a misreading of John's text, which certainly states[7] that he was arrested and put aboard a ship late one evening, but nowhere specifies which evening it was. In fact, Sokrates and Sozomen[8] (here he is not simply copying Sokrates but has independent information) are positive that the government could do nothing for three days because of exceptionally violent demonstrations in John's favour. As we noted above,[9] the mob was already in a turbulent mood during the earlier sessions of the synod. Immediately its verdict became known, angry crowds rushed to Hagia Sophia, kept watch there throughout the night, and prevented the officers sent to arrest John from doing so. Meanwhile they were clamouring for a more authoritative council to adjudicate the affair. The historians' version is confirmed by the warm tribute John was shortly to pay to his congregation for their devoted support 'for so many days'.[10]

II

The timing of John's arrest is not a matter of merely academic interest. The recognition that there was a gap of three days before it took place enables us to restore to its rightful position an important, in some respects controverted, sermon of John's which, where the alternative view prevailed, had to be relegated to limbo.

It was on the morning of the second day, probably, that John stepped forward to the ambo of his packed cathedral and delivered what he intended, certainly in its opening paragraphs, to be a dignified farewell

[4] See above, pp. 168-71.
[5] *SC* 342.114.
[6] E.g. Baur, 2,263: cf. 2,270 n. 4.
[7] *SC* 342.78, lines 1-4. The previous sentence, which speaks of his being 'driven from the church', has nothing to do with his arrest, but refers to Theophilos' relentless persecution of him.
[8] Sokrates 6.15 ad fin.; Sozomen 8.18.
[9] See above, p. 224.
[10] *PG* 52.430.

address. A text, five sections long, which purports to be this address has come down,[11] and while critics remain divided about the closing two sections, there has been a reasonable consensus that the first three are authentic. Although plainly an abbreviation of the original, they leave a strong impression of John's style, language and characteristically direct, outgoing approach. His object, clearly, is to prepare his worried listeners for his imminent exile. Instead of getting alarmed or turbulent, he urges them to sustain him with their prayers.[12] So he dwells eloquently on his own readiness to face whatever disasters are in store, on the invincibility of the church so often demonstrated in history, on the bond between a bishop and his flock which, like that between husband and wife, makes them inseparable. With Christ's promise, 'Lo, I am with you always' (Matt. 28.20) ringing in his ears, what has he to fear? Above all, he places his confidence in the trust and loyalty of his devoted people wonderfully displayed in the courageous vigils they have been keeping for him recently.

Themes like these criss-cross in the opening sections. In the closing two the tone changes abruptly: John turns from affectionate pleading and exhortation to polemical abuse. They have come down in what seem to be two redactions which at points repeat, at points supplement each other.[13] The text of both is confused, even chaotic, and the Greek seems occasionally hardly to make sense. In both redactions John angrily asks why his persecutors are so keen to depose him. It is because he has refused to indulge in the soft life of luxury himself, and also refused to sanction their gluttony and avarice. In the second he takes a swipe at Theophilos without naming him: just as long ago the Egyptian Potiphar tried to seduce Joseph, so an Egyptian today – in vain – seeks to separate John from the flock which is his spiritual bride. Even Arkadios (again not named) is asked to reflect that David, the model king, made no attack on true religion, never made ill-gotten gains his aim, and never allowed himself to be led by his wife. In both there are warnings to misguided women who shut their ears to the truth, give bad advice to their husbands, or wage war against the immaculate church while wallowing themselves in a life of sensuality. In both the figures of Jezebel and of Herodias, John the Baptist's persecutor, are paraded – 'once again Herodias is dancing, and seeks the head of John'. In one daring passage the preacher exclaims, 'In the evening she called me the thirteenth apostle, today she has branded me as Judas. Yesterday she sat with me conversing freely, but today pounces on me like a wild beast. But … we must not forget the words of Job who, when he suffered so much affliction, could only proclaim, "Blessed be the Lord's name forever." '[14]

---

[11] *Sermo antequam iret in exsilium* (PG 52.427-32). Sir Henry Savile and Bernard de Montfaucon, the greatest of John's editors, accepted the genuineness of the three first sections.
[12] *PG* 52.430 ad init.
[13] *PG* 52.431-2; 435-8 (the latter is separately designated *Sermo cum iret in exsilium*).
[14] *PG* 52.437-8.

These texts clearly present something of a problem. In traditionalist circles they have generally been pushed to one side[15] – although this does nothing to tackle the question how they originated in the first place. On the other hand, scholars of the calibre and independence of O. Seeck[16] and H. Lietzmann[17] had no doubts about their authenticity. According to them, they represent, not shorthand notes of John's actual address (if they had been such, they would have been much less disjointed), but bits and pieces of it as remembered by friendly listeners. To the present writer a solution along these lines seems much the most satisfactory.[18] It is not easy to imagine stenographers taking down, much less preserving copies of, such politically sensitive material. Two further points deserve mention. First, there is a clear link between these fragments and the three earlier sections, not only in their common preoccupation with John's exile, but in such themes as the resemblance between a bishop's relationship with his flock and that of husband and wife. Secondly, the genuineness of at any rate part of the second redaction is supported by the fact that, in his very next sermon,[19] John was to remind his audience that he had appealed to the words of Job cited above when setting out for exile.

However provocative the finale of his farewell address, John was in no mood for a head-on clash with the emperor. As her pastor he was ready enough, when the occasion seemed to warrant it, to rebuke Eudoxia for what he considered feminine follies, but his consistent attitude to Arkadios, as to his father Theodosius I, was one of unwavering respect and deference. If the imperial orders meant exile, he was fully prepared, as his sermon had made plain, to accept it, placing his trust in God. So the following day, at noon when the heat was at its most intense and the streets were deserted,[20] he quietly slipped out of the church and, without fuss or publicity, surrendered himself to the chief of police (*kouriosos*). Although we have no proof of it, we may suspect that he had privately notified this high official of his intention. The last thing he wanted, the historians emphasise, was that there should be more rioting and civic uproar on his account. Late that evening, with an enormous crowd surging around the little procession, he was escorted under guard down to the port and bundled (*eneballomen* is the word he uses) aboard a waiting boat. As it sailed in the darkness from the Bosporus into the Sea of Marmara, he was still loudly demanding a more authoritative court to review his case. He was being

[15] Moulard, for example (341-2), fully agrees that John gave the address, but confines his summary to the first three sections.
[16] *Geschichte des Untergangs der antiken Welt* 5, 361 and 581 n. 31.
[17] PW IX.2.1822.
[18] See also K.G. Holum, *Theodosian Empresses* (California 1982), 74-5.
[19] See below, p. 236.
[20] Sokrates 6.15; Sozomen 8.18. In *Ep. 1 ad Innocentium* (*SC* 342.78) John seems to suggest that his arrest and embarkation both took place in the late evening, but this is probably the result of the compression inevitable in such a brief account.

taken to Praenetos, a market-town and developing port on the south coast of the Astacene Gulf between Helenopolis and Nikomedia. It was the preferred starting-point for travellers to Nicaea who had sensibly avoided the tedious land route from Constantinople.[21]

III

Praenetos was probably intended as a temporary halting place. We have no clue to the locality the government had planned (if indeed it had yet reached a decision) for John's permanent exile, but in any case he was never to reach it. Against all expectation the authorities suddenly reversed their policy in regard to him.

Predictably, the news of his deposition, and of his departure from the city under guard, provoked a furious outburst of popular indignation, directed in the first instance at the sovereigns, but even more at the bishops who had taken part in The Oak, especially at Theophilos and Severian of Gabala.[22] The fact that Severian judged this the moment to declaim from the pulpit that John had richly deserved his fate if only because of his insufferable arrogance ('God is prepared to forgive other faults, but scripture teaches that he resists the proud') was like pouring petrol on a bonfire. What was decisive, however, in forcing an about-turn on the authorities was not mob violence but some disaster which they interpreted as a divine warning. Theodoret identifies it as 'a tremendous earthquake' which took place on the night after John's arrest,[23] but the evidence we should expect confirming it is lacking. Palladios' account[24] is diplomatically vague, but suggests a personal tragedy: 'on the following day a misfortune (*thrausis*) occurred in the imperial bedchamber.' O. Seeck took this to be an accident to Eudoxia's daughter Flacilla which resulted in her death,[25] while Baur explained it as a miscarriage suffered by Eudoxia herself.[26] Baur's conjecture, apparently, is supported by 'Martyrios' in language which, although full of 'laborious circumlocutions', is unmistakable in its meaning.[27]

Intensely superstitious, the empress inevitably took this to be a signal of God's anger at the expulsion of his consecrated representative, and begged Arkadios to order John's immediate recall (a request the emperor is likely to have welcomed). To persuade John himself to agree she dispatched one of her favourite eunuchs, the chief chamberlain Brison, a friend and admirer of John's,[28] to Praenetos to bring him back. She even sent John

---

[21] A.H.M. Jones, *Cities of the Eastern Roman Provinces* (Oxford, 2 ed. 1971), 164-5.
[22] Sokrates 6.15; Sozomen 8.18.
[23] *HE* 5.34.5 (*GCS* 44.335).
[24] *Dial.* 9 (*SC* 341.180).
[25] Op. cit., 5.362. K.G. Holum, op. cit., 75, is inclined to take the same view.
[26] 2,265.
[27] F. van Ommeslaeghe, *AB* 99 (1981), 337 (he does not quote the text).
[28] See above, p. 138; also p. 255.

an agonised note, which he was shortly after to cite with satisfaction,[29] protesting before God that she had had no part in the plot which wicked, depraved people had concocted against him, but deeply revered him as the priest who had baptised her children. The royal emissaries had considerable difficulty in finding him; John claims that they had no clear idea of his whereabouts,[30] so that one wonders if he had somehow gone into hiding. When Brison eventually tracked him down, John was evidently in no hurry to return. He insisted that, as he had been deposed by a synod, he could not properly resume his former position until a subsequent synod had overruled that verdict. His obstinacy added to the court's impatience, and no fewer than three groups of imperial messengers were sent to put pressure on him.[31] He eventually agreed to be taken back to the outskirts of Constantinople, and Theodoret has left a colourful picture of the vast flotilla of boats crowding the mouth of the Bosporus to welcome the returning hero. John, however, insisted on staying outside the walls at a suburban villa called Marianai which Eudoxia placed at his disposal; he was adamant that he would not enter the city itself until the injustice of his deposition had been formally recognised.[32]

The delay, which seems to have been prolonged, exasperated the populace, and there were renewed demonstrations against the imperial couple. What finally induced him to change his mind was a quite unforeseen, near-disastrous development of which historians have only recently begun to take notice – the temporary occupation of the Great Church by swarms of rampaging monks, followed by their forcible expulsion by government troops. John himself makes two unmistakable allusions to the shocking incident. First, in a sermon delivered shortly afterwards, he recalls[33] how Theophilos' supporters had fought with clubs in the church, and how although they had been vanquished by the prayers of the faithful the baptistery had been spattered with blood. Then in his letter to Innocent I he describes[34] how the emperor, just before his own recall, had 'driven from the church those who had shamelessly invaded it.' In the past students could make little or nothing of the latter passage, while they tended to dismiss the former on the ground[35] that the sermon must be inauthentic, or at any rate tampered with, since it was in the following year, at Easter 404, that the baptistery was the scene of bloodshed.[36] A fuller, much more explicit account of the affair is given by the pagan Zosimos,[37] who reports that, before John's return, 'the city was filled with tumult, and the church

---

[29] *Sermo post reditum* 4 (*PG* 52.445).
[30] *Sermo post reditum* 4 (*PG* 52.445-6).
[31] Theodoret, *HE* 5.34.6 (*GCS* 44.335).
[32] Sokrates 6.15; Sozomen 8.18.
[33] *Sermo post reditum* 2 (*PG* 52.444).
[34] *Ep. 1 ad Innocentium* (*SC* 342.78).
[35] See, e.g., Montfaucon in *PG* 52.437-8; Baur, 2,272 n. 27; Moulard, 344.
[36] See below, p. 244.
[37] 5.23.4-5.

of the Christians was taken over by the so-called monks ... who prevented the crowds from participating in the customary prayers.' The ordinary citizens, he adds, were infuriated by this behaviour and joined with the military in launching attacks on the black-robed fanatics, butchering them until the building was filled with corpses. This important evidence, too, has until recently been largely overlooked.

Today scholars have been obliged to take a fresh look at these texts; as a result they have been enabled for the first time to reconstruct in plausible outline the short-lived emergency to which they refer. This has been brought about in part by the publication of a hitherto unknown passage[38] of 'Martyrios' which confirms in a remarkable way the glimpses of it given by both John and Zosimos. He too testifies that, in the anxious period when John was laying down conditions for his return, a mob of his opponents occupied the church, filling it with stones and bludgeons, challenging would-be worshippers either to denounce their bishop or else suffer physical violence. He even adds, strikingly bearing out the evidence of John's sermon, that the sacred place where baptisms were administered was stained with the blood of injured catechumens. There are readily understandable differences between our three witnesses. Zosimos alone tells us that the intruders were monks. Only he and John (by implication, in his letter to the pope) speak of government troops being moved in. Reading John and 'Martyrios', one would infer that the victims were all innocent worshippers; it is only Zosimos who reveals that numerous black-robed monks were among the dead.

These differences apart, their convergent testimony leads to one fairly safe conclusion. The reversal of John's banishment had been a shattering blow to all who had been working for his downfall. The most furious reaction, however, had come from the monks of the capital, who gave their allegiance to his arch-enemy Isaac, now hand in glove with Theophilos, and whom he had criticised from the start of his ministry as an indisciplined rabble.[39] In a desperate move, characteristic of their fanaticism, they barricaded themselves in Hagia Sophia, spreading terror among ordinary people and threatening his loyal supporters. So alarming was the situation that the government felt obliged to send in troops. The people, aware that John's return had been settled in principle by the authorities, were only too eager to join forces with them and assist in punishing his irreconcilable enemies.

This reconstruction, incidentally, helps to clear up a passage in Sokrates which has long puzzled scholars, his report[40] of a violent conflict, in the

---

[38] See F. van Ommeslaeghe, *AB* 99 (1981), 333-9, who cites the text (P 501a-b) in a French translation on p. 337. The contribution of T.E. Gregory, *Byzantion* 43 (1973), 63-81 was fundamental.

[39] See above, pp. 123-5.

[40] 6.17: also Sozomen 8.19. Tillemont (xi.19) long ago queried Sokrates' account.

period of John's banishment, between 'Alexandrians' and 'Constantinopolitans' which resulted in numerous persons being wounded, several killed. Sokrates links this implausibly with an attempt by Theophilos to have Herakleides, John's unpopular choice as bishop of Ephesos,[41] deposed; it seems much more likely that he was referring, confusedly and on the basis of incomplete evidence, to the affray in the church.[42]

IV

In this atmosphere of excitement and violence, 'Martyrios' confirms,[43] the emperor and empress put renewed pressure on John to overcome his scruples and return. When they backed this with letters containing solemn promises to convene a council charged with re-examining his case in all its aspects, he consented. By this time Theophilos, with his attendant Egyptian bishops, and Isaac had boarded a ship by night and were on their way to Alexandria.[44] Severian, too, and the other bishops who had banded together against John at The Oak had also been quick to take their departure. John seems to admit[45] that they had had no hand in the monks' occupation of Hagia Sophia, but recognised its criminality and distanced themselves from it. Nevertheless, once it became known that the court was bent on recalling John and was planning a synod to review his case, they knew that the tide had turned against them. Theophilos had been well advised to go. His reappearance in Constantinople (he had crossed the Bosporus from Chalkedon) at the very moment of John's expulsion had exasperated the masses, and there were ominous threats of having him thrown into the sea.[46]

John's re-entry into the city in early October was a triumphal one. Writing to the pope, he simply recalls[47] that the emperor had sent a secretary of the imperial consistory (*notarios*) to conduct him, and that more than thirty bishops came out to escort him. In fact, immense, exultant crowds received him, thronging the streets and squares, singing psalms and carrying lighted tapers.[48] They included, 'Martyrios' (who claims to have been present) insists,[49] numbers of affluent people as well as the poor, and these showed their zeal by not only providing flaming torches but holding them aloft themselves. When the procession reached Holy Apostles,

---

[41] See above, p. 174. For Herakleides' imprisonment after John's definitive exile, see Palladios, *Dial.* 20 (*SC* 341.398).
[42] So too van Ommeslaeghe, art, cit., 339 n. 23.
[43] P 501a-b.
[44] Sokrates 6.17; Sozomen 8.19: also John's letter to Innocent I (*SC* 342.78-80).
[45] *Ep. 1 ad Innocentium* (*SC* 342.78 lines 106-7).
[46] Palladios, *Dial.* 9 (*SC* 341.180).
[47] *Ep. 1 ad Innocentium* (*SC* 342.80).
[48] Sozomen 8.18.
[49] P 501b-503a.

the people at John's bidding swarmed into the church, where he delivered a short, extempore address; the Greek original is lost, but two independent Latin versions which, it is generally agreed, reproduce its substance survive.[50] Recalling that he had used Job's exclamation, 'Blessed be God', in his last sermon to them,[51] he declares that he is glad to repeat the words now – 'Blessed be God, who allowed me to go into exile; blessed also be God, who has ordered me to return.' His enemies had hoped to separate him from his people, but their efforts had only won him more friends. Previously the church alone had been filled, today the entire city square has been transformed into a church. Best of all, although there is horse-racing in the hippodrome, there are no spectators there, for everyone has thronged to church. What especially rejoices him is that, while the flock assembled here is so numerous, the wolves, the robbers, the adulterers who tried to seduce his bride have all been dispersed. And they have been routed, not by any spear or sword of his, but by the tears and continuous prayers of his faithful people.

The following Sunday, in spite of his initial refusal, his reiterated protests that he must be rehabilitated before resuming his episcopal functions, he was prevailed upon, by popular demand, to take his seat on the throne of Hagia Sophia and, at the start of the service, to give the liturgical greeting 'Peace be with you' to the congregation. This was a right reserved to the bishop, and the people's insistence that he should exercise it was a public acknowledgement that in their view his deposition was invalid.[52] The incident is reported, in slightly differing accounts, by Sokrates and Sozomen;[53] 'Martyrios' is silent about it, but it is understandable that he should not record such a rash move. He also preached an exultant celebratory sermon.[54] It opened with what Sozomen called an elegant comparison between Theophilos, who had tried to seduce John's bride, his church in the capital, with that Pharaoh (was not Theophilos nicknamed the Egyptian Pharaoh?) who (Gen. 12.10-20) was struck by the beauty of Sarah, wife of Abraham (who was passing her off, in the interest of his own safety, as his sister) and took her into his harem, only to be stricken by God 'with great plagues'.[55] Theophilos' dastardly attempt had been frustrated, and the church's honour remained unstained. John then showered extravagant compliments on his people, who had not only thwarted Theophilos but, during his own absence, had shown unexampled faith, courage and devotion, and who, when his return became known, had braved the sea to greet

---

[50] *PG* 52.439-42. It is Sozomen (8.18) who reports the extempore address, but he confuses it with the sermon to be discussed below.

[51] See above, p. 230.

[52] On this see F. van de Paverd, *Zur Geschichte der Messliturgie in Antiocheia und Konstantinopel gegen Ende des vierten Jahrhunderts* (Rome 1970), 442-3.

[53] 6.16; 8.18.

[54] *Post reditum a priore exsilio* (*PG* 52.443-8).

[55] According to the Jewish midrashic tradition Sarah (Sarai) remained inviolate.

his ship and had turned the forum into a worshipping church. But his most effusive praise is reserved for Eudoxia. He brings her in, he observes, not to flatter her, but to celebrate her piety, zeal, outstanding virtue. He describes how desperately she had worked to bring about his restoration and how, once she had achieved it, she had assured him that she counted this a crown more splendid than her diadem. The sermon ends with a promise that henceforth he will do nothing except in concert with both the people and 'our most devout Augusta', whose pastoral concern it is that the church should sail its course unbuffeted by the waves.

According to Sozomen, the sermon was rapturously received, with the crowded congregation cheering the imperial couple to the skies, and John had to break off before he had reached his finale. Some modern students have been less indulgent.[56] Finding it hard to believe that John could have used such blatant flattery, or drawn such a manifest travesty of Eudoxia's role, they have claimed that it can be no part of his genuine oeuvre. In fact, its authenticity has never been seriously questioned.[57] The one serious argument which used to be brought against it,[58] that the bloodshed in the baptistery referred to in section 2 surely points to a later author, has lost its force now that we know the story of the monks' occupation of Hagia Sophia. The critics' squeamishness does more credit to their good taste than to their appreciation either of the complexity of John's character or of the diplomatic ambivalences considered acceptable in Byzantine court rhetoric.

V

For several weeks John enjoyed something of a St Luke's summer. His recall contrary to all expectations, brought about partly at any rate as a result of their demonstrations, redoubled his popularity with the masses. His deferential tributes ensured that his relations with the court were once again on an amicable footing. He was nevertheless fully aware of the delicacy of his position and, by his own account,[59] repeatedly put pressure on the emperor to summon an authoritative synod which would redress the wrong done to him at The Oak. Arkadios, he reports, complied with his request, dispatching messengers in all directions to summon the bishops to a fresh synod. Theophilos in particular was commanded to present himself in the capital along with his supporting Egyptian bishops. He was called upon, as John expressed it, 'to give an account of all that had happened, and not to suppose that the unjust acts he had dared carry out, unilaterally, in my absence and in defiance of so many canons, would suffice for his defence'. Not surprisingly, Theophilos decided to remain in Alexan-

---

[56] E.g. Baur, 2,272 n. 27; Moulard, 344.
[57] It was accepted, for example, by Savile, Montfaucon, Tillemont and Stilting.
[58] See above, p. 233.
[59] *Ep. 1 ad Innocentium* (SC 342.80).

dria; the excuse he sent, according to John, was that he feared that his devoted people would riot if he left them.

In the meantime, Sozomen reports,[60] some sixty bishops met in conclave, solemnly declared the decisions of The Oak null and void, and confirmed John as the rightful bishop of the see. At first sight he seems to imply that this happened shortly after John's return. If this is correct, the total must have been made up of John's own supporters supplemented by a number of bishops who had come to the capital for the abortive council to judge Theophilos, and had delayed their departure. It seems more likely, however, that the meeting took place somewhat later, and that many of the participating bishops were early arrivals for the new council ordered by the emperor.[61] In passing, there is no reason to suppose, as has sometimes been suggested,[62] that Arkadios himself had convened the meeting. The gathering, it is clear, was an informal one, designed to provide John with assurances which would quieten his scruples pending the forthcoming general council. It had no canonical authority, and it is significant that John makes no mention of it in his letter to Innocent I. Whatever its status and date, however, John's confidence was evidently at a high level. It must have seemed certain to him that, when the new council met, he would be finally vindicated. Disregarding therefore the risk he was running, he resumed presiding in his cathedral, ordaining clergy, and exercising all the normal episcopal functions.[63] Thus when Paul of Heraklea, who had presided at The Oak, died shortly after his own return from temporary exile, he consecrated the priest Sarapion as metropolitan of Thrace in his place,[64] thereby removing from the capital a confidant on whom he placed complete reliance but who was widely detested as a trouble-maker.

For all his assurance John was in fact playing with fire, for nothing could have been more brittle than the patched-up harmony between himself and the palace. Although Theophilos and the cohort of Egyptian bishops he had brought to The Oak had returned to Alexandria, he still had a host of enemies in the capital. He himself complains to the pope of 'certain Syrians' of Theophilos' entourage whom the patriarch had left behind;[65] this suggests that although Antiochos, Akakios and Severian had temporarily made themselves scarce, one or two of them were soon back in Constantinople. Although they could do nothing while he apparently basked in the court's favour, they were only waiting for him to make a false or indiscreet move. The moment came sooner perhaps than they dared hope. About mid-November the city prefect Simplikios had a silver statue of Eudoxia,[66]

[60] 8.19: cf. Sokrates 6.18.
[61] So Baur, 2,270; Moulard, 345.
[62] É. Demougeot, *De l'unité à la division de l'empire romain* (Paris 1951), 324.
[63] Sozomen 6.18 ad fin.
[64] Sokrates 6.17; Sozomen 8.19.
[65] *Ep. 1 ad Innocentium* (*SC* 342.82).
[66] Sokrates 6.18; Sozomen 8.20.

arrayed in the distinctive mantle of an Augusta, set up in front of the senate-house, well within earshot of Hagia Sophia. It stood resplendent on a column of porphyry; the base bore a bilingual inscription,[67] four complimentary Greek hexameters on the left, and on the right a brief summary of their content in Latin. The statue was formally dedicated one Sunday, and Simplikios arranged for the occasion to be celebrated with spectacles of mimes and dancers 'as was then the usual practice when statues of the emperors were erected'.[68] Unfortunately the music, singing and clamorous applause interrupted the service in the cathedral, where John was presiding at the liturgy. Instead of courteously asking for the celebrations to be discontinued (as Sokrates suggests would have been appropriate), he lost his temper, and in a public address complained that these noisy entertainments were an insult to the church, and witheringly denounced their organisers.

While John's irritation was understandable, his outburst was, to say the least, politically maladroit. The setting up of this statue was a significant occasion for the imperial family; this is confirmed by the way the event was singled out for mention by later chroniclers.[69] There is evidence that, ever since her elevation to the rank of Augusta,[70] the eastern government had been striving in its propaganda to promote the recognition of Eudoxia's imperial status; as western complaints at the highest level reveal,[71] it was having images of her, arrayed in the honorific mantle and diadem appropriate to an Augusta, distributed throughout the empire, including (to the annoyance of the authorities there) the western parts. A report of his sermon was immediately taken to the empress. Although he seems to have avoided mentioning her personally, it was inevitable that she should interpret it as an attack on herself, an attack all the more wounding as the homage implied in the silver statue fully accorded with the divinely appointed role which she and the court generally regarded as devolving on her as Augusta.[72]

So infuriated was she, we are told,[73] that she even began planning another synod against John, this time because of his temerity in resuming his duties as bishop before being formally exonerated. She had conveniently forgotten that it was only in response to her frantic appeals that he had agreed to return from exile, and that whatever ecclesiastical functions he had undertaken had been with the full knowledge and connivance of the

---

[67] *CIL* 3.736.
[68] Sozomen, loc. cit.
[69] E.g. Marcellinus Comes, s.a. 403 (*MGHAA* xi.67).
[70] See above, p. 151.
[71] *Collectio Avellana* 38.1 (*CSEL* 35: 1.85 – a letter from Emperor Honorius dated late June 404).
[72] For this para. see K.G. Holum, *Theodosian Empresses* (California 1982), esp. 65-7; he cites also her representation on the imperial coinage.
[73] Sokrates 6.18; Sozomen 8.20.

court. Almost certainly it was the news of her change of attitude, so contrary to her earlier blandishments, which provoked him into a further tirade, this time on the occasion, apparently, of some ceremony in honour of his name-saint John the Baptist. It started dramatically with the words, 'Again Herodias is enraged, again she dances, again she seeks to have John's head on a platter.' Like other preachers then and now, John was evoking famous biblical figures to press home his homiletical message, and we can be sure that he pointed no finger overtly at the empress. But in the fevered atmosphere of the capital people could not fail to detect in his words a veiled comparison between his own predicament facing the irate Eudoxia and the fate of the Baptist, whom the tetrarch Antipas had had reluctantly beheaded at his queen's behest.[74] Apart from its exordium the sermon has disappeared (an address which had proved so offensive to the palace was not likely to remain in circulation), but both Sokrates and Sozomen knew it, and described it as 'much spoken of', 'notorious'.[75]

VI

Reports of John's sermon, as Sokrates observed,[76] only added to the empress's exasperation, with the result that the fragile reconciliation patched up between him and the court now lay in tatters. The altered atmosphere was not slow in making itself felt. According to Palladios,[77] the first bishops arriving in the capital in response to Arkadios' summons entered into communion with John. It seemed to them the proper thing to do, especially as they took it for granted that his formal rehabilitation would be a matter of course. To their astonishment they were informed that 'those in power' (*hoi kratountes*) disapproved; Palladios was too prudent to mention names. By December more and more bishops were pouring in, some of them well disposed to John, but others, like Akakios of Beroea, Leontios of Ankyra, Ammonios of Laodikeia and Brison of Philippopolis, his sworn enemies. The news that the palace was distancing itself from John must have revived their spirits and, joining forces with Severian and others like-minded, they wrote to Theophilos urging him to change his mind and come to Constantinople to lead a new campaign against its bishop; failing that, they sought his advice on the tactics they should adopt.[78] Recalling his earlier experiences, Theophilos preferred to direct operations from Egypt, but dispatched three bishops to the capital armed with instructions which, if followed, he was sure would irretrievably ruin any hope of John's sentence of deposition being overturned.

---

[74] Mark 6.16-28. It was not Herodias but her daughter who danced.
[75] The sermon printed in *PG* 59.485-90 is not authentic: see J.A. de Aldama, *Repertorium pseudochrysostomicum* (Paris 1965), 138-9 (no. 381).
[76] 6.18.
[77] *Dial.* 9 (*SC* 341.184).
[78] Palladios, *Dial.* 9 (*SC* 341.180-2).

The breach between John and the palace became official as Christmas approached. It was the custom of the imperial family to forsake the chapel in the Sacred Palace on that day and worship with their subjects in Hagia Sophia. Now Arkadios sent John a curt message informing him that he and Eudoxia would not be present since they could not, in conscience, hold communion with him as their bishop until he had been canonically cleared of the charges of which he had been found guilty at The Oak.[79] Although John's disgrace and the imperial disfavour were evident for all to see, there was a curious stalemate from Christmas until almost Easter 404, with the authorities apparently unsure about their next move. All the bishops summoned to the council were now in Constantinople except Theophilos, who was however closely following events from Alexandria. There was intensive lobbying, by the bishops ill-disposed to John but also by people close to the court, to drop their allegiance to him. Palladios reports that one of these, Theodore of Tyana, who would have liked to remain loyal, judged it prudent to leave the city rather than give offence in high quarters.[80] Another, Pharetrios of Caesarea (in Cappadocia), felt so intimidated that he cravenly went over to the enemy camp. It looked as if the council which had originally been assembled to overturn the decisions of The Oak was going to be transformed into one to ratify them. Meanwhile John, who had forty-two bishops firmly attached to him,[81] continued to draw vast crowds to his sermons, and to protest his readiness to defend himself.

In fact, no formal council was held. There are passages in Palladios[82] and Sokrates[83] which at first sight seem to suggest that there was 'a second synod', but in both cases the reference is almost certainly to an informal meeting or meetings of John's enemies.[84] In his letter to Innocent I John himself is emphatic that all his demands for a tribunal before which he could plead his case went unanswered.[85] The truth seems to be that, faced with his defiant attitude and supreme self-confidence, his opponents drew back; as Sozomen put it (using material not available to Sokrates), his accusers took fright and had not the courage to follow up their charges.[86] Clearly they could not be sure that the verdict would go in their favour. Moreover, John's popularity with the masses must also have been a deterring factor; the government, they well knew, had no wish to risk a repeat of the violent demonstrations which had attended his first exile. What was really decisive, however, was the advice which they had recently received from Theophilos. This was that they could get rid of John quietly,

---

[79] Sokrates 6.18; Sozomen 8.20.
[80] *Dial.* 9 (*SC* 341.184-6).
[81] Palladios, *Dial.* 9 (*SC* 341.190 lines 110-11).
[82] *Dial.* 9 (*SC* 341.186 line 156).
[83] 6.18 (*PG* 67.720-1).
[84] See below, p. 243.
[85] *SC* 342.82.
[86] 8.20.

without the embarrassment of letting him plead his case publicly, by calling in aid the canons of the famous synod held at Antioch in May 341 (the so-called Dedication Council). The fourth[87] of these canons (of which Theophilos had sent them a copy) had laid it down unequivocally that, if a bishop who had been deposed by a synod resumed his functions on his own responsibility, without first having his sentence quashed by another synod, he was excluded from office henceforth, without the possibility of an appeal. When they studied it, they at once perceived that it provided a solution to their problem. They therefore decided, as Sokrates put it,[88] to drop all further investigation and rely exclusively on the fact that John was in clear breach of this canon.

Their stance placed John and his supporters in an awkward position. While canon 4 (with the related canon 12) had been drafted with the object of preventing Athanasios, the champion of Nicene orthodoxy, who was then in exile, from returning to his see, the Antiochene canons were held in high esteem in the east; canon 4 in particular reappears in the respected Apostolic Canons[89] (late fourth century), and was to be appealed to at the fourth session of the council of Chalkedon (451). They therefore resorted to denouncing the Dedication Council as having been Arian. Historically, this was a travesty of the truth;[90] the participating bishops had explicitly repudiated Arius and his distinctive teaching. Nevertheless they had deliberately sought to bypass the then controversial new formula 'of one substance', and their own middle-of-the-road position, judged by the orthodoxy current *c.* 400, could be plausibly misrepresented as tainted with Arianism.[91] This was therefore the line that John's friends adopted. At a joint meeting of the opposing parties held in the emperor's presence (Palladios is our sole informant of it)[92] we find them protesting that appeal to the canon was illegitimate in the present case since (a) John had not been canonically deposed, but simply expelled by government officials; (b) he had not returned to his see on his own initiative, but at the express command of the emperor; and (c) the canons of Antioch were in any case the fabrication of Arian heretics. They seem to have had some initial success in winning Arkadios over to their viewpoint, for (if we can trust the story) he expressed warm approval when the leader of John's group, Elpidios of Laodikeia, challenged Akakios and Antiochos to sign a declaration that they personally accepted the canons and shared the theological position of the bishops who had framed them. Greatly daring, the two assured the meeting that they were ready to sign, and the scruples of the emperor, who was convinced of their orthodoxy, were set at rest. The

---

[87] Hefele-Leclercq, *Histoire des conciles* 1.745-6.
[88] 6.18.
[89] Included in *Apostolic Constitutions* 8.47 (Funk, I, 564-91).
[90] Cf. J.N.D. Kelly, *Early Christian Creeds* (London, 3 ed. 1972), 263-74.
[91] See above, pp. 10f.
[92] *Dial.* 9 (*SC* 341.188-90).

objections of John's supporters were therefore overruled, and the official view which prevailed seems to have been that he was disqualified for office by the disputed canon.

VII

The approach of Easter 404 brought the stalemate to an end; the great feast, preceded by a solemn vigil and the mass baptism of catechumens during the night, called for a public clarification of John's position. By his own account he had been, incessantly and insistently, clamouring for a council, a court of law, a tribunal, at which he could have the charges against him rehearsed and be able to marshal his defence.[93] This his opponents, the majority of bishops in the capital, steadfastly refused to grant him, being satisfied that the Antiochene canons made such a council not only unnecessary but also improper. At some point, probably soon after the debate between both parties mentioned above, they must have held a meeting, taken a formal decision to this effect, and communicated it to the emperor. It was their verdict at this meeting which Arkadios had in mind when, as Sokrates reports,[94] he now informed John that he could not attend his Easter services 'since he had been condemned by two synods'. At the same time, yielding to pressure from Antiochos and his associates, he reluctantly instructed John to cease functioning in Hagia Sophia.[95] As John himself tersely expressed it,[96] 'I was once again expelled from my church.' When John protested that he had received his church from God and would not abandon his sacred charge unless forced to do so, the emperor responded by forbidding him, pending further action, to leave his episcopal residence. In his eagerness to exonerate Arkadios from all blame, Palladios describes how the worried man summoned Antiochos and Akakios and warned them not to give him bad advice,[97] only to be confidently assured that they were prepared to take full responsibility for what effectively amounted to John's deposition.

By the beginning of holy week it had become known to the people that their bishop, now a prisoner in his own palace, would not be officiating at the Easter services in his cathedral. On Good Friday, when the emperor and empress customarily visited certain martyrs' shrines, some forty Johnite bishops (again it is Palladios who recounts the story)[98] waylaid the royal procession and made a last desperate attempt to persuade them, in consideration of the holy season and of all the catechumens waiting to be baptised, to restore to the church its beloved bishop. Their petition was

---

[93] *Ep. 1 ad Innocentium* (*SC* 342.82).
[94] 6.18.
[95] Palladios, *Dial.* 9 (*SC* 341.190-2).
[96] *Ep. 1 ad Innocentium* (*SC* 342.82).
[97] *Dial.* 9 (*SC* 341.192-4).
[98] *Dial.* 9 (*SC* 341.194).

rebuffed. It may have been Eudoxia who took the lead in spurning it,[99] for one of the bishops, Paul of Krateia, had the courage to warn her to fear God and not do anything which might bring his wrath down on her children.

It was on Easter Sunday itself (17 April), more particularly on the evening preceding it, that the lengths to which John's enemies in high places, prodded by Antiochos, Akakios, and Severian, were prepared to go were revealed.[100] Arrangements had been made for the baptism during the night of the scores of catechumens who had been preparing for it throughout Lent. In spite of the ban imposed on John but undoubtedly with his agreement, the clergy loyal to him were determined to go ahead with these arrangements, and the mass of ordinary citizens, including the catechumens, showed themselves resolved to support them. This was a display of independence which the authorities had perhaps not bargained for, but which, when they learned that the baptisms were proceeding, they felt bound to resist. The master of the offices, Anthemios, according to Palladios, was at first reluctant to have recourse to violence, and when persuaded to intervene made it plain that he did so under protest. Thus, when evening fell and John's clergy were beginning their services in Hagia Sophia and Hagia Eirene, some four hundred young recruits commanded by a pagan officer Loukios forced their way into the baptisteries with orders to break up the solemn gatherings. There followed extraordinary scenes of brutality and sacrilege, with officiating clergy being driven out with cudgels, women catechumens who had undressed in preparation for immersion fleeing half-naked, the water in the fonts turned red with the blood of the wounded, and unbelieving soldiers forcibly entering the place where the holy sacrament was kept and desecrating its contents. Sozomen, a devout man who had detailed information about what happened, remarked that he would not elaborate on it in case his work should fall into the hands of non-Christians and bring the church into disrepute.

There is in fact close agreement among our sources about the horrors perpetrated.[101] Both John and Palladios also agree in their concern to exonerate the emperor; as John exclaims, 'All these violent deeds were committed against the wishes of our religious sovereign ... they were organised by the bishops.'[102] But two discrepancies between the sources deserve attention. First, according to Palladios and Sokrates the baptism of catechumens and the soldiers' attack took place in the Baths of Constantius,[103] close to the church of the Holy Apostles, and most historians have followed their account, arguing that the clergy and their charges must have

[99] Baur, 2, 283.
[100] For the story told in this para. see esp. John's letter to Innocent I (*SC* 342.82-6); also Palladios, *Dial.* 9 (*SC* 341.194-8); 'Martyrios' (P 508b-512b); Sozomen 8.21.1-4.
[101] For a detailed comparison of the accounts of John and Palladios, see A.M. Malingrey, *SC* 342.52-8.
[102] *Ep. 1 ad Innocentium* (*SC* 342.86).
[103] For their location see R. Janin, *Constantinople byzantine* (Paris 1950), 346.

transferred themselves there after finding that they were forbidden to use Hagia Sophia. John himself, however, Sozomen and (as we now know) 'Martyrios' all speak unequivocally of 'the churches' or 'the church'. Secondly, while John places the army break-in 'in the evening', Palladios says it occurred 'in the second watch', i.e. at midnight or a little later. In both cases it seems reasonable to prefer the evidence of John, who wrote his letter to the pope within a few weeks of the events, and of 'Martyrios', who claims to have been an eye-witness.

Ejected forcibly from the churches, John's clerical and lay supporters assembled next morning in the Baths of Constantius to celebrate the Easter liturgy. For this again we have the explicit testimony of 'Martyrios' and Sozomen;[104] John's abridged narrative passes over this move. Meanwhile the Great Church stood virtually empty – embarrassingly so, for the imperial family was due to worship there. In spite of efforts to pack a congregation into it,[105] Arkadios seems to have had to absent himself from the service. Before long, however, the multitude crowding the baths was again driven out by armed force, and reassembled for worship in the open air some distance from the centre, north-west of the city, at a place called Pempton, which Constantine the Great had arranged for horse-racing. It was from this date that John's devoted adherents began holding separate meetings for worship, in one place or another, and that the Johnite schism came into being.[106] When the emperor took a ride later in the day in that region, he and his escort came across this motley gathering of worshippers, the recently baptised still wearing the white garments they had been given after receiving the sacrament. Palladios, who alone reports this episode, says they numbered 'about three thousand',[107] but the figure should be treated with caution; it is an edifying reminiscence of the number baptised by the apostles on the first Whitsunday (Acts 2.41). A number of clergy and even more layfolk were, according to Palladios, arrested.

VIII

For two full months John was allowed to remain, under government surveillance, in his official residence. Although prohibited from appearing in public, he had several friendly bishops with him, and was able to keep in touch with sympathisers and maintain correspondence. He is even reported,[108] when a poor deranged man attempted to break into the palace armed with a dagger, to have sent some of his bishops to the city prefect to plead with him to exercise leniency. There was apparently one genuine plot

---

[104] P 508b-512b; 8.21.1-4.
[105] Palladios, *Dial.* 9 (*SC* 341.196).
[106] Sokrates 6.18; Sozomen 8.21; 'Martyrios', P 508b-511b.
[107] *Dial.* 9 (*SC* 341.200).
[108] Sozomen 8.21.

to assassinate him,[109] the hired killer being a slave of the priest Elpidios, who had testified against John at The Oak; according to 'Martyrios', when the attempt was foiled and the culprit taken before the city prefect, he was given only a token punishment. Henceforth John's keener supporters took it in turns to mount guard over his residence by day and night.[110] It is evident that the schism between the Johnites, comprising at this stage the mass of ordinary citizens, and the established authorities in church and state was continuing unabated, and was rapidly spreading beyond the capital.

Some students have found the prolonged inaction of the government surprising, but it is easy enough to surmise possible reasons for it, even if we lack the means of assessing the probable weight attaching to each. There is no evidence that Arkadios, in any case always irresolute, had any special animus against John. Even Eudoxia, for all her violent tantrums against him, seems to have had a warm feeling and a deep, ultimately superstitious reverence for him; having already been punished by God once (as she devoutly believed) for having sent the holy man into exile, she may well have been wary of courting further chastisement. A rather different factor which should not be overlooked is that the authorities were in all probability momentarily stunned by the appalling events of Easter weekend. They must have been disturbed by the popular reaction to them, and anxious to avoid making things worse by taking stern action against the people's hero. It must have been during this indecisive period that an attempt was made to break the deadlock by trying to persuade John to abdicate voluntarily, as his predecessor, the great theologian Gregory of Nazianzos (who was only too eager to do so), had done in 381. We owe our knowledge of this manoeuvre to 'Martyrios', who describes how the empress herself put the proposal to him, and when he raised objections of conscience promised to take the responsibility on herself.[111] His rejoinder, that each man is responsible for his own actions, and that he could no more shelter behind her than Adam had been able to blame his sin on Eve or Eve hers on the serpent, only made her explode with indignation. According to 'Martyrios', who was probably retailing gossip leaked from the palace, she complained to Arkadios that John had insulted them both, comparing them to Adam and Eve.

While confined to his palace, John took a step of great importance. At some date between Easter and Pentecost (7 June), probably quite soon after the former, he wrote for support to the pope, Innocent I, and, in identical terms, to the two other leading patriarchs of the west, Venerius of Milan and Chromatius of Aquileia. Written under the stress of emotion, breathless in tone and repetitive, in general careless of style but with occasional

---

[109] 'Martyrios', P 516a-517b; Palladios, *Dial.* 20 (*SC* 341.402); Sozomen 8.21.6-8.
[110] Sozomen 8.22 ad init.
[111] F. van Ommeslaeghe, *AB* 97 (1979), 152-3 (citing P 506b-507a).

flashes of rhetoric, this remarkable document[112] (of which abundant use has been made in this chapter) is an anguished recital of the disasters caused by Theophilos, to John and the church of Constantinople, from the moment of his being summoned from Alexandria to stand his trial to the recent bloody events of Easter. There are gaps in his story which tantalise modern readers; for example, he says nothing about the circumstances, of his temporary recall. But it was not his object to give a complete account; he could rely on the letter's bearers to supply missing details. His ostensible aim was to alert the western bishops to the turmoil and division into which the churches of the east had been thrown by Theophilos' machinations, and to warn them that if his presumptuous interference in a province far removed from his own were to remain unchecked, the entire Christian world would be reduced to chaos. While the letter is at every point careful to shield the emperor, its silence on the subject of Eudoxia could be read as an accusation.

It was entirely natural that John, now effectively primate of the eastern churches, should resort to Innocent in his hour of crisis. His move in no way implied that he recognised the holy see as the supreme court of appeal in the church (much as the pope would have relished it if he had). Such an idea, absent from his sermons and other writings, is ruled out by his simultaneous approach to the two other western patriarchs. In writing to Innocent and his western colleagues he was concerned, in a general way, to mobilise their moral co-operation in calling a halt to the 'illegal behaviour which is devastating the churches'. Secondly, he perhaps also hoped, although this nowhere comes out in his text, that the western leaders would persuade the government of Honorius, since 402 settled at Ravenna, to lean on Arkadios to modify his policies. Thirdly, however, when he called on his venerable correspondents to declare in writing that his condemnation, in his absence and by people without any authority to sit in judgment on him, was invalid,[113] he was taking steps to safeguard his own position. That this was a prime objective comes out clearly in the hope he expressed that they would continue that exchange of letters and of other tokens of brotherly fellowship which he had enjoyed with them in the past, and which (this he did not say in so many words, but clearly implied) would assure himself and the world that they did not recognise his purported deposition and were still in full communion with him.[114]

---

[112] Critical edition, with French translation, by A.M. Malingrey in *SC* 342 (Paris 1988). The letter has hitherto been printed as ch. II of Palladios' *Dialogue*, since it appears as such in Medicaeus IX. 14, the only complete MS of the latter; Malingrey has demonstrated that it forms no part of the original text of the *Dialogue*.

[113] *SC* 342.90.

[114] This, rather than A.M. Malingrey's 'veuillez nous gratifier d'une prompte réponse ... comme auparavant', seems to be the true bearing of lines 218-22 of p. 90. The adverb *sunethos* ('as hitherto') should be retained rather than the unsupported *sunechos* ('promptly') which she substitutes.

John nominated an impressive delegation to carry his letter to the west: four bishops – Pansophios of Pisidia, Pappos from Syria, Demetrios of Pessinos and Eugenios from Phrygia – and two deacons, Paul and Cyriacos. His ability to make these arrangements illustrates, incidentally, the large measure of freedom of action he still enjoyed. The delegates carried two other important documents with them, a letter to the pope from John's forty loyal bishops, and another to him from the clergy of the capital who still stood by him.

IX

The stalemate dragged on, with the court irresolute and the authorities thereby prevented from acting, until the Thursday after Pentecost, 9 June. On that day his four leading adversaries – Akakios, Severian, Antiochos and Cyrinos of Chalkedon – their patience exhausted, sought an audience with Arkadios and put pressure on him to take decisive action.[115] Public order, they assured him, could never be restored until John, the source of all the trouble, had been finally got rid of. The emperor, it would appear, continued hesitant, reluctant to make a move, and only agreed to sign the decree of exile when they declared that they would take full responsibility themselves; the accounts of Palladios and Sozomen are at one in this. Even so, he procrastinated for more than a week, and it was only on 20 June that he sent a notary, Patrikios, to convey to John his decision that he must leave his church and city and go into exile forthwith.[116]

John accepted the emperor's orders, which he must have been expecting for days, even weeks, calmly. He first protested, however, that he was being expelled by force, without the legal trial which even common criminals had a right to expect.[117] He then left his official residence and, probably in the sacristy of Hagia Sophia, held a last meeting with the bishops still faithful to him. There he was warned that a company of armed soldiers, commanded by none other than the Loukios who had been responsible for the bloody events of the evening before Easter, was standing by in case of resistance. He was also told that the mass of citizens were in a state of intense agitation, and that there was a real danger that they might clash with the troops in an effort to save him. He bade farewell to the bishops and other clergy, and then, in the baptistery, to his faithful deaconesses Olympias, Pentadia, Procla and Silvina, an aristocratic widow, all devoted workers on his cathedral staff. According to Palladios, who paints an edifying picture of these parting

[115] Palladios, *Dial.* 10 (*SC* 341.204): cf. Sozomen 8.22.
[116] The date is given by Sokrates 6.18, and appears in *Chronicon paschale* s.a. 404 (*PG* 92.781).
[117] Sozomen 8.22.

greetings, he instructed them to show loyalty and obedience to anyone consecrated bishop in his place provided he had not intrigued to obtain the office and was generally deemed worthy of it: 'The church cannot continue to exist without a bishop.'[118]

[118] *Dial.* 10 (*SC* 341.206-8).

Final Exile

I

It was on the afternoon of 20 June that John left Constantinople for good. The city was in uproar as rumours that his expulsion was at hand spread, and an enormous crowd packed itself into Hagia Sophia desperate to catch a last glimpse of their bishop. As at his earlier banishment he was determined, our main sources agree,[1] that his arrest should not provoke popular demonstrations, and therefore adopted a simple ruse. To distract attention he ordered the mule on which he normally moved about the city to be saddled and placed as if awaiting him outside the great west door of the cathedral; meanwhile he himself slipped out almost unobserved by a side entrance, and there surrendered himself to an armed guard. He was accompanied by his faithful friends, bishops Cyriakos and Eulysios, and several other clergy. Led by a young officer named Theodore, the party went unobtrusively to the harbour, boarded a small vessel and set out across the Bosporus. Landing on the Bithynian shore (for this second exile the more irksome landward route had been chosen), John and his escorts travelled eastwards to Nikomedia (Izmit), and then southwards to Nicaea (Iznik), scene almost eighty years before of the first ecumenical council. The journey must have been uncomfortable in the sweltering heat of mid-summer, but in letters[2] to Olympias written from Nicaea John reported that he was in excellent health and spirits, enjoying the pure air. He also commented on the considerate treatment he was receiving from the soldiers escorting him; they were so attentive to his needs that he scarcely noticed the absence of servants.

Back in the capital reports of John's arrest had created tumult in Hagia Sophia, where the crowds inside struggled to force their way out. The doors, however, had been deliberately barricaded in case there should be a mass attempt to rescue him; they had to be broken down, with some people pulling them inwards, others battering them with stones.[3] In the turmoil

---

[1] 'Martyrios', P 518a-520a; Palladios, *Dial.* 10 (*SC* 341.208 – describing the ruse); Sozomen 8.22.

[2] *Epp.* 11 and 10 (*PG* 52.609; 608): I.106-8; II.110. From now on John's letters to Olympias are cited, first, by their number and column in *PG* 52, then by their number and page (Greek text) in A.M. Malingrey's critical edition (*SC* 13bis: Paris 1968).

[3] Sozomen 8.11.

an unknown hand started a fire near the bishop's throne;[4] fanned by a north-east wind, this spread to the nearby hangings and woodwork. Within three hours the entire building, with the exception of the small section serving as cathedral treasury, as well as the adjacent senate-house, with its remarkable collection of works of art, had been gutted. Palladios, characteristically, attributes the disaster to the avenging hand of God, but suspicion inevitably fell on John's supporters (even, implausibly, on John himself). This is reflected in the accounts of Sokrates[5] and the pagan Zosimos,[6] who adds that in their desire to prevent the appointment of another bishop the Johnites were resolved to burn the whole city down, starting with the cathedral. 'Martyrios', perhaps surprisingly, does not exclude the possibility that over-zealous Johnites might have been the culprits, but also puts forward the interesting suggestion that these may have been hired agents of John's enemies.[7] Sozomen's picture is of Johnites and anti-Johnites hurling accusations and counter-accusations at one another.[8]

The government, hitherto so hesitant, seems to have been goaded into activity by the destruction of both cathedral and senate-house. First, a high-powered commission was immediately set up to discover the arsonists. The city prefect, Stoudios, was in charge of it.[9] He was a friend of John's, who later in the year was to send him a consolatory letter on his brother's death,[10] but at least one other member was an implacable enemy, count John, Eudoxia's favourite, now finance minister (*comes sacrarum largitionum*).[11] As the Johnites were the prime suspects, one of the commission's first acts was to order the arrest of the bishops and other clergy accompanying John. They had scarcely landed with him on the Bithynian coast when they were seized, put in chains and imprisoned at Chalkedon.[12]

Then, less than a week after John's deportation, a successor bishop was installed in the church of the Apostles.[13] He was Arsakios, younger brother of John's predecessor Nektarios. A mild and ineffectual octogenarian, caricatured by the malicious as 'dumb as a fish, inactive as a frog',[14] he had been a hostile witness at The Oak. Sokrates and Sozomen[15] stress his piety

---

[4] Palladios, *Dial.* 10 (*SC* 341.210-14).
[5] 6.18.
[6] 5.24.3-4.
[7] P 518a-520b.
[8] 8.22.
[9] Sokrates and Sozomen suggest that Optatos was in charge, but he only became city prefect in November 404. Both Palladios (*Dial.* 3: *SC* 341.78) and the decree calling off the investigation (see below, p. 253) confirm that he was Stoudios.
[10] *Ep.* 197 (*PG* 52.721-2).
[11] Palladios, *Dial.* 3 (*SC* 341.78).
[12] *Dial.* 11 (*SC* 341.214); *ep.* 174 (*PG* 52.711).
[13] *Chronicon paschale* s.a. 404 (*PG* 92.781).
[14] Palladios, *Dial.* 11 (*SC* 341.216).
[15] 6.19 and 8.23.

and gentle disposition, but these qualities did not make him acceptable to the public generally, much less to the Johnites, in whose eyes he was an unlawful intruder. They persisted, therefore, in holding their separate assemblies in outlying parts of the city. When Arsakios complained to the emperor, the authorities reacted by sending soldiers to break up these meetings. Brutal violence was used, on women as well as men, and many of John's more prominent or devoted adherents were gaoled.[16] The government was determined to stamp out all manifestations of disloyalty to the official bishop, and imposed harsh penalties on those who attended, or allowed those for whom they were responsible to attend, 'riotous assemblies'. There must have been specific legislation authorising this, but it has disappeared. Its broad tenor, however, can be inferred from a later decree[17] directing provincial governors to insist on orthodox Christians holding communion with the chief bishops recognised by the authorities.

The persecution of Johnites, which was to continue for years (even after John's death), rapidly spread to the provinces, including of course Syria. At Antioch Bishop Flavian is commonly held to have died in late September and to have been then succeeded by the priest Porphyrios. This seems impossible, however, in view of the recorded circumstances of Porphyrios' appointment. When Flavian died, the trio Severian, Akakios and Antiochos were soon on the scene and, taking advantage of the fact that the bulk of the population was out at Daphne attending the Olympic games, unscrupulously rushed through the election and consecration of Porphyrios, who shared their hostility to John.[18] If this account is correct (there is no reason to doubt it), Porphyrios' installation must have taken place in July-August, when the games were customarily held,[19] probably in July, and Flavian cannot have long survived John's deposition. Palladios, in a neglected passage,[20] confirms this, stating that 'the death of Flavian ... coincided with the exile of John'. The action of the trio caused great offence in the city, where the popular choice would, according to Palladios, have been Constantios, Flavian's adjutant and a trusted friend of John's. The result, inevitably, was the birth in Antioch of a militant Johnite schism at the time when John himself was still on the first lap of his journey to his place of exile.

Meanwhile the investigation into the fire was carried out with relentless rigour. It was fortunate for John that the guardians of the cathedral treasury, Germanos and the deacon Cassian,[21] had prepared and were able to submit an authenticated inventory of all the gold, silver and precious

---

[16] Sozomen 8.23.

[17] CT 16.4.6 (18 Nov. 404): see below, p. 272.

[18] Palladios, *Dial.* 16 (*SC* 341.304-12 – including a critical portrait of Porphyrios and a flattering one of Constantios).

[19] G. Downey, *A History of Antioch in Syria* (Princeton 1961), 418 n. 25.

[20] *Dial.* 11 (*SC* 341.308, lines 1 and 2). His use of *sunakmazo* in the sense of 'coincide' has not been noted in dictionaries.

[21] Later founder of monasteries at Marseilles and famous for his ascetic writings.

objects it contained;[22] he had been accused at The Oak of appropriating church property,[23] and this time too his enemies were only biding their time to bring similar charges. The commission of inquiry did not hesitate to employ torture, and the Johnites were to compile an impressive list of martyrs who had suffered at its hands.[24] Olympias herself, known to be the leader of John's deaconesses and a sympathetic friend, was brought before it.[25] When asked why she had set fire to the church, she retorted that, having spent considerable sums of money building churches, she was not likely to start burning them down. When the examining magistrate tried a softer line, offering to leave her and her nuns in peace provided she acknowledged Arsakios as her bishop, she spiritedly replied that nothing would induce her to act contrary to what the divine law enjoined. In the end a huge fine of two hundred pounds of gold was imposed on her.

After more than two months' work the commission had to admit that it was getting nowhere. An imperial decree,[26] addressed to the city prefect Stoudios, was published on 29 August ordering that, since it had proved impossible to identify the arsonists, the imprisoned clergy should be released from gaol. They were, however, to be put on board ship and packed off home. In fact, as well as proscribing all who took part in 'riotous assemblies' separate from the official churches, the decree required all non-resident bishops and clergy to quit 'this most sacred city'. This injunction applied not only to the many Johnite bishops in Constantinople (e.g. Palladios),[27] but also to the many (like Severian, Akakios and Antiochos) who were John's adversaries. The government was evidently getting impatient with the presence of so many quarrelsome clerical busybodies in the capital.

II

John was held in Nicaea for several days. Presumably his military escort were awaiting instructions about the place of exile to which they were to conduct him. This was a matter of great concern to him. He was hoping it might be a populous, accessible city, perhaps even Sebasteia (Sivas), capital of Armenia Prima, which seems to have been talked of and where a wealthy friend, Arabios, was eager to place his mansion at his disposal.[28] As he waited, bad news kept filtering in from the capital – the appointment of Arsakios in his place, the persecution of dear friends, the brutal deposition of bishops he had appointed (especially Herakleides of Ephesos, who was

[22] Palladios, *Dial.* 3 (*SC* 341.76-8).
[23] See above, p. 222.
[24] Sozomen 8.24.
[25] Sozomen 8.24.
[26] CT 16.2.37.
[27] See below, p. 275.
[28] *Ep.* 121 (*PG* 52.676).

kept in gaol at Nikomedia for four years),[29] etc. It must have distressed him to learn that, just so soon as the authorities had ordered his banishment, the rich citizens who had objected to his plans for a great leper hospital had halted all work on it and had even pounced on the funds he was collecting to finance the project.[30] He was worried, too, about Olympias, especially as he had received no letter from her; he wanted to know not only how well she was, but even more whether she had managed 'to scatter the dark cloud of depression'.[31] He was no less concerned, however, for his clerical friends, locked up in chains on suspicion of arson in the filthy, smelly gaol at Chalkedon, and dashed off a note of characteristically bracing encouragement to them.[32] Their lot, he assures them, calls for congratulation and rejoicing since they are enduring it because of their faith. 'A golden crown does not bring so much honour to the head that wears it as his chains do to the prisoner whose right hand has been fettered in God's service.' Whatever they do, 'never cease giving glory to God in all things'.

At last official notification arrived that his place of exile was to be, not some great centre of social and commercial life, but Cucusos (*Koukousos*). This is described by Theodoret, writing in the first half of the fifth century, as 'a small city' which had earlier been attached to Cappadocia but now belonged to Armenia Secunda.[33] It had probably been raised to the rank of a city when Armenia Secunda was created by emperor Valens in 371/2. It was a natural enough choice for the government, which had used it before, and would use it again, for important exiles; a previous bishop of Constantinople, Paul, had been deported there in 351 (and had been strangled by his guards). But John, knowing that it was a fairly isolated place in the mountains, was deeply disappointed. He seems to have written at once to friends urging them to arrange with the authorities, in view of his fragile health, for some more congenial centre to be designated for his residence. Their efforts proved fruitless; a few weeks later he was bitterly complaining that, 'in spite of having so many rich and influential friends, I have not succeeded in obtaining what even criminals are granted, transfer to a nearer locality, with a more satisfactory climate. Notwithstanding my broken, enfeebled condition and the ever-present threat of Isaurian brigands, this modest and inexpensive favour has not been granted me. Nevertheless glory be to God for this too.'[34]

---

[29] Palladios, *Dial.* 20 (*SC* 341.398).
[30] 'Martyrios', P 495b. For the hospital see above, pp. 119f.
[31] *Ep.* 10 (*PG* 52.609): II.110.
[32] *Ep.* 118 (*PG* 52.673).
[33] *HE* 2.5.2 (*CSC* 44.99). See A.H.M. Jones, *Cities of the Eastern Roman Provinces* (2 ed. Oxford 1970), 182.
[34] *Ep.* 120 (*PG* 52.674-5).

III

It was on 4 July or shortly after[35] that John and his military escort set out on their long, wearisome journey. Their route can be followed, in broad outline, with the aid of the Antonine Itinerary (*Itinerarium Antoninianum*), a fourth-century military road manual covering the entire empire, which features not only the larger cities through which they passed, but also Arabissos, another small city of Armenia Secunda where John was to stay, and Cucusos itself.[36] It took them, as John was to tell his friend Brison,[37] eunuch and choir-master, some seventy days to reach their destination. While the soldiers marched, John was able to use a litter (*lektikion*) strapped to a mule.[38] Although his guards treated him considerately – especially their commanding officer, Theodore, with whom he established a friendly relationship – he had a wretched time, even worse, he complained,[39] than the lot of criminals kept chained or condemned to the salt-mines. In the same letter he spoke bitterly of the filthy water, mouldy and hard bread, the lack of baths – indeed, of most basic necessities. On top of all, he was almost continuously ill, racked with high fever and without medical attention. As the party moved south, it was constantly threatened with attacks by marauding Isaurians, a warlike tribe which had its strongholds high in the Taurus mountains and periodically descended to plunder and terrorise the settled population. Yet in the earlier stages, at any rate, of the long trek his spirits were from time to time cheered when, as the sad little procession made its way past farmsteads or through villages and towns, ordinary folk came out in crowds to gaze, with wonder and pity, tears in their eyes, at the famous exile.[40]

The two principal cities on the route were Ankyra (Ankara) and Caesarea (Kayseri), capitals of Galatia and Cappadocia respectively. In spite of his exhaustion and need of medical care, John knew he could not look for a friendly reception at Ankyra. Its bishop, Leontios, although commended by Theodoret[41] as 'adorned with many virtues' and by Sozomen[42] as having previously been one of the two outstanding monks in Galatia, had taken the initiative in proposing an appeal to the Antiochene canons as a certain means of destroying him.[43] Nevertheless the two men seem to have met when John and his escort reached the city. It must have been an awkward confrontation, for all that John records of it is that 'the Galatian all but

---

[35] *Ep.* 10 (*PG* 52.608): II.110: also *ep.* 221 (*PG* 52.734).
[36] O. Cuntz, *Itineraria Romana* (Leipzig 1929), e.g. 31.
[37] *Ep.* 234 (*PG* 52.739). For Brison see above, p. 138.
[38] *Ep.* 9.3 (*PG* 52.615): IX.228.
[39] *Ep.* 120 (*PG* 52.674).
[40] *Ep.* 9 (*PG* 52.608): III.112.
[41] *HE* 5.27.4 (*GCS* 44.329).
[42] 6.34 ad fin.
[43] Palladios, *Dial.* 9 (*SC* 341.186). See above, p. 242.

threatened me with death'.[44] He and his guards, we may suppose, did not linger long in Ankyra, and were soon making their way to Cappadocia. As they approached Caesarea, travellers they met brought him messages from its bishop, Pharetrios, assuring him how keenly he was looking forward to receiving him. He wanted to show hospitality and affection, and had even put his religious houses, male and female, on the alert for his arrival. Although he disclosed his inner doubts to no one else, John was later to tell Olympias how sceptical he had been about this promised welcome.[45] He was well aware that, when the conspiracy against him at Constantinople was taking shape, Pharetrios, a cautious man always anxious to be on the winning side, had stayed at home but assured its leaders by private letters of his support.[46]

John's suspicions were to prove all too accurate. He was more dead than alive, he wrote,[47] exhausted and suffering from recurrent bouts of fever, when the little party reached Caesarea. They put up at an inn on the very fringe of the city, and he was at last able to sleep on a bed, eat decent food and drink clean water, have a proper bath, above all be looked after by first-class doctors. Although still in grave danger, his spirits revived. To his gratification, the top administrative and military officials, the leading professors, all the clergy and many religious turned out to meet him and showed him every consideration. Everyone, in fact, was there except Pharetrios himself. Stung with jealousy, as John suspected, all he now wanted was to have him ejected from his city. As John, who was quick to take the hint, was preparing to resume his journey, his departure was held up by a terrifying rumour that a wild horde of Isaurians had burst into the province, spreading fire and devastation and threatening the city. Then at dawn one morning he found his lodging surrounded by scores of fanatical monks, incited apparently by Pharetrios, loudly demanding that he should get out; otherwise they would burn the roof over his head. His military guards were terrified; even the civil governor, who had been alerted, was helpless with the hysterical mob, and was reduced to begging Pharetrios to hold his hand for a few days until John's health improved.

Even this had no effect, for the monks were back next morning. In spite of renewed fever, John had no option but to quit the city, accompanied by sympathetic local clergy who had, however, no power to help him. For a moment it seemed that all might be well, for a wealthy lady, Seleukeia, gave him hospitality in one of her country houses 8 km away. Pharetrios, however, was furious when he heard of this, and ordered her with threats to get rid of him. At first Seleukeia refused to be intimidated, even inviting John to stay in her private mansion, a heavily fortified building, but he

---

[44] *Ep.* 14.1 (*PG* 52.613): IX.220.
[45] *Ep.* 14.1 (*PG* 52.613): IX.220-2.
[46] Palladios, *Dial.* 9 (*SC* 341.184-6).
[47] For this para. see *ep.* 14.2-3 (*PG* 52.613-16): IX.222-30; also *ep.* 120 (*PG* 52.674).

declined. In the end even Seleukeia had to give in to her bishop and felt obliged to turn him out of doors in the middle of the night. To save her honour, she had concocted an alarmist rumour that another Isaurian onslaught was imminent. John's description of the adventures of that terrible night, when he and his companions had to flee her house, is one of the most dramatic he ever wrote.[48] As there was no moon, he had ordered torches to be lit, but a priest called Evethios who accompanied him caused them to be extinguished in case they betrayed their position to the (imaginary) Isaurians, and he had to leap to the ground, and then had to be dragged by Evethios along the precipitous mountain path.

Writing to a highly placed friend, Paeanios, John was to describe Pharetrios' behaviour towards him as abominable and unforgivable.[49] But he begged him not to breathe a word about it to anyone. He made an identical request to Olympias.[50] His unjust sufferings, he assured her, would help to efface his sins, and should be a ground for rejoicing. Leave it to his military guards, when they returned to the capital, to tell the story; they too had been exposed to frightful dangers. This insistence on silence has seemed surprising, but his real motive comes out in the letter to Paeanios: he feared that, if reports about his brutal treatment were made public by his known friends, the news would exasperate Pharetrios' clergy, all of whom stood firmly on his side, as well as his other supporters, with disastrous consequences for everyone, including himself. Pharetrios' conduct, like that of Leontios, lays bare the relentless hatred with which the hard core of anti-Johnites were still prepared to pursue their *bête noire*. Their attitude, it is interesting to note, contrasted strikingly with that of the authorities in Constantinople. There the official policy, for the present at any rate, seems to have been that, while John had, understandably, to be detained at a remote centre where he was unlikely to cause trouble, the conditions of his exile should be as relaxed and comfortable as was reasonably possible. His escort, for example, clearly had instructions to treat him with consideration, and no objection seems to have been raised to his having social relations with, or accepting hospitality from, prominent citizens, even top-ranking officials like provincial governors.

IV

We have no details of John's journey from Caesarea, but it was probably made more bearable because one of the 'skilled and highly reputed doctors' he met there had volunteered to accompany him.[51] Eventually, probably about 20 September, the party reached Cucusos, represented today by the

[48] *Ep.* 14.3 (*PG* 52.615): IX.228.
[49] *Ep.* 204 (*PG* 52.725). For Paeanios see p. 263 below.
[50] *Ep.* 14.3 (*PG* 52.616): IX.230.
[51] *Ep.* 12 (*PG* 52.609): IV.116.

agricultural village of Göksun, some 175 km north-east of Adana in southern Turkey. Then it was a small city, with a bishopric, in the Cilician Taurus, over 1400 m above sea-level, approachable by difficult passes, resembling an oasis surrounded by mountains.[52] To John, as he never tired of repeating,[53] it seemed the most forsaken corner of the world, 'possessing neither a public square nor shopping facilities'.[54] To some extent this reaction reflects the shock felt by a man accustomed all his life to populous and splendid capitals on being transported to a small provincial centre. In fact, his initial impressions were favourable. Its pure air, he noted, recalled the climate of his native Antioch.[55] It had a garrison, and the sight of numerous well-armed soldiers banished for the moment his dread of Isaurian raiders.[56] A wealthy resident, Dioskoros, moved out to his country estate and lent him his town house, going to trouble and expense to equip it with everything needful, especially in view of the coming winter. Friends in Constantinople with property in the neighbourhood instructed their stewards to make life comfortable for him. The provincial governor, Sopater, was kindness itself.[57] In spite of her great age the deaconess Sabiniana, almost certainly his aunt, had arrived the same day as he, having courageously overcome the hazards of the difficult journey from Antioch; while his devoted friend, the priest Constantios, also from Antioch but the victim of much abuse there, was expected at any moment.[58]

To add to his satisfaction, his health had markedly improved, at any rate for the early months of his stay. To Firminos,[59] a layman of Caesarea, he wrote simply, 'I am well', and to Paeanios,[60] 'Although Cucusos is a deserted spot, I enjoy peace here, and through sitting indoors regularly have been able in large measure to cure the illnesses contracted on my journey.' He could assure Olympias[61] that he now felt physically stronger than when he lived in Constantinople. In spite of being constantly aware of the Isaurian menace, his optimism was now so great that he tried to stop his friends from lobbying for his transfer to a more congenial detention centre. He had no wish, he told Paeanios,[62] to undergo again the discomforts of travel which such a change was bound to entail. He was even more open with Olympias in his first letter from Cucusos.[63] His well-wishers, he pleaded,

[52] See F. Hild, _Das byzantinische Strassensystem in Kappadokien_ (Vienna 1977), 134, with photos 96 and 97.
[53] E.g. _epp._ 234, 235, 236 (_PG_ 52.735-40).
[54] _Ep._ 14.1 (_PG_ 52.612): IX.218.
[55] _Ep._ 14.4 (_PG_ 52.616): IX.232.
[56] _Ep._ 13 (_PG_ 52.610-11): VI.126-8.
[57] _Ep._ 64 (_PG_ 52.644).
[58] _Ep._ 13 (_PG_ 52.611): VI.130.
[59] _Ep._ 80 (_PG_ 52.651).
[60] _Ep._ 193 (_PG_ 52.720).
[61] _Ep._ 14.4 (_PG_ 52.617): IX.232.
[62] _Ep._ 193 (_PG_ 52.720).
[63] _Ep._ 13.3 (_PG_ 52.611-12): VI.128-30.

should make no effort to move him from it unless (a faint hope, as he must have realised) he were allowed to choose the alternative himself. What he feared, he confessed, was that he might be sent to an even more distant and inhospitable location. He was terrified, too, of having to set out on the road afresh: 'to me travelling is more painful than any number of banishments.' If she wanted to help him, she should use all her finesse to discover where the authorities were minded to send him. If it were somewhere near Constantinople, Cyzikos perhaps or Nikomedia, then she should encourage the arrangement. But not if it were some spot more remote than, or even as remote as, Cucusos.

John was to remain in Armenia for almost three years, but he was very soon forced to adopt a more realistic view of Cucusos. First, the winter of 404-5, as he was to tell Olympias,[64] was exceptionally severe; as a result he suffered a painful recurrence of stomach upsets, headaches, loss of appetite, sleeplessness night after night. Because of the intense cold he had to shut himself in a single small room, with his eyes smarting from the smoke of his fire, never venturing out of doors. Much of the time he had to remain in bed, covered with layers of thick rugs, but even so he could not keep warm. Thus he passed 'two whole months in a worse condition than if I had been a corpse'. There was a dramatic change when warmer weather returned with the spring, but his digestive system had become so impaired that he was obliged to stick to an extremely light diet. The arrival of summer brought miseries of its own. On the one hand, he found the great heat no less upsetting than extreme cold; on the other, 'we live in a state of continuous siege, all the time terrified by repeated Isaurian attacks'.[65] In addition, there was a shortage of doctors and essential medicines. With all these troubles it is surprising that he was able to assure his correspondents that his physical state was reasonably good and his spirits high.

Then the following winter there were trials no less severe and even more alarming to be faced. With characteristic resilience John had been looking forward to it with confidence. His health was excellent, he told his friend bishop Elpidios,[66] the Isaurian incursions had for the moment ceased, and experience had taught him how to cope with the rigours of winter – for example, staying indoors when temperatures dropped. He was soon to be disillusioned, not this time by the cruel climate, but by the unexpected renewal of ferocious plundering raids by the Isaurians. Normally they kept themselves in winter to their inaccessible villages and towns in the mountains, but this winter seems to have been exceptional. They were, indeed, almost continuously active, in spite of strong repressive measures taken by the government, from 404 to 408.[67] 'Here there is nothing', John exclaimed

[64] *Ep.* 6.1 (*PG* 52.593): XII.316.
[65] *Ep.* 146 (*PG* 52.698-9).
[66] *Ep.* 142 (*PG* 52.627).
[67] É. Demougeot, *De l'unité à la division* (Paris 1951), 343-4; F. Paschoud, *Zosime* (Paris 1986), III, 189-90.

in one letter,[68] 'except butchery, wild confusion, bloodshed and blazing buildings, with the Isaurians ravaging whatever they come across with sword and fire.' The situation became so perilous that he and the civil population had to evacuate Cucusos precipitately, 'in the very depth of winter', and for days a panic-stricken rabble was fleeing from place to place, camping in snow-bound forests and ravines.[69] Eventually they found refuge in Arabissos[70] (Afsin: today a small village), a frontier fortress town described by the Antonine Itinerary[71] as 52 Roman miles (= 77 km) from Cucusos, almost 1000 m high in the Amanus range. John himself was lodged in the citadel. He complained that it was 'worse than a dungeon'; and with so many people packed into the small town there was a real danger of famine.[72] He was at any rate so secure that he was able one night to sleep undisturbed while three hundred Isaurians temporarily wreaked havoc in the lower town.[73]

John made friends with Otreios, the bishop of Arabissos,[74] but was seriously ill during most of his stay there. It was only in the spring of 406 that he recovered. How long he remained at Arabissos has been debated. Palladios seems to imply that he was detained for only one year at Cucusos;[75] but he was dependent for this on hearsay, and spoils his story by adding that he was sent to Arabissos by the malice of his enemies, a suggestion contradicted by John's own letters. Some have argued that, as the Isaurians continued to be exceptionally active throughout 406 and 407 (his letters abound in references to their atrocities), he may have been permitted to enjoy its relative security until 407. On balance it seems more likely that, as Cucusos was his nominated place of exile, he returned there after his health was restored in summer 406. This is supported by a letter[76] in which he claims to have *sent* someone to Bishop Otreios to collect certain valuable relics from him, and also by his last letter[77] to Olympias (probably early 407), in which he mentions 'all those trials I had to endure after my sojourn at Arabissos'.

V

Throughout these years of exile John carried on a vast correspondence. Some 240 of his letters have survived;[78] there can be little doubt that there

[68] *Ep.* 61 (*PG* 52.642).
[69] *Ep.* 127 (*PG* 52.687).
[70] *Ep.* 69 (*PG* 52.646).
[71] O. Cuntz, op. cit., 31.
[72] *Ep.* 69 (*PG* 52.646).
[73] *Ep.* 135 (*PG* 52.693).
[74] *Ep.* 126 (*PG* 52.687).
[75] *Dial.* 11 (*SC* 341.220).
[76] *Ep.* 126 (*PG* 52.687).
[77] *Ep.* 4.4 (*PG* 52.594): XVII.382.
[78] *PG* 52.549-748. Only the 17 to Olympias have received a critical edition.

were others which have perished. Addressed to more than one hundred individuals in Constantinople and elsewhere, they are the precious sources of such knowledge as we possess of his personal experiences and thoughts during this trying period. Yet it is a surprisingly unequal, not to say disappointing, collection. A score, perhaps, of the letters are intensely personal and revealing. A number are rich in descriptive detail. But an even greater number, probably the majority, are conventional and flat, repeating well-worn topics in stereotyped language and lacking the liveliness and personal touch one looks for in correspondence. But they all make it plain that, used as he had been to living in great cities, with a daily load of multifarious business, John missed the company of people and an outlet for his energies. The letters are full of his sense of loneliness and inactivity; many contain insistent, sometimes reproachful demands for return-letters from his correspondents and for news of their doings and welfare.[79]

In fact, he was not so deprived of society or of pastoral opportunities (of a modest kind, perhaps) as he would like one to believe. From time to time, as the letters reveal, increasingly as the months slipped by, visitors found their way to Cucusos. After all, the road through it, although snow-bound in winter and cut off by Isaurian invaders in the open seasons, was an important military thoroughfare from Sebasteia in the north to not-too distant Antioch in the south. One such visitor, out of many, was a bishop named Seleukos, who had braved the icy roads in his eagerness to see him. John sent him on his way with letters of commendation,[80] one to another bishop, Tranquillinos, and a second to a physician with a request to treat his severe cough. One or two adventurous friends even penetrated as far as Arabissos in winter.[81] Towards the end of his exile, according to both Palladios and Sozomen,[82] large numbers of his admirers were making a pilgrimage from Antioch and other Syrian cities to set eyes on their revered preacher and hear his voice again. In addition to preaching as opportunity offered, he was active pastorally. Sozomen reports[83] that he had ample funds at his disposal, supplied by Olympias and other friends, and these he expended sometimes on helping the destitute of Cucusos and Arabissos, sometimes on ransoming wretched people who had been dragged off into slavery by Isaurian captors.

The letters illustrate the range of his contacts and concerns, as well as his determination to keep in touch with the people who still respected him as their bishop. A great many reveal his preoccupation with 'the common tempest afflicting the church and the shipwreck spreading throughout the world'[84] as a result of the events leading up to and flowing from his

[79] E.g. *ep.* 185 – to Pentadia; 190 – to Brison (*PG* 52.716; 718).
[80] *Epp.* 37-8 (*PG* 52.630-1).
[81] E.g. *epp.* 135 and 136 (*PG* 52.693-4).
[82] *Dial.* 11 (*SC* 341.220-2); 8.27.
[83] Loc. cit.
[84] *Ep.* 113 – to Palladios (*PG* 52.669).

deposition. In some of these[85] he urges his clerical correspondents to use all their efforts, particularly unremitting prayer, to resist and reverse these disasters. In others[86] he congratulates individual bishops or groups of them who have stood firm in the crisis, begs them to continue their struggle and assures them of the heavenly rewards that await them. In still others[87] he challenges friends to maintain the hostility they have so far shown to those who have thrown the churches into disorder and scandal. Quite a number[88] are addressed to women who have proved steadfast under the terrible ordeals to which they have been subjected; they can be sure that 'blessings passing all understanding' will be theirs in the world to come. Two of these were to Pentadia,[89] once his faithful deaconess. In one he praises her unflinching courage in the face of brutal judicial interrogation; in the other he seeks to dissuade her from visiting him on the ground that her presence in the capital will be an inspiration to others threatened with persecution.

Several show him making a brave attempt to maintain the semblance of directing his church. In two,[90] for example, he rebukes priests for neglecting their preaching duties and absenting themselves from divine service. In two more we find him maintaining close contact with the community of Gothic monks he had established on 'the estate of Promotos' in Constantinople.[91] In one[92] he expresses sympathy with them in the harassment to which they have been exposed since his departure. This, he promises them, will redound to their eternal glory. In the meantime they should keep up their patient efforts to prevent disturbance or dissension from upsetting the church of the Goths. In the other[93] he seeks to enlist Olympias' help in ensuring that a worthy successor is found for the community to replace Unila[94] as bishop of the Goths settled on the north-west shores of the Black Sea. He is worried lest the choice should be made by those at present in control of the church in the capital, who could not be relied upon to nominate a man of the right calibre. In another to Olympias[95] he advises her that it might be best for Herakleides, whom he had controversially appointed bishop of Ephesos,[96] and who was the object of virulent attack at The Oak and brutal imprisonment thereafter, to resign and so be rid of everything. In the meantime he told her that he had written to Pentadia asking her to do everything in her power to relieve his present troubles.

---

[85] E.g. *epp.* 113; 114; 121 (*PG* 52.669; 670; 675).
[86] E.g. *epp.* 150-6 (*PG* 52.700-3).
[87] *Epp.* 88-90 (*PG* 52.654-5).
[88] *Epp.* 29; 40; 60; 103; 133 (*PG* 52.627; 632; 662-3; 681-92).
[89] *Epp.* 94 and 104 (*PG* 52.657-9; 663-4).
[90] *Epp.* 203 and 212 (*PG* 52.724; 729).
[91] See above, p. 143.
[92] *Ep.* 207 (*PG* 52.726-7).
[93] *Ep.* 14.5 (*PG* 52.618): IX.236-8.
[94] See above, pp. 143f.
[95] *Ep.* 14.4 (*PG* 52.617): IX.234.
[96] See above, p. 174.

Quite a few letters are purely personal. There are three, for example, to a society lady, Carteria, one thanking her for a rather special ointment which she had personally prepared for him.[97] Again, there is a charming note to bishop Cyriakos asking him to be kind to the son of Sopater, governor of Armenia, and introduce him (the lad was a student at Constantinople) to people in a position to make his stay there more agreeable.[98] A deeper note is struck in a letter to one Malchos consoling him and his wife on the death of their daughter; rather, it bids them rejoice since, like farmers with their first-fruits, they have presented their first-born to 'the common Lord of all'.[99]

Several are to important civic or state functionaries whose friendship John wishes to retain or cultivate. In one letter,[100] for example, John offers somewhat stilted congratulations to Gemellos, once a pupil at Libanios' school and now promoted prefect of Constantinople (404-8), on his appointment. In another[101] he urges him (he was obviously a devoted admirer) not to put off his baptism until he himself is free to administer the sacrament, but to be baptised as soon as possible by loyal friends of his. Another close friend and correspondent who was also urban prefect was Paeanios.[102] Most intriguing is a congratulatory letter to Anthemios,[103] who as master of the offices had been reluctant to use violence in Hagia Sophia on the eve of Easter 404.[104] and who was soon to become virtual ruler of the eastern empire and master of John's fate. John piles up effusive compliments on his appointment as consul for the year and praetorian prefect (405-14), recalling his own affection for him and making it unambiguously plain that everyone suffering unjust treatment will be looking to him for relief. With his habitual optimism he was nursing hopes which were not to be fulfilled.

Several of John's correspondents, it is interesting to note, were men and women of high social position living at Rome. The Candidianus, for example, to whom he wrote in warm terms,[105] probably quite early in his exile, and who was clearly a friend of long standing, was a high-ranking general, husband of Vasianilla, a devout Christian whose ascetic achievements Palladios admired.[106] Two other Romans to whom he wrote,[107] thanking the first for her support and the second for the generosity with which she and her companions had, in difficult circumstances, received friends whom he

---

[97] *Ep.* 34 (*PG* 52.629-30).
[98] *Ep.* 64 (*PG* 52.644).
[99] *Ep.* 71 (*PG* 52.647-8).
[100] *Ep.* 124 (*PG* 52.678). For Gemellos see *PLRE* 1, 388.
[101] *Ep.* 132 (*PG* 52.690-1).
[102] *PLRE* 2, 818. For John's letters to him see above, pp. 257; 258.
[103] *Ep.* 147 (*PG* 52.699). See *PLRE* 2, 93-5.
[104] See above, p. 244.
[105] *Ep.* 42 (*PG* 52.633). See *PLRE* 1, 179.
[106] *Lausiac History* 41 (Butler 128).
[107] *Epp.* 168 and 169 (*PG* 52.709).

had commended to her, were Proba and Juliana. The former[108] was the
wealthy widow of S. Claudius Probus, four times praetorian prefect, the
latter[109] wife of Olybrius, consul for 359. Both received letters from
Augustine too, and as members of the *gens Anicia* belonged to the old
aristocracy.

Although their significance can be exaggerated, great interest attaches
to a handful of letters which graphically illustrate the oversight John
struggled to maintain, within the limits of his constricted situation, over
his campaign to convert non-Christians, chiefly but not exclusively in
Phoenicia (roughly modern Lebanon). His interest in this mission dated
back to his early days as bishop,[110] when he had entrusted its administration to a priest at Antioch, his friend Constantios[111] – a capable man who
had been bishop Flavian's adjutant, and would undoubtedly have succeeded him but for the machinations of John's enemies.[112] When he reached
Nicaea in July 404, he learned to his distress that it was undergoing a
disturbing setback. He at once wrote to Constantios urging him,[113] notwithstanding his present difficulties, to carry on with the good work, and to
send him up-to-date information about the construction of churches, the
number of helpers, and the general progress of the Christian cause. He also
sent him a monk whom he had found living enclosed at Nicaea to assist
him. Other letters[114] over the next two years show how energetically he
kept on exerting himself to organise the dispatch of money, supplies and
qualified manpower to Phoenicia. A final letter,[115] written probably in 406,
reveals that there had been bitter fighting between the missionaries and
the pagans; John pressed a priest called Rufinos to hasten there at once to
restore order. He begged him to spare no pains in getting the churches still
under construction securely roofed before winter set in; he need be in no
anxiety about martyrs' relics, for he was arranging to get some absolutely
authentic ones from Otreios, bishop of Arabissos, and would be sending
them to him shortly.

Further evidence of John's restless concern for missionary work is
provided by a letter to Olympias[116] and another to his old friend Agapetos.[117]
In the former he calls on Olympias to get in touch with Maruthas, bishop
of Martyropolis in Mesopotamia, in spite of his having acted as one of the
judges at The Oak (in fact, such an approach, he suggests, might well help

---

[108] *PLRE* 1, 732 and 736-40.
[109] *PLRE* 1, 468 and 639.
[110] See above, p. 142.
[111] See above, pp. 252; 258.
[112] See above, p. 252.
[113] *Ep.* 221 (*PG* 52.732-3).
[114] *Epp.* 21; 53; 54; 123 (*PG* 52.624; 637-8; 638-9; 676-8).
[115] *Ep.* 126 (*PG* 52.685-7).
[116] *Ep.* 14.5 (*PG* 52.618): IX.236.
[117] *Ep.* 175 (*PG* 52.711-12).

in dragging him back from the abyss). As we noted earlier,[118] John's interest in the christianisation of Persia had been aroused by the bishop some years previously. He seems to have borne him little resentment, had sent him two so far unanswered letters, and was particularly eager to discover what success he had had in Persia, and why he had returned to Constantinople. In the latter he begs Agapetos to give generous assistance to the priest Elpidios, who had been striving to win over pagan inhabitants of the Amanos mountains (between Cilicia and Syria), and had already achieved numerous conversions as well as building churches and founding monastic communities.

VI

Ever since Photios singled them out for their usefulness and careful composition,[119] the seventeen letters (there are likely to have been more originally) which John sent to Olympias at irregular intervals between his arrival at Nicaea in June 404 and the early months of 407 have always attracted special attention. They had last seen each other in the baptistery of Hagia Sophia immediately before his arrest, and they were never to meet again. For the first year of their correspondence she was in Constantinople, much of the time seriously ill. In spring 405 John fulsomely congratulated her not only on her 'repeated triumphs' (presumably in the judicial proc-esses from which she had emerged as the moral victor), but on the extraor-dinary example she was setting, confined though she was to her sick-room, 'to that great and populous city' by her fortitude in bearing her sufferings.[120] At some unknown date, however, in 405 she withdrew of her own choice from the capital and settled at Cyzikos (Erdex peninsula) on the Sea of Marmara.[121] But her struggle against relentless pressure had taken its toll. The correspondence indicates that for many months she continued ill, suffering from a double break-down both of physical health and, even more grievously, of morale. She was shattered by the cruel division in the church, by the persecution of so many of her friends, above all by the seemingly inexplicable disaster which had befallen John and by her interminable separation from him.

John and Olympias had to rely on such couriers as they could be sure were trustworthy. A letter written from Arabissos contains a chill warning to her against employing anyone for this service unless he was making the journey on other business, for otherwise there was a real danger of his being murdered.[122] (This was written in 406, when the government's attitude may

---

[118] See above, p. 144.
[119] *Bibliotheca* 86 (ed. R. Henry, Paris 1960: 2, 11).
[120] *Ep.* 6.1 (*PG* 52.599): XII.318-20.
[121] Sozomen 8.24.7.
[122] *Ep.* 15 (*PG* 52.620): XV.358-60.

well have been hardening.) The letters themselves vary greatly in length, style and content. If the early ones and a few others are short notes rushed off to give the latest news, there are some (e.g. 1 (VII), 2 (VIII), and 3 (X)) which develop into sustained and closely argued treatises. While the language is always polished, John now and then slips into almost conversational Greek;[123] at other times he deploys all the artifices of structured rhetoric. Invariably he addresses Olympias with a deferential courtesy ('Your excellency', 'Your grace', 'Your reverence') which modern readers, unused to ancient conventions, often find off-putting. Yet everywhere, even in those lengthy passages which are virtually homilies, the letters reveal, with a vividness which has few parallels in ancient correspondence, the intimacy and deep mutual trust which bound together these two remarkable spirits, the one assured and self-reliant but greatly in need of a confidante, the other no less strong-willed but baffled and disoriented by the course of events.

Their close rapport is evident in the naturalness with which John pours out (while her letters are lost, we may be sure that Olympias fully reciprocated) all the minute incidents of his daily life, the excitements, dangers and disappointments he experiences, the ups and downs of his health, his reaction to the cruel winter, such details as his struggle to keep warm, his fits of vomiting and the medicine he takes to check them.[124] It is evident, too, in his unquestioning reliance on her to carry out confidential commissions for him and to keep him supplied with information.[125] It comes out, again, in his eagerness to hear from her, in his restless interest in her health, in the desolation he feels when letters fail to arrive from her.[126] But it is most tenderly, and eloquently, expressed when he seeks to console her for what he knows distresses her most, her separation from 'the nothingness that is all I am' (*tes oudeneias tes hemeteras*).[127]

Here we are brought face to face with an ever-present concern in all these letters, the overriding one in several – John's desire to help Olympias to shake off 'the tyranny of depression' (*athumia*) which has fastened its grip on her.[128] To achieve this he continually reminds her of certain confidently held beliefs which should be, and are, as self-evident to her as they are to him. For example, if the church is like a ship battered by storms, God is 'the pilot of the universe' and will set it on its true course in his own good time.[129] If her friends are victims of unjust treatment, confiscations, false accusations, banishment itself, all these apparent disasters are only transitory; the one thing which should be dreaded and make one downcast is

---

[123] E.g. *epp.* 13.1 (*PG* 52.610): VI.128; 14.2 (*PG* 52.613): IX.222.
[124] For examples see section IV above.
[125] E.g. *ep.* 14.5 (*PG* 52.618): IX.236 (Maruthas).
[126] E.g. *ep.* 10 (*PG* 52.609): II.110.
[127] *Ep.* 2.11 (*PG* 52.568): VIII.202.
[128] Ibid.
[129] *Ep.* 1.1 (*PG* 52.549-50): VII.134-6.

sin. Christ himself was maltreated, vilified, and betrayed. The first disciples were persecuted, but so far from impeding the church this was the stimulus to its progress.[130] The fact is, as he constantly insists, suffering here, in the providence of God, both allows a man to expiate his sins and procures ineffable rewards in the life to come.[131] Olympias should abandon her gloom, turning her eyes away from the distresses of the moment to contemplate the deliverance and the ultimate recompense which will surely be hers.

It is Job, stripped of everything but nevertheless exclaiming, 'The Lord gave, the Lord has taken away; blessed be the Lord's name', who sums up John's consistent message of grateful acceptance of whatever comes to pass.[132] So he can encourage Olympias to believe that the greater one's suffering, the more fruitful it becomes provided one is thanking God.[133] Even separation from such a loved friend as himself will bring a measureless reward if she bears it courageously, 'never letting a bitter word escape her lips, but glorifying God for all she has to bear'.[134] But the cure of moral prostration demands the active co-operation of the sufferer, just as the cure of physical illness that of the patient.[135] So he assures her, with his invincible faith in the efficaciousness of personal effort, 'What we are aiming at is not just to rid you of your depression, but to fill you with immense and lasting joy. This is possible if you will it. For it is not on the immutable laws of nature, which it is impossible for us to manipulate or alter, that our good dispositions depend, but on the free decisions of our will, which we can easily control.'[136] Here, as elsewhere in his elaborate argument (e.g. in his tireless insistence that the experiences generally rated disastrous are really matters of indifference), we catch echoes of the great Stoic commonplaces which he had inherited from his upbringing. As he expounds them, however, they are almost always interwoven with distinctively Christian themes such as the hope of rich rewards in the life to come and the acceptance of suffering, not with Stoic resignation, but with the joyous outpouring of thanks to God.

We have no means of knowing whether John's earnest, repetitious efforts to lift Olympias out of her dejection were successful, but one suspects that they were not. John himself seems to admit as much, a little impatiently, in his last letter to her. After sending her a reasoned summary of his familiar arguments, he suggests that, properly studied, this should prove an effective medicine for her if only she makes up her mind to use it. He then adds, 'But if you obstinately resist me and do not heal yourself, if while receiving endless counsel and consolation you decline to drag yourself from

---

[130] *Ep.* 1.4-5 (*PG* 52.553-6): VII.146-56.
[131] *Epp.* 14.1 (*PG* 52.612-13): IX.220; 2.3 (*PG* 52.559): VIII.170.
[132] *Ep.* 2.11 (*PG* 52.568): VIII.204.
[134] E.g. *ep.* 16 (*PG* 52.621): XIV.352.
[135] *Ep.* 2.1 (*PG* 52.556): VIII.158-60.
[136] *Ep.* 3.1 (*PG* 52.572-3): X.242-4.

the stagnant pond of depression, I for my part shall not find it easy to comply with your request to keep sending you frequent, lengthy letters from which you are not going to derive any improvement in your spiritual condition.'[137] His ill-success is not really surprising; in her deep prostration she needed something more than intellectual reassurance and brisk admonition to pull herself together. For all his affection and devotion John was temperamentally unsuited to enter sympathetically into her psychological predicament. One small but significant evidence of this is the rebuke he once gave her for rejecting his pleas: 'If you go on repeating, "I should like to, but I haven't got the strength", I too shall go on repeating, "Mere excuses and pretexts!" For I know how strong the sinews of your deeply religious soul are.'[138]

VII

Meanwhile John had decided to disseminate the message he had been giving Olympias to a wider public, and put together two pieces amplifying his ideas on the seemingly inexplicable trials which befall ordinary decent people. He intended them primarily for the hard core of Johnites in Constantinople, but also for Olympias herself. In his last letter, written in spring 407, he recalls that he had sent her the first of these 'recently' (*proen*), and then describes the second, which he enclosed with the letter, as 'carrying on the same combat'.[139] It was this latter piece, as we noted in the preceding paragraph, which he had hoped she would find to be an infallible remedy for her depression. These were the last of his formal compositions, but neither shows any flagging of his powers as a writer of high-flown rhetoric.

The first and much shorter of the two, *No Man Can Be Harmed Save By Himself*,[140] in several MSS entitled 'Letter written from Cucusos to Olympias and to all the faithful', is in fact a treatise prepared in the style and with all the rhetorical features of a spoken address. Its object is to convince John's adherents in the capital and elsewhere, victims since his deposition of every sort of persecution at the hands of both the civil and the ecclesiastical authorities, that this treatment is incapable of doing them any real damage provided they retain, through their own firm resolve, their personal moral integrity. The reason for this is that a man's true worth does not reside in riches, health, reputation, freedom, or even life itself, but in that very moral integrity, which John defines more precisely as 'a thorough

[137] *Ep.* 4.4 (*PG* 52.595): XVII.384-6.
[138] *Ep.* 2.3 (*PG* 52.558): VIII.166.
[139] *Ep.* 4.4 (*PG* 52.595): XVII.384.
[140] *Quod nemo laeditur nisi a seipso*: *PG* 52.459-80. There is a first-class critical edition, with French translation, by A.M. Malingrey in *SC* 103 (Paris 1964), to which the present writer is much indebted.

grasp of the true doctrines coupled with strict integrity of behaviour'.[141] This no one, not even the Devil, will be able to take from him provided he is careful to keep it intact. Thus it cannot be affected by such apparent disasters as exile, enslavement, torture, death itself; it is only when, like Adam, he abandons it through negligence or lack of vigilance, and so slips into sin, that he sustains real injury.[142] John winds up his stern but bracing message by recalling the three young Jews who, according to Daniel 3, were thrown into 'the burning fiery furnace' for refusing to worship the golden image which Nebuchadnezzar had set up.[143] They had been subjected to much the same injustices and cruelties as the Johnite supporters for whom he was writing, but they emerged from their ordeal not only scatheless but bathed in a special radiance.

As he expounds it, John's thesis is an elaboration of the paradox set out in the title, to which he constantly returns as he develops his argument. The paradox itself is a neat distillation of an axiom traditional in Greek thinking from Sokrates and Plato right down to the later Stoics, the idea that it is always better to suffer injustice than to inflict it, and that for the good man who remains true to himself no evil is possible either in this life or after death.[144] This is a theme which underlies much of John's teaching; what is a little startling is that, whereas he usually sets it in a patently Christian context, this is almost wholly lacking here. In other works he stresses, for example, that the experience of suffering is an opportunity for thanksgiving,[145] or argues that no one can make us truly wretched while we fear the Lord and receive his grace,[146] or celebrates the disciple who bears every kind of disaster in the knowledge that nothing can separate us from the love of Christ (Rom. 8.35),[147] or claims triumphantly that no one in the world can inflict real harm on the man who is a Christian.[148] By contrast there is little or no attempt in this essay to give a Christian slant to the successive themes developed. The illustrations, it is true, are drawn from scripture, with Paul held up as the heroic exemplar, but the substance of the argument might have been drawn from a Stoic manual.[149] The Christian element is minimal, with only perfunctory references to Christ. There is a problem here which has embarrassed some students, but no satisfactory solution to it has been proposed.

[141] *Quod nemo laeditur* 3 (*PG* 52.463).
[142] *Quod nemo laeditur* 4 (*PG* 52.464).
[143] *Quod nemo laeditur* 17 (*PG* 52.478-80).
[144] E.g. Plato, *Apol.* 32d; 41d; *Gorgias* 469bc; 477e; 509c; *Repub.* 10.608d-609a; 12.613a; Epiktetos, *Discourse* 1.1.21-5; 4.1.127-31.
[145] *De incomp.* 4.4 (*PG* 48.735-6).
[146] *Ad pop. Antioch. hom.* 18.4 (*PG* 49.186).
[147] *De res. mort.* 3-04 (*PG* 50.425).
[148] *In Act. hom.* 51.4 (*PG* 60.356).
[149] See esp. É. Amand de Mendieta, *Byzantion* 36 (1936), 353-81.

The second piece,[150] which John hoped would prove particularly helpful to Olympias, aptly named by its most recent editor *On God's Providence*, is also a treatise with many of the characteristics of an address. It, too, is aimed at giving reassurance to the Christian community in Constantinople whose faith has been shaken by the dreadful events happening to themselves and like-minded fellow-Christians. As in its briefer predecessor, much of the argument rests on widely accepted Stoic presuppositions; for example, the axiom that the man who keeps himself free from wrong-doing cannot be injured by anyone, or even by death itself, has an important place in it.[151] Here, however,these considerations take second place to a powerful presentation of distinctively Christian themes, such as the certainty of God's love for man (surpassing all the forms of love we know),[152] or the reminder that the cross, a scandal in the eyes of most people, meant for Christ himself his glorification (John 17), while for Paul it was the ground for his boasting (Gal. 6.14).[153] Combined with these is a characteristic emphasis on man's inability to understand God's providence, and a challenge to Christians in the capital to imitate those heroes of the Old Testament who, 'although they had no clear knowledge of the resurrection and witnessed events quite contrary to God's promises, did not allow themselves to be scandalised or upset, but committed themselves to his inscrutable providence ... Confident of the power and resourcefulness of his wisdom, they looked forward to the outcome, indeed well before the outcome bore whatever adversity was perpetrated with thanksgiving, glorifying the God who permitted these things to happen.' Those who can read the New Testament are even better placed, for they have the Lord's assurance, 'He who endures to the end will be saved' (Matt. 10.22).[154]

For all its fine formal structure, this letter-treatise is no detached discussion of great philosophical and religious issues. Its language is eloquent, and it throbs with the emotion of personal involvement. From time to time, especially towards the end, this erupts in scarcely disguised allusions to current events and personalities. The centre-piece of the section just quoted is a poignant description of 'the church rent asunder, with its most illustrious members harassed and scourged, its chief pastor exiled to the ends of the earth'.[155] Later John bitterly contrasts his faithful congregation (swollen by an inflow of people hitherto devoted to the theatre and race-course) obliged, as a result of the removal of their rightful clergy, to celebrate the liturgy on their own in the wild countryside, with the false

---

[150] *Ad eos qui scandalizati sunt ob adversitates* (*PG* 52.479-528): critical edition, with French translation, by A.M. Malingrey – *J. Chrysostome: Sur la Providence de Dieu* (*SC* 79: Paris 1961).
[151] E.g. *Ad eos qui scandalizati sunt* 15-16 (*PG* 52.516-18).
[152] Ibid., 6 (*PG* 52.488-91).
[153] Ibid., 17 (*PG* 52.516-18).
[154] Ibid., 9 (*PG* 52.499-500).
[155] Loc. cit.

bishops who, after deceiving the world with a pretence of sound religion and charitable conduct, have been exposed as the impostors they are.[156] He even lampoons 'the high-priest who has become vicious and ravages his flock more cruelly than a wolf would' (this can only be Attikos, bishop of Constantinople since March 406), and 'the highly placed magistrate who shows himself ruthless in the extreme'[157] (almost certainly Optatos, city prefect 404-5, always detested by Johnites for his severity). This was dangerous language if the treatise found its way, as it was likely to do, into the hands of the authorities, but at this stage John seems, for reasons hard to explain, to have been optimistic about his prospects of a come-back.[158] In any case, he was evidently pleased with what he had written, and begged Olympias to read it continually, aloud if her health permitted.

[156] *Ad eos qui scandalizati sunt* 19 (*PG* 52.520-1).
[157] Ibid., 20 (*PG* 52.521).
[158] See below, p. 282.

19

Last Journey

I

During his three years of exile John was eagerly watching events unfold, in Constantinople and the greater world beyond, impatient to assess their bearing on his fortunes. One such event, of more than ordinary importance, was the death of Eudoxia on 6 October 404. A few days before a hail-storm of unprecedented ferocity, with hail-stones as big as walnuts, had beaten down on the capital and its suburbs.[1] Emotionally upset by it, perhaps also guilt-stricken, she had suffered another miscarriage, one which this time ended her life. She was buried in the Holy Apostles. We should dearly like to know John's reaction to the wholly unexpected passing of the volatile, impulsive empress, once his eager supporter and friend, but later fatally estranged, but no mention of it survives, or is likely ever to have figured, in his correspondence. The Johnites, inevitably, were quick to interpret her death as manifest proof of divine displeasure at his ill-treatment and as a vindication of their cause.

If they hoped the government would relax its severity, they were greatly mistaken. The opposition to John extended far beyond her and her circle, and was deeply entrenched. In any case, a new situation had been created by the appointment of Arsakios as bishop, and the authorities were determined to maintain it at whatever cost. About mid-November they replaced Stoudios, a detached and perhaps covertly sympathetic city prefect,[2] with Optatos, a non-Christian with a reputation for imposing harsh penalties;[3] for the next eight or nine months the implementation of the penal legislation lay in his hands. Then on 18 November, alarmed at the rapid spread of the divisions caused by John's deposition, they published a fresh edict extending the ban on dissident worship to the provinces.[4] This instructed provincial governors to outlaw all services held by orthodox Christians in places other than the official churches, and made communion with Arsakios, Theophilos and Porphyrios of Antioch, the three government-recognised patriarchs of the east, obligatory.

---

[1] Sokrates 6.19; Sozomen 8.27; *Chronicon paschale* s.a. 404 (*PG* 92.781): the last mentions her burial place.
[2] See above, p. 251.
[3] *PLRE* 1, 649-50.
[4] CT 16.4.6.

Early in 405 a further edict,[5] dated 4 February, made it impossible for bishops sympathetic to John who had been deposed to recover their sees by requiring them to be held in custody far from their episcopal cities, without any right of appeal. Finally, when the aged Arsakios died on 11 November 405,[6] and the Johnites hoped against hope that the return of their hero might be arranged, the government after four months' delay pushed through the election of the Armenian priest Attikos, whom Palladios was to describe correctly as the architect of the conspiracy against John.[7] A dull preacher, but a man of warm personality and immense charitableness, he was also a capable administrator.[8] It was probably the combination of this quality with his record of antipathy to John that prompted his choice as bishop: the authorities reckoned that he was better equipped to carry out their policies energetically than his elderly, indolent predecessor. Under him the legislation penalising anyone, clerical or lay, who refused to hold communion with the officially recognised bishops was intensified.[9]

II

If the prospects for John and his adherents in Constantinople looked bleak, more encouraging signals were coming from the west. About the time of Eudoxia's death[10] two letters from the pope, Innocent I, reached the capital, one to John, to be forwarded to him at Cucusos, and the other to the clergy and people loyal to him. Separately, but at roughly the same time and closely linked with the second, a third letter of importance arrived from Ravenna, where the western court had moved in 402: it was from Emperor Honorius to his elder brother Arkadios. Palladios, who came to Rome in autumn 404 and thoroughly briefed himself on recent events there, has left a detailed and, to all appearances, trustworthy chronicle of the successive pressures which were brought to bear on the pope during the preceding months, and which culminated in the writing of all three letters.

The first official report about what had been happening in Constantinople to reach Innocent was a terse note from Theophilos which simply announced that he had deposed John.[11] Its clear implication, whether stated or not, was that it was no longer proper for the pope to maintain communion with him. As leading patriarch of the east (as he still believed himself to be), bishop of a see with close traditional ties with Rome, Theophilos was doing nothing exceptional in making this *démarche*; if he

---

[5] CT 16.2.35.

[6] Sokrates 6.20.

[7] *Dial.* 11 (*SC* 34.216).

[8] For balanced, well documented accounts of him see *DCB* 1, 207-9 (E. Venables); *DHGE* 5, 161-6 (M. Th. Disdier).

[9] Palladios, *Dial.* 11 (*SC* 341.216-24).

[10] Sozomen (8.27) dates the arrival of these letters to the time of the hail-storm.

[11] Palladios, *Dial.* 1 (*SC* 341.62-4): source for the whole paragraph.

had refrained from notifying Rome about The Oak until now, that was because its decisions had been almost immediately suspended. Nevertheless Innocent was disturbed that Theophilos was the sole signatory of the letter, and that he had given no explanation of his drastic action. Meanwhile a deacon Eusebios, probably John's business representative in Rome, advised him against precipitate action. Just three days later there arrived the delegation[12] carrying John's impassioned and circumstantial appeal to the pope, as well as letters from the forty loyalist bishops and from the faithful clergy. As John had drafted his appeal towards the end of April and two or three weeks must be allowed for its transmission, both it and, three days earlier, Theophilos' curt message must have been delivered to the Lateran palace by mid-May at latest.

Innocent's reaction to these two communications (they had been written, it should be noted, quite independently of each other) was cautious but by no means neutral.[13] He dispatched letters to both John and Theophilos informing each that he was in full communion with him. This amounted to a rejection of Theophilos' request that he should break off communion with John. He demanded, moreover, that a fresh, impartial synod composed of western as well as eastern bishops, with declared enemies of either side excluded, should be convened to adjudicate the affair. His attitude sharpened, however, when, a few days later he received from Theophilos a copy of the acts of The Oak, along with an assurance that, in deposing John, the canons of the council of Antioch had been invoked. The acts made it plain to Innocent that John had been condemned in his absence, on largely trivial charges and by a synod packed with Egyptian bishops. He therefore sent the patriarch a markedly stiffer letter,[14] repeating that he remained in communion with both John and him, but adding that he could not reasonably break off communion with John on the strength of such frivolous proceedings. If Theophilos insisted on sticking to his verdict on John, he would have to submit it to a properly constituted synod at which the canons of Nicaea, the only ones recognised by the Roman church, would be authoritative.

So far John's fate was still unknown at Rome, but in early July a Constantinopolitan priest, Theoteknos, representing the Johnite bishops, brought the pope a full account of his banishment to Armenia, as also of the burning of the Great Church.[15] Then throughout the summer and autumn, as the eastern government's penal legislation made their residence there untenable, a stream of refugees from Constantinople poured into Rome, each the bearer of an anguished complaint or a grim story of

---

[12] See above, p. 248.
[13] Palladios, *Dial.* 3 (*SC* 341.64).
[14] Palladios, *Dial.* 3 (*SC* 341.66-8). He is the sole source of this letter, no. 5 in Innocent's correspondence.
[15] Palladios, *Dial.* 3 (*SC* 341.68).

persecution. Palladios, who himself arrived in September, driven out (as he hints) by the decree of 29 August,[16] methodically records their names.[17] They all gave full reports to Innocent, who notes that he questioned them closely.[18] There must also have been intense interest in the news they brought, and discussion about it, in the imperial court, for Honorius and his chief minister Stilicho were in residence in Rome from November 403 until 25 July 404; the letter of Honorius to Arkadios mentioned above reveals how fully informed he was about everything that had been happening in the eastern capital. Others in Rome who undoubtedly listened eagerly to the refugees' alarming stories were the small but influential group of John's sympathisers and friends there – the aged Melania, whom Olympias had taken as her role-model in asceticism,[19] and her granddaughter Melania the Younger (both had returned to Rome from the holy land in 400), as well as aristocratic ladies such as Proba and Juliana, with whom John would soon be corresponding.[20] The younger Melania, we know,[21] gave generous hospitality at this time to Palladios and numerous others visiting Rome to forward John's interests.

It was not only desperate Johnites who were doing all they could to lobby the pope. Hard on Theoteknos' heels a priest Paternos arrived with a sheaf of abusive letters from Antiochos and other virulently anti-Johnite bishops.[22] But Innocent had already come down firmly on John's side; what he was not so clear about was the action he should take. After his second letter to Theophilos[23] he had ceased acknowledging the approaches of John's adversaries. The cautious reply he sent to Theoteknos,[24] however, betrays the difficulty in which he found himself. While confirming his continued communion with John, he counselled patience since he himself could do nothing against the powerful forces determined to destroy John. This was a veiled allusion to the eastern government, on which protests from even the leading bishop of the west were unlikely to have the least effect. It was apparent to him that, if influence was to be brought to bear on it, this could only be through a direct approach by the western government. It seems certain, in fact, that before the court left for Ravenna at the end of July, there had been close consultation between himself and Honorius and his advisers, and that a common policy had been worked out. For several weeks Innocent took no steps to implement this; he was waiting for the opportune moment. In late September, however, when the priest Germanos and the

---

[16] See above, p. 253.
[17] *Dial.* 3 (*SC* 341.68-80).
[18] *Ep.* 7.4 (*PL* 20.506-8).
[19] See above, p. 112.
[20] See above, p. 264.
[21] Palladios, *Lausiac History* 61 (Butler 57).
[22] Palladios, *Dial.* 3 (*SC* 341.70-2).
[23] *Ep.* 5 (*PL* 20.493-5): see above, p. 274.
[24] Palladios, *Dial.* 3 (*SC* 341).

deacon Cassian presented him with a petition from all the clergy loyal to John in Constantinople,[25] he decided that that moment had arrived and sent off letters to both John and his clergy. It is likely that he also notified Honorius, so that he could dispatch the letter he was planning to send to his brother.

III

Innocent's letter to John[26] was in largely general terms. While taking his innocence for granted and making a scathing comment on the 'hubris' of his oppressors, it made no direct reference to the wrongs done him. It sought to remind him of what, as 'the teacher and shepherd of so many peoples', he already knew full well, that it is often the best of mankind who are tested by afflictions, and that 'the man who can rely on God first of all, and then on his own good conscience', should be able, as the example of the saints abundantly proves, to bear whatever comes to him.

Innocent was more specific, and much more outspoken, in his message to John's loyalist clergy and people.[27] He had read and re-read, he assured them, the story of their wretched plight as set out in the letter brought by Germanos and Cassian. He compared their sufferings to those of the saints of old, and promised that, if they showed patient endurance, God would speedily bring them to an end. In the meantime he felt himself punished along with them. It was intolerable, he then declared, that all these misfortunes should have been brought about by 'the very people whose special concern it should be to promote peace and harmony'. It was preposterous that bishops who were guiltless should have been deposed. 'John, our brother and fellow-minister, your bishop, has been the first to receive this unjust treatment, without being allowed a hearing, without an accusation being brought or heard.' It was against all precedent, too, that a new bishop should have been installed while the rightful holder of the see was still alive. Innocent then deplored the reliance of John's persecutors on church canons that were heretical rather than on the Nicene ones, which alone were binding. The only means of checking the storm that had arisen was, as he had long been arguing, a proper synodical investigation. This alone would bring calm to the disordered situation brought about by the Devil in order to try the saints. He was now giving earnest thought to how such an ecumenical synod could be assembled.

If Innocent's letter was outspoken, that of Honorius to his elder brother[28] was testy, not to say ill-tempered. It opened with some peevish grumbles

---

[25] Palladios, *Dial.* 3 (*SC* 341.76-8).
[26] *Ep.* 12: preserved only by Sozomen, 8.26 (*GCS* 50.385-7).
[27] *Ep.* 7 (*PL* 20.502-7): preserved only by Sozomen, 8.26 (*GCS* 50.385-7).
[28] No. 38 in the *Collectio Avellana* (*CSEL* 35.85-8).

about the unseemly parading of Eudoxia's images[29] (it was apparently written before news of her death had reached Ravenna) and about the devastation carried out by Alaric the Hun in Illyricum. Honorius then deplored at length the tumult and violence which had recently disgraced Constantinople at the holy season of Easter, the imprisoning of clergy at the time when amnesties were normally granted, the bloodshed desecrating the sanctuary, and the driving of 'venerable bishops' into exile. Actions like these were an insult to God, who had shown his displeasure in the burning down of the Great Church. Turning to more recent history, he struck at the eastern government's intervention in church affairs. Disputes about religion ought to be settled by the bishops, to whom the interpretation of divine things belonged; the role of princes was to respect the faith. As regards the dispute over John, he recalled that both parties had been at one in sending representatives to Rome to seek its arbitration, and condemned the precipitate haste with which, before the matter had been properly examined and judgment given, the accused bishops had been bundled off into exile. It was all the more outrageous as those to whom the final decision had been entrusted had judged it proper to remain in communion with John pending the settlement of his case. The letter's analysis of the crisis was, as we should expect, closely in line with Innocent's as shown in all his dealings with it, but it criticises and rebukes the eastern authorities with a frankness which the pope was in no position to use. As it has been aptly remarked,[30] Honorius made an admirable intermediary for conveying the condemnation of the holy see to the court at Constantinople.

IV

Whether Innocent's letter to John came to the attention of the eastern government we do not know, but it is likely to have been infuriated by the other two, which gave open support to a condemned trouble-maker. Innocent's could only fuel the dangerous schism it was striving to stamp out; Honorius' must have been regarded as unwarranted interference. It is scarcely surprising that Arkadios declined to acknowledge it, notwithstanding its being followed by a second letter requesting a reply to it.[31] Meanwhile appeals to the pope continued to pour in from Constantinople. One of the latest recorded by Palladios,[32] complaining of the harsh methods employed by Optatos, the city prefect, to force women of rank and deaconesses to accept communion with Arsakios, gives us a date at the end of 404 at least, more probably well into 405. By this time, according to Palladios,[33]

---

[29] See above, p. 239.
[30] Ch. Pietri, *Roma Christiana* (Rome 1976), 1, 1319.
[31] Palladios, *Dial.* 3 (SC 341.82), where Honorius describes the letter cited below as 'my third'.
[32] *Dial.* 3 (SC 341.78-80).
[33] *Dial.* 3 (SC 341.80): *meketi karteresanta.*

Innocent had reached the end of his patience. It is likely, although specific evidence is lacking, that he was also under pressure from John's influential friends living in Rome.[34] More important, probably, were the disappointment and frustration which the evident failure of Honorius' approach to his older brother must have inspired both at Rome and Ravenna. He therefore sent off to Honorius a comprehensive summary of all the reports and complaints he had received from the east. As a result of this move, made probably early in 405, the collaboration between pope and emperor entered on a fresh, more active phase.

First, as Innocent must have expected and had probably planned, Honorius' response[35] was to request him to convene a council of Italian bishops to adjudicate on the great issue of John's deposition. It was now their policy, Honorius' personal approach to his brother having proved fruitless, to confront the east with the canonically formulated judgment of the west on the divisive question. Innocent duly assembled a representative synod; as well as bishops in the vicinity of Rome, it included several from the north (e.g. Chromatius of Aquileia), and also refugee bishops from the east (notably Palladios). The synod, which probably met in early summer 405,[36] rejected the charges which had been brought against John, treated Theophilos, Arsakios, and their partisans as excommunicate, and, guided by Innocent, besought the emperor to invite his brother to summon a council of eastern bishops, reinforced by a delegation of westerners, to meet at Thessalonica. The meeting-place proposed was geographically convenient for both parties; the choice also cohered with Innocent's policy, inherited from his predecessor Siricius (384-99), of making the bishop of Thessalonica his vicar, and thus maintaining the ecclesiastical authority of Rome in territory which was politically subject to Constantinople. The Roman synod's determination to have John rehabilitated was made crystal-clear in its stipulation that, while he would be expected to appear at the projected council, he must first be given back his see and title as bishop, and restored to ecclesiastical fellowship.[37]

Secondly, Honorius fully endorsed the synod's report and agreed to write to Arkadios asking him to arrange for the great council it had proposed to be held at Thessalonica.[38] At his request Innocent organised an impressive delegation to convey the imperial letter, as well as letters from himself and other Italian bishops and the acts of the Roman synod, to Constantinople. The delegation consisted of five Latin bishops, two priests and a deacon, and was accompanied by four of the eastern bishops who had fled to Rome,

---

[34] Ch. Pietri, *Roma Christiana* (Rome 1976), 1, 1319.
[35] Palladios, *Dial.* 3 (*SC* 341.80-2).
[36] Ch. Pietri, op. cit., 1, 1321 n.2.
[37] Palladios, *Dial.* 4 (*SC* 341.86): an extract, apparently, from the synod's proceedings.
[38] Palladios, *Dial.* 3 (*SC* 341.82).

including Palladios.[39] Honorius' letter[40] to his brother was superficially less aggressive in tone than his earlier rancorous communication. He made much, for example, of his concern for the peace of the church, with which the welfare of the empire was bound up, and professed himself ready to revise his views on John in the light of the projected council's deliberations. He made no attempt, however, to disguise his present conviction that John was the innocent victim of a sinister conspiracy; what he in fact was asking for was the 'correction' (*diorthosis*) of the sentence passed on him. He also insisted that the presence of Theophilos, the man responsible for all the trouble, at the council was indispensable. For a fuller exposition of the views of the west on John he referred Arkadios to two letters which he enclosed, one from Innocent and the other from Chromatius of Aquileia.

Although backed by Honorius and carrying his letter, the delegation was actually a pontifical one; as such it was granted the privilege of travelling by the imperial post.[41] The date of its departure is debated, a favourite choice being late autumn 405.[42] But this seems much too early: Attikos, who was probably appointed bishop in March 406, had already been installed when it reached the vicinity of Constantinople. It is more likely to have set out early in 406, at the very start of the sailing season, i.e. 11 March. For all its impressiveness, it is hard to imagine what Honorius and Innocent expected it to achieve. Perhaps they were hoping that, bishop Arsakios having died in November 405, the eastern authorities might be prepared to modify their policy in regard to John.[43] If so, they were doing nothing to help them, for their mandate was to demand a complete climb-down by Constantinople. In any case, this was a time of growing friction between the two governments. From the start of 405 Stilicho, Honorius' all-powerful minister, had refused to recognise the consulate of Anthemios, now praetorian prefect of the east; while the eastern government was fully aware that Stilicho was planning, from 405 at least, to bring eastern Illyricum (the Balkans, apart from former Yugoslavia) back under western control.[44] As for Anthemios, whatever his personal feelings about John, he was clearly in no mood to gratify the hopes of the Johnites; it must have been with his approval that Attikos was appointed as Arsakios' successor.

In fact, reports of the embassy caused great resentment in the capital; a campaign seems to have been mounted to portray it as an insult to the eastern government.[45] It is scarcely surprising, therefore, that Anthemios saw to it that every obstacle was placed in the way of the unwelcome visitors once they had penetrated the provinces under Arkadios' suzerainty. From

[39] Palladios, *Dial.* 4 (*SC* 341.84-6).
[40] Palladios, *Dial.* 3 (*SC* 341.82-4): cited only here.
[41] Palladios, *Dial.* 4 (*SC* 341.84).
[42] So, e.g., É. Demougeot, *De l'unité à la division de l'empire romain* (Paris 1951), 346.
[43] E.g. Ch. Pietri, *Roma Christiana* (Rome 1976), 1, 1324.
[44] A. Cameron, *Claudian* (Oxford 1970), 60-2; 157-8.
[45] Sozomen 8.28.

the moment they had rounded the Peloponnese and were sailing in the direction of Athens they were kept under continuous military surveillance.[46] Although they were carrying letters from the pope to the bishop of Thessalonica, Anysios, they were prevented by the authorities from entering the great harbour there, let alone from landing; Illyricum was forbidden territory for suspect westerners. Instead the two groups were separated and placed on different ships, the Latins on one and the Greeks on another, and peremptorily ordered to sail on, storm-tossed and for three days without adequate provisions, to the capital. Here too the harbour police dashed their hopes of going ashore. They were obliged to reverse course, and were interned in the Thracian fortress of Athyras, several kilometres west of the city (probably the present Büyükçekmeçe).[47] The Latin party was confined to a small apartment, without a servant to attend to them; the Greeks were locked up separately. Although the emperor was in Constantinople, he flatly declined to offer the western delegation the audience they expected; when they protested that they were ambassadors and could only deliver the letters they were carrying, including that of Honorius to his brother, to him personally, a military tribune wrested the sealed documents violently from them. A clumsy attempt was then made to bribe them (3,000 gold pieces was the sum proposed) to enter into communion with Attikos, drop their concern for John, and stop talking about the need for a fresh council. Faced with this final humiliation, they demanded to be permitted to return in peace to their homes. This request at least was granted. They were taken, under a heavy escort and in an unseaworthy vessel, across the Propontis as far as Lampsakos, at the northern mouth of the Hellespont (Dardanelles). There they were put on board a more serviceable ship, and after some twenty days at sea landed on the Calabrian coast, having achieved nothing and utterly disconsolate. Their fate was at least less wretched than that of their four eastern companions, who were all dispatched to remote places of exile.

The deliberately hostile reception of the delegation, carrying as it did a letter from Honorius as well as one from the pope, was a slap in the face for the western government. It was a calculated blow, however; Anthemios was aware that he could act as he did without fear of retaliation. Stilicho's position had changed dramatically for the worse. He was now perforce concentrating all his efforts and attention on striving to check the Ostrogoth Radagaisus, who since the closing months of 405 had been ravaging the north of Italy.[48] Until August 406, when he was able to crush the barbarian hordes at Fiesole, his hands were too full for him to spare a

---

[46] We owe the story of the expedition and its fate to Palladios, *Dial.* 4 (*SC* 341.86-92), who was a member of it.

[47] So called from the river of that name, between Selymbria (Silivri) and Constantinople: see Strabo, *Geog.* 7, 331 (frag. 56).

[48] Cf. CT 7.13.16 (17 April 406): encouraging the mobilisation of slaves.

thought for the luckless embassy or for John. So far from reaching an accommodation with them, the eastern government stepped up its persecution of the Johnites, and replaced the name of Arsakios with that of Attikos in the edict requiring all bishops to be in communion with the three officially recognised patriarchs of the east.[49] The rebuff to the pope was equally insulting. His reaction was to renounce fellowship with Attikos, Theophilos and Porphyrios, and all the other leading opponents of John, pending the holding of the general council which had always been at the centre of his policy.[50]

V

When news of the ambitious embassy the west was planning on his behalf filtered through to him, John was naturally excited, and rushed off several letters of thanks and encouragement to the Latin bishops and priests who were going to take part in it.[51] Written in almost identical terms, they were all curiously general, almost conventional in content; they also made no mention of the persons for whom they were intended. This omission was probably due to the fact that, at the moment of writing, he was still unaware of their names, and expected the presbyter (Evethios) who was acting as courier to distribute them to the appropriate persons when they had been identified. In a similar vein, again without naming the addressees, he wrote to the eastern bishops who he understood would be accompanying the delegation.[52] Nor did he forget Chromatius of Aquileia,[53] one of his stoutest supporters who had played an influential role in the consultations which had resulted in the expedition. It is interesting to note that, while invariably commending his correspondents and pressing them to maintain the struggle, John seems in some of these letters to entertain doubts about the likely result of their endeavours. In one,[54] for example, he assures its anonymous recipient that, whether his efforts are crowned with success or 'the originators of all these troubles' persist in their contentiousness and refuse to accept conciliation, he at any rate can be certain of the reward awaiting him.

This suggests that he may not have been either surprised or unduly cast down when he learned of the embassy's failure. We have no idea when reports of this reached him, but such news is likely to have travelled swiftly, if not directly from Constantinople, at any rate from Antioch, from which frequent visitors found their way to him. Certain of his letters (e.g. 182 to Venerius of Milan and 184 to Gaudentius of Brescia)[55] have sometimes been

[49] Palladios, *Dial.* 11 (*SC* 341.218-20).
[50] Palladios, *Dial.* 20 (*SC* 341.430-2); Theodoret, *HE* 5.34 (*GCS* 44.336).
[51] *Epp.* 157-61 (*PG* 52.703-6).
[52] *Epp.* 165-7 (*PG* 52.707-9).
[53] *Ep.* 155 (*PG* 52.702-3).
[54] *Ep.* 160 (*PG* 52.705).
[55] *PG* 52.714-15; 715-16.

interpreted as expressing gratitude to western leaders for backing the luckless venture.[56] If this reading of them is correct, the mood they reveal is one of unshaken resolve; he is insistent that his correspondents should redouble their efforts. Early in 407, when he drafted his last surviving letter to Olympias, his spirits were certainly confident. In it he assured her that, if it was her continued separation from himself that caused her depression, she could afford now to be cheerful, for it would soon be brought to an end.[57] It is not clear what grounds he can have had for believing, least of all at this juncture, that his return to Constantinople was imminent; it is more than likely that we have here yet another instance of his incurable optimism. He was in a more sombre mood when he wrote, somewhat later in the year, to Innocent.[58] He thanked the pope for giving him all the support of a loving father; if the issue had rested with him, all the wrongs which scandalised the Christian world would by now have been put right. Since this had not come about, he begged Innocent to continue the struggle in so great a cause with unremitting zeal. Even if he achieved nothing, it was the sure knowledge of his trust and affection which gave John, now (as he complained) in the third year of his weary exile, an inexpressible consolation – a consolation which would sustain him even if he should be relegated to an even more remote and desolate place of exile.

This letter, it seems, dates from spring or very early summer 407,[59] for its closing sentence indicates that John had heard rumours, at least, of the fate in store for him. The government had, in fact, decided to substitute a more distant, much harsher exile for his relatively easy house-detention in Armenia. An imperial edict was issued ordering his removal, as a matter of urgency, to Pityus on the eastern shores of the Black Sea.[60] Now Pitsunda, some 75 km north-west of Sukhumi in the Georgian republic of Abkhazia of the former Soviet Union, it was then the most easterly Roman outpost, more than 1100 km by sea from Constantinople. It had a strong fortress and an excellent harbour, but was incessantly plagued by attacks by barbarian tribes even more savage than the Isaurians, who descended from the slopes of the Caucasus.[61] It had been the place of exile, as John well knew, of Abundantios,[62] one of the generals whose ruin had been brought about by Eutropios.

---

[56] So, e.g., Moulard, 392.
[57] *Ep.* 4.4 (*PG* 52.594: XVII.382). Baur held (2, 399) that John's confidence was based on his hopes of the success of the Roman embassy; but the letter's date (see *SC* 13bis.98) excludes this.
[58] *PL* 52.535-6.
[59] It is usually dated late 406, but he cannot have heard of his projected removal to Pityus so early: see the letter to Olympias just cited (early 407).
[60] Palladios, *Dial.* 11 (*SC* 341.222).
[61] Theodoret, *HE* 5.34.7-8 (*GCS* 44.335): see A.H.M. Jones, *The Cities of the Eastern Roman Provinces* (Oxford 1971), 173.
[62] See above, p. 111; also *PLRE* 1, 4-5. Jerome (*ep.* 60.16: *CSEL* 54.570) pictures him as living there 'in destitution' (*egens*).

According to Palladios,[63] this sharp aggravation of his sentence (which would make visits to him impossible, and cut him off from the network of friends he had established in Armenia) resulted from a frenzied appeal to the court from Porphyrios of Antioch and other Syrian bishops, his old adversary Severian being prominent among them. Cucusos was becoming a place of pilgrimage, they complained, with swarms of John's admirers streaming north from the Syrian capital and elsewhere to visit him and listen to his words, and bringing back rapturous reports of his preaching. His extraordinary popularity stung them with jealousy, and they were impatient to have him transported to somewhere completely out of reach. It is likely enough that factors like this played their part, but to concentrate on them exclusively and ignore the political dimension is to oversimplify. Sozomen[64] sets the move in the context of the growing demand in the west for a general council, something the eastern authorities wished at all costs to avoid. Their decision should in any case be seen as a by-product of the great resentment created in Constantinople by the west's persistent intervention on John's behalf, most recently exemplified in the papal embassy. They must have feared, too, that the balance was once again swinging in the west's favour, for Stilicho, having decisively defeated Radagaisus at Fiesole in August 406, would soon be again well placed to champion the Johnite cause. He was not likely, if John was still around and easily accessible, to leave the humiliating rebuff administered to the western delegation unrequited.

VI

There is some uncertainty when the deportation order, with the detachment of praetorian guards who were to carry it out (there seem to have been just two of them) reached Cucusos (or Arabissos, if the alternative hypothesis is accepted). All the information, meagre as it is, that we have about John's last journey and its tragic outcome is supplied by Palladios.[65] 'Martyrios' throws no light on them; all we gather from his exordium[66] is that news of John's death has reached Constantinople, without any details of how it happened or of events preceding it. Palladios, we may be sure, was careful to ransack every scrap of evidence bearing on this last phase of John's life that filtered through to him, but even so it does not amount to much. He describes 'that most cruel' journey as having lasted three months (*trimenon*).[67] If this is correct, the order must have arrived, and John and his escort must have set off, around mid-June 407. But three months has always struck scholars as an inordinately long time, implying as it does

[63] *Dial.* 11 (*SC* 341.222).
[64] 8.28.
[65] *Dial.* 11 (*SC* 341.224-28).
[66] P 532b-533c.
[67] *SC* 341.224, line 116.

that, although the soldiers had orders to proceed with all possible dispatch, they only covered about three or four kilometres a day on average. There is therefore much to be said for the suggestion that Palladios may have misunderstood the reports given to him, and that the duration of the journey was in fact three weeks.[68]

If this is accepted, the praetorian guards with John would have taken to the military road leading north to the Black Sea around 25 August. In accordance with their instructions, they pressed ahead with brutal disregard for the frail physique and fragile health of their prisoner. If we can trust Palladios (it may have been just a rumour current in Johnite circles), they did not trouble to conceal the fact that they had been promised promotion if he succumbed on the way. One of them, we are told, felt genuine compassion for him, but he dared not show this except secretly. Much of the route covered difficult, often mountainous country, and the little party made forced marches of some 20 kilometres a day; this time John had no litter or mule at his disposal. As was to be expected in early autumn, pelting rainstorms alternated with blazing sunshine. When they reached a town or village where the elementary comforts he needed (e.g. the warm baths he had so often told[69] Olympias were indispensable to his health) might have been obtained, his escort hurried past without stopping. This was not necessarily an example of deliberate harshness; his identity was no secret, and demonstrations of public sympathy were the last thing his guards wanted. More questionable was the way in which (according to Palladios), when travellers they met made suggestions aimed at easing his sufferings, their leader brushed them contemptuously aside.

On 12 September they reached Dazimon (today Tokat), in the rocky and well forested valley of the river Iris (Yeşil Irmak). They had completed about three-quarters of the way to Polemonion (just east of the little port of Fatsa) on the Black Sea coast, where, judging by their route, they probably planned to board a ship bound for Pityus.[70] John was utterly exhausted, racked with fever and with his face burnt brick red by the sun, but they pressed on next day, crossing the Iris (the ancient bridge can still be seen) and passing the important city of Comana Pontica (close to the village of Gömenek) without a moment's halt. Some eight kilometres beyond they reached a hamlet (today Bizeri) clustered around the shrine of a local martyr Basiliskos, whom Palladios represents (probably mistakenly)[71] as a bishop of Comana who had perished in 312, a victim of the persecution of Maximin Daia (308-12). Here they decided to spend the night, close to the martyr's tomb. Palladios relates, in one of the rare

[68] E.g. D. Stiernon, *BSS* VI.684 (taking up a suggestion of Baur's, in 2, 420).
[69] E.g. *ep.* 4.4 (*PG* 52.595): XVII.384.
[70] Baur, 2, 240.
[71] He is more likely to have been a soldier who was exposed as a Christian. For a good discussion see *BSS* IV.54-6 (G.D. Gordini).

intrusions of the miraculous in his story, how as John slept Basiliskos appeared to him in a dream and bade him take heart, for on the following day they would be united together. The saint, he adds, was said to have appeared a short while before to the priest in charge of the chapel, and to have warned him to prepare a place 'for my brother John'. Like other Christians of that age, Palladios accepted these manifestations without question; some years later he was to describe,[72] in almost identical language, the death of a woman recluse to whom the martyr Kollouthos had appeared with a similar message.

Next morning, 14 September, John, feeling at the end of his tether, begged the soldiers to postpone departure until the fifth hour (11 a.m.), but they insisted on setting out at once. He managed to drag himself on for four or five kilometres, but weakness then overcame him and he collapsed. His guards had no option but to bring him back to Basiliskos' chapel. From this point Palladios' generally sober narrative takes on a heightened tone as he draws an idealised sketch of John's last moments. First, he asked for 'the white garments which befitted his life'. Then, having changed into these, he distributed his discarded clothes to the bystanders, received the holy sacrament, and made his final prayer aloud in their hearing. Finally, he stretched himself out on a bed, and was 'gathered to his fathers'.[73] His last words were the thanksgiving which, as Palladios remarks, had been habitually on his lips, and which summarily expressed one of his deepest convictions, 'Glory be to God for everything.'[74] If our reckoning that he was born in 349 or thereabouts is correct, he was about fifty-eight years old. His body was interred close by that of Basiliskos; in the now ruinous little church at Bizeri an empty grave has traditionally been shown as his original resting-place.

[72] *Hist. Laus.* 60 (Butler 154). See Baur, 2, 429; P. Devos, *AB* 107 (1989), 262-5.
[73] 1 Macc. 2.69. Palladios assimilates his death to that of the patriarch Jacob by using the expression (Gen. 49.33) 'having drawn up his feet', i.e. into the bed.
[74] *Ep.* 93 (to Paeanios: *PG* 52.719-20) can be read as an eloquent commentary.

EPILOGUE

Triumphal Return

I

More than thirty years were to elapse before John would return to the capital he had left, deposed but believing himself still its lawful bishop, in June 404. On his death his partisans in Constantinople, Antioch and other cities where hostile bishops were installed, while refusing to participate in the official services or doing so with sullen resentment, were careful not to elect a successor and so create a continuing schism.[1] The government therefore had no motive for keeping up its harassment of them and, in the interest of communal peace, published some kind of amnesty.[2] Even Theophilos, now that his *bête noire* was out of the way, urged Attikos,[3] since 406 bishop of Constantinople, to desist from reprisals against the Johnites. As a realist he knew that nothing was to be gained by perpetuating divisions, and that his move might assist bridge-building with Rome. So far from being appeased, however, the Johnites now took the offensive, calling for their hero's name to be inscribed in the diptychs, i.e. the formal list of dead (and living) persons commemorated in the liturgy. This would be a first step to his complete rehabilitation, implying that his deposition had been uncanonical and that he had remained bishop until his death. Their demand received powerful support from Innocent I and other western bishops; the pope made compliance with it the indispensable condition for his resumption of communion with the eastern churches.[4]

This demand was quite unacceptable to John's victorious enemies, and for years they turned a deaf ear to it. The first break in their ranks came, appropriately enough, at Antioch, where public sympathy for him and his cause were particularly strong. The hated Porphyrios, who had succeeded Flavian in 404,[5] died in 412, and his successor Alexander, a man of ascetic training and a peacemaker by temperament, was determined to end the divisions in his community.[6] He first dealt with the lingering Antiochene

---

[1] Theodoret, *HE* 5.34.10 (*GCS* 44.336).
[2] Synesios, *ep.* 66 (*PG* 66.1408-9). He uses the term *amnestia*.
[3] Synesios, loc. cit.
[4] Theodoret, *HE* 5.34.11 (*GCS* 44.336).
[5] See above, p. 252.
[6] Theodoret, *HE* 5.35.1-5 (*GCS* 44.337-8).

schism; going over with his congregation to the church where the remaining Eustathians worshipped, he charmed them by persuasive blandishments and led all but a handful of them in procession to the Golden Church. He sealed the union by accepting the priests and deacons ordained by Paulinos and Evagrios among his own clergy. He then turned his attention to much the largest body of dissidents in Antioch, the Johnites, and won them over at a stroke by including John's name in the diptychs. What is more, as metropolitan of Syria he arranged for Elpidios and Pappos, devoted friends of John who had had to lie low for three years,[7] to return to the sees from which they had been ejected. He then sent a delegation to Rome to report what he had done, and the delighted pope, sitting in synod with twenty Italian bishops, wrote back enthusiastically announcing that he was admitting Antioch to communion.[8]

Alexander died in 416. His successor, Theodotos (417-29), initially tried to reverse his policy, erasing John's name from the diptychs, but was immediately forced by a popular outcry to replace it.[9] But if John's rehabilitation was carried out relatively swiftly in the Syrian patriarchate, the process took longer and proved rather messier at Constantinople. At Antioch it was simply a case of appeasing Johnite malcontents, something Alexander was happy to do and which cast no doubts on his own position. For Attikos placing John's name in the diptychs was tantamount to admitting that he himself had been an intruder on the see for at any rate his first two years. Pressure on him to do so was, however, mounting. In the main it came from the large proportion of Christians in the city who shunned his services. The pope too, however, wrote to his nuncio in the eastern capital, Boniface (to become pope in 418), telling him to advise those who were pleading for the recognition of Attikos by Rome that he would have to accept exactly the same conditions as Alexander had recently accepted at Antioch.[10] More alarming still, Alexander himself turned up in Constantinople and, as well as using his personal influence with his brother bishop, did not scruple to incite the people to force his hand. Eventually, faced with excited calls for John's name to be inscribed in the diptychs and growing threats of public disorder, he consulted the youthful Theodosios II, sole eastern emperor since Arkadios' death in 408. His reply, dictated (we may assume) by his praetorian prefect and guardian Anthemios, was to the effect that there could surely be no harm in placing a dead man's name on a tablet if thereby peace and harmony could be ensured.

So, grudgingly and with blustering protests, Attikos capitulated. To explain and justify his conduct he sent a detailed account of the affair to

---

[7] Palladios, *Dial.* 20 (*SC* 341.398).

[8] *Ep.* 19 (*PL* 20.540-2; JW 305).

[9] So we must deduce from a letter of Attikos of Constantinople to Cyril of Alexandria: *PG* 77.849D.

[10] *Ep.* 23 (*PG* 20.246-7; JW 309).

Cyril,[11] who had succeeded his uncle Theophilos as bishop of Alexandria in 412, inheriting his hatred of John as well as his despotic disposition. He had been forced to give way, he claimed in this extraordinary letter, because of the alarming situation, against his better judgment. Even so, he had not transgressed the canons, for the names not only of bishops, but of priests, deacons, laymen, even women, figured in the diptychs. He concluded by challenging Cyril, 'for the sake of securing peace throughout the entire world', to instruct the churches of Egypt to have 'the name of that dead man inscribed in the diptychs'. Cyril's reply[12] dissected Attikos' excuses with cold contempt. According to his information, he pointed out, John's name had not been inscribed at Constantinople in the lists of lay folk, but in that of bishops. That was the equivalent of restoring Judas to the ranks of the apostles. If Attikos was really concerned for church unity, he should at once erase the name of a man who had ceased to be a bishop from the lists of genuine bishops.

Yet, for all his domineering tone, Cyril himself found it prudent before long to fall into line. Alexandria could not forever remain isolated from the other eastern churches or from Rome. Among the factors weighing on him may have been pressure from the government in Constantinople.[13] When or for what precise reasons he made the, to him, unpalatable gesture, is not clear. A date around 418, however, seems plausible, for the council of Carthage of May 419 requested Pope Boniface to obtain certified copies of the Nicene canons from the great sees of the east, including Alexandria.[14] Whatever the date and circumstances of his climb-down, it is certain that he made it for political reasons, and that he remained convinced until his death of the legitimacy of The Oak and of John's culpability.

II

It is often suggested that 'the first and chief credit' for John's formal rehabilitation belongs to Innocent I, who masterminded it by uncompromisingly insisting that there could be no communion between Rome and any of the eastern churches until they inscribed his name in their diptychs.[15] But this verdict, which would have gratified that forceful promoter of papal authority, rests on a misreading of the evidence. At Alexandria Cyril's reluctant capitulation was in part determined by his need to restore the special relationship with Rome, but equally he could not afford to maintain a stance which clashed so markedly with imperial policy. Antioch,

---

[11] *Ep.* 75 in Cyril's correspondence: *PG* 77.347-52. It is the main source of the previous paragraph.
[12] *Ep.* 76 (*PG* 77.352-60).
[13] See Baur, 2, 450-1.
[14] *CCL* 149.160.
[15] So Baur, 2, 232: cf. A. Moulard, 403; É. Demougeot, 351; etc.

too, was keen to renew its ties with Rome, but this was at least in part because it needed the pope's support in getting rid of the Eustathian schism. As for Constantinople, it is obvious that, although Attikos was eager for peace with the holy see,[16] he found Innocent's conditions totally repugnant. But all this is beside the point. What the evidence overwhelmingly suggests is that, in inscribing John's name in their diptychs, the authorities at both Antioch and Constantinople were responding, gladly in the former case and with grave misgivings in the latter, to immense popular pressure.[17] In particular, there is not the slightest hint, in Attikos' fairly detailed letter to Cyril, of the desirability of placating the pope. Everything points to the conclusion that John owed his restoration to the honour and dignity of which he had been stripped exclusively to the insistent demands of his activist followers and of the ordinary people whose affection he had always courted.

Notwithstanding their success, his admirers in Constantinople still remained dissatisfied. The diptychs of churches, as Attikos had remarked in his astonishingly frank letter to Cyril, sometimes included the names of schismatics (e.g. Paulinos and Evagrios at Antioch) and other persons of dubious repute which the authorities had inserted, or allowed to remain there, in the interest of peace and unity. They demanded, therefore, a fuller, more signal acknowledgement of John's exceptional status. The more determined and fanatical of them refused to rest content so long as his body lay in a humble grave in faraway Pontus, where no one could visit his shrine or draw strength from contact with it. Both groups had to wait several years for their aspirations to be fulfilled, but in the end they were. The first step was taken on 26 September 428, when John's memory was for the first time solemnly celebrated in the liturgy.[18] The bishop who must have presided at the mass, enthroned only in April of that year, was Nestorios, like John a monk and priest who had been summoned from Antioch to the capital, like him to be deposed (431), but in his case for heresy. It is pleasant to reflect that it was he who, with the court's consent and in the interest of communal reconciliation, had promoted what was in effect the canonisation of his countryman.

The climax came some nine years later, when John's remains were brought with magnificent ceremony to Constantinople. A new bishop, Proklos (434-46), with the ready support of the emperor and his elder sister Pulcheria, had had them fetched from Comana. The ship conveying them from the Asian coast reached the mouth of the Bosporus on the night of 27 January 438.[19] It was surrounded by so many boats illuminated by torches that, in the colourful language of the historian,[20] the sea seemed to have

---

[16] Theodoret, *HE* 5.34.12 (*GCS* 44.337).

[17] See esp. E. Caspar, *Geschichte des Papsttums* (Tübingen 1930), 325.

[18] Marcellinus Comes, *Chronicon* (*MGAA* xi.77).

[19] For the date see Marcellinus Comes, *Chronicon* (*MGAA* xi.77); Sokrates 7.45.

[20] Theodoret, *HE* 5.36.1-2 (*GCS* 44.338), the source of most of this paragraph.

become an extension of the mainland. When the precious reliquary was carried ashore, Theodosios II, son of Arkadios and Eudoxia, was there to receive it. Bending low, fixing his gaze on it and pressing his forehead against it, he offered prayers on behalf of his parents, begging John to grant them pardon for all the injustices they had done him in ignorance. A triumphant procession then accompanied it through the city to the church of the Holy Apostles, traditional burying-place of bishops and emperors. There John's body was ceremonially placed,[21] not far from the spot where the bodies of Arkadios and Eudoxia had been interred. It was to remain there until, after the capture of Constantinople in 1204 during the Fourth Crusade, the plundering Venetians seized it and carried it off as a precious relic to Rome, where it was installed in St Peter's basilica.[22]

The return of John's remains to Constantinople and their interment in the church of the Holy Apostles represented, in the thinking of devout Christians of that age, his final vindication. The small body of die-hard Johnites in the capital who had hitherto kept themselves stubbornly apart now conceded that honour had been satisfied, and felt able to join in communion with Proklos and the orthodox congregation of the city.[23] It is fascinating to note that, a generation later but in exactly the same way, the last flickering embers of the seemingly endless Antiochene schism were extinguished when the body of Eustathios was in 382 solemnly brought back to Antioch from Philippi in eastern Macedonia.[24] As in the dispute over the diptychs, John had once again owed his triumph to the unyielding loyalty and insistent demands of ordinary people.

[21] Sokrates 7.45.

[22] The claims of numerous other places to possess relics of John's body have created needless doubts about the traditional story. For a brief discussion see *BSS* VI, 685 (D. Stiernon).

[23] Sokrates 7.45 (where he expresses puzzlement that John had been rehabilitated so soon whereas Origen still remained under a cloud).

[24] Theodoros Lector, *HE* 2.1 (*PG* 86 (1).181).

Appendix A

Some Ancient Sources

1. JOHN'S letters are a primary source of unique value. Certain of his homilies (see Chapter 7.VII) can be shown to throw light on his activities, but in general he rarely refers to events in his life in his writings. The great exception is the account of his boyhood and early manhood which forms the setting of the dialogue *Priesthood*. In Chapter 2.II it is argued, against current scepticism, that these recollections, although set down in middle age and worked up for dramatic effect, can be trusted as regards the key facts they record.

2. 'MARTYRIOS' designates the unknown author of the so-called Life of John erroneously attributed to Martyrios, orthodox bishop of Antioch, 459-71. The complete Greek text is found only in MS Paris gr. 1519 (eleventh century). It has never been published in full, although the closing paragraphs were printed in *PG* 47.xliii-lii. J.P. Migne recognised that the work is not a biography proper, but a panegyric which touches on several key episodes in John's career; F. van Ommeslaeghe has shown[1] that it was pronounced in 407 within a few weeks of John's death on the reception of the news at Constantinople. Whoever the author, he was a passionate supporter of the dead bishop, having been baptised and ordained by him; he claims to have been an eye-witness of many of the events described. Where it can be checked, his accuracy in matters of detail seems firmly established, and the panegyric is now accepted as an authoritative source for John's life. It is remarkable that C. Baur, who had studied the MS and appreciated its worth, eventually decided[2] that it was a mid-fifth-century compilation based on Palladios, Sozomen, and others. A critical edition in *Subsidia hagiographica* has been promised by van Ommeslaeghe for more than twenty years. This had not appeared by January 1994, but repeated announcements of its imminent publication have deterred the present writer from having his own transcription of the MS made. He has therefore had to rely for information about it on valuable (but inevitably selective) articles by van Ommeslaeghe in *AB* 95 (1977), 97 (1979), 99 (1981) and 110 (1992). References to the Paris MS are by page and column.

---

[1] *Studia patristica* 12 (Berlin 1975 = *TU* 5), 498-83 .
[2] 1, xxxii.

3. PALLADIOS'[3] (364 – c. 430) *Dialogue*[4] on John's life, completed in exile at Syene (Assouan) in 408, is generally regarded as a trustworthy source.[5] This verdict is based in part on his close involvement, often as an eye-witness, in the main events of the critical years 400-4, and on the intense interest he evidently took in John personally, noting his habits and even mannerisms.[6] This makes it likely that, being so much in John's company (sometimes for weeks on end), it was from him that he derived the carefully drafted summary of his early life included in *Dial.* 5. In addition, he was exceptionally well qualified to report on Theophilos' treatment of the Nitrian monks and their sojourn in Constantinople, since he had met Isidore and the Long Brothers in Egypt,[7] and can hardly have failed to seek them out when they came to the capital. The credibility of his work is enhanced by the pains he clearly took (a) to give precise details of time, place, numbers, etc. wherever possible,[8] and (b) to include references to, or excerpts from, great numbers of official letters and other documents.[9] But if for reasons like these Palladios' general reliability seems assured, there are important qualifications to be made. First, he was not a detached historian, but a partisan concerned to vindicate John and depict him as the model bishop. We must expect him, therefore, to gloss over incidents which might seem damaging to him (e.g. the uproar following his appointment of Herakleides as bishop).[10] Conversely, we should not look for objectivity in his portraits of John's enemies. Secondly, when he had no first-hand knowledge he could either make serious mistakes (e.g. in explaining John's move from Cucusos to Arabissos)[11] or seek refuge in edification (e.g. in describing John's death).[12] Thirdly, he was not, and did not claim to be, either systematic or exhaustive, and his narrative therefore often needs to be corrected or supplemented by our other sources. A striking case of this is his account of The Oak,[13] where 'Martyrios' gives a fuller and more accurate report on the course of the trial and Photios alone supplies the complete charge-list.[14]

4. SOKRATES (c. 380 – c. 450), a barrister, was born and spent his life in Constantinople. His *Church History*,[15] written 438-43 and covering the period 306 to 439 in seven books, was intended as a continuation of that of Eusebios. Adopting a plain, unadorned style so as to reach ordinary people

---

[3] For his career see A.M. Malingrey, *SC* 341 (Paris 1988), 10-18; more fully, E.D. Hunt, *JTS* 24 (1973), 456-80.

[4] Critical editions by P.R. Coleman-Norton, Cambridge 1929; A.M. Malingrey, op. cit.

[5] Cf. Altaner-Stuiber's 'historisch wichtig' (*Patrologie* 240: Freiburg, 8 ed., 1978).

[6] A.M. Malingrey, op. cit., 25.

[7] E.D. Hunt, art. cit., 466; 468.

[8] A.M. Malingrey, op. cit., 35.

[9] P.R. Coleman-Norton, op. cit., lxxii-lxxv.

[10] See p. 174.

[11] See p. 260.

[12] See p. 285.

[13] See p. 221.

[14] Cf. F. van Ommeslaeghe, *AB* 95 (1977), 389-413, esp. 412-13.

[15] *PG* 67: best ed. still R. Hussey, Oxford 1853.

as well as the learned (1.1; 6.prooem.), he gave his narrative a firm chronological framework, drew on a wide range of sources (including letters and official documents), mentioning and frequently reproducing them, and from Book 6 on (6.prooem.) used his own recollections and the reports of eye-witnesses. He evaluated his sources critically, since he aimed, not without success, at impartiality and objectivity. Thus, coming across fresh documents which showed up the errors of one of the chief of them (the Latin historian Rufinus), he drastically revised Books 2 and 2. That he extended the revision to the others is clear from the survival, at the end of Book 6, of a lengthy fragment (important for John's story)[16] which differs markedly from the current text. An orthodox Christian who appreciated Greek culture (3.16), stood up for Origen (6.12-13), and was refreshingly tolerant of heretics (e.g. 7.6), he himself was sympathetically disposed to the Novatians (though classifying them with the Arians: 5.20). His account of John takes up much of Book 6. In general he seems to respect him for his character, eloquence, and hold over the people, but is puzzled by his severity and aloofness, and freely reports criticism of him on these grounds. While trying to be fair, he himself was also critical of him for his harshness to the Novatians (6.19) and shocked by the freedom with which he offered forgiveness to sinners (6.21).

5. SOZOMEN(OS) was born *c.* 400 at Bethelia, a village near Gaza, educated by monks, and settled in Constantinople after 425; there he practised as a barrister. His *Church History*,[17] written between 439 and 450 and dedicated to Theodosios II, was intended (see Dedication) to cover the period 324-439, but the concluding sections (425-39) are for some unexplained reason missing. Although composed in a more elegant, high-flown style, designed to attract a cultivated lay readership, much of it is a recasting, without acknowledgment, of Sokrates' *History*; but Sozomen abandons his predecessor's chronological framework, is sparing with dates and prefers, save in exceptional cases, to refer to letters and documents rather than cite them. But if inferior to Sokrates in critical method, his work is given special importance by his insertion of independent material bearing (a) on the persecution of Christians in Persia under Shapur II, and (b) on the development of Syrian monasticism, with accounts of individual monks. He took a relaxed view of dogmatic controversy, for example ranking the extreme Arian Aetios among great church teachers; on the other hand, he was credulous to a degree. In contrast to Sokrates' distinctly reserved attitude, he was a warm supporter of John, suppressing anything in his predecessor's account which might reflect badly on him and going out of his way to cite in full documents which tended to vindicate his cause (8.26).

6. THEODORET(OS) (393-466) was born at Antioch, brought up by monks,

---

[16] See p. 184.
[17] *PG* 67: critical edition by J. Bidez and G.C. Hansen (*GCS* 50: 1961).

and in 423 became bishop of Kyrrhos, *c.* 60 km north-west of Beroea (Haleb), a town important for the religious life of Syria. From then until his death, while diligent in looking after the spiritual and temporal needs of his flock, he was greatly involved in the fierce christological controversies of the time. Antiochene in his sympathies, he was deposed by the council of Ephesos in 449, but in 451 was reinstated after reluctantly anathematising Nestorius; in 553 certain of his writings were condemned by the fifth ecumenical council (Constantinople). His literary output was vast and extremely varied, covering exegesis, apologetics and dogmatic theology. Here we are concerned with two of his historical works. His *Historia religiosa*,[18] written *c.* 444, recounts the lives and practices of 28 male and 3 female ascetics. As most of them lived near Antioch and were personally known to him, the work is a rich source for our knowledge of Syrian monasticism. His *Church History*,[19] completed during temporary exile in 449-50, covers the years 323 to 428 (discreetly breaking off before the Nestorian controversy). Uncritically put together and unashamedly apologetic, it is nevertheless valuable for the mass of original documents on which it is based.

7. PHILOSTORGIOS (*c.* 368 – after 425), a Cappadocian by birth, settled in Constantinople when 20 and spent most of his life there, making occasional trips to Palestine and Antioch. Among other works his *Church History*[20] in twelve books, covering the period 320-425. Quite early he had met the radical Arian Eunomius (d. 394), and became his wholehearted disciple. His *History* was heavily biased in favour of Arianism, so that Photios[21] (who, with reservations, praised its style) described it as 'not so much a history as a eulogy of the heretics and a barefaced critical onslaught on the orthodox'. Because of this the complete text has not survived. Substantial extracts from it, however, were published separately by Photios and, in addition, numerous fragments have been preserved by Suidas and others. These make it plain that he used first-rate sources, including acts of councils and Arian documents not available elsewhere. His work has considerable interest, both because of the information it supplies about the controversy and its leading figures, and as illustrating the attraction intellectual Arianism had for cultivated Christians.

8. ZOSIMOS, according to Photios[22] a count (*comes*) who had held the position of counsel for the crown (*advocatus fisci*), wrote between 498 and 510 his *New History*[23] of the Roman empire from Augustus. A militant

---

[18] *PG* 82.1289-1496: critical edition by P. Canivet and A. Leroy-Molinghen in *SC* 234 (1977) and 257 (1979).
[19] Critical edition by L. Parmentier and F. Scheidweiler, *GCS* 44 (1954).
[20] Critical edition (exceptionally thorough) in *GCS* 21 (3 ed. 1977) by J. Bidez and F. Winkelmann.
[21] *Bibliotheca* 40 (R.Henry, 1.23-5).
[22] *Bibliotheca* 98 (R. Henry, 2.65-6).
[23] F. Paschoud, *Zosime: Histoire nouvelle* (text and French translation, with full notes: Paris 1971-81), 6 vols.

pagan, a leading idea of his work was that the decadence of the empire was due to the abandonment of the old religion. He was heavily dependent on his sources, the principal one for the sections cited in this book being Eunapios of Sardes (345/346 – c. 420), a pagan like himself. Photios, indeed, who had studied both writers, remarked that Zosimos had not so much written a history as transcribed that of Eunapios. There is general agreement that Zosimos himself was a very mediocre historian, careless of chronology and frequently muddled, but that since his sources often contained valuable material the student who makes the effort to 'sift the wheat from the tares'[24] can be rewarded. Eunapios, it is certain, had first-hand information about important public events occurring during John's time as bishop.

---

[24] F. Paschoud, op. cit., 1, lxx.

Appendix B

The Chronology of John's Earlier Life

It seems reasonably certain that John was born between 340 and 350. This can be deduced from his own statement,[1] when seeking to console a young widow whose husband has died before attaining the prominence for which he seemed destined, that while nine emperors have reigned 'in our lifetime' (*geneas*), only two of them have died natural deaths. His point is that, even if the young husband had lived and achieved greatness, she and he would not necessarily have been happy, since men in great positions lead imperilled lives. John gives no names, but states that five of the nine perished in violent ways which he briefly describes. As for the current sovereigns (plainly Gratian and Theodosius I), they too illustrate his thesis, the one being young and inexperienced, the other involved from his coronation to the present day in barbarian wars, both causing great anxiety to their wives. Since John clearly includes these two among the nine (if not, why mention them and their troubles at all?), the other seven can only be Constans (d. 350), Gallus Caesar (d. 354), Constantius II (d. 361), Julian (d. 363), Jovian (d. 364), Valentinian I (d. 375), and Valens (d. 378). Of these the third and sixth died ordinary deaths, the others violently in ways which, it should be noted, tally exactly with John's descriptions. Some earlier scholars, including Tillemont,[2] assuming unnecessarily that all nine must be dead, started the list with Constantine I and Constantine II. This solution, however, overlooks John's distinction between 'past history', to which these surely belonged so far as he was concerned, and 'our lifetime', faces the awkward fact that Constantine I died in his bed, and makes nonsense of John's pointed references to the reigning emperors. The case for the identifications given above was made out centuries ago by J. Stilting,[3] but has been freshly re-argued by G.H. Ettlinger.[4] The conclusion must be that John's birth fell in the reign of Constans, i.e. 340-50.

Apart from random reminiscences of his own and one or two scraps preserved by Sokrates, all the material bearing on John's early chronology is contained in a summary account which Palladios drafted with obvious

---

[1] *Ad viduam iuniorem* 4-5 (*PG* 48.605-06). Its date is 380/1: see above, p. 47.
[2] XI.556.
[3] *AASS* Sept. IV (Antwerp 1753), 437.
[4] *Traditio* 16 (1960), 373-80.

care.[5] His own reminiscences include a conversation he had when a student of 'twenty' with his pagan professor;[6] an attempt by church leaders at Antioch to have him and his friend Basil ordained;[7] and an alarming experience which he had at Antioch when 'a boy' (*meirakion*), and which can be dated to winter 371/2 when emperor Valens was in the city.[8] Sokrates reports[9] that his teacher of rhetoric was Libanios, and that he studied at the ascetic school of Diodore and Carterios. Palladios' compressed narrative supplies the following facts: John was eighteen when he left his rhetorical school; falling then under the influence of Meletios, orthodox bishop of Antioch, he was baptised, attended on the bishop for three years, and was made reader; at some point he withdrew to the nearby mountains, where he spent six years as a monk; he then returned to Antioch, 'served the altar for two years in addition to the three' (i.e. the previous three), and was then ordained deacon by Meletios. It is a reasonable surmise,[10] in view of his close contacts with him during most of 400-4 and his intense personal interest in him, that Palladios derived this information from John himself; and this surmise is strengthened by the precision with which he sets down his facts. The objection[11] that John's recollections of his earlier life may have been blurred carries scepticism too far. He was only in his early fifties, and events like his baptism, retreat to the mountains, and ordination must have remained fixed in his mind.

When we attempt to piece our miscellaneous data together, it becomes clear that Meletios' movements provide the regulative framework; the hapless bishop, exiled soon after his installation in 351, only managed two stays in Antioch – 362-5 and 367-71 – between that date and his final return in autumn 378 on the death of the Arian emperor Valens in August.[12] It was during this final stay (378-81) that he ordained John deacon. Not immediately, however. Palladios' careful statement that, before being ordained, John served the altar for two further years obliges us to narrow the date down to late 380 or early 381. Again, since John's return to Antioch from the mountains followed closely on, and was probably connected with, Meletios' resumption of office, it can be confidently placed in late 378 or very early 379. His six years of monastic seclusion must consequently have covered the years 372-8.

John's earlier association with Meletios – his baptism, three years' lay attendance on him, appointment as reader – can only be assigned to the

[5] *Dial.* 5 (*SC* 341.104-10).
[6] See above, p. 7.
[7] See above, pp. 25f.
[8] See above, pp. 24f.
[9] 6.3.
[10] See more fully Appendix A (1).
[11] R.E. Carter, *Traditio* 18 (1962), 357. This article (pp. 357-64) is much the fullest and best discussion of John's early chronology available.
[12] *PW* 15 (1931), 500-2 (W. Ensslin).

bishop's residence in Antioch during 367-71; apart from being too early, his earlier stay during 362-5 is too short for all the events we have to squeeze in. They can be fitted, exactly and conveniently, into 367-71 if we assume that he was baptised by Meletios in 367 or, more probably, 368, then assisted him for three years, and was appointed reader in 371 before he was again forced into exile by the return of Valens to the city in winter 371/2. Since Diodore accompanied Meletios to Armenia,[13] John's ascetic initiation under him is likely to have coincided with his attendance on the bishop; while the failed attempt to ordain him should be placed after Meletios' departure, when there was an urgent need to recruit clergy. According to Palladios, Meletios was 'ruling the church' when John, aged eighteen (the normal age), left his rhetorical school: this is likely to have been 367. As the normal date for leaving school was the end of July,[14] and for administering baptism Easter, he was probably baptised at Easter 368; the normal two-year catechumenate was usually dispensed with in the case of children of Christian parents,[15] and in any case may not have been thought necessary for so earnest a young Christian as John.

The conclusion to which this reconstruction points is that John was born in 349 or thereabouts. There are two apparent discrepancies which have needlessly worried students: his description of himself as being about twenty when his professor complimented his mother, and as being a *meirakion* (boy) at the time of the alarming experience in 371, when on our reckoning he must have been twenty-two. The former is simply an example of his habit, irritating but derived from his rhetorical training, of rounding off numbers.[16] The latter rests on a misunderstanding of the connotation of *meirakion*. Often assumed to refer exclusively to boys of around fourteen, writers as varied in date and style as Hippokrates, Menander and Epiktetos define it as applying quite normally to young men from puberty to twenty-one.[17]

---

[13] Basil, *ep.* 99.3 – written in 372 (Courtonne 1.217).

[14] A.J. Festugière, *Antioche païenne et chrétienne* (Paris 1959), 135.

[15] Baur 1, 81 and 86 n. 8.

[16] C. Baur, *ZKTh* 52 (1928), 404 n. 5.

[17] In addition to Liddell and Scott's *Greek-English Lexicon* (1968), see A.W. Gomme and F.H. Sandbach, *Menander: A Commentary* (Oxford 1973), 140.

Appendix C

Charges Brought against John at The Oak

1. Charges preferred by the deacon John[1]

(1) He accused Chrysostom of having treated him unjustly by excluding[2] him for having beaten his own servant Eulalios. (2) A monk, John, had, as he alleges, on Chrysostom's instructions been beaten, taken into custody, and put in chains along with possessed persons. (3) He sold off a large number of valuable objects.[3] (4) The slabs of marble belonging to St Anastasia which Nektarios had set aside for the decoration of the church had been sold off by him.[4] (5) He disparages his clergy as men without honour, corrupt, dissolute,[5] good-for-nothings. (6) He called the sainted Epiphanios a babbler and a little weirdo. (7) He contrived a plot against Severian, letting his flunkeys[6] loose on him. (8) He composed a slanderous pamphlet against the clergy.[7] (9) He convened a meeting of his entire clergy and cited three deacons, Akakios, Edaphios and John, accusing them of stealing his monk's cloak,[8] suggesting they might have taken it for a rather different purpose. (10) He consecrated Antonios in spite of his having been convicted as a grave-robber. (11) He informed against count John during the army mutiny.[9] (12) He failed to offer prayer either when setting out for church or when entering it. (13) He had carried out ordinations of deacons and of priests without an altar.[10] (14) He ordained four bishops at a single service of consecration. (15) He receives women entirely on his own, excluding all others. (16) He used the services of Theodoulos to sell the inheritance bequeathed by Thekla. (17) No one has any idea where the revenues of the church have gone. (18) He ordained Sarapion priest while still subject to a charge.[11] (19) He had people who were in communion with the whole world shut up in prison by his own decision, and when they died

---

[1] The translation is based on the Greek text presented by A.M. Malingrey in *SC* 342.100-14.
[2] I.e. suspending him from communion and/or his functions as deacon.
[3] I.e. church property.
[4] See above, p. 119.
[5] *Autoparachretos*: a word not found elsewhere and of doubtful meaning.
[6] *Dekanous*: the sense is not clear.
[7] Probably the pastoral mentioned on p. 121 above.
[8] *Maphorion*: meaning not wholly clear.
[9] See above, pp. 154-6.
[10] An ordination was expected to be followed by a mass.
[11] Presumably of discourtesy to Severian.

there he paid no attention to them and did not even think fit to give due honour to their remains.[12] (20) He insulted the venerable Akakios and did not even address a word to him.[13] (21) He handed over the priest Porphyrios to Eutropios to be exiled.[14] (22) He also handed over the priest Venerios in an insulting manner. (23) He has his bath heated for himself alone; after he has bathed, Sarapion shuts off access to it so that no one else may take a bath. (24) He had ordained many persons without witnesses. (25) He takes his meals alone, living gluttonously as Cyclopes do. (26) He acts as accuser, as witness, and as judge: this is evident from the affair of Martyrios, the archdeacon, and, it is said, from that of Proairesios, bishop of Lycia.[15] (27) He gave a blow with his fist to Memnon in the church of the Apostles, and while the blood was still flowing from his mouth offered him holy communion.[16] (28) He takes off and puts on his vestments at the throne, and eats a morsel of bread.[17] (29) He also gives money to the bishops he consecrates so that through them he can oppress the clergy.

2. Charges preferred by Isaac

(1) With regard to the monk John,[18] already mentioned several times, he had been thrashed out of regard for the Origenists.[19] (2) Blessed Epiphanios refused to hold communion with him because of the Origenists Ammonios, Euthymios, Eusebios and also Herakleides and Palladios. (3) He brings hospitality into discredit, making a habit of eating alone. (4) He says in church that the holy table is filled with Furies.[20] (5) In church he brags loudly, saying 'I am beside myself with love'; but he ought to explain who are the Furies, and what he means by 'I am beside myself with love'. For the church is unfamiliar with this language. (6) He offers sinners immunity with his teaching, 'If you sin again, again repent', and, 'As often as you sin, come to me and I shall heal you.' (7) He blasphemes when he asserts in church that, although Christ prayed, he was not listened to because he did not pray in the right way. (8) He is inciting the populace to demonstrate against the synod. (9) He has welcomed pagans who have done Christians much harm, and keeps them in the church and protects them. (10) He trespasses on provinces outside his jurisdiction and consecrates bishops.[21]

---

[12] These were the agents whom Theophilos had sent to slander the Long Brothers and who were gaoled: see above, p. 201.

[13] Bishop of Beroea: see above, p. 117.

[14] Nothing is known of this or the next incident.

[15] Both these incidents are unknown.

[16] Memnon is not known.

[17] For John's practice see Palladios, *Dial.* 8 (*SC* 341.162).

[18] Referred to in item 1 of the first dossier; he later brought charges on his own against Herakleides.

[19] I.e. the Long Brothers: cf. the three mentioned in the next charge.

[20] For brief discussions of this and the following three charges see above, pp. 224f.

[21] A reference to John's activities on his Asian tour.

(11) He insults bishops, and orders them to be ejected from his house without letters of commendation.[22] (12) He insults his clergy with unprecedented rudenesses. (13) He has forcibly seized deposits belonging to other people. (14) He carries out ordinations without consulting his clergy in synod and against their wishes. (15) He gave hospitality to the Origenists; but when people in full communion with the church who had arrived with letters of communion were flung into prison, he not only did not get them released, but when they died there did not concern himself about them.[23] (16) He has consecrated as bishops other men's slaves who had not been freed and who were actually of ill repute. (17) It has come about that this Isaac has himself suffered much evil at their hands.

[22] A more measured reference, perhaps, to his attempt to send Severian home complained of by the deacon John in his seventh charge.
[23] A repetition of the deacon John's nineteenth charge, contrasting however John's warm welcome of the Long Brothers with his neglect of Theophilos' agents.

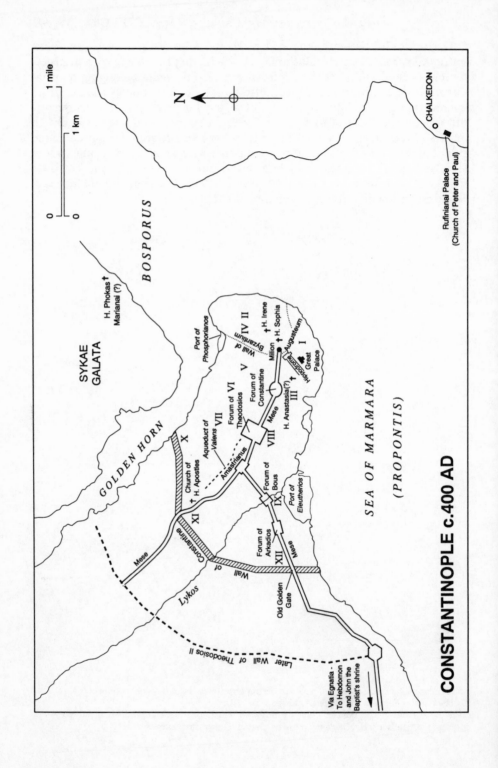

CONSTANTINOPLE c.400 AD

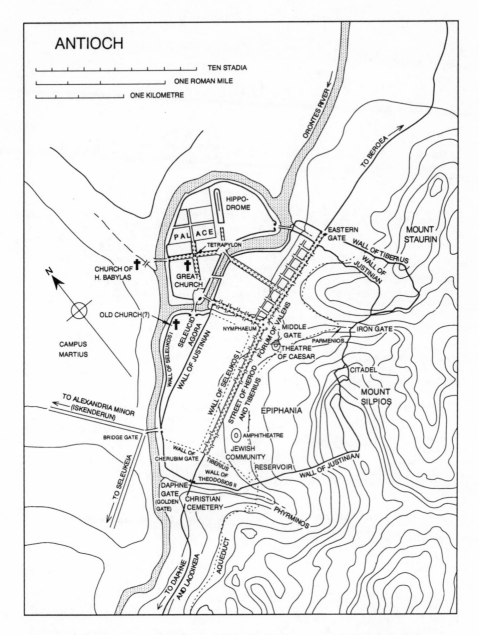

This plan reproduces, with adjustments, that printed in G. Downey, *A History of Antioch in Syria* (Princeton 1961). In John's time the walls of Theodosios II and Justinian did not exist.

Index